BUSINESS SOLUTIONS
FOR THE GLOBAL POOR

JOSSEY-BASS

BUSINESS SOLUTIONS FOR THE GLOBAL POOR

Creating Social and Economic Value

V. Kasturi Rangan, John A. Quelch,
Gustavo Herrero, and Brooke Barton

Foreword by C. K. Prahalad

John Wiley & Sons, Inc.

Published by Jossey-Bass
A Wiley Imprint
989 Market Street, San Francisco, CA 94103-1741   www.josseybass.com

Jossey-Bass books and products are available through most bookstores. To contact Jossey-Bass directly call our Customer Care Department within the U.S. at 800-956-7739, outside the U.S. at 317-572-3986, or fax 317-572-4002.

Jossey-Bass also publishes its books in a variety of electronic formats. Some content that appears in print may not be available in electronic books.

Library of Congress Cataloging-in-Publication Data
Conference on Global Poverty: Business Solutions and Approaches (2005 : Harvard University)
  Business solutions for the social poor : creating social and economic value / [edited by] V. Kasturi Rangan, John Quelch, Gustavo Herrero, with Brooke Barton ; foreword by C. K. Prahalad. — 1st ed.
    p. cm.
  Papers presented at A Conference on Global Poverty: Business Solutions and Approaches held at Harvard University, on Dec. 1-3, 2005.
  Includes bibliographical references and index.
  ISBN-13: 978-0-7879-8216-4 (alk. paper)
  1. Social responsibility of business—Congresses. 2. Poor—Congresses.. 3. International business enterprises—Moral and ethical aspects—Congresses. 4. Social responsibility of business—Developing countries—Congresses. 5. Poor—Developing countries—Congresses. 6. International business enterprises—Moral and ethical aspects—Developing countries—Congresses. I. Rangan, V. Kasturi. II. Quelch, John A. III. Herrero, Gustavo. IV. Title.
  HD60.C624 2005
  362.5'5765091724—dc22
                        2006034762

Printed in the United States of America
FIRST EDITION
HB Printing   10 9 8 7 6 5 4 3 2 1

CONTENTS

PART TWO: MEETING THE BASIC NEEDS OF THE POOR

PART THREE: BUILDING THE BOP VALUE CHAIN

PART FOUR: BUSINESS AND LEADERSHIP MODELS

PART FIVE: THE ROLE OF GOVERNMENT AND CIVIL SOCIETY

PART SIX: MEASURING SUCCESS

FOREWORD

C. K. Prahalad

Paul and Ruth McCracken Distinguished University Professor,
Stephen M. Ross School of Business, University of Michigan

The idea that the private sector can contribute to the goal of poverty alleviation is a relatively new concept. There has long been an implicit compact between the private sector on one side and the UN, the World Bank, aid agencies, national governments, and civil society on the other. They agreed, on the basis of historical evidence, that the private sector was an unlikely vehicle for dealing with poverty. The goals of profits, growth, and innovation were assumed to be contrary to the task of poverty alleviation. *The purpose of this book is to continue challenging this deep-seated, ideologically grounded assumption.*

The convergence of the interests of the world's poor and the private sector are driven by their specific needs. The poor, who represent 80 percent of humanity, are eager to reap the benefits of globalization: high-quality products and services at affordable cost as well as access to global markets. Today they are not constrained by ignorance of what is possible. Ubiquitous connectivity—through television, radio, cell phones, and PCs—is systematically breaking down barriers to information.

Managers, in turn, are searching for new markets. In their quest for sustained growth, telecoms such as Nokia, Motorola, and Vodafone have broken many a dogma. The industry expects three billion people (half the world's population) to be connected by cell phone by 2009–2010. People at the bottom of the economic pyramid (BOP) are driving this growth.

New business models—phone ladies in Bangladesh, prepaid cards as a mechanism for promoting affordable consumption, and increasingly flexible regulatory environments for telecom services—are showing that the poor can be a market, one that propels global growth and has an impact on costs and prices worldwide. Further, BOP consumers, though value-conscious, have proved that they can rapidly adapt to new technology. They are also willing to pay for what they receive. The growth of Celtel, a wireless service in sub-Saharan Africa, and MTN in South Africa, Nigeria, and now in Iran demonstrates that working with the BOP markets need not lead to lowering profitability or market capitalization. In fact, the opposite is true.

Experiments in a variety of industries, from fast-moving consumer goods (Unilever) to microfinance (ICICI in India), housing (CEMEX in Mexico), retailing (Casas Bahia in Brazil), personal computing (AMD, Intel, Microsoft), and health (Aravind and Narayana Hrudayalaya in India), have shown that the opportunity is real. The debate is not whether the BOP is a true market or whether it can be profitable. The question is, How can it be tapped?

This opportunity forces managers and others to challenge their assumptions. They must come to terms with *the need for innovations to serve BOP markets*—not just in creating new hybrid technologies (for example, PCs running on car batteries in a hut) but for entirely new business models. Equally important are (1) creating the capacity to consume, (2) cost structures that are a fraction of those in developed markets, and (3) innovations in distribution and logistics.

The works in this volume describe successful BOP business models from around the world. They represent interesting experiments if considered one study at a time, but *collectively they reveal a new way of doing business.* By focusing on a range of industries—from housing to microfinance, from agriculture to health—and covering a geographical spread from India to Mexico and South Africa, the collection helps managers and public policy makers anchor their thinking on the role of the private sector and market-based solutions to poverty alleviation. It is a manifesto on how to combine profits and poverty alleviation.

What is the long-term impact of private sector involvement in poverty alleviation? First, it brings choice to BOP consumers. Access to world-class products and services at affordable prices and the benefits of choice are critical elements in developing self-esteem and dignity for BOP consumers. Consumption also creates new forms of entrepreneurial activity leading to new sources of livelihoods. For example, in India there is a new phenomenon of thousands of entrepreneurs who sell prepaid cards and charge cell phones for a fee. Second, the private sector enables BOP consumers to access global markets, as in the case of ITC. The two sides of the equation—consumption and new livelihood opportunities—are at the core of poverty alleviation. Finally, private sector involvement, when profitable, promotes new investments and scaling. Multinationals can create a global market for a successful experiment held in one locale. Consumption, new livelihoods, and scalability are the elements that lead to *democratizing commerce*, making the benefits of a global economy accessible to all.

This is our new challenge. This collection of studies represents a significant step in facilitating the process of engaging business in the most pressing problem we face.

ACKNOWLEDGMENTS

Although each of us has been independently engaged on topics related to the role of business in poverty alleviation, the idea of hosting a conference to bring focus to this area germinated quite informally. Two of us had an initial concept for such a gathering, which was further developed with the input from a number of our colleagues at the Harvard Business School (HBS).

This conference would not have been possible without the support of the school's Division of Research and Faculty Development. Three people in the division in particular deserve our thanks: Dean Jay Light, Senior Associate Dean Krishna Palepu, and former Dean Kim Clark. Each of them gave the necessary encouragement at various critical times in the planning of the event.

The conference from which this book is drawn—*A Conference on Global Poverty: Business Solutions and Approaches*—met December 1–3, 2005. Nearly 120 academics and practitioners from around the world attended the conference. We thank them and their sponsoring organizations for taking the time to earnestly examine what may be one of the most pressing issues facing global business today. They are far too many to name in this section, but a complete listing and their affiliations are found in the Appendix. We are particularly thankful to the six keynote speakers who addressed the conference at various points over the three days, challenging them with innovative ideas on the role of business in addressing poverty: David Ellwood (dean, Harvard University's Kennedy School of Government), Kurt Hoffman (director, Shell Foundation), George Lodge (professor emeritus, Harvard Business School), Andrew Natsios (administrator,

USAID), Ray Offenheiser, (president, Oxfam America), and C. K. Prahalad (professor, University of Michigan's Ross School of Business).

We are also extremely grateful to the numerous faculty members at HBS and Harvard University who went to extraordinary lengths to make this conference a success. Their unusual dedication and participation in both the conference and the book is a testament to the cross-disciplinary thinking and intellectual excellence that the problem of global poverty requires. Here we would like to especially acknowledge the roles played by James Austin, Joe Bower, David Brown, Allen Grossman, Linda Hill, Robert Kaplan, Tarun Khanna, Herman Leonard, and David Upton in moderating sessions and leading discussion groups.

As editors, we would like to congratulate the contributors to this volume for a job well done. Each paper had to undergo revision, and the authors stayed focused on the task in good spirit, enhancing the quality of the collection. We believe that their work—and the work of others like them—will affect the critical task of formulating lasting solutions to global poverty.

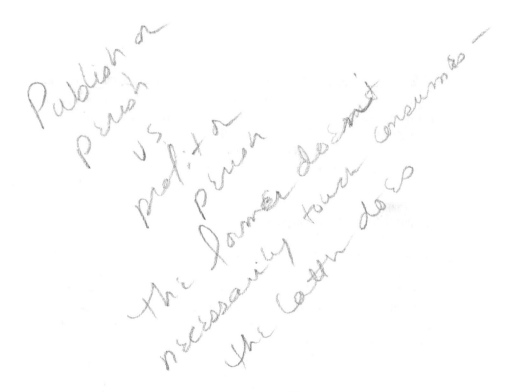

BUSINESS SOLUTIONS FOR THE GLOBAL POOR

INTRODUCTION

The problem of global poverty is ubiquitous and enduring. Although sustained economic growth in countries such as India and China has brought down the overall poverty level, we are still far from achieving the UN's top Millennium Development Goal[1] of halving the number of people living in extreme poverty by 2015.[2] We have all heard the statistics: nearly half of the world's 6.5 billion people survive on less than $2 a day, and 1.2 billion get by on just half that amount. We know that widespread hunger and malnutrition are among the many grim consequences; according to the United Nations, more than 800 million people routinely do not have enough to eat.[3]

Despite these sobering facts, the women and men who dwell at the base of the pyramid (the so-called BOP) have begun to capture the attention of corporate executives and senior managers. This emerging interest has been driven by the innovative work of a growing number of businesses that are redefining their interaction with the poor from a secondary activity to one integral to continued business growth and profitability. Their approach has been showcased by C. K. Prahalad, Stuart Hart, and Allen Hammond,[4] scholars whose work has awakened business attention to a potential "fortune at the bottom of the pyramid."[5] Not only is there a vast, untapped BOP market for goods and services, these authors argue, but business can play a critical role in connecting these underserved consumers to the economic mainstream, with tremendous social benefits to the poor themselves.

We believe, however, that the BOP represents less of a "fortune" than a solid market opportunity that can be cultivated only through the hard work of market development bolstered by cross-sector collaboration. Indeed, successful BOP initiatives offer a refreshing take on the age-old problem of poverty alleviation precisely because their approach reenvisions how governments, nonprofit organizations, and private enterprise might collaborate to redefine good business practice. Such initiatives draw to the fore latent business opportunities in what has long been an overlooked, undervalued market.

There isn't enough tax money in the world to make a dent in poverty. It's got to be done privately. And we know that one of the answers is promoting domestic businesses. But we also know that for a domestic business to flourish, it requires the nourishment that comes from global attachment, from integration into the world economy, from access to markets, credit, and technology. And where does this come from? This comes from the 63,000 multinational corporations that are now the engines of globalization.

George Lodge, professor emeritus, Harvard Business School, keynote speaker, HBS Conference on Global Poverty, December 2005

Those business opportunities are not insignificant. A recent article estimated the BOP market for goods in the eighteen largest developing countries at $1.7 trillion.[6] This does not include the potential investments in other aspects of poverty alleviation such as infrastructure for energy or transportation. One estimate put the value of such investments at more than $300 billion in 2003.[7]

As more and more businesses target their share of the BOP "fortune," there is ample need to critically examine the success factors in and obstacles to operating in this market. How do businesses formulate BOP strategies? What are the key components of such a strategy? What are the characteristics of successful enterprises and leaders? What steps have they taken to address the managerial, operational, and cultural challenges of working with and serving the poor? Just what impact are these approaches having on the bottom line and on poverty itself? Finally, is business alone a sufficient force to help the poor climb the economic ladder?

To answer these questions, in December 2005 Harvard Business School convened its first-ever conference on business approaches to poverty alleviation. Entitled "A Conference on Global Poverty: Business Solutions & Approaches," the event assembled 120 academics and practitioners from around the world to explore how doing business with the poor can be both a profitable—and a socially beneficial—undertaking.

The aim of the conference was not so much to direct business attention to the fortune at the base of the pyramid. Instead, our goal was to analyze and draw practical lessons from the actions and approaches taken by successful enterprises engaging the BOP segment.

Building on the richness of three days of discussion, we are pleased to bring together in this volume thirty-two papers presented at the conference. Most chapters are coauthored by academics and corporate, nonprofit or public sector managers. Each is anchored to one or more concrete case examples. All told, they draw on initiatives undertaken by more than fifty enterprises in twenty countries and deliver practical and powerful how-to insights gleaned from leading BOP ventures around the world.

> *When business is faced with a problem it can't look up to the heavens and pray for a solution. It rolls up its sleeves and solves the problem. Because if a company doesn't solve the problem, it goes out of business. This problem-solving capacity is why I think the private sector can provide tremendous social value in tackling poverty.*
>
> Kurt Hoffman, director, Shell Foundation,
> keynote speaker, HBS Conference on Global Poverty

The book is divided into six thematic parts structured to reflect the multifaceted nature of poverty and the broad range of actors—multinational and local businesses, entrepreneurs, civil society organizations, and governments—that play a role in its alleviation. Nonetheless, it must be kept in mind that this book is a collection of papers developed for a conference, and as such they may not all fall neatly into one of the six parts we have created for them; nor do they fully exhaust each theme. Furthermore, many papers address multiple themes and could have easily appeared in another section of the book.

Part One: Just Who *Are* the Poor?

It hardly needs to be said that the poor represent a vast market; as of 2006, nearly four billion people lived on less than $5 a day. Without doubt, the four billion people represented in Figure I.1 are too numerous and varied to be treated as a single group. In fact, they are extremely heterogeneous, representing a variety of subgroups that differ by socioeconomic status, culture, and gender.

Figure I.1. The Global Income Pyramid.

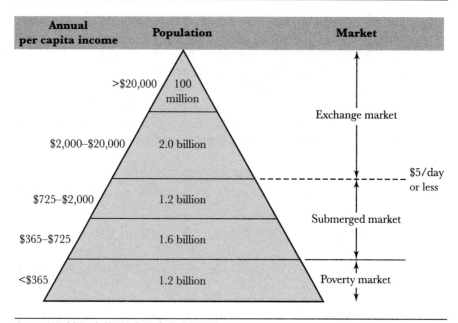

Annual per capita income	Population	Market
>$20,000	100 million	
$2,000–$20,000	2.0 billion	Exchange market
$725–$2,000	1.2 billion	$5/day or less
$365–$725	1.6 billion	Submerged market
<$365	1.2 billion	Poverty market

Source: World Bank (2001a); Prahalad (2002).

We find that the true rock bottom of the economic pyramid consists of what might be called a "poverty market," where most people still lack the basic necessities of life: sufficient food, clean water, and adequate shelter. The sheer precariousness of their daily existence may preclude them from meaningfully participating in the market, as consumers or producers. Poor health, lack of nutrition, financial vulnerability, and a dearth of marketable skills shut the so-called ultrapoor out of the economy and, if they are lucky, into the hands of nonprofit agencies and government relief programs.

In contrast, those individuals at the middle of the base of the pyramid, with incomes between $1 and $5 per day, participate in "submerged markets,"[8] often indulging in consumption of packaged goods, apparel, and appliances much like those at the top. These submerged markets, as with conventional markets the world over, are driven by voluntary exchanges of goods and services for money or monetary equivalents. Nevertheless, they are often extremely inefficient and lack the infrastructure and supporting institutions that characterize the "exchange" markets at the top of the pyramid. For example, submerged consumers may not have bank accounts or access to formal credit, but they may be able to obtain loans from money lenders or other channels at above-market rates. Similarly, they may have physical access to markets and commercial centers but are forced to walk miles to reach them, and once there they are able only to exchange goods through barter.

Chapters One through Three take a close look at these differences and examine the characteristics, preferences, and habits of both the ultrapoor and those already engaged in submerged markets.

Part Two: Meeting the Basic Needs of the Poor

To add value to the exchanges taking place at the higher levels of the BOP, companies must first come to grips with the day-to-day needs of those living at the rock bottom. These are the men and women who spend their waking hours struggling to meet their families' minimum needs for physical security, food, water, shelter, health care, and energy. The hierarchy of these basic needs may be a matter of debate, but unless the poor have access to the full bundle it is impossible for them to ascend the pyramid and participate as consumers in market exchange.

Chapters Four through Ten look at this challenge through a series of case studies that examine the role of business in meeting the poor's basic needs for security, health care, and utilities such as water, gas, and electricity. Without a clear pathway to profit, private investors are not normally motivated to meet the poor's basic needs. In fact, many successful cases of private provision to poor consumers owe their profitability to enlightened government policies that enable adequate returns for investors. Such policies seem to have a common characteristic: they provide just enough incentive to attract the private entity to develop the infrastructure but leave it to the companies to collect the rest of the return from consumers of their service. This crucial link has forced innovative market mechanisms to emerge in terms of product and service design, and delivery and compliance.

Part Three: Building the BOP Value Chain

By creating a positive business environment, providing the right tools for entrepreneurship and trade, and offering private sector partnerships, you open the door to people to pursue their own development. There is no development approach which is more edifying to a person, and in turn, more durable in results, than this.

Andrew Natsios, administrator, USAID, keynote speaker,
HBS Conference on Global Poverty

The poor engage in a range of economic activity; they are both consumers and producers. However, because of variation in their purchasing power, level of economic and geographic integration, and risk-taking ability, their consumption and production patterns are often markedly different. Chapters Eleven through Fourteen examine a series of case studies about companies that have successfully adapted their value proposition to the needs of low-income, submerged market consumers in the retail, technology, and consumer goods sectors. In Chapters Fifteen through Seventeen, we look at the role of business in creating employment opportunities at the BOP, as well as how the private sector can facilitate integration of the poor into the global production system.

The Poor as Consumers

The poor differ from affluent consumers in a number of ways. Low-income consumers tend to shop frequently and buy in small quantities. Their purchasing habits are driven by low and highly variable incomes (which they often earn on a weekly or even daily basis), as well as by other constraints, such as lack of storage space or appliances to preserve and cook food. Because of their economic vulnerability, the poor also have a much lower tolerance for risk taking than their wealthier counterparts. This tendency is exacerbated by the fact that many rural poor live in "media-dark" areas characterized by extremely low penetration of electronic media and a high level of illiteracy. Thus they lack access to essential information about products or services—information commonly available to wealthier consumers. This situation of low risk-taking ability and imperfect information often manifests itself in a reluctance to switch brands or adopt new products, because doing so may pose higher financial risk than sticking to the status quo, even when the products are sold at a discount. For companies seeking to overcome existing brand loyalties, this means finding ways to allow low-income consumers to experience a new product or service in a risk-free, firsthand manner—whether through product demonstrations or the recommendation of friends and neighbors.

The Poor as Producers

Much has been made (and deservedly so) of the potential consumer market at the base of the pyramid. However, consumption is inherently linked to income, and for many observers the drive to sell consumer products to the unemployed and underpaid is putting the proverbial cart before the horse. Indeed, companies may best make use of the BOP by leveraging the productive capacity of the poor as an input—in both supply and distribution chains—to business. Bringing BOP-produced goods to market is not easy, however; poor producers often lack the information, infrastructure, and risk-taking ability to commercialize their products without the intervention of rent-extracting intermediaries. However, as contributors to this volume show, improving information flow and market access can go a long way toward empowering the poor and reducing procurement costs for companies.

On the distribution end, companies have looked to the poor themselves as a primary channel to the BOP market. For example, low-income, community-based salespeople can be extremely effective in building demand for goods in the hard-to-service rural market. What's more, because such salespeople have deep knowledge of the economic situation and reliability of their neighbors, they furnish the market intelligence critical to building a creditworthy customer base.

Part Four: Business Models at the Base of the Pyramid

The fourth part of the book offers three integrative chapters that provide overarching business principles for serving the base of the pyramid. They also highlight the fact that companies seeking to operate at the BOP face a number of unique challenges:

- Because of the unintended, but nevertheless, real cultural distance and lack of engagement between corporate decision makers and the poor, companies may overlook crucial business opportunities if they do not proactively transform their organizational culture.
- A lack of essential infrastructure in developing countries and poor markets makes operating at the BOP a difficult, and potentially costly, undertaking.
- Finally, companies are challenged to find ways to bring BOP initiatives to scale and sustainability within the time frames dictated by traditional corporate targets.

To be truly responsive to low-income clients, companies must strengthen bottom-up market intelligence and outreach, while also ensuring that corporate leadership sets a tone of openness and engagement from the top. Making this change requires a shift in worldview and hard-wiring a sensitivity to the poor throughout the business. Companies that work successfully with the BOP typically have organizational cultures that are entrepreneurial, and they frequently possess leadership that sets the vision externally while internally reinforcing the openness and patience needed to support new, sometimes risky, BOP ventures.

Companies interested in engaging BOP markets often operate in an environment devoid of the valuable physical, legal, and institutional infrastructure that undergirds mainstream markets. For instance, a basic lack of physical connectivity—be it by road, air, or rail—characterizes many rural markets and poses tremendous challenges for companies seeking to operate profitably in this space. In many developing countries, companies seeking BOP customers must learn to adapt their business model in the context of uncertain (or virtually nonexistent) legal institutions that fail to protect essential property rights. As detailed in Part Four, success may rely on community-based agents and leveraging the poor's social capital in order to build incentives for all actors to "play by the rules." The role of social capital is also significant in overcoming obstacles related to weak economic institutions. In the absence of formal credit bureaus, many microcredit organizations, for example, rely on the self-selection and mutual monitoring of a group of entrepreneurs to reduce credit risk and minimize default.

A final challenge lies in the fact that companies are under inevitable pressure to quickly bring their BOP ventures to scale. In many such ventures, the true profit driver lies in volume, rather than in profit margin. However, because of the challenges already outlined (ill-equipped organizational cultures and the serious institutional and infrastructural deficits that characterize the BOP environment), few BOP ventures can be expected to reach scale at the pace seen in their mainstream counterparts. Indeed, those BOP ventures that do quickly reach scale often credit some of their success to support from governments, multilateral donors, and nonprofit organizations. Others that grow more slowly have benefited from enlightened managers who take the view that a BOP venture's steep start-up costs are a long-term investment.

Part Five: The Role of Government and Civil Society

Chapters Twenty-One through Twenty-Seven elaborate on the theme that supportive government structures, vibrant civil societies, and empowered entrepreneurs are drivers for reaching the BOP and essential partners. Although the profit motive reigns supreme in many of the cases examined in this volume, the conditions that make serving the poor profitable are frequently shaped by nonmarket actors. Government intervention—or the mere threat of such intervention—is one powerful driver. In South Africa, government-led initiatives to empower the country's long-oppressed black population spurred private sector actors to voluntarily take steps to integrate black-owned businesses into their value chain.[9] In the United States, efforts by the federal government to end discriminatory lending practices through the Community Reinvestment Act have spawned profitable new markets for banks targeting low-income individuals.[10] In some cases, companies (particularly public utility providers) choose to serve the poor because if they do not their goodwill with community groups and civil society—and therefore their ability to serve any customer segment at all—may be at risk.

Oxfam is interested in NGO-corporate partnerships that address obstacles to development, empower stakeholders, and build corporate accountability. I'm convinced, though, that it's not any easier for an NGO to transform itself into a suitable partner for companies than it is for a company to transform itself into a suitable partner for NGOs. I think it's hard for both of us to engage in these new kinds of relationships. However, once we get beyond the adversarial rhetoric and distrust to a place where civil conversation can begin, both for-profits and not-for-profits must focus on a common set of questions.

First, how do we find mutual interests in our core missions? Is that actually something that's possible? Second, how do we identify win-win outcomes that we can build upon? Is it possible for us to actually do a deal? And finally, how do we find systemic market-based solutions to fundamental social problems? Is that a pipe dream or is that something we might be able to pursue together?

Ray Offenheiser, president, Oxfam America,
keynote speaker, HBS Conference on Global Poverty

Business engagement with NGOs, local community groups, and entrepreneurs figures prominently in many of the chapters in Part Five. Alliances with civil society groups, whether formalized nonprofits, self-help groups, or community associations, can give companies strategic insight and access to new customers or suppliers. Organizations that have long-standing relationships with target groups can play the role of bridge builder between companies and communities. Through partnership, companies can leverage the strengths of their civil society counterparts—including deep knowledge of local conditions and legitimacy as local representatives—to dramatically lower their costs of market entry and operation. Partnerships with local entrepreneurs and businesses can play a similar role, enabling companies to reach scale and profitability. Government partners are essential for companies that may be attempting to build new markets where existing infrastructure is weak. In addition, to create a secure environment for business to operate, governments can also play a role in helping companies to provide socially beneficial services (particularly in sectors such as water, energy, and health care) by subsidizing service provision to certain consumer groups (for example, those who cannot pay), or by furnishing the seed funding necessary to reduce cost structures and generate the incentives for business involvement.

Part Six: Creating Economic and Social Value

The final part of the book examines the relationship between economic and social value creation at the base of the pyramid. "Social value" casts a broad net and can be measured by an array of variables, including improved quality of life, empowerment, security, and income. Specifically, the papers in Part Six ask, Under what circumstances can companies maximize both types of value? Are financial returns for investors and social returns for the BOP consumer or producer ever at odds? Do specific types of venture yield significantly more social value to the poor than others?

Work is what works best. A variety of government welfare efforts have been tried. But at the end of the day, getting somebody into a private sector job has proven over and over again to be the most effective long-term solution to poverty. This is not to say that selling cheap products more cheaply doesn't help. It really does. But still, employing the poor to create and provide products and services— as well as consume them—is what really generates income. And in generating income, it's especially important that this income stay in the community and feed other economic activity.

David Ellwood, dean, Harvard University's
Kennedy School of Government,
keynote speaker, HBS Conference on Global Poverty

To begin answering these questions, companies must first rigorously examine their business models to determine if they are really creating net economic gains for base-of-the-pyramid communities. Increasing the consumption of certain goods on the part of poor consumers can lead to improvement in their quality of life, but it may also displace consumption of other locally produced goods and services, thus reducing income for others in the community. Similarly, certain goods sold to BOP consumers may satisfy their immediate needs, but other products and services may go even further by also improving the productivity and income-earning potential of these individuals. To the degree that companies produce goods that enhance the productivity of the poor, or even employ the poor to produce such goods, more social value is created. Thus companies that are serious about maximizing the poverty alleviation impact of their business model must carefully account for the full range of income and productivity effects produced by their interactions with the poor.

Microfinance—provision of small business loans for low-income entrepreneurs—is a well-known example of a product that has strong income-generation effects on the "consumers" of the loan. In response to the high demand for financial services among the poor, the microfinance industry has grown rapidly in the past thirty years and proven itself to be a legitimate commercial market with returns equal or superior to those of conventional banking in many developing countries. However, having shown its financial value, how can microfinance also demonstrate the social value it confers to low-income entrepreneurs? For some, the mere existence of market demand for a product or service—that is, the willingness of customers to pay—is evidence enough that microcredit creates social value for the poor. Others argue that without measuring the ultimate social impact of the loans—in terms of income created, and quality-of-life improvements in health care, nutrition, and education—microlenders cannot understand their true impact, and by extension cannot maximize the poverty-alleviating aspects of their business model.

Even when companies do carefully consider the economic and social impacts of their products on the poor, they may still face reputational threats if their BOP ventures are seen as "excessively profitable." Of course, it can be argued that without this profit businesses targeting the poor will not attract the level of investment necessary to be sustainable or scaleable across the entire BOP. According to this view, above-average profitability should be seen as a sign of success, one that will no doubt invite competition and thereby bring down prices, ultimately benefiting the poor. To minimize negative public perception, however, companies that find themselves "profiting from the poor" must be willing to publicly address the profit debate, work collaboratively with NGOs and governments, and also measure and report on the social value they are creating for the poor.

In conclusion, companies should not look to the poor merely to exploit their untapped purchasing power or dip into low-cost labor pools. Over the long run, such a cursory and extractive approach will draw the attention of governments and NGOs—many of which already question the legitimacy of the private sector's involvement in BOP operations. To succeed in serving this market, companies must strike a delicate balance, keeping in mind both their legal obligation to return profits to their investors, as well as their social obligation to the societies in which they operate—and on which their long-term success depends. Only those who identify and cultivate their internal capacities and gain the collaboration of other interested parties within or outside their sector are likely to succeed. In short, there is not a fortune at the base of the pyramid, but much opportunity that may be converted to value for all concerned through the hard work of market development.

PART ONE

JUST WHO ARE THE POOR?

Because of the vast economic, cultural, and social disparities that exist in most societies, many businesspeople have only limited understanding of the poor and their daily lives. As a result, they may be at risk of misunderstanding or overgeneralizing the needs, capacities, and resources of the low-income sector. Chapters One through Three shed considerable light on the lives of the extremely heterogeneous group known as the global poor. The authors find that this heterogeneity is not merely economic but also gendered, geographic, and cultural. Women, who number among the poorest of the poor in many societies, are a crucial demographic that must be segmented with a careful eye to cultural as well as economic variables. Furthermore, because the poor represent a group of culturally diverse individuals (between and within countries, states, or even villages), segmentation may require completely new methodologies grounded in sociocultural, rather than socioeconomic, variables.

In the first chapter, Fauzia Erfan Ahmed takes an ethnographic approach to understanding the distinct needs of rural women who are clients or potential clients of the Grameen Bank in Bangladesh. Her case studies of three poor women in "Microcredit, Segmentation, and Poverty Alleviation Strategy for Women: Who Are the Customers?" reveal that marital, social, cultural, community, and household characteristics are all essential variables for effective segmentation. Her studies reveal that microcredit institutions and others serving the BOP can more effectively meet the needs of the poor if they fine-tune their segmentation models.

In the paper "Understanding Consumers and Retailers at the Base of the Pyramid in Latin America," Guillermo D'Andrea and Gustavo Herrero examine purchasing habits and preferences of Latin America's low-income consumers. On the basis of focus groups and interviews from six countries, the authors conclude that the poor in this market segment are not focused solely on purchasing the lowest-priced products. In fact, they found these consumers take a very sophisticated approach in assessing total purchasing costs. Like many of their more affluent counterparts, they value brand names, store cleanliness, and customer service. However, the authors also argue that the poor have distinct shopping habits, store selection criteria, and attitudes toward brand loyalty, calling for more precise segmentation strategies.

In Chapter Three, "Marketing Programs to Reach India's Underserved," Kunal Sinha and colleagues discuss a variety of mainstream marketing adaptations that companies have used within India to segment and serve culturally diverse markets. The authors highlight marketing techniques that leverage peer approval, word-of-mouth recommendation, and product sampling as particularly effective for attracting risk-adverse, conservative rural consumers.

CHAPTER ONE

MICROCREDIT, SEGMENTATION, AND POVERTY ALLEVIATION STRATEGY FOR WOMEN

Who Are the Customers?

Fauzia Erfan Ahmed

As never before, poverty reduction dominates the international donor agenda, and microcredit has emerged as the major market-based poverty alleviation strategy of the millennium. Pioneered by the Grameen Bank, a bank that gives small loans to poor women, this paradigm is being replicated in various parts of the world through the Microcredit Summit Campaign, which aimed to reach one hundred million poor women and their families by the end of 2005.[1]

The benefits of microcredit and other market-based poverty alleviation approaches are being debated in a variety of fora. But these discussions fail to explore variations among the poor, a group that is by no means homogeneous. Segmentation, admittedly a fundamental component of any marketing strategy, should also be applied to low-income populations. The question is not simply whether the poor should be regarded as customers and not as beneficiaries,[2] but *which* group among the poor can be customers. The contexts of poverty are also the contexts of doing business with the poor; they form the distinguishing characteristics of each segment. This context-specific segmentation[3] is particularly relevant to poor women for whom socioeconomic, cultural, familial, and religious contexts pose serious obstacles to poverty alleviation. If the private sector wants to help women get out of poverty, as a first step it must understand the realities of their everyday existence. This knowledge has to be

This research was made possible by the generous support of the American Institute of Bangladesh Studies in 2001.

the source of feasible segmentation; it means understanding who poor women really are and what creates value for them.

In Bangladesh, a predominantly Muslim country, minorities are among the poorest groups and minority women lie at the very sediment of rural society. In this chapter, I compare and contrast the contexts of three Bangladeshi women from the minority Hindu and Rishi (untouchable) populations. Broadly separated by marital status, they are Saraswati, a Hindu widow; Mohua, a Hindu wife; and Brinda, a Rishi divorcee. The case studies reveal that marital status is only one variable of segmentation, and that an increasing level of sophistication is required to distinguish one segment from another. These three women, even though they live within a few miles of each other, in fact belong to different segments of the low-income customer base. Drawn from a larger sample of two hundred villagers, these case studies are based on my field research in Bangladesh in 2001,[4] where I lived in a village with sharecropper Grameen Bank families to investigate microcredit, gender empowerment, and poverty alleviation.

These examples are used as a backdrop to explore two questions basic to the *what* and *how* of segmentation. First, what do village women themselves think of microcredit as a poverty alleviation mechanism? Second, how do social, economic, cultural, household, and religious characteristics distinguish one segment from another?

What Creates Value for Poor Women?

Low-income women know what a good life means to them. They want financial security, peace within the household (*shanghare shanti*), individual dignity (*shonman rekhe chola*), and equal gender representation in village legal and political institutions.

Lending money to a low-income man is not the same as lending to a low-income woman. She faces many obstacles; disenfranchisement and vulnerability are common themes in her microenvironment. Women not only face economic vulnerability but also low social status, discrimination in the workplace, and violence at home and outside. The social and economic status of a woman in rural Bangladesh is dependent on that of her husband and male kin.

Poor women want security. Given their low social status, this security has to be broadly defined, at the financial, societal, and household levels. Economic security consists not only of asset building but also of asset protection. Female property ownership and control[5] and salaried jobs are viewed as essential assets. In the household, security means a husband who supports his wife's entrepreneurial activities and makes decisions with her on how to manage the household. It also means safety. Women need protection from violence at home and from harassment in the workplace. Microcredit creates value only to the extent that it contributes to security and reduces vulnerability in all these arenas.

Saraswati: A Widow with Some Assets

If it hadn't been for the Grameen Bank, I would have lost the roof over my head. With the loan, I thatched my roof. I have a grocery shop and I eat three meals a day.

SARASWATI, BAROI (LOWER CASTE) WIDOW

Saraswati is an older widow. She belongs to the Baroi caste and has two daughters and one son. Her son, who is married, is estranged; even though they live in the same compound they do not eat together. He does not take care of Saraswati in any way. (I suspect that this was because his wife did not get along with her.) The younger daughter is mentally retarded, but neighborhood families help out by paying her for simple domestic chores.

Before his death, her husband managed a neighborhood grocery store out of their home. With the help of the Grameen Bank, Saraswati is now able to run the store herself. Business is good. As she says, "Mine is a neighborhood grocery store. We have always been here, so everyone comes to buy from me first." Because she belongs to the Barois, a betelnut leaf-growing caste, Saraswati also has betelnut leaf groves.

The Grameen Bank considers Saraswati a good risk. As an older widow, she does not face sexual harassment. She already owns a grocery shop, has no competitors, and possesses at least some of the know-how to run it—important assets from the lender's perspective. The local Grameen Bank manager helped to arrange Saraswati's older daughter's marriage to a Baroi family who did not take dowry, thereby enabling her to protect her assets. With the help of a loan and the business workshops that the Grameen Bank provides, this older widow is able to manage the grocery store profitably and to repay the loan in a timely manner. Through bereft of a "male protector," Saraswati, a successful entrepreneur, is able to live with dignity in the neighborhood. Indeed, as the next case study depicts, a married woman cannot always count on her husband to protect her.

Mohua, a Wife with an Abusive Husband

Getting along with everyone is important. I can get peace by getting along with everyone. I suffered for a whole year—there was strife. No one loved me.
Mother-in-law, brother-in-law, sister-in-law, everyone used to beat me. I have been beaten by everyone. . . . I have also been beaten by my father-in-law.

MOHUA, KAYASTH (UPPER CASTE HINDU WOMAN)

Terrified of her husband, Mohua would praise him in public even more so than other wives. In his presence, she always said that serving one's husband is tantamount to serving God (*swami seva ishwar seva*)—the common refrain of the dutiful Hindu wife. But in private she admitted that this was difficult. "For women, serving the husband is serving God. In fact, serving God comes after serving the husband. This causes much difficulty. . . ."

Despite the fact that she has three grown-up sons, Mohua has remained an outsider in her extended family. More educated than her husband, Mohua learned how to take out loans and became an entrepreneur. But a cycle of verbal and physical abuse and lack of solidarity with other female family members combined to deprive her of voice. As the quote indicates, she knew that the only way to survive was to please everyone and to keep quiet about her husband's violence.

Manik, the Husband

Q. Many people say if the wife earns money, then she won't listen to the husband. What do you think?

A. No, I don't agree. My wife earns a lot but there is one rule. She doesn't sell anything without asking me first—not even one egg! Yes, of course, I give her freedom. But if she goes to someone's house without reason, she has to tell me before she goes.

Q. What causes trouble in the household?

A. If she is secretive. Maybe she has saved 200 takas. If she doesn't hand it over when there is need, and if I find this out later, then there will be trouble.

MANIK, KAYASTH (UPPER CASTE HINDU MAN)

Manik strongly believed that Mohua should be subordinate to him. The implied threat of "there will be trouble" was real; he beat Mohua regularly. He gave her no independence, and lost no opportunity to devalue her. He did not appreciate her earnings from the loan investment; he saw this income as his due. Manik liked the money she brought in, but as the quote clarifies he was not going to allow Mohua to gain any dignity through her income.

His resentment of Mohua was not abstract. He had specific complaints about her lack of dowry.

Q. Do you think that women should get property in their own name?

A. Yes. When Hindu women get married, they get hundreds of thousands of *takas* as dowry. That is why they don't get property. But I didn't get anything when I married (my wife).

Manik was particularly resentful because, as the eldest brother in his own family, he had to find the dowry to marry off his sisters (he had nine siblings). He had hoped to recoup this loss by getting a good dowry from Mohua's family. Manik's hostility to Mohua was rooted in his disappointment at being denied the expected dowry.

So far, Mohua has been a "good" loanee of the Grameen Bank. She has been able to make the weekly repayments. But the income that she works so hard to earn is not hers to spend, and Manik uses violence to ensure that she doesn't "rise above him" through her profit-making activities.

Brinda: A Divorcee, Educated, but Unemployed

Educated people should get the respect that their education deserves. My husband was only educated up to class four or five. After high school, I went on to college. I loved it. We had weekly exams, and English was my favorite subject. I was [a] good student. But looking at me now you might find this hard to believe. . . . Rich people used to say, "Why is this girl from a poor family studying so hard and doing so well? We will lose face." But no one could keep me down. . . . Why did my parents marry me off at a young age? I could have got my master's. I have lost everything. I don't even have a husband to take care of. When I look at my books now, I cry. Once there was a way out, once there was direction (in my life). . . . Only God can understand my anguish.

BRINDA, YOUNG RISHI (UNTOUCHABLE) WOMAN

Highly educated for a low-income rural environment, Brinda finished high school and two years of community college at the intermediate level. She was then married to a man who did not even have a primary school education. He used to drink and beat her. Brinda finally left him after he contracted syphilis. No one in her family had ever completed primary school. They were illiterate; her father told me that when times were difficult, he had to beg for a living.

Her siblings, who were also illiterate, worked as sharecroppers in the field, but Brinda stayed home and searched for work she considered appropriate to her status. Her family also did not want her to do manual labor. Alternatively the object of scorn and jealousy, Brinda wanted badly to get out of the *para* (neighborhood). She wanted a white-collar job.

Segmentation Criteria: Gendered Contexts of Poverty

Segmentation should be based on the contexts that shape women's lives. These contexts include obstacles as well as possibilities. For poor women, poverty doesn't simply mean lack of income but also vulnerability to domestic violence, social disapproval, and discrimination. Minority low-income women face greater barriers. They can be divided, therefore, into segments along several context-specific variables: caste, age, education, income, and marital status (Table 1.1).

Caste

It is all too easy for the outsider to dismiss caste as wrong. But anyone who wants to engage the Hindu community in microcredit activities must first try to understand what caste means to them. Caste defines who a villager is. People derive strength and solidarity from belonging to the same caste as their forefathers, even if they are lower-caste. There are connections between caste and entrepreneurship activity since caste also determines income patterns. The Barois grow betelnut leaf (*pan*), but it is not just how they earn a living. For Barois, caste is tradition, culture, and identity. "*Pan* growing is like our mother tongue," said an older Baroi woman. Indeed there is a special *puja* (Hindu religious ceremony) ceremony for betelnut leaf, which is widely celebrated throughout the neighborhood. At first glance, it would seem practical for the Grameen Bank staff to advise Saraswati to sell her pan groves and concentrate on the grocery business. But the Grameen Bank cannot do so for cultural and religious reasons.

Higher caste (Kayasth) does not necessarily mean greater assets, as Mohua's example reveals. Notions of respectability restrict such higher-caste women from working the land. Mohua took out a loan for home-based activities; she could not work in the fields, a serious constraint in a country where agriculture remains the largest employer. Limited opportunities for work make these women even more dependent on their male relatives.

TABLE 1.1. CONTEXT-SPECIFIC SEGMENTATION.

Woman	Caste	Age	Education	Income	Marital Status	Loanee	Customer Potential
Saraswati	Low	Older	No	Moderately poor	Widow	Yes	+ Prime
Mohua	High	Older	Yes	Moderately poor	Abusive husband	Yes	− At-risk
Brinda	Untouchable	Young	Yes	Extremely poor	Divorcee	No	+ Hidden

Untouchability

What does it mean to be an untouchable? Rishis are outcastes. Despised by Muslims and caste Hindus (also a minority) alike, Rishis suffer from extreme discrimination, and this can result in exploitative income patterns. Many men said that they had to leave their homes for an extended period of time to beg for a living. Rishi women still worked as domestics in homes of the well-to-do for a meager in-kind payment, a hallmark of the traditional feudal master-servant relationship.

Discrimination also affects relationships between Rishi men and women. When Rishi men gain formal education, as a response to intense discrimination they do their best to leave the community and "pass" for Christian. Their strategy is to marry outside the community and lose touch with their neighborhood, a phenomenon that is striking in a culture where family is identity. As the case of Brinda indicates, educated Rishi women have less mobility and often are compelled to marry uneducated Rishi men, which invariably leads to problems.

Age

In a gerontocratic society, age is a key variable; status and mobility directly affect whether women can access microcredit. Older women, even if they are widows, have more status than younger women, and they are less prone to sexual harassment by the men in the neighborhood. Purdah[6] restrictions are much less stringent for these women who occupy a dominant position in the hierarchy of the extended family. Had Saraswati been younger, she could have lost control over her grocery store. But her age protected her. As an older woman, she also enjoyed greater mobility and could go unaccompanied to purchase goods for her grocery business.

Education

The link between education and security is not linear, especially for minority women. Education for low-income women translates into increased status only if it results in a commensurate job. Such minority women face many obstacles as they try to get work appropriate to their educational level. Brinda, a young, untouchable divorcee, faced discrimination on at least three fronts as she tried to get a white-collar job. First, rich people resented her because as an untouchable she studied with their children and surpassed them. She also had no mentors at school who could advise her, and in the neighborhood she was isolated, being the only woman who had studied up to the intermediate level. Education without suitable employment has in fact increased her vulnerability.

Husband

A supportive husband is perhaps the most important asset a woman can have in rural Bangladesh. Loanees need help from their husbands to pay back the weekly installments and encouragement from family members to develop business and leadership skills through Grameen Bank workshops. Women have made economic gains through microcredit not just for themselves but mainly for their families, as illustrated by a study[7] showing that women spend a greater part of their earnings on household needs. Despite this contribution, a woman's efforts to become a successful entrepreneur can also lead to unresolved tensions within the household, tensions sometimes characterized by violence. Given the volatile family situation in which she lives, it is unclear how much longer Mohua will be able to continue being a loanee.

Recent quantitative studies about microcredit, decision making, and violence in Bangladesh show that violence increased within loanee households. A study of 2,038 married women indicated that violence peaked when credit was introduced[8] but tapered off when other inputs were introduced.[9] Goetz and Sen Gupta's path-breaking study in 1996 of 253 loanees showed that 63 percent of interviewees had no direct control over credit. Thanks to "status inconsistency," described as a situation where the husband is threatened by the wife's perceived higher status,[10] wife-beating can increase even as the woman's economic status increases. Women whose education or income is higher than their partners (status-inconsistent) are at greater risk, particularly since "most conflicts involve making it clear who is in charge."[11] Other family members and patterns of violence within the household itself also play a role in increased domestic violence.

It is not surprising, as these studies reveal, that male relatives frequently control the loan. My findings indicated that violence decreased over time, not because of other inputs but because the loanee surrendered to her husband. As in Mohua's case, the wife hands over the loan in order to keep peace at home. Allowing male relatives to control the loan may be a woman's way of managing a status imbalance in the household that could otherwise result in domestic violence.

Income

In their excellent book *Who Needs Credit?* Wood and Sharif[12] segment the poor into three major groups on the basis of per capita income: the extreme poor, 40 percent below the poverty line; the moderate poor, who live just under the poverty line; and the vulnerable nonpoor, who reside precariously just above the poverty line.

But as Saraswati's case illustrates, per capita income should be distinguished from assets, just as asset protection needs to be distinguished from asset building. For poor women, however, assets can have an ephemeral quality. They can be easily eroded by dowry, which remains one of the biggest threats to financial security for poor families.

Despite the Dowry Prohibition Act, ratified in 1980, which outlawed dowry in Bangladesh,[13] dowry is seen as an investment to secure a daughter's future with her in-laws. The amount of dowry is much larger for Hindu families and results in no property rights for minority women. The groom's family may demand at least 30,000 *taka* (approximately US$600) in cash with gold ornaments, a bicycle, and a watch. In some Hindu communities, the cash amount demanded is 100,000 *taka* (US$2,000), which is many times more than a poor family's annual income. Saraswati would have had to borrow money for the dowry from the local moneylender at 150 percent interest and mortgage her grocery store to get her daughter married. This would have made serious inroads on her assets. Had she taken this step, Saraswati might have become a high-risk entrepreneur and therefore ineligible for a microcredit loan.

Women Customers: Segments and Characteristics

The context-specific segmentation presented in this chapter reveals that there are at least three segments among poor women: prime customers, customers at risk, and hidden customers (see Table 1.1). Clearly, Saraswati has benefited from the loan; women like her constitute the prime customer base. Mohua repays on time, but the loan has not created value for her. Microcredit has made her more vulnerable; she is therefore a customer at risk. Brinda is not a loanee. The current microcredit product, designed for illiterate women to pursue agricultural activities, does not appeal to her, and she will not buy it. But she represents a hidden customer base for the Grameen Bank.

Prime Customers

Key characteristics of prime customers are defined as much by their intangible resources as by their tangible assets: age, a supportive husband, business savvy, and ownership of some kind of infrastructure. Though not explicitly stated, the microcredit paradigm relies on this borrower profile for its success. Microcredit for the grocery shop has made financial security an attainable dream, if not a reality, for Saraswati, who possessed these assets even before she became a Grameen Bank loanee. Prime customers pay back the weekly installments on time and rise within the Grameen Bank committees to assume a leadership role.

Customers at Risk

It is only too easy to mistake such women for prime customers. They dutifully come each week to the Grameen Bank committee meetings and fulfill the repayment requirements. But a closer look reveals that the oppressive family contexts in which such women are compelled to live ensure that the microloan activities do not create value for these customers at risk. A telltale sign is their reluctance to display their leadership skills in the Grameen Bank, in contrast to the prime customers who speak out with impunity during meetings. The loan has made Mohua more vulnerable. Because of status inconsistency, wife beating can increase even as the woman's economic status increases. Male relatives frequently control the loan.

Hidden Customers

The Grameen Bank customer base today is not the same as it was thirty years ago, when it started in 1976. Bangladesh has shown remarkable progress in the past three decades. As a result of government programs, fertility has been reduced to an average of 3.2 children per woman and primary school enrollment is 100 percent for both boys *and* girls.[14] The high primary school enrollment rate and reduced fertility rate also reflect profound changes in this customer base. The low-income woman now has different needs and aspirations for herself and her children. There is a growing segment of educated women in the low-income customer market in Bangladesh. Contrary to a widespread belief in the development community, these women do not want to be "educated sharecroppers." Despite a bumper harvest in the region in 2001, Brinda was extremely poor, unlike the other illiterate Rishi women who were earning a good income as sharecroppers. She would not work in the fields. Such women want white-collar jobs. Yet the bulk of Grameen Bank loans are given for agricultural purposes such as livestock rearing and rice trading, a product mix that is more suited to an idealized static view of the customer as an illiterate woman. Women like Brinda represent a hidden customer segment for the Grameen Bank, who can use microcredit to become white-collar entrepreneurs.

Conclusion

The face of poverty is not uniform. Segments exist among poor women just as they do in other markets. Segmentation is as crucial for any private sector enterprise seeking to serve poor women as it is for mainstream marketers. The case studies presented in this chapter illustrate that, in addition to prime customers, there are also customers at risk and hidden customers.

Segmentation of the low-income customer base must be derived from knowledge of the environments in which poor women live. Context-specific segmentation based on caste, age, education, income, and marital status leads to feasible segments and therefore to appropriate poverty alleviation strategy. In a dynamic and rapidly changing environment such as rural Bangladesh, an idealized customer profile can become static. Low-income women want financial security, physical safety, social status, and equal opportunities for work and peace at home. Respect for whether poor women think this market-based mechanism creates value along with sensitivity to cultural, social, and religious contexts are essential to an effective microcredit program.

CHAPTER TWO

UNDERSTANDING CONSUMERS AND RETAILERS AT THE BASE OF THE PYRAMID IN LATIN AMERICA

Guillermo D'Andrea, Gustavo Herrero

This chapter focuses on low-income consumers in Latin America, and on the retailers that serve their needs. We first highlight some macroeconomic data on the region, describe the research method followed, and then cover our major findings about low-income consumers (such as brand preference, frequency of purchase, ticket size, store selection criteria, their buying decision process, and so on). We then look at the retailers that serve these consumers' needs and try to understand their business model and value proposition. Finally, we analyze both the performance and the fiscal behavior of smaller retailers.

Latin America

Latin America is home to the largest income inequality on earth. In 2003, the richest decile of the population earned thirty times that of the poorest decile.[1] By the end of 2004, 43 percent of Latin America's 517 million people lived below the poverty line, with 19 percent living in extreme poverty.[2] Although the region is inhabited by people with similar cultural heritage and traits, there are significant socioeconomic differences among countries.

After a decade of reform and moderate growth, Latin America still shows highly dualistic social structures, where the affluent represent 8–15 percent of the population but concentrate 45–65 percent of total purchasing power. Nevertheless, there is a vast segment of middle-, lower-middle-, and lower-class consumers who make little money but are not destitute and thus represent a significant share of spending in the region.

Our Research

Our research focused on how the Latin American retail sector addresses the brand and product needs of consumers who make up the region's low and middle socio-economic strata. The scope of the project covered six countries—Argentina, Brazil, Chile, Colombia, Costa Rica, and Mexico—that are home to 71 percent of the region's population and encompass 81 percent of the region's GDP. Four focus groups were conducted in each country, and 217 interviews were carried out with retailers in all of them. These data were supplemented with information on the region's macro-economic context. Our work draws largely from field work sponsored by the Coca-Cola Retailing Research Council (Latin America) and commissioned to Booz Allen Hamilton and IBOPE.

Emerging Consumers

A closer look at the low-income or "emerging" consumer segments shows that the key differentiator resides in employment, which drives income and access to home supplies. A typical household has one wage earner, who is employed in a working-class activity and earns anywhere from \$80 to \$300 per month.[3] Individually—and compared to their counterparts in higher classes—they buy less, but the portion of their income devoted to food and consumer products is significantly higher. Thus emerging consumers, though considered poor by many, in fact have a considerable amount of money to spend on consumer products as a group.

Consumer products are the number one spending category across Latin American countries, with housing or rent, transportation, and communications typically absorbing a large part of the remainder. However, although consumer products make up roughly 30–35 percent of spending for the average consumer in a given country, emerging segments allocate a disproportionately larger share of their income to these products—anywhere from 50–75 percent, with the lowest socioeconomic strata claiming to spend nearly all their income on these purchases. Hence, the net effect of this phenomenon is that household purchases in these segments can still amount to a substantial sum over time[4] and consequently represent a significant share of the consumer goods markets.

The vast majority of lower-income consumers can hardly be described as desti-tute. It is true that Latin America has its share of poverty, and that there are social classes who are classified as marginal or indigent, but many households today have running water, electricity, and basic appliances that bear an impact on purchasing behavior. Nearly all "C" and "D" households (see Figure 2.1) have a television set, radio, and refrigerator (90–100 percent household penetration), and in countries such as Mexico and Costa Rica the penetration of washing machines, VCRs, and access to cars in urban areas is high.[5]

Beyond the rather large fraction of the budget that these purchases represent, household expenditures have a much greater meaning to emerging consumers. For the women who control the majority of these purchases, consumer products are a key mechanism by which they fulfill the overlapping roles of wife, mother, economist, and "self." Discussion groups revealed that considerable self-esteem is derived from man-aging this spending in the best way possible to care for the family.

In terms of consumer products, emerging consumers represent a market larger in value than upper segments in all of the markets covered in our study, ranging from 51 percent in Brazil to 69 percent in Chile (Figure 2.1).

Brands

Surprisingly, consumers showed strong preference for leading and intermediate brands over low-priced, economy brands. This preference was linked not only to aspiration and image but also to perceptions of quality, performance, and support. With less dis-posable income, poor consumers also have less margin for error in their purchases, therefore steering their preferences toward established, proven brands.

The product and retail format needs of emerging consumers are better described as "basic" than "simple." These consumers purchase more basic foodstuffs and perishables, but they are willing to pay for intermediate and leading brands in basic categories. They also may shun low-cost retail formats such as hard discount stores.[6]

There is a well-established link between affordability and category penetration of consumer products in low-income households. The shopping basket of these con-sumers is weighted toward staple products, some of which are common across coun-tries while others are not. Typically the more expensive, higher-value-added categories such as frozen foods, ready-to-eat meals, yogurt or flavored milk drinks, and fabric soft-ener are less prevalent in these households, driven in part by the low penetration of household appliances such as freezers and microwaves.[7]

It is worth noting that brand loyalty (for purposes of this study, defined as *purchasing* a brand as opposed to just *preference* or *purchase intent*) differs by category.

FIGURE 2.1. SOCIOECONOMIC SEGMENTS IN LATIN AMERICA (PERCENTAGE OF TOTAL POPULATION VS. PERCENTAGE BUYING POWER FOR CONSUMER PRODUCTS).

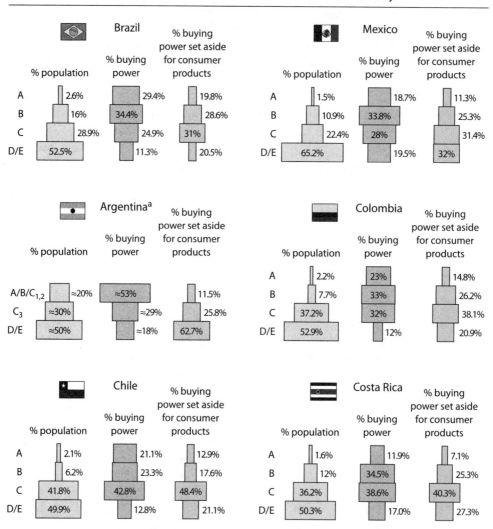

Notes: [a] percentage of household income; A/B/C$_1$ and C$_2$ percentages reported together for 11/02.

Source: Strategy Research Corporation; UN Demographic yearbook, UNESCO statistical yearbook; CCR Latin Panel; Sigma; IAE Universidad Austral in Buenos Aires analysis.

Interestingly, we found the highest loyalty to brands on staples such as rice and cooking oil. Loyalty was also high for aspirational categories such as soft drinks, or categories that have an impact on self-esteem as a caregiver (for example, laundry detergent), but economic reality overrode purchase intent more often. Overall, less loyalty was observed in personal care and cleaning products, even though brand preference was still high (especially in personal care categories that appeal to consumers' sense of vanity). Hence, brand attitudes and purchasing patterns represent quite rational and savvy behavior on the part of emerging consumers, who are fulfilling their need for performance in categories that make up the bulk of the daily diet or that showcase capabilities as a caregiver. These observations are in line with existing theory, which holds that a consumer's "level of involvement" with a category is positively correlated with loyalty.[8]

Acceptance of dramatically lower-priced (and low-cost) "value brands" is growing in some countries; nevertheless, emerging consumers are still drawn to traditional brands. In Brazil and Argentina, emerging consumers were more open to trying value brands, especially in cleaning products. Economic necessity clearly plays a role in increasing the trial of these products, as do word-of-mouth testimonials from friends and family regarding performance. However, intermediate and leading brands still represent the largest share of purchases, and emerging consumers hesitate to try value brands. Low price points are attractive but can also generate mistrust and skepticism about product quality. *Lo barato sale caro* (what's cheap ends up being expensive) was a frequently heard comment.

Buying Behavior

However, low-income segments did differ from other segments in the size and frequency of purchases. Because of less stable income and lack of available room for storage, the shopping process is driven by day-to-day needs. The lower percentage of formally working women in these segments allows daily shopping. Several stores are visited two and three times per week, and in the case of fresh produce some consumers may make two trips to the store on the same day.

Emerging consumers are certainly price-sensitive, but purchasing decisions are generally driven by a desire to minimize "total purchasing cost"—which is quite different from retail shelf price. Total purchasing cost represents a fully loaded cost for a basket of goods, and retail shelf prices naturally make up an important part of the equation. However, we found that emerging consumers mentally factor in transportation costs to arrive at a final price for the shopping basket. In addition, they have strong awareness of "hassle factors" (such as finding child care or coping with children's demands while in the store), logistical constraints for bringing purchases home, and time spent commuting or standing in line. Ideally, to recover this total cost low-income consumers would seek to purchase in bulk and shop less frequently to minimize transaction costs. But this approach to cost savings lies beyond the reach of their wallet. Scarce and variable income translates into smaller-size purchases, making meaningless the discounts offered by big box retailers on bulk items. This makes the tradeoff of physical proximity and pricing a key determinant of store and product choice.

Format needs do differ for daily and large or stocking-up purchases, but physical proximity is the first-order determinant of store choice in both cases. Consumers do not like to travel very far, and they consider the transportation costs of even round-trip bus fare or a short taxi ride to be significant.[9] When asked to explain the difference between a store that is considered close by versus far away, most consumers define both of these extremes within a relatively small physical distance: "one block" versus "seven to ten blocks away," or "within a five-minute walk" versus "three or four bus stops away." Most emerging consumers in urban areas (by far the bulk of the population in these segments in Latin America) have numerous store formats nearby and thus need travel only minutes to make daily or even stocking-up purchases.

Frequent shopping and daily cooking give poor consumers deeper knowledge of product quality and prices, and of the best place to buy each category. Street and open air markets are perceived as having both better quality and price, with the added benefit of enabling social interaction with neighbors. The produce and meats sold in these markets are seen as fresher, more natural, and less uniform than those found at supermarkets. These attributes combine to make such markets appealing to a range of consumers, not only those from lower-income segments. These markets also give consumers the option to buy the products they need in specific quantities and from a broader range of qualities, and prices may vary through the day, coming down as the daily closing time approaches.

The right assortment of brands and products is important, as well as the emotional validation from interacting with the store owner. For low-income consumers, a wide product assortment and broad acceptance of credit cards are less important than hygiene and dignified treatment. Product variety may be a point of attraction but also a source of frustration, and the type of credit required by these consumers is strictly related to the amount of cash they can access short-term.

Preferred Retailers

Small stores make Latin America's retail landscape unique in its composition. Diverse retail formats both between and within countries offer a sharp contrast to what is often unkindly referred to as the "cookie-cutter commerce" of chain stores in more mature markets.

Within this diversity of formats, we identified five basic smaller service models. *Traditional* stores tend to be quite small (25 to 50 square meters) and offer mostly behind-the-counter service. *Small supermarkets* are self-service businesses, ranging from small self-service outlets with one cash register manned by the sole proprietor to bustling, independent supermarkets that stock a broad range of products and have as many as five or six checkouts. *Street* and *open air* formats—the least homogeneous of all models—are characterized by semipermanent or mobile infrastructure, for example, an easily moved cart or stall that may be mounted in the same location every day or in multiple locations that vary by day of the week. *Category specialists* such as butchers, bakers, and greengrocers concentrate their business on limited fresh categories, usually sold from behind a counter—with some exceptions, such as self-service fruit and vegetable stores (*sacalões*) in Brazil. Lastly, *convenience* outlets sell primarily candy, gum, tobacco, and limited general merchandise (pens, newspapers) through small (less than 10 square meters) but permanent kiosks.

Increasingly, the lines between service models are blurring. For example, many traditional stores sell dry goods across the counter but have some self-service racks for high-velocity items such as soft drinks, ice cream, packaged breads, cookies, and snacks. Additionally, many countries have formats (bakeries, for example) that combine the sale of on-premise, ready-to-eat foods along with goods for future consumption.

Given the range and diversity of formats, we focused our research on a subset of small retailers that operate in relatively similar fashion across all six countries: traditional stores, small self-service (a subset of small supermarkets), and open-air street fairs.

Customer-facing value drivers such as location, product assortment, price and value, people, and services were examined along with selected ratios from the *Strategic Resource Model*.[10] The results offered a few lessons to be learned for those who seek to attract emerging consumers as customers, or who view small retailers as inherently inefficient.

The Store

Location is a compelling advantage that many small retailers offer emerging consumers, many of whom make small daily purchases. To an eye trained on the layout of chain stores, small retailers show a cluttered and less tidy physical appearance. Goods appear to be stocked randomly; product seems haphazardly stacked on the shelves or floors. Narrow aisles and poor lighting appear to add to the unattractive infrastructure.

Naturally, physical appearance varies a great deal between small-scale stores, but on the whole emerging consumers find the infrastructure of small stores perfectly acceptable. Hygiene matters, and most sole proprietors are careful about it. In fact, many emerging consumers equate modern infrastructure with cost and point out that it is the customer who ultimately bears the final bill for such luxuries.

Product

Small-scale retailers offer the "right" assortment; they are able to optimize the mix to the micromarket they serve, offering only the categories, brands, and sizes that their customers demand. The assortment at traditional and small self-service stores focuses on fresh foods, drinks, and basic dry goods, along with a limited selection of cleaning products, personal care items, and luxury food items such as canned fish, deli meats, cookies, and condiments. In most countries, leading brands dominate the assortment—especially in traditional stores, where approximately 80–90 percent of the stock-keeping units (SKUs) stocked are first-tier brands. Additionally, small-scale retailers serve daily purchase needs effectively by offering a higher proportion of smaller sizes, and by "fractioning" products such as dry pasta, cereals, sugar, and cigarettes. In many countries, the smallest size of powdered laundry detergent sold by large chain supermarkets is 500 grams. Small retailers, on the other hand, commonly carry sizes as small as 150 or 250 grams. Open-air markets give customers exactly the quantity desired, no matter how small the amount. In comparison, consumers express feeling shame when asking for a very small quantity in a large chain supermarket.

Price

Despite a shelf-price disadvantage, affordability is not a major issue for many small retailers. Our survey found that shelf prices for exact substitutes (that is, same SKUs) were anywhere from 5–20 percent more expensive compared to large supermarkets. Argentina was the only exception; shelf prices were 1–3 percent lower.[11] This is not surprising, given that small retailers by definition lack the scale to earn the significant volume discounts or trade allowances granted to large chains. Interestingly, emerging consumers perceive a poor price-value trade-off at large chain supermarkets, because they think in terms of total purchasing cost. Furthermore, street and open fairs do have a clear shelf price advantage in fresh produce; products typically come direct from farmers, their agents, or vast wholesale markets. Besides lower prices overall, their service model better matches the consumer demand curve. Chain supermarkets usually offer only first-grade produce, but street and open-air formats offer several grades of quality.

People

Small-scale retailers benefit from the presence of the local owner/operator who can tailor the business model to local needs and lend a personal touch. Shopkeepers claim to know most of their customers (more than 60 percent) by name. Local owners observed during store surveys made product recommendations, shared neighborhood news, or simply made a point to engage and greet almost every customer who entered the shop. The end result of this treatment is an emotional proximity that makes emerging consumers feel comfortable and in a familiar environment. Adding to this, owner/operators may be actively involved in community activities.

Service

Small-scale retailers offer limited services compared to large chain supermarkets. A few accept credit cards, offer home delivery, state that they offer "extended operating hours," or run promotions such as free product with purchase. Although promotional vehicles and merchandising activities are less prevalent, small-scale retailers' techniques are simple yet appropriate. Some independent supermarkets fund their own promotions (ranging from raffles to temporary price discounts) or even distribute one-page flyers in the neighborhood with pricing and promotion information.

Credit

Small retailers offer credit in one of two forms: "informal credit," where the owner/operator writes the name of the debtor in a small notebook, or through a "virtual wallet," when the customer is short of small amounts of cash at the register and is allowed to pay the next time. Informal credit, when offered, acts as a sort of loyalty program; once the customer uses this service, there are strong incentives to continue shopping at the store (versus switching to other small neighborhood shops). Typically, the social cost of defaulting on this sort of debt is high for consumers in this segment, since noncompliance usually becomes public knowledge in the neighborhood.

In summary, affordability, total purchasing cost, the right assortment, and the quality of fresh produce, combined with a satisfactory personal interaction, all enhance the emerging consumers' preference for small neighborhood stores over impersonal modern retailers. They also end up spending less.

Retailers' Performance

It is difficult to speak of the small retailer business model without first acknowledging that, conceptually, these businesses operate under a different perspective from large chain stores. Small retailers care almost exclusively about cash flow—that is, whether they can cover costs each month and have money left to replenish inventory. They typically do not run their businesses using traditional management tools. That said, standard frameworks are useful for highlighting some distinctive advantages of the small-scale retail business model that go beyond attributing their success to fiscal informality.

Looking at sales productivity, one finds that sales per store can be quite low—in the region of US$2,000–4,000 per month.[12] Small independent supermarkets may reach US$6,000–14,000 per month, but this is still a fraction of what is sold in larger chain stores, partly because of smaller ticket sizes. For the traditional stores surveyed, sales per square meter were only about 10 percent the amount for the large-scale trade.

Small-scale retailers face procurement handicaps, since middlemen supply a large portion of their product mix and small-order quantities raise final delivered cost. Yet most small retailers set prices with a markup in the range of 20–30 percent, with actual markups higher for slower moving items (such as bath soap) and lower for high-speed items (soft drinks). The higher retail shelf prices observed at small-scale retailers are consistent with a higher delivered cost of sales. Shopkeepers' pricing practices preserve an average gross margin in the area of 20–25 percent, similar to or lower than gross margins for chain supermarkets, which for a small sample of chain retailers ranged from 20–32 percent.[13] Hence, similar or lower gross margins combined with lower sales per square meter yield relatively lower gross margin return on sales (GMROS) for small-scale retailers.

Regarding employee productivity, small retailers tend to work with no more than two to five employees in the store, traditional shops and street or open air formats typically having only one or two staff. Employees are often family members and may not work full-time in the shop. Owner/operators take on numerous roles that in a large chain store could formally be described as store management, purchasing, human resources, security, cashiering, merchandising, and general administration (these general expenses typically account for 3.5–10 percent of sales for the large chain retailers). Some of the small-scale retail stores surveyed show monthly sales per full-time employee of as little as US$1,000–2,000—results that would be a cause of concern for a large chain retailer.[14] Similarly, gross margin return on labor (GMROL) for these stores was low.

The business model of small retailers excels at inventory turnover, which is more than twice as high as that of large chain supermarkets. Traditional shops and small self-service stores stock significantly fewer SKUs compared to a typical chain supermarket, and the product assortment consists of relatively fewer general merchandise categories, which often have lower turnover.

The cash nature of the business introduces rigorous discipline into inventory management; the consequences of ordering mistakes are large for the sole proprietor. Stores are quite small, making mistakes glaringly obvious to the owner: an empty space on the shelf, a customer asking for a preferred brand, product that sits on the shelf for a painfully long time. Not surprisingly, small-scale retailers replenish frequently—more than three times per week for fresh products and drinks and a little less than once per week for basic food items.[15]

Therefore, even though small retailers have low GMROS and GMROL, their business model is quite efficient in converting inventory into cash, observing high gross margin return on inventory (GMROI), one of the keys of retailing. The small-scale retailers surveyed have surface productivity (GMROS) that is only 25–30 percent that of large players, but their GMROI is double or triple the figure of large chain retailers (Figure 2.2).

A look at net operating profits holds further valuable lessons as to why small retailers have a sustainable business model. Beyond gross margin, small retailers have reduced or nonexistent operating costs, which can be quite significant for a large chain supermarket retailer. Labor costs are generally lower and more variable than those of organized trade. Leveraging family members allows the small retailer greater flexibility to adapt hours worked to fluctuations in store traffic. Another benefit is that it can lead to lower shrinkage from theft. Additionally, the small retailer has the ability to defer cash salaries in the event of a liquidity crisis.

FIGURE 2.2. STRATEGIC RESOURCE MODEL RATIOS (SMALL-SCALE VS. LARGE-SCALE RETAILERS).

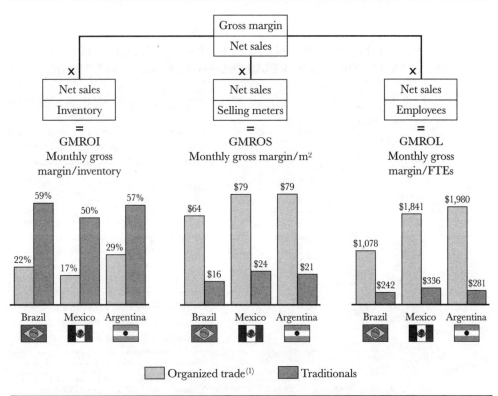

Note: [1]Organized trade is CBD in Brazil, WalMex in Mexico, and Disco in Argentina.

Source: 2002 annual reports; field interviews; Booz Allen analysis.

When it comes to rent expense, many small retailers (from 20 percent to 60 percent) own the site where they operate as either a freestanding business or as a store co-located within their residence. In Colombia and Argentina, for example, between 40 percent and 50 percent of traditional shop owners also live in the store, which helps them to save on security and share other expenses. For those small retailers who own their stores, noncash depreciation or return on invested capital is not viewed as an operating cost; in these cases, depreciation is often not even a good proxy for the minimal capital expenditure made to maintain property. For those who rent, charges are less in the lower-income zones where shops are located, and small retailers do not opt for overly large sites with parking and warehouse space.

In total, small retailers show lower or similar operating expenses as a percentage of sales than their chain supermarket counterparts (Figure 2.3). Admittedly, the comparison is somewhat artificial for reasons discussed earlier about rent and depreciation expense and because labor expenses for the small-scale retail sector usually do not include a salary for the owner/operator (net income from the business is typically his or her compensation). To complicate the comparison further, most small-scale

FIGURE 2.3. OPERATING EXPENSES AS PERCENTAGE OF SALES FOR SMALL RETAILERS AND LARGE-SCALE TRADE.

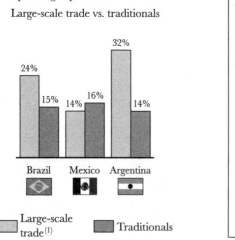

Estimate
Operating expenses as % of sales
Large-scale trade vs. traditionals

Brazil   Mexico   Argentina

Large-scale trade[1]   Traditionals

Comments

• Labor expenses do not include a salary for the owner since net income from the business is his/her compensation

• Main items included in operating expenses for small retailers:
  - Rent (when they are not owners of the site)
  - Electricity and other utilities
  - Telephone
  - Car maintenance and expenses
  - Insurance (seldom)
  - Advertising and promotional expenditures (very seldom)
  - Banking fees, cash management
  - Accounting, legal support

Note: [1]Large-scale trade is CBD in Brazil, WalMex in Mexico, and Disco in Argentina.

Source: 2002 annual reports; field interviews; Booz Allen analysis.

retailers qualify for small business tax regimes, which typically simplify a plethora of sales, social, business income, and value-added taxes (VAT) into one flat tax with revenues as a calculation basis.[16] The total tax pie is higher under the standard tax regime applied to large retailers, compared to small-business tax regimes. So regular small-scale retailers enjoy a perfectly legal, structural cost advantage—as long as they stay small.

Taking all into account, the average net income after tax for the small retailers surveyed ranged from 4 percent to 11 percent of sales. Though this is an enviable figure for the large chain supermarket retailer, scale must be considered. In fact, this higher percentage translates into a rather small absolute amount, anywhere from two to three times the minimum monthly wage.

Fiscal Considerations

Regarding fiscal behavior, there are many creative means by which informal players may reduce their VAT, sales, and business income tax burden. Informal players may understate revenues to take advantage of small-business tax regimes, purchase from suppliers or sell to customers without invoices and tickets, or sell with "half invoices" that list only a fraction of the volume delivered. With labor taxes, employers can neglect to register all or some employees in an attempt to avoid paying social contributions and labor benefits (such as the "thirteenth salary" that is standard practice in many Latin American countries).[17] Informality is present, and its relevance cannot be denied.

The economic benefits of tax evasion are enhanced when informal practices are present along the whole value chain. Informality is probably more characteristic of categories such as fresh produce and for value brands in general. Potential tax evasion could reach upwards of 20 percent of sales for informal value chains, by one estimate.[18]

Yet complete evasion of these taxes by small-scale retailers is unlikely even in countries with higher prevalence of informality. For one thing, large companies and multinational manufacturers (who sell formally) supply the majority of consumer products in Latin America. When these companies sell through intermediaries, tax compliance tends to "travel" along the value chain since middlemen have strong incentives to also sell formally and recover VAT credits. Moreover, many of these companies are trying to sell directly to small retailers (candy, cookies, packaged breads, ice cream, soft drinks, beer), introducing tax formality to a large portion of small retailers' sales.

Once retailers purchase formally, it is more difficult for them to evade VAT, sales, and business income taxes. Second, in some countries government agencies are improving their inspection capabilities and small retailers perceive a higher probability of being caught. For example, Chile has implemented an extensive information matching system that allows the collections agency to discover tax evaders with greater precision. In Brazil, the tax authorities are linking sales tax and financial operations information, making it easier to identify inconsistencies. In most countries, cash registers with recording devices are being introduced.

Lastly, labor litigation risks introduce some self-policing with respect to labor contributions. Most small-scale retailers need fewer employees to operate their stores to begin with. Even for those retailers that require a small number of employees and choose not to comply with the law, there is risk of a judicial process or claim. In most countries, labor law infractions are dealt with severely, and fines or litigation costs are high.

To better understand how informality affected performance, we looked at the *stated* tax payments of the small-scale retailers' surveyed and made two adjustments: simulating increased labor costs to include higher contributions and benefits, and applying the statutory rate under small-business tax regimes. This *presumes* some degree of informality—not necessarily a correct assumption, given that effective and statutory tax rates may differ for perfectly legal reasons. If the difference between stated and statutory tax payments were evasion and full taxes were paid instead, then the retailers surveyed would need to increase prices by anywhere from 2 percent to 8 percent above existing levels to recover the increased labor and tax expenses. For those informal players unable to raise prices, lower margins or business failure could be the result. Yet, even with these "full taxes," simulated net income was still close to or slightly above one minimum salary—so rehabilitated informal players would not necessarily exit the retail business.

Therefore informality in Latin America is not the main driver of the continued presence of small-scale retailers. Our research shows that small retailers run a solid business, consistently attracting emerging consumers with a combination of correct assortment and affordable sizes, offered at convenient distance from their homes or workplaces, with the required level of service and personal attention. Their low-cost operations combined with careful inventory management give their owners an income comparable to or higher than an average salary.

Conclusions

The intent of our research was to show the relevance of emerging consumer segments and to build better understanding of their needs and consumption habits. We found that even though these consumers have less disposable income than their upper-segment counterparts, they do allocate a significant portion of their income to consumer products and represent a market of larger aggregate value. What is more, they do not limit their consumption to basic products but also have interest in other product categories.

Their buying decisions are not simplistic, driven by product price alone. Our research shows that emerging consumers aren't necessarily attracted just by low prices but instead concentrate on minimizing the total purchasing cost, which includes a range of nonprice factors.

In addition, emerging consumers do not show uniform patterns but rather have differing shopping habits, store selection criteria, and attitudes toward innovation and brand loyalty, calling for more careful segmentation. This explains the resilience of the traditional small retailers that characterize Latin America and other emerging regions. That they meet those particular needs explains their appeal not only to emerging consumers but often to consumers from upper levels, especially in the produce categories. By adopting some modern trade practices such as home delivery, self-service, in-store displays, and multiple check-outs, they are increasingly updating their value proposition.

We find that informality and tax evasion fall short of explaining the endurance of small-scale retailers. Manufacturers have also recognized the importance of these channels and are paying more attention to these traditional or down-the-street stores, by adjusting their supply in terms of product sizes and packaging as well as logistics and promotions designed for these segments.

Although many large retailers have yet to make emerging consumers their primary target, their future growth will probably be conditioned by their ability to adjust their offering to this vast segment of the population.

CHAPTER THREE

MARKETING PROGRAMS TO REACH
INDIA'S UNDERSERVED

Kunal Sinha, John Goodman, Ajay S. Mookerjee,
John A. Quelch

During the first forty years after India's independence, major Indian companies and multinational corporations focused on the country's rich and upper-middle-class urban consumers, to the exclusion of the country's immense low-income population, which was seen to lack sufficient purchasing power and accessibility. As the effects of economic liberalization kicked in during the 1990s, companies began shifting their focus to India's burgeoning middle- and lower-income classes, a market of between 300 and 500 million people.[1] There was growing recognition among companies that even though revenue realized per customer in the "elite" market was up to five times higher than in the lower-income market, the latter contained twenty-five times more customers.[2] Indeed, India's 125 million poor households have a combined income of $378 billion[3] and significant demand for low-price consumer products and services.

Representing 60 percent of India's GDP, rural markets are an important segment of the overall poor market. Consumer goods have increasingly penetrated rural households, accounting for 53 percent of all fast-moving consumer goods (FMCGs), 59 percent of consumer durable sales, and 38 percent of sales of the two-wheeler market (which includes motorcycles, motor scooters, and mopeds). In 2002–03, Life Insurance Corporation of India sold 50 percent of its policies in rural India. Of Bharat Sanchar Nigam Limited's two million mobile phone connections, 50 percent are in small towns and villages. Today, forty-two million rural households access banking services, in comparison with twenty-seven million urban households. Overall, the rural market has grown at 12–13 percent over the last decade, while urban markets have grown only 7–8 percent.[4]

The implications for managers—especially those whose training ground has been in marketing to India's "haves"—are profound. First, the poor market represents the biggest potential growth opportunity for consumer marketers. Demand among poor young consumers has increased, thanks to rising exposure through mass media and more frequent travel in search of a better livelihood. Second, to succeed all marketing mix variables often have to be redesigned. This redesign can lead to superior streamlined business models with better products and distribution that can challenge traditional elite market models. Third, the perceived high cost of doing business in poor markets, especially in rural areas, has deterred many players. Because organized competition in the poor market is scarce, market entrants lack requisite support infrastructure such as suppliers, distributors, and consumer education.

For the last decade, the communications agency Ogilvy & Mather (O&M) has operated a division in India that specializes in helping its clients reach low-income consumers. This division has developed a network of some fifty thousand subcontracted staff to implement communication strategies to this market, on behalf of O&M's clients.[5] Based on O&M's research, this paper first defines the low-income market opportunity in India and the new market research and communications techniques used by O&M to serve this market. Next, we describe what O&M and its clients have discovered about how businesses can make money serving the poor. We highlight commercial techniques and business models that have proven successful and ways in which mainstream firms have had to adapt their marketing, organization, and product design.

O&M interviewed sales and marketing managers at Castrol Engine Oils, CavinKare, Kodak, and Bajaj Auto to uncover case studies of business model redesign. We also examined how businesses can add social value while profitably serving the poor. Finally, we suggest how corporations should create and sustain relationships and how they should understand and use existing social networks in their efforts, rather than build communication and distribution networks from scratch.

Defining the Underserved Market

India's one billion citizens constitute roughly 193 million households, 53 million of which are high- to middle-income households, with annual income in excess of US$3,000 ($18,000 purchasing power parity). Farther down the pyramid, we find approximately 125 million low-income households with annual income ranging from US$360 to $3,000. Below this are the remaining 15 million, below-poverty line households surviving on less than a dollar per day.[6]

Consumption

Poor consumers spend a greater proportion of their monthly expenditure on food, clothing, and footwear than the wealthy. One significant trend is the growing emphasis on education; real expenditure on education has increased from 575 rupees per person per year in 1993–94 to Rs. 1,158 per person per year in 2001–02.[7] Consumption patterns and asset ownership are the most commonly used proxies to define the poor market. In O&M's experience, an important factor characterizing poor consumers is lack of access to organized, nonexploitative finance that would facilitate acquisition of durables.

Geographic Spread

The geographic dispersion of the poor can deter marketers. In addition to the more than 3,700 urban cities or towns and rural feeder towns, an estimated 593,000 villages make up rural India. But 17 percent of these villages account for 50 percent of the rural population and 60 percent of rural wealth. These larger villages, with an average population over two thousand, offer a greater concentration of prospective consumers and therefore a more attractive point-of-entry.[8]

Researching the Underserved

Conventional market research techniques come unstuck when we use them to understand the poor, often illiterate consumer. To overcome this problem, O&M adapted participatory rural appraisal (PRA) techniques pioneered by development agencies to understand the needs, motivations, and drivers of poor communities, as well as to map communication opportunities in rural India. The methodology differs from conventional survey methods in several ways. It takes into account the fact that poor consumers have ideas and perceptions far different from our own, which are expressed in their own way and do not fall into our existing frameworks. Most researchers fail to accurately understand the poor consumer because their reference points and investigation techniques focus on individual, rather than group, decision making.

The PRA technique involves immersing oneself into the lives of respondents and engaging them to collectively describe the kinds of lives they lead. It examines the dynamics of their complex social environment, which we must be sensitive to in designing and implementing marketing communications. For example, a village mapping exercise, whereby groups of villagers get together and draw out a map of the village, reveals caste and community clusters, important congregation points, and where and when group communications occur and can be influenced. It is not only the map itself that provides vital clues but also the map-making process. For example, a group of women might position a health center or a hand pump closer to their homes on their map than a post office—even if this representation is not accurate—because the perceived importance of the former is greater.

A wealth mapping exercise yields economic stratification data, along with information about symbols of wealth in a community such as land and consumer durables ownership. It also tells us about villagers' aspirations, which they are often reluctant to articulate in any direct interrogation. A "time line" (which is a freewheeling conversation with a village elder) allows us to map changes in the community over several decades. It brings to light significant events that have altered the community (the first tractor, the first TV, a flood or a drought, connection to the outside world via a paved road) and identifies those people who were early to adopt change. Through such tools, we define clusters of consumers and determine their propensity and motivations for change. These visual and story-led methods of consumer research result in the compilation of a rich vocabulary that can be used in designing local communications.

Communicating with the Underserved

Having thoroughly researched the underserved, companies can use this information as the basis for developing their communication strategy.

Media Reach and Geography

Lack of exposure to the mass media is the biggest challenge in communicating with poor consumers. O&M specializes in identifying regions and communities that have little or no access to conventional media (TV, radio, print, cinema) and then creating and implementing new media forms for brand promotion. Lack of media data at the district level—the unit of implementation planning—poses problems for planners. O&M's planners created a media index that combines media reach data, available at the sociocultural region level, with a district-level rural purchasing power index. Districts are classified into media-live (media index > 57), media-gray (media index between 57 and 34), and media-dark (media index < 34). According to the classification, only 13 percent of rural India is media-live, 45 percent is media-gray, and 42 percent is media-dark. This allows O&M to determine the relative roles and weights of mass media (TV, radio, print, and cinema) versus new media and to optimize where and how client money is allocated. In the state of Haryana, for example, there are twelve media-live districts and four media-gray districts. Here, clients are advised to invest in traditional advertising via television and radio for creating brand awareness. A different approach would be recommended, however, in the neighboring state of Uttar Pradesh, where forty-one districts are media-dark, twenty are media-gray, and only two are media-live.[9]

Sociocultural Parameters for Communication Design

Language and culture are more important in identifying opportunities for communication than geography and income. O&M uses the parameter of sociocultural region (SCR) to understand consumer and communication opportunities. Each macrogeographic unit or state usually comprises three or four distinct SCRs, each with its own dialect and visual styles, key components in developing any kind of grassroots-level communication. For example, in Uttar Pradesh, rural communication must be conducted in the Avadhi, Brajbhasha, and Bhojpuri languages in the central, western, and eastern regions of the state, respectively. Adapting a Madhubani style of illustration in north Bihar is likely to elicit greater empathy than a neutral photographic style.

Technology for Planning Communications for the Poor

Most communication to poor consumers is seemingly low-tech, but technology is the backbone of any implementation plan. O&M developed a system that places every one of the 579,361 villages and 3,696 feeder towns on their media planners' desktops, along with key data about the audience and the infrastructure available in each village (communication facilities, education infrastructure, medical facilities, electricity and water sources). This database was derived from traditional sources such as the primary census abstracts and market rating studies including the Mudra Rural Market Ratings and Market Potential Value. GIS mapping software places the villages on a map, relative to the district headquarters, main roads, and feeder towns. The data enable two kinds of micro-level planning. First, knowledge of village-level infrastructure informs decisions on where to locate communication activities. Visual depiction of roads and distance of a village from a feeder town helps O&M plan routes and coverage for communication activities. For example, it can be used to determine if folk performances can be held in more than one village a day, or how many villages can be covered in a week by a team putting up shop signs and tinplates.

Business Models

Business models targeting low-income consumers require managers to change their mind-set from one focused on revenue and margin maximization to one concerned with sales volume and market penetration. Since the revenue potential of the underserved markets can be as much as five times that of the elite market, sacrificing short-term unit margin for volume and market share can improve long-run profitability. However, to succeed, traditional assumptions about managing the marketing mix must be challenged.

Products for poor markets have to be cheaper and therefore simpler, stripped down to the key elements most important to the consumer. Distribution is often more reliant on direct, relationship-oriented channels, leveraging the power of third parties. To keep costs low, O&M and its clients have found it useful to synchronize distribution and communication channels. Most of the communication that O&M organizes for its clients in traditional *haats* (weekly bazaars) and *melas* (fairs) includes product sampling and direct selling. Since word-of-mouth plays a significant role in poor communities, the retailer and his shop are the key to successful communication.

Reaching the poor requires less reliance on brand-building advertising than on targeted promotions and support services. The task for the marketer is to introduce and build the category. Targeted promotions—including sampling—help to change long-entrenched behaviors and shift consumers from commodities to brands. For the Hindustan Lever shampoo brand Clinic Plus, the challenge was to create dissonance among users of mud, natural herbs, and low-cost local shampoos. O&M created a "Mother-Daughter Day," a talent competition in which teams of mothers and daughters displayed their talent in the fields of study, handicraft, painting, cookery, and rural folk arts. Shampoo demonstrations were carried out during the event, creating a memorable brand experience. Some 250 million rural consumers participated in these events, resulting in an 8 percent increase in users.

Some of O&M's clients have recognized the need to approach the poor market differently from how they do business in more prosperous urban markets. The examples presented here illustrate how these companies have changed their business models to succeed in the low-income consumer segment.

Castrol Engine Oils

To reach the low-income market, the company first redesigned its products with a low unit price and smaller packaging, for example, engine oil pouches priced at Rs. 3 per pouch for all two-stroke engines (scooters and mopeds) and four-stroke motor bikes. Castrol also strengthened distribution from twenty thousand outlets in 1992–93 to ninety thousand by 2005, many of which were mom-and-pop *kirana* stores, *haats* (bazaars), and *melas* (fairs), all new points of sale in the lubricants category. Castrol's mainstream marketing organization had to adapt to this market by focusing on building long-term relationships, rather than just achieving short-term sales targets. More than sixty field marketing specialists drummed up demand by driving vehicles equipped with projection systems and amplifiers to carry out *haat* and *mela* promotion. They also spent time educating the consumer and held training boot camps in small towns and villages for mechanics who were key opinion leaders for the category.

CavinKare Ltd. (CKL)

CKL is a successful consumer packaged goods company headquartered in Chennai. CKL starts its marketing planning with a price point affordable to the poor consumer and then designs the product, distribution system, and other elements of the marketing mix to achieve this price. CKL has developed unique formulations, such as herbal shampoos and vegetarian toothpaste, to meet the preferences of poor consumers. CKL also uses creative packaging to reduce costs. Its Chinni brand pickles, for example, are packed into sachets commonly used for personal care products. CKL finds poor consumers are inherently more brand-loyal because they are less familiar with brands and perceive a higher financial risk in switching brands. Though they can be easily switched by discounts, they are unlikely to buy again at full price. Building distribution channels to suit the shopping patterns of the poor market is another key to CKL's strategy; Chinni sachets are sold through an army of cyclists who distribute to small shops.

Kodak India

Kodak targets "intenders"—rural consumers who have some experience with a camera, whether by borrowing one from a friend or from having had a picture taken at a studio. Consumers in villages take pictures only on special occasions, and their cameras cannot let them down. Hence the product must be reliable, branded, and easy to use. Kodak has designed special, low-priced, high-quality products such as its KB10 Manual Camera, which is priced at Rs. 499 and includes a film roll and a two-year warranty. Kodak built its own distribution network, appointing distributors and franchises for film processing. Kodak also invested in consumer education and product demonstrations, teaching consumers how to load and unload a camera.

Bajaj Auto

India's second-largest two-wheeler manufacturer, Bajaj Auto was traditionally focused on the urban elite market, with its flagship scooter propelling the company to market leadership. However, the scooter was unsuitable for bad road conditions in rural areas. In response, Bajaj designed two entry-level motorbikes, the Boxer and CT-100, to address poor commuters' needs. They also introduced a linked consumer finance scheme called "999" (an installment program of Rs. 999 per month) with the tagline "Why dream when you can drive?" Although consumer finance schemes normally depend on collateral assets that poor people lack, Bajaj instead relied on informal checks of the reputation of prospective customers, knowing that people would be very concerned about keeping their reputation intact. Bajaj did not have to hard-sell the two-wheeler to the poor; it only had to enable people to buy. This required attention to finance and distribution. Owning a consumer finance company helped. Bajaj's mainstream and mass marketing organization also had to adapt its business cycle to crop cycles that determine when rural consumers have money to spend.

Creating Social Value

Are brands that market to the poor being exploitative, persuading already cash-strapped people to spend money on unnecessary goods? O&M has reason to believe otherwise, and so do its clients. There are significant positive social impacts to be gained through marketing to the poor.

Rather than merely transfer urban communications approaches, O&M recognized that traditional folk performances have a tremendous appeal to rural consumers. They carry within them the entire folk culture, reflecting the local cults, customs, rituals, and beliefs that have been transmitted over generations. O&M catalogued the folk forms that existed throughout India and established commercial sponsorship programs to promote folk art. In many places, folk performers remain idle for much of the year, called on only during festival seasons. Using folk performances to promote brands gives these artists more regular income and keeps the art forms alive.

It was important for O&M to consider how to tastefully communicate a brand message at a folk performance that has drawn a crowd. This was achieved in several ways: creating visibility of the brand through the stage backdrop, banners, and costumes; integrating the brand into prepublicity of the folk performance; and interspersing the brand message in the performance. Some folk forms tend to be a better fit for communicating a brand's properties than others. For example, the *Bagha Nach* (tiger dance) of the Jharkhand region is an obvious opportunity for association with Hindustan Lever's Lipton Tiger tea brand.

Companies also create social value by directly supporting customers in times of need. When drought hit western India, Castrol saw engine oil sales drop, as tractors stood idle on farmers' parched land. Rather than wait for the rains to reverse fortunes, Castrol and O&M embarked on a massive drought relief program, working with local nongovernmental organizations in 557 villages, directly benefiting thirty thousand farmers. Through an exercise in watershed management (constructing sixteen check dams, eight drinking water tanks, twenty-two farm bunds, and forty-four thousand feet of canal repairs) and by educating the rural community on drought-proofing their land, Castrol and O&M created tremendous goodwill for their engine oils. Unaided category recall of the brand CRB Plus rose from 45 percent to 91 percent during the campaign period. Eighty-five percent of consumers and community perceived the brand as friendly and caring, one that facilitated solution-seeking behavior in times of adversity.

Companies also see that their products have a direct positive social impact. Kodak believes its mass market business is built on the importance of sharing memories through pictures, which strengthens the institution of the family. For example, migrant workers take back pictures of the city to their village families to illustrate their stories about life in the city. Bajaj Auto believes it has created social value by simply enabling people in the villages to travel farther and thus realize their potential. In addition, by creating a service network of mechanics, Bajaj created self-employment opportunities in poor areas.

Key Implications for Managers

- Poor customers represent the largest growth market opportunity. Success requires a change of mind-set. Marketers have to shift their focus from high-value individual consumers to a higher-volume, lower-margin segment. Soft data on the poor are hard to come by; hence significant investment in consumer outreach is required to understand their behavior. New approaches to segmentation are needed, based on behaviors and attitudes grounded in culture rather than on economic variables such as household or disposable income.
- The marketing mix must be redesigned. The first mover certainly has an advantage, but it is essential to recognize that low pricing alone does not guarantee penetration of the poor market. Low-income consumers are extra careful with their money but will spend more if they get good value. Distribution is critical, and often expensive as a percentage of sales. Building partnerships through local networks and using weekly markets can help optimize distribution efficiency.
- Since the cost of reaching a rural village is high relative to the prospective returns, it is essential to combine educational communication with selling. Personal selling allows two-way communication rather than one-way message delivery and is therefore more likely to convert and retain consumers. It allows immediate evaluation of communication effectiveness. Managers can measure how many trials were generated or how many inquiries were made.
- Brands targeting the poor can benefit by leveraging social networks. Targeting groups rather than individuals makes sense because peer approval, which lowers the emotional cost of adoption of new behaviors, is the key. Since rural societies are conservative and consumers lower risk by shopping together and comparing notes, social endorsement through reference groups can help brand adoption. Such reference groups have to include opinion leaders belonging to the same social class as the rural audiences themselves—because their aspiration is to belong, not to stand out. These are situations when the *we* moves the *me*—quite unlike urban societies where self-actualization and independence are greater motivators.
- Besides facilitating group behavior, this one-on-one selling approach has another distinct advantage. It lends itself extremely well to product demonstration. O&M

has discovered that demonstration is a far more effective communication tool than analogies and metaphors. This is because urban advertisers not only have little understanding of the metaphors that influence the rural mind but also because analogies and metaphors (which are grounded in culture) are likely to change every few hundred kilometers in rural India. Demonstrations, on the other hand, allow the rural audience to immediately see the benefit associated with the behavior change that is being advocated. The simplicity of the product's use and its benefits often dispel their doubts and motivate them to change.

- From a long-term perspective, it is essential to invest in building relationships. Unlike mass media, which can be used to reach consumers as and when required, the focus in reaching the rural poor has to be on creating spokespersons for the brand at the community level, and on retaining satisfied users through positive word-of-mouth. They then become the brand's best sales force.

- These adaptations require significant changes across all elements of the marketing mix, and in business models, financial structures, and ultimately in business philosophy. If an organization's focus is on short-term profits alone, chances are it will not succeed in serving the poor market. If, on the other hand, the objective is to catalyze social and economic change at the grass roots, the long-term payoff is likely to be significant.

PART TWO

MEETING THE BASIC
NEEDS OF THE POOR

Physical security, health care, and energy are among the most basic needs faced by human beings everywhere. Although the public sector has historically been called to address these needs, many governments have failed to meet them for all of their citizens. Increasingly, private sector actors are pioneering new ways to meet these needs profitably. In doing so, they have the potential to fill a critical development gap for developing countries, many of which face serious institutional deficits.

The first chapter in Part Two highlights the critical role effective government (and governance) plays in creating favorable conditions for business development and poverty alleviation. In "Brcko and the Arizona Market," Bruce Scott traces the development of an outdoor market that blossomed in the most unlikely of places: postwar Bosnia, when a NATO commander encouraged the growth of spontaneous commercial activity that emerged at a guarded checkpoint under his command. Shored up by military protection and a rudimentary infrastructure, this informal marketplace grew to become the largest shopping mall in the Balkans, drawing buyers from more than a hundred-mile radius. Scott concludes that rule of law and physical security were fundamental preconditions for the market's growth and by extension are necessary precursors to true business success everywhere.

David Bloom and Tarun Khanna consider the opportunities for private health care provision in developing countries in Chapter Five, "Health Services for the Poor in Developing Countries: Private vs. Public vs. Private *and* Public." In particular, they discuss the Narayana Hrudayalaya Heart Hospital—an example of private and profitable health care provision in India—and the partnerships the hospital has developed with local public sector organizations.

In "Fighting AIDS, Fighting Poverty," Rohit Deshpandé and Zoë Chance present case studies of three pharmaceutical companies that made significant contributions to the fight against HIV/AIDS. They find that the three organizations share a customer-centric model that allows them to identify patient needs and work backwards from these needs to develop profitable solutions.

In Chapter Seven, "Meeting Unmet Needs at the Base of the Pyramid: Mobile Health Care for India's Poor," Pablo Sánchez, Miguel Rodríguez, and Joan Ricart analyze Philips India's DISHA project, a mobile health care diagnostics initiative that serves rural, low-income villagers. Drawing from the DISHA case, the authors identify and generalize three factors that reduce cost structures and generate the knowledge and trust that companies need to succeed in low-income markets: use of new and advanced technologies, partnerships to develop total solution delivery systems, and integration into social networks.

The ability of poor people to climb the economic ladder depends significantly on the infrastructure that affects how they live and do business. The aspect of infrastructure most important in facilitating business growth is perhaps provision of reliable, fairly priced utilities.

In Chapter Eight, "Energizing the Base of the Pyramid: Scaling up Successful Business Models to Achieve Universal Electrification," David Jhirad and Annie Woollam examine three distributed energy business models using solar or other low-cost energy sources. The authors find that bringing these models to scale presents a significant challenge and that creative multisector project finance—notably including private sector participation—is essential to success.

In a similar vein, in "Utilities and the Poor: A Story from Colombia," Carlos Rufin and Luis Arboleda explore options for lowering the cost of water, a scarce resource for an estimated 1.2 billion people around the world. Privatization and deregulation of utilities were the norm in many emerging economies during the 1990s, but these initiatives often failed to expand service to the poor. However, the example of the AAA water utility in Barranquilla, Colombia, shows how a company with a concerted plan to address the needs of poor communities can do well at the same time as doing good.

Community involvement is a key theme in Chapter Ten, "Bringing Natural Gas Service to Poor Areas: The Case of Buenos Aires's Moreno District," Marcelo Paladino and Lisandro Blas's paper on provision of piped natural gas to four thousand families in a poor district of Buenos Aires. Seed funding from the World Bank to a local NGO enabled a neighborhood survey to be conducted, assessing the willingness of the community to pay for gas service and calculating the return on investment at a number of price points. Once the project was implemented, average monthly fuel expenses in participating households fell dramatically, freeing up household income for other daily necessities or investment into microenterprise.

CHAPTER FOUR

BRCKO AND THE ARIZONA MARKET

Bruce R. Scott

The founding and subsequent growth of a market along Route Arizona in the Bosnian countryside some fifteen kilometers outside Brcko is testimony to the fundamental importance of security and the rule of law to the capitalist system. The market, which started as an informal open-air flea market, was gradually transformed into the largest fresh produce market in the region. Within five years it comprised almost two thousand stalls with an estimated sales volume of US$100 million per year. Meanwhile, the surrounding countryside was characterized by "peace"—in the sense of an end to hostilities—following the Dayton Peace Accords. But this formal assurance of freedom, private enterprise, and democratic rule was of little avail in restarting the Bosnian economy, which was still experiencing stagnation and an estimated 40–50 percent unemployment rate ten years after the signing of the accords.

The market enjoyed several critical advantages related to its location and the protection it was afforded by NATO forces. First, it held a natural commercial advantage due to its location on the main north-south highway into Bosnia from much more prosperous Croatia. Second, the market benefited from the protection afforded by a NATO checkpoint, where all vehicles had to stop for inspection. Third, these inspections were soon supplemented by an emergent system of market regulation drawn

---

This paper is based on the Harvard Business School case "Brcko and the Arizona Market," case no. 9-905–411, Harvard Business School Publishing, Boston, revised December 5, 2005, as well as supplementary interviews with three of the four supervisors for the Brcko district.

up by local civilians under the supervision of local NATO officers. Fourth, and of crucial importance in its early years, the market had the peculiar advantage of having been deliberately located in the Zone of Separation between the two entities that together constituted the new Bosnia-Herzegovina, on land that was controlled by NATO rather than any civilian authority. This protected the market from hostile takeover by any of the nearby civilian authorities (including U.S. civilian authorities).

Overview

In December 1995, NATO troops entered Bosnia with the mission to enforce the recently negotiated Dayton Peace Accords that had brought a close to a bitter three-year civil war among Serbs, Croats, and Bosniacs. Almost immediately, the NATO troops insisted that all barriers to free movement of goods or persons along the highways be removed. At the same time, they established a checkpoint of their own to monitor traffic on the major north-south highway, renamed "Route Arizona," that traversed Serb territory to link Bosnia and Croatia. All vehicles crossing the checkpoint were required to stop and submit to a search for weapons and explosives. This largely defensive step, in a rural location, would soon set in motion a series of developments that transformed the checkpoint and the surrounding rural area into a self-sustaining market and a bustling site of commercial activity. At the same time, this spontaneously generated market would become the focus of repeated attempts at hostile takeover by nearby political authorities. An exploration of these two developments—the spontaneous growth of the market and the attempts at hostile takeover—yields important insights into the fundamentals of capitalism, fundamentals easily overlooked in more stable situations.

By 2005, the Arizona Market was made up of an estimated two thousand small retail establishments covering some three hundred acres stretching along Route Arizona for approximately half a mile. In the interim, administrative oversight of the market shifted from local NATO commanders to the Brcko supervisor, and operational management shifted from small independent stalls to Ital Project, an Italian property developer who had invested much of a planned US$100 million to upgrade various aspects of the market, including basic utilities and the retail structures. This remarkable but localized development was surprising because it took place in the midst of pervasive economic stagnation. Why did a market flourish within an economy beset by high unemployment and rampant crime, while neighboring and presumably better-placed commercial areas did not? To what extent might the Arizona Market be a model for helping restart the economy in other parts of Bosnia, or indeed post-conflict situations anywhere? Answers to these questions might suggest lessons for members of civil society interested in nurturing poles of growth in their own economy, with or without the help of an army.

The Emergence and Growth of the Arizona Market

Colonel Gregory Fontenot, brigade commander in charge of establishing order in the Posavina Corridor, chose a strategic site for his roadblock, at the intersection of the corridor and Route Arizona. The Posavina Corridor was the strategic lifeline for the Serbs, connecting the eastern and western sections of the rump Serbian entity known as Republika Serpska; its continued control had been nonnegotiable at the Dayton negotiations. The corridor was traversed by an east-west highway, Route Texas, a vital lifeline for the Serbs during the civil war, while Route Arizona, the north-south highway that cut across the corridor, connected Muslims and Croats to Croatia and thus to a world beyond Serb control. The roadblock, located at the junction of Route Arizona and the interentity boundary line (IEBL) between Serb and Bosniac/Croat territory, occupied what had been the meeting point of three ethnically distinct neighborhoods before the war (see map in Figure 4.1). Fontenot posted troops and tanks at the roadblock to ensure that all vehicles stopped for inspection, and that no troop movements by the previously warring parties could pass.

Within a few days, civilians were gathering in the roadway to meet friends and relatives separated by the war; the checkpoint allowed members of the three ethnic communities to safely convene and renew acquaintances. As Fontenot recalls: "At first they would call to one another to reestablish contacts that had been broken during the war. Soon people were selling cigarettes, then gasoline and a few other commodities. Then one day a van pulled up, the driver slid open a door, and out came a huge container of coffee, and a light went on for me. This looks like a market, I thought."

Rather than suppress this spontaneous initiative as a traffic hazard, Fontenot and his fellow officers took action to protect and nurture it, aware that the nascent market demonstrated that NATO troops could be a positive and impartial source of security for all sides in these tense circumstances. Not long thereafter—and before the combatants' weapons were locked up—Fontenot telephoned Maj. Gen. William Nash to ask permission to "widen the road." Nash hesitated initially but soon gave his OK, admonishing Fontenot, "Be careful."

Both Fontenot and Nash were highly conscious that widening the highway entailed risks and indeed the possibility of an unfortunate incident that would call their decisions—and even their careers—into question. There were still an estimated one million mines in Bosnia (NATO troops were forbidden from removing them by the Dayton Accords), some of which, it was expected, lay beside the highway. Fontenot arranged with Croats, Muslims, and Serbs to clear the mines, hoping that this could be accomplished without injury. As the market grew in succeeding months and years, this process of clearing mines and improving the roadway was repeated until about three hundred acres were cleared in all.

FIGURE 4.1. MAP OF THE REGION.

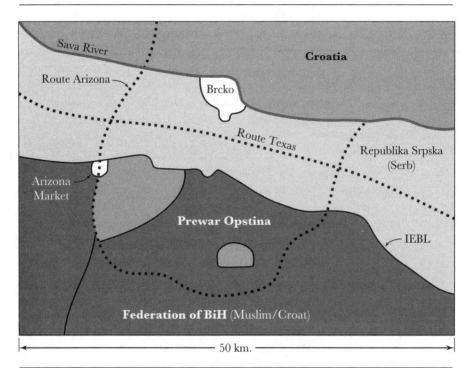

Note: "Opstina" indicates a county. The medium gray shading in Bosnian territory refers to prewar Croatian areas. Light gray shading indicates Serbian holdings; dark gray, Bosnian.

Initially, the Arizona Market was under the direct, if informal, supervision of NATO officers, but this direct supervisory role went beyond the assigned NATO mission. So Fontenot arranged for a Croat civilian to become the formal administrator of the market, responsible for supervising local police who would ensure security within the bounds of the market, and he arranged for a Serb to secure its approaches. This local supervision was bolstered by frequent personal inspection visits by U.S. civil affairs officers as an additional informal form of supervision.

Over time the market grew from a mere "wide spot" in the road into a rough-and-tumble destination off the highway, complemented by off-road parking. But because it was outside the limits of the nearby city of Brcko, and outside the territory under the control of the Brcko supervisor, the Arizona Market was an unregulated affair without running water or sanitary facilities; its source of electricity consisted of informal taps on the local wholesale distribution system. In addition, it was established without formal permission from the landowners whose property it occupied.

Nash and his officers undertook their unofficial supervisory role essentially on their own initiative. The Arizona Market was not officially recognized by the Dayton Treaty, by NATO headquarters in Belgium, or indeed by the high representative who supervised civil affairs for Bosnia. All the same, the officers established a set of regulations whereby the market supervisor rented space by the square meter to all individuals who wished to sell within its limits. No sales taxes or other indirect taxes were authorized. The officers also attempted to limit traffic in undocumented or stolen goods, though this proved challenging. NATO and U.S. civil affairs officers brought a second level of supervision and possible dispute resolution within the market, but they could not be expected to ensure the authenticity of the goods that were for sale. As the variety of articles increased, so did the range of prices and the quality of the goods, with the provenance of many items remaining obscure.

In 1997, a preliminary arbitration settlement was handed down, formally recognizing that the city of Brcko and a surrounding area of approximately three hundred square kilometers, including the road junction of the north-south and east-west highways, were to constitute a NATO protectorate under the administrative control of a supervisor named by NATO—and, in effect, by the U.S. government. The Arizona Market was located just outside this protectorate in the Zone of Separation (ZOS), a strip of land some four kilometers wide that separated the Serbian-controlled portion of the former Bosnia (51 percent of the area) from the portion controlled by the Croat-Muslim federation (constituting 49 percent). The ZOS was placed under the exclusive control of the U.S. Department of Defense pending final disposition of issues such as the fate of the Brcko protectorate. Since NATO commanders were rotated about once a year, the "sovereignty" of the market fell to the discretion of the local commanding generals, none of whom could expect to have a long-term role in Bosnia. It was a very imperfect yet important set of arrangements.

Almost from its inception, the Arizona Market came under attack from various political authorities. Nearby mayors wanted to send their police to "protect" the market (and, one supposes, take charge of the rental fees paid by those who set up shop within its boundaries). On another occasion, the market came under attack by the Bosnia-Herzegovinian government in Sarajevo, which sent thirty armed policemen to protect it. In this instance, the brigade commander had been advised of the expected arrival of the policemen. He conferred with his commanding general, and they agreed that this added protection was not needed. Hence a detail of troops backed by armor were assigned to greet the visiting police. In an early morning encounter, the police were informed that their help was not needed, and they returned to Sarajevo.

In 1999, the preliminary arbitration award for the Brcko protectorate came up for review. The award, finalized in 2000, enlarged the protectorate to about five hundred square kilometers, an area that encompassed the Arizona Market. At the same time the sweeping powers of the supervisor (often described as comparable to those of a British viceroy) were reaffirmed. With the expansion of the Brcko district, the supervisor now controlled the Arizona Market. This transfer of power was to have far-reaching, if unanticipated, implications.

Soon after the final arbitration award, the autonomy of the market was threatened by the high representative in Sarajevo, who wanted the market shut down because its infrastructure and health standards did not meet European norms. Henry Clarke, the newly appointed Brcko supervisor, responded he would look into the situation immediately and soon decided that privatization would be a preferable solution. Clarke then set out to find potential bidders and was lucky enough to find two. He selected Ital Project to take over the market. The developer pledged to put up about US$100 million to purchase and redevelop the land. The redevelopment included moving the businesses to proper stalls built in an adjacent area. In addition to larger, better buildings, the rebuilt Arizona Market would have running water, sewage, a formal electricity supply, and an appropriate internal network of roads. Although the developer's contract was with the local government of Brcko, in fact his security depended on the continued existence of the Supervisory District, and thus ultimately on the implied backing of NATO forces should a real challenge to its position materialize. Without that backing, a local government with more muscle than the Brcko Protectorate could try to take control and raise the taxes or even annul the Ital contract in favor of a local developer.

By 2005, the Arizona Market was the crown jewel not just of the Brcko District but of the Bosnian economy. Some claimed that it had become the largest shopping mall in the Balkans, drawing buyers from more than a hundred-mile radius and merchandise from much farther afield. Visiting the market in 2004, after a seven-year absence, Nash found it almost unrecognizable. The former enclave, now clean and orderly, and boasting an array of branded goods as well as local items, was announced by a hundred-foot neon sign trumpeting the Arizona Market. Susan Johnson, the incumbent Brcko supervisor, saw the market as a crown jewel in another sense: the developer was paying taxes amounting to about US$17 million per year into the coffers of her local government.

Why Did the Arizona Market Survive and Flourish?

Why did commerce flourish in the Arizona Market and not in the nearby fields, and indeed more than in Brcko, which was only fifteen kilometers away? The war was over, there had been no combat deaths in more than ten years, and tourists could circulate freely from one ethnic area to another. All of Bosnia could be said to have "freedom, democracy, and private enterprise"; yet the country was still characterized by economic stagnation and unemployment. What distinguished the Arizona Market from its surroundings, near and far? The initial evidence points to development of security and the rule of law. But there were also additional commercial reasons, notably its position at the entrance to Bosnia on the main north-south highway.

The success of the Arizona Market amid a stagnant Bosnian economy is a stark reminder that stopping a war is not remotely the same as bringing about peace. Establishing peace requires that inhabitants be assured of physical safety and the rule of law, at night as well as in the day, and at home as well as in public places. Most wars do not take place between or within democracies but instead between societies with patron-client power relationships, where a few patrons can intimidate their less powerful neighbors through extrajudicial means. The military can stop large-scale, overt intimidation, but it cannot expect to establish or reestablish the safety and rule of law that are so essential to healthy capitalism. The Dayton Accords did not require NATO forces to take any responsibilities for the state building required to protect people. It was only at the insistence of U.S. Ambassador Richard Holbrooke that the accords allowed local commanders to take on such responsibilities, if they so desired.

NATO troop strength in Bosnia was initially about sixty thousand, with twelve thousand in the U.S. sector. But even with this relative troop strength, U.S. commanders could not bring security, let alone rule of law, to their zone of operations. To do so would have required that authorities have the power and determination to break down the illegitimate structures of power that sprouted almost immediately after the accords, as well as the troop strength and economic incentives to keep these powers in check.

Americans attempting to bring peace to Bosnian society had to confront the challenge of overturning their mental models, which assume that societies are basically egalitarian, in a Jeffersonian model. Let's call the model of a relatively egalitarian society A. Alternatively, B stands for an unequal society, where land is distributed in a pattern that involves great differences in wealth and power, including the power of a few to intimidate others. See Figure 4.2 for an illustration of these social structures. If each four-sided piece of territory represents a piece of land, with a house proportionate to the size of the land, then B is a very inegalitarian society. The owner of the large plot in the upper-left-hand corner can be thought of as living in a chateau, while many of his neighbors live in hovels. Township A has an extreme egalitarian structure, simply to establish the contrast.

NATO officers found that Bosnia had a power structure like that of B—a society that is not fertile ground for democracy but rather for a free-for-all among gangs of thugs, often under the command of former military personnel. The Arizona Market, in contrast, implied relatively egalitarian relationships ("leave your guns outside the market") and transactions based on the rule of law. The market was a small outpost from the beginning, an island with a structure like A in a sea of localities like B.

The true measure of power in Bosnia was the capacity to mobilize a political coalition to take control of government. In such a context, control of a market meant the

FIGURE 4.2. THE SOCIOECONOMIC FOUNDATIONS OF DEMOCRACY.

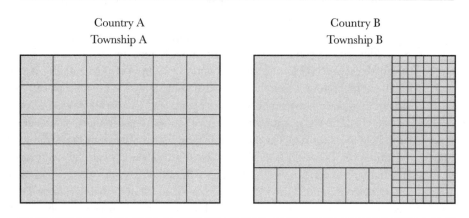

ability to tax it, and thus the power to control a revenue stream as the basis of a political party, perhaps backed by thugs. Power was determined not by ownership of land but by the control of wealth or income with which to hire supporters to intimidate opponents.

Lessons from the Arizona Market

The Arizona Market got started and initially grew on the basis of four key advantages: (1) a good location on a major north-south highway that was the gateway into Bosnia; (2) physical safety guaranteed by NATO; (3) a set of rules for trading, supervised by local police but overseen by NATO personnel; and (4) a substantial tax advantage relative to nearby towns. Mayors in nearby towns were reported to charge much higher taxes, sometimes offering a tax reduction for merchants who would contribute directly to their regimes and their political power. Each of these advantages might be considered part of a transferable model, but they all depended in turn on a more fundamental initial advantage that is not nearly so broadly transferable: its location in the Zone of Separation.

The Dayton Accords placed the ZOS under exclusive control of the U.S. Department of Defense. Since the DOD was scarcely aware of the existence of the market, the local commander of the U.S. sector exercised de facto sovereignty there. The market was thus protected against the designs of local political authorities, who eyed it either as a potential source of additional revenues or as a rival for their existing markets in nearby cities.

But these political and institutional advantages did not fully account for its success. Another checkpoint, established farther west on Route Texas, had an initial success but soon withered. Located much deeper within Bosnia, it did not have much by way of natural advantages to sustain it. As is apparent from the map, the Arizona Market had a natural advantage in terms of location—both by its placement along a major north-south highway and by being technically in Bosnia yet close to Croatia. Since much of Croatia had escaped damage in the war, Croats could use the market to peddle supplies to impoverished Bosniacs.

Given these peculiar circumstances, one must be very careful in drawing lessons. The presence of NATO troops and their sovereignty in the ZOS were absolutely essential to the initial growth of the market. NATO officers' use of power in this situation highlights some fundamental lessons about capitalism. The success of this market, in the midst of the stagnation and lawlessness of Bosnia, makes abundantly clear that the two essential foundations of a capitalist economy are physical safety for its participants and the rule of law. NATO was a trusted sign of safety and the rule of law, as contrasted with the free-for-all in the remainder of Bosnia. The Arizona Market prospered because it was a far more stable and transparent context in which to do business than the unregulated circumstances to be found in nearby fields or towns, in spite of their apparent freedoms and superficially democratic government.

What lessons might a private sector entrepreneur draw from this experience in terms of scope of freedom or responsibility to take action? In answering this question, I think it is useful to ask what General Nash stood to gain from authorizing Colonel Fontenot to "widen the road," or indeed what Fontenot might gain from organizing the mine clearing. Neither man had any inkling that the Arizona Market would achieve even a small fraction of the size and scope that it had by 2005. Its eventual success did not increase the likelihood of either man earning a promotion or bonus, even if the growth were to happen before they retired from their service in Bosnia.

Thus their rationale for clearing the mines and laying the gravel along the Arizona Highway stemmed from a moral imperative, a belief that this was the right thing to do. It was a way to help promote a return to normalcy after three years of a brutal civil war. Both Nash and Fontenot—as well as a number of their successors— recognized that security was essential to a peaceful Bosnia, but security itself was insufficient to ensure that normal economic activity and growth would take place. Reestablishment of the rule of law was also important, and the market illustrates the positive role of both security and rule of law.

Nash was asked to play a developmental role because he had power, economic and political as well as military, and he had the training and experience to know how to use it. He did not seek a state-building role, but it was his because of the circumstances. Nash and Fontenot held some forms of power not available to most entrepreneurs, but entrepreneurs similarly have command of a hierarchy of skilled personnel, plus equipment and a budget. In addition, entrepreneurs have within themselves and their organizations the analytic capabilities and the capacity to envision how they can achieve coordination among various groups of people to produce results unlikely to stem from the efforts of a single individual. Most important, entrepreneurs can take a much longer time perspective. The NATO officers could be expected to be rotated out to a new assignment in less than twenty-four months; as private actors, entrepreneurs have the possibility of seeing the job through over an extended period of years.

How might an entrepreneur recognize such opportunities to use his or her organizational capabilities to promote economic development? First of all, like the NATO commanders entrepreneurs must always be cognizant that this developmental activity is *not* their primary responsibility. They must remain attentive to their formal job responsibilities if they are to retain their power to intervene in the economy.

Second, business leaders should be open to the possibility that they can achieve a measure of voluntary coordination of societal resources through their initiative and leadership abilities, on the basis of the respect they have earned for surviving in a capitalist society. Business leaders have earned credibility from proven competence in their own form of combat, as with an army officer. Putting something back to help others can be highly satisfying, especially if it helps others who have had fewer opportunities in life.

CHAPTER FIVE

HEALTH SERVICES FOR THE POOR IN DEVELOPING COUNTRIES

Private vs. Public vs. Private *and* Public

David E. Bloom, Tarun Khanna

In much of the developing world, the poor lack access to adequate health care and are particularly vulnerable to the economic impacts of ill health. To address this situation, new models for health care provision are needed. This paper considers opportunities for private health care initiatives to address some unmet needs for health care in developing countries. In particular, it discusses the Narayana Hrudayalaya Heart Hospital—an example of private, profitable health care provision in a developing country—and the partnerships this hospital has developed with public sector organizations. More broadly, it considers how this and similar initiatives and partnerships can be most effective in the face of significant challenges.

The Unmet Need for Health Care

In much of the developing world, poor health is a major impediment to both quality of life and economic development. Life expectancy is much lower in developing regions than in developed ones, infant and child mortality are much higher, malnutrition is more widespread, and people living in developing countries are more

The authors are grateful to Helen Curry, Larry Rosenberg, and Mark Weston for their extremely helpful assistance.

vulnerable to infectious diseases and health shocks caused by environmental degradation and natural disasters.

Numerous factors lead to weak health in developing countries. Vast disparities in political and economic power between and within countries set the context in which developing countries struggle to find resources to shore up the health of populations. One major problem stems from living conditions. Poor countries lack the water and sanitation infrastructure of industrialized nations; their people therefore rely on an unclean water supply and ineffective sanitation, both of which create fertile conditions for the spread of infectious disease.[1] Use of biomass for cooking and heating is also much more common, leading to widespread respiratory illness.[2] In addition, many developing countries are in the tropics; 93 percent of Africa is tropical, for example. Climatic conditions in tropical regions inhibit food production and increase the threat of infectious disease. The latter is more prevalent in the tropics than in temperate zones even after controlling for per capita income level, and life expectancy is significantly lower.[3]

In addition to poor living conditions, another major cause of poor health is the weakness of health systems. Physical barriers such as bad roads, unreliable sources of energy, and the remoteness of rural communities make it difficult to reach the poor with health services. In many cases, political will is also lacking, with health given a low priority by decision makers. Developing country governments spend a lower proportion of their gross domestic product on health than their wealthier counterparts do. Countries classified by the United Nations as having a high level of human development spend an average of 5.1 percent of their GDP on health; in "low human development" nations, the proportion drops to 2.4 percent.[4] Some of the results of this are clearly evident. In high human development nations, 97 percent of births are attended by skilled health personnel. In developing countries, this occurs with 59 percent of births, and in the least developed countries with just 34 percent.[5] Immunization rates differ markedly too, with 93 percent of one-year-olds in high human development countries immunized against measles, compared to 75 percent in the developing world.[6]

Even where there is the will to improve health, policies are often misguided. Perhaps even more than in developed countries, preventing health setbacks generally receives less attention and budget support in developing countries than treatment and care, and the health of wealthy groups often takes precedence. In both rich and poor countries, the poor lack the power to direct resources to diseases that affect them, even though they heavily outnumber the rich. Diseases of and care for the wealthy are therefore prioritized, and partly as a consequence the relationship between poor people and health services suffers. Health officials working in poor communities receive low salaries and sometimes demand bribes. This in turn reduces patients' trust and deters them from accessing the limited services that are available to them.[7]

Who Provides Health Care in Developing Countries?

In the past century, the public sector has had considerable success in improving health in developing countries. National governments, foreign donor governments, and multilateral agencies such as the United Nations and World Health Organization have combined to improve nutrition, sanitation, and water purity; tackle infectious disease; and strengthen sexual and reproductive health services, among other advances. As a result, infant, child, and maternal mortality have declined; the threat of infectious disease has receded; and life expectancy has increased in all developing regions.

However, some health problems remain intractable, and the emergence of new threats places continued strain on public sector health services. If working in isolation, governments face significant implementation and resource problems. Government-run health programs face particular challenges in accessing geographically isolated or otherwise difficult-to-reach populations, in furnishing sufficient oversight of program administration to avoid corruption, and in ensuring that health subsidies are directed to the people who most need them.

Because resource constraints and underperformance using available resources contribute significantly to the health gap between rich and poor nations, governments have turned to a variety of nongovernmental partners and international donors to bolster their resources and their programs' effectiveness. Some studies suggest that a high proportion of health care in developing countries is delivered by private providers who charge fees for their services.[8] A review of some twenty-five developing countries found that, although public sector provision accounts for the majority of inpatient treatment, private organizations are dominant in the sphere of outpatient care.[9] Studies of public and private provision of health care are complicated by the fact that many public sector physicians have extensive private practices.[10]

The majority of partnerships between governments and external actors have involved not-for-profit nongovernmental organizations (NGOs). In most developing countries, these groups have sprung up to fill the health care void in the absence of government action. NGOs have often proved particularly effective at working with poor communities. Many developing world governments lack the will or else the ability to reach the poor, and NGOs have been able to establish a high level of trust with these otherwise alienated groups. NGOs' work to distribute food, health care, and shelter after the December 2004 tsunami in Southeast Asia is an example of their ability to reach those with whom governments have difficulty connecting. A recent study in Guatemala, meanwhile, showed that agreements for NGOs to provide health services have resulted in a large increase in immunization rates and prenatal care coverage.[11]

The for-profit private sector is a major player in the health care arena in nearly all countries. Individuals are willing or able to pay for many health services, which stimulates private provision of health care. As in any market, there is competition based on price, and there may also be competition based on quality or other characteristics of providers.

Businesses involved in the health sector, whether in direct service to the ill or in supplying goods or services to direct care providers, are, like all businesses, profit-seeking entities. As a result, their aims do not always coincide with the needs of all those seeking health care. Businesses will not provide services that do not result in a profit or that result in less profit than extending other services. They will, in general, be more ready to offer services to those who can afford to pay more. Although some companies may flourish by supplying stripped-down, low-cost services to the poor, it is likely that in a business-only health care environment the poor will not be adequately served.

This means that at least some level of public intervention is required to ensure that the poor receive health care in places where it is at least partially privately financed (that is, nearly everywhere). The level of intervention may be as light as fostering a leg-islative and regulatory environment in which private organizations can operate freely while adhering to national standards of safety and quality. It may involve slightly more public sector intervention, with governments offering tax incentives or subsidies to di-rect private providers toward a country's priority health problems. Deeper coopera-tion might take the form of a government contracting out all or part of a health service to a private entity, while maintaining varying levels of supervision over operations.[12] Within these scenarios, there may be distinct roles in terms of the financing and provision of services: combinations of public and private investment are possible with respect to both.[13]

The Narayana Hrudayalaya Heart Hospital

The Narayana Hrudayalaya Heart Hospital in Bangalore, India, is one example of a private sector health organization making a profit while at the same time improving the health of the poor. Its skills lie in providing inexpensive, cost-effective, and high-quality cardiac care, and it uses these skills for both profit-making and philanthropic purposes. It also has established partnerships with the government and other organi-zations to extend its services to an even greater number of people.

Like many other parts of the developing world, India is in the midst of a health transition. As infant and child mortality declines and life expectancy increases, chronic illnesses and diseases of aging are replacing infectious disease as the major cause of ill health. Heart disease is emerging as a significant threat to health, with around 2.4 million Indians needing heart surgery each year. Cardiac problems are not limited to the elderly; more than one-quarter of the 5 million annual deaths from cardiovascular disease occur in people below age sixty-five, and 224,000 newborns are affected by heart disease every year.

India spends just 1.3 percent of its GDP on publicly funded health care; this is one of the lowest ratios in the world.[14] Private spending takes up much of the slack, accounting for 79 percent of total health expenditure.[15] However, with more than 250 million people living in absolute poverty and thus unable to afford most private for-profit services (only 14 percent of the population has health insurance), quality health care is inevitably skewed toward the wealthiest.

Narayana Hrudayalaya (NH) Heart Hospital was founded in 2001 to pursue a dual strategy of making profits and providing cardiac care for the poor. It aims to attract patients who pay the full price of treatment and uses some of the profits from these services to offer at-cost or below-cost care to those who cannot afford the full fee. In 2004, the hospital employed approximately ninety cardiac surgeons and cardiologists, most of whom had extensive experience both in India and abroad.

For the hybrid approach to work, quality has to remain high while costs are kept as low as possible. An indicator of the high quality of care is that mortality and infection rates during bypass operations are comparable to those in U.S. hospitals. To keep costs down (NH's fees for open heart surgery are the lowest in India) the hospital performs a high number of operations per day (eight times the Indian average), which lowers the unit cost of each operation. It uses short-term agreements rather than long-term contracts with suppliers to allow flexibility in purchasing when prices fall. It embraces new technology, such as digital rather than film X-rays. Finally, it offers a package for wealthier individuals whereby instead of paying US$2,400 for a standard open heart surgery package (including surgery and hospitalization fees for a bed in a ward) they can pay US$3,100 for a private room. The treatment and care does not differ across packages.

NH's dual strategy has had some success in treating poorer patients. In 2004, 63 percent of patients paid full price for open and closed heart surgeries, 18 percent paid the break-even cost, a further 18 percent paid below break-even cost, and 1 percent received free treatment.[16]

NH works largely independently to supply treatment to the poor, with the government playing a regulatory role to ensure minimum standards of care. However, it has also initiated programs with the government and other partners. Its telemedicine project has established nine coronary care units in remote parts of India to improve access of the poor to health care. NH trains physicians at the units to carry out checks on patients and submit the results electronically to specialists at NH and the

Rabindranath Tagore Institute of Cardiac Sciences in Calcutta, who advise the physician on treatment. The telemedicine program is run by NH, but it receives financial support from the government of Karnataka and technical support from the state-run Indian Space Research Organization, which furnishes free satellite connectivity to the coronary care units.

Likewise, a health insurance program set up by a team at NH also relies to some extent on government infrastructure. The scheme, which offers cheap insurance to farmers in Karnataka, targets members of state-controlled farming cooperatives, and the government of Karnataka adds 2.5 rupees to every 5 rupees paid in to the scheme by farmers. The government has also allowed its post offices to be used to collect premiums and issue membership cards. Twelve percent of the NH hospital's surgeries in 2004 were performed on members of the health insurance program.

The NH case illustrates a general principle followed by some successful entrepreneurs in developing countries: identify institutional deficiencies in the public sphere and look for a way to compensate for them through private activity. Absence of financial markets spurs NH to help create and foster insurance arrangements; absence of a well-functioning market for housing near the hospital encourages NH to facilitate creation of affordable temporary accommodation for families accompanying patients.[17]

Within the broad Narayana Hrudayalaya project, there are varying degrees of public and private involvement. The heart hospital is run entirely by the for-profit private entity, with government's role limited to regulation. The telemedicine and insurance programs, also run by NH, receive financial and technical support from the public sector, with each side fulfilling the role to which it is best suited in order to improve efficiency and keep down costs.

Bridging the Financing Gap: Building on NH

Despite NH's success, there are significant structural limits to its reach. The program operates to a significant extent by charging well-off patients for both fixed and variable costs, whereas the poor are asked to pay only the variable costs (or some fraction of them). This cross-subsidy is an effective redistributive mechanism, so far as it goes. But even the variable costs are high, and in any case there are too many poor in India for even a significant fraction of them to be served by such a scheme, or multiplicity of schemes. Finally, after taking into account India's status as a developing country (that is, controlling for GDP per capita), India depends to an extraordinary extent on private funding for health services. Note India's extreme place in Figure 5.1, which shows the share of private expenditures out of total health care expenditure in selected countries.

There appears to be little means, at least under current arrangements, for government to step into the breach to make NH-type care available to all.

NH and similar efforts therefore cannot reach all of India's poor people, nor address the many noncardiac health problems these people face. It is possible, however, that the NH model can have more widespread effects in developing countries if supported by health insurance programs or other initiatives.

Government insurance schemes in developing countries are generally limited to those working in the formal sector. In India, this means they reach just 10 percent of the workforce,[18] leaving most people bereft of security against a health shock. Only a small minority of informal sector workers can afford private health insurance, and poor communities remain excluded from both state and private insurance. By giving more patients the ability to pay for their health care, health insurance would enhance the economic sustainability of hospitals such as NH, allowing them to provide free treatment only to those who truly need it and to subsidize it with payments from the wealthy (and perhaps those in insurance schemes). But the level of insurance that would be needed to allow payment for NH's services will be limited for the foreseeable future to India's middle class—not a small group by any means, but such coverage will be much easier to achieve than will reaching the much larger number of poor or semipoor.

Where governments cannot by themselves guarantee funding for the health care of the poor, and the reach of private sector programs such as NH is limited by geography or funding, community-based health insurance offers one way of reducing costs while increasing access, even if such programs cannot hope to extend access to expensive procedures to a broad swath of the poor.

Community-based health insurance has been implemented by some NGOs in India and elsewhere. SEWA, a labor union for women workers in the state of Gujarat, set up a health insurance scheme in 1992 that now has more than a hundred thousand members.[19] The scheme charges members 85 rupees per year, which covers them for up to Rs. 2,000 (US$45) of inpatient treatment. A lifetime membership scheme is also available. This involves payment of a lump-sum deposit of Rs. 1,000, which is repaid when the member reaches age sixty. The SEWA scheme has proved financially sustainable with only limited support from external funders (the German company GTZ makes available some funding for administration). Income from premiums and the interest on lifetime membership deposits have always exceeded payments for claims.

Although the effect of the scheme on the health of its members has not been measured, as can be seen from the gulf between SEWA's maximum annual payout (Rs. 2,000) and the cost of open heart surgery at Narayana Hrudayalaya (Rs. 110,000), the program has stringent limits. Certain forms of treatment are clearly beyond the scope of the scheme. One hundred thousand members, though impressive, is a drop in the ocean in a state with a population of 50 million.

FIGURE 5.1. SHARE OF HEALTH EXPENDITURES THAT ARE PRIVATE (SELECTED COUNTRIES).

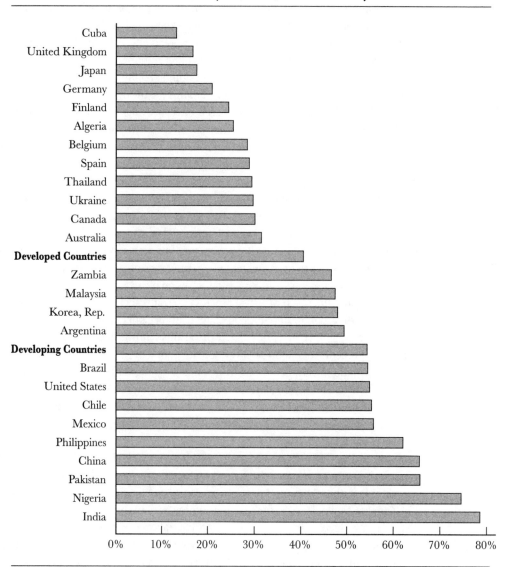

Source: World Bank, *World Development Indicators 2004.* Data for 2002.

Microfinance programs may be another, nonhealth means of improving access to treatment. These community-run schemes open savings and loan facilities to poor individuals. Interest rates on loans are usually low, and they have enabled many poor families who would otherwise struggle to raise funds to invest in education, microenterprises, and other areas. According to an extensive study of longitudinal data from the Indonesia Family Life Survey, microfinance can have long-term positive impacts on health.[20] Participation in microfinance schemes was found to be associated with an increase in health knowledge, greater knowledge about contraception and pap smear tests, and a higher incidence of health-seeking behaviors such as more vaccinations for children, greater food consumption, and reduced indoor air pollution.

Microfinance and community-based health insurance are promising ways of shrinking the deficit between poor people's ability to pay and the cost of health care. It is likely that these and many other indirect methods (such as education) will need to be deployed if poor communities are to access all the health care they need.

Conclusions

The public sector has made great strides in improving health in developing countries, but standards of health care nevertheless lag far behind those of the industrialized world. Private sector involvement in health would be socially beneficial if companies could effectively apply their resources, knowledge, and expertise to tackle the diseases that governments have been unable to control, and more generally to improve health.

For some private sector firms, such as the Narayana Hrudayalaya Heart Hospital, there are obvious business motivations for involvement. In many cases, however, for developing-world populations the benefit of business intervention in health heavily outweighs the incentives for individual firms.

In these circumstances, partnership between public and private sectors offers the best solution. The examples of the NH telemedicine and health insurance schemes show public and private sector organizations dividing responsibilities. Governments have expertise in identifying social goals and designing programs to achieve them. They also have funds, which can create incentives where there would otherwise be none. Businesses, on the other hand, have skills in implementation and innovation, as well as the proven ability to reach targets and deliver products and programs to large numbers of people.

Identifying areas where partnership is needed, and the roles each partner should fulfill, is clearly a key challenge for governments seeking to improve health in developing countries. In some cases, as the NH Heart Hospital shows, governments can leave most of the work to the private sector, with its own role limited to regulation of markets. In others, notably vaccine development, public sector institutions such as universities, which carry out much of the basic research on immunization, will need to work with private companies, with governments perhaps providing the financial carrot to make business involvement worthwhile.

Such partnerships are at a fledgling stage, though there is increasing recognition among all parties that they are needed. Investment in health care can help both businesses and public sector organizations achieve their goals. If they can find effective ways to work together, the health gap between rich and poor countries may at least begin to abate.

CHAPTER SIX

FIGHTING AIDS, FIGHTING POVERTY

Customer-Centric Marketing in the Generic Antiretroviral Business

Rohit Deshpandé, Zoë Chance

By 2005, HIV/AIDS had become the most lethal epidemic in recorded history.[1] Sixty-five million people had been infected, and most of the forty million living would die without treatment. Even though 95 percent of those infected lived in the developing world, 90 percent of the patients receiving treatment lived in the richest nations. In this paper, we present case studies from three organizations that attained success in the fight against HIV/AIDS: Aspen Pharmacare in South Africa, Cipla in India, and the National AIDS Program in Brazil. The common pattern we find is a customer-centric marketing paradigm: first identifying patient needs and then working backward to develop profitable solutions.

HIV/AIDS and Poverty

HIV/AIDS and poverty exist in a vicious cycle. The poorer a person is, the more likely he is to contract HIV/AIDS[2]; and if he becomes ill, he will grow poorer. In many African countries in the early twenty-first century, the population is shrinking and life expectancy has been reduced by a decade or more. The World Bank estimated that in a country with a 20 percent prevalence rate, annual loss of potential GDP due to AIDS could be as severe as 2.6 percent, leading to a two-thirds deficit after twenty years, in comparison to a no-AIDS scenario.[3] The trend of treatment coverage, however, is positive. Facilitated by increased availability and affordability of generic drugs, antiretroviral drug (ARV) coverage in developing nations doubled between 2004 and 2005 to reach one million patients.[4]

South Africa

At the time of our study, South Africa was home to more people living with HIV/AIDS than any other nation in the world. About 5.3 million people were infected with the virus, 21.5 percent of adults aged fifteen to forty-nine. In some areas, the local unemployment rate was as high as 60 percent. Average life expectancy had dropped by twelve years owing to AIDS, reversing half a century of progress.

For many years, South Africa was one of the few African nations with Western-style intellectual property laws and a local pharmaceutical industry.[5] The country's first foray into the global AIDS battle came in 1997, when the legislature, under then-President Nelson Mandela, approved the Medicines and Related Substances Control Act and subsequently faced withdrawal of U.S. foreign aid and a lawsuit by thirty-seven pharmaceutical companies.[6] Provisions in the act permitted compulsory licensing (generic reproduction of patented drugs with a royalty paid to the patent holder) and parallel importing (purchasing patented drugs from other nations with negotiated price reductions), guaranteeing lower prices for life-saving drugs. On learning about the lawsuit, activists across the globe demonstrated publicly against the drug companies that "would rather cure a bald American than a dying African."[7] The plaintiffs eventually dropped the case, volunteering price reductions of up to 90 percent.

In 2004, the government found itself embroiled in American party politics: both the Clinton Foundation, a nongovernmental organization started by former U.S. President Bill Clinton, and U.S. President George W. Bush's President's Emergency Plan for AIDS Relief (PEPFAR) were vying to negotiate pricing and procurement terms for the country's new AIDS relief program. The Clinton plan was more favorable, guaranteeing access to low-priced generics, but the PEPFAR initiative had more funding for patented AIDS drugs and treatment programs. Adopting either plan could have had negative political repercussions; however, Aspen Pharmacare was able to help South Africa realize the benefits of both the Clinton and the PEPFAR plans.

Case Study: Aspen Pharmacare

Founded in 1997 in a suburban home in the Kwa-Zulu Natal province, where the HIV/AIDS prevalence rate reached 33 percent—the highest in the nation[8]—Aspen Pharmacare soon grew to become Africa's leading generic pharmaceutical manufacturer.[9] 2005 was a record year for the firm, with earnings per share (EPS) growth at 40 percent, revenue up 30 percent, and earnings before interest, taxes, depreciation, and amortization (EBITDA) up 32 percent over 2004. It was no wonder Aspen Pharmacare was a rising star on the Johannesburg Stock Exchange, combining solid financial performance with an unmatched core competence in business diplomacy.

Aspen Pharmacare was the first African firm to enter the ARV market, and the first firm in the world granted voluntary licenses for development and manufacture of patented ARVs. Working with the national government on an ARV rollout program, Aspen Pharmacare launched a licensed version of Bristol-Myers Squibb's patented stavudine in 2003, followed by Boehringer Ingelheim's nevirapine, for preventing mother-to-child transmission, and GlaxoSmithKline's lamivudine-zidovudine cocktail in 2004. These nonexclusive licensing agreements extended patient care, increased revenues to Aspen Pharmacare, and prevented price erosion of patented drugs in other markets. The GlaxoSmithKline agreement waived the licensing royalty in exchange for a donation of 30 percent of sales to local HIV/AIDS programs,[10] and the Boehringer Ingelheim agreement was royalty-free. Additionally, the latter agreement—the multinational firm's first nonexclusive voluntary license—would allow Aspen Pharmacare to export nevirapine to thirteen other African countries.

When in 2004 the Clinton-Bush dilemma hung in the balance, it seems that Aspen Pharmacare was successful in negotiating deals with all the major stakeholders. Because the firm was manufacturing patented drugs, it was eligible for PEPFAR funding and became the first generic firm approved by PEPFAR. Additionally, the firm's manufacturing costs were low enough to supply drugs at the Clinton Foundation's floor price, and it became the Clinton Foundation's first approved supplier. Aspen Pharmacare also negotiated a fourth ARV marketing agreement, this one with biopharmaceutical firm Gilead Sciences, for the rights to sell Gilead's ARVs in ninety-five countries around the world. The South African government rewarded Aspen Pharmacare with the lion's share of its public tender for drugs to treat 1.2 million HIV/AIDS patients. The governments of Nigeria and Uganda soon followed suit, placing orders for their own national AIDS programs.

India

With 5.1 million people afflicted, in 2005 India had the second highest number of AIDS cases in the world. The World Bank estimated that during the next ten years as many as 35 million people in India could become infected—nearly doubling the total number of HIV/AIDS patients in the entire world. The epidemic was still nascent, with a national prevalence rate of only 0.8 percent, so expedient action might contain it.

Changes in India's patent laws had stimulated major shifts in the country's pharmaceutical sector, and more major changes lay ahead. From the early 1900s until 1970,

India had obeyed English-style patent laws. However, in 1970, local drug manufacturers convinced Parliament to pass a Patent Ordinance prohibiting product patents in the key areas of food and medicine.[11] Indian generic drug companies soon surpassed the multinational pharmaceutical firms that had dominated the Indian market for decades, and access to drugs expanded as prices dropped dramatically.[12] Patients in other countries benefited too, as Indian firms sold their generic drugs and bulk ingredients where laws permitted. By 2005, 50 percent of all generic ARVs distributed in developing countries came from India.[13]

In 2005, Indian generic firms were at a crossroads: India was required to comply with restrictive World Trade Organization intellectual property laws in January of that year, and all patents submitted since 1995 would be considered. Since less than 1 percent of drugs produced in India were under patent in 2005, there would be little effect on current offerings; however, patents submitted in 1995 would cover drugs only just reaching the market, so the future impact would be much greater.

Case Study: Cipla

One of the firms on which India's pharmaceutical future rested was the country's top drug company, Cipla, a global success by any measure. From 1995 to 2005, Cipla's revenues rose 25 percent annually, and in 2004 sales growth outpaced the national pharmaceutical industry by 400 percent. The firm maintained a healthy 17 percent net profit, matching the bottom line of multinational companies charging up to twenty times more for identical drugs.

For seventy years, Cipla had pursued novel strategies for improving the health of the impoverished while enriching its shareholders.[14] During World War II, when drugs were in short supply, Cipla began manufacturing basic active pharmaceutical ingredients (APIs) for British pharmaceutical companies and after the war continued producing APIs as well as a variety of generics. Yusuf Hamied, chairman and majority shareholder of Cipla, partnered with other generics manufacturers in lobbying the government for the patent reform that would make food and medicine protected categories in 1970. Though Cipla was the fifty-sixth largest pharmaceutical firm in India in 1970, the firm gradually surpassed all the foreign multinationals and secured the top spot in 2005. As the company grew, Hamied focused the business on his country's greatest medical needs: lifesaving drugs and chronic medicines. Under India's revised patent laws, Cipla was permitted to reverse-engineer any patented drug and sell it at an affordable price.

By the late 1990s, so-called ARV drug cocktails requiring patients to take three separate drugs were proving effective for treating AIDS. However, patent ownership was divided, and no firm manufactured a combination of drugs. The cocktail regimen sold for US$10,000 per person per year in most of the world, putting it out of reach for the vast majority.[15] According to Vachani and Smith's pricing model,[16] on the basis of one thousand patients in the developing world who were then being treated at a price of US$10,000, a price reduction to below US$1,000 would have increased the customer base by a factor of 50 to 80. Cipla's leaders seized the opportunity, reverse-engineering the most promising and cost-effective anti-retroviral drugs on the market.[17] The process led to creation of Triomune, a patient-friendly, triple-therapy cocktail in one tablet that could be sold for less than US$200 per patient per year. By 2005, Cipla's ARV business had grown to cover 150 countries and 25 percent of all the ARV drugs in the world.[18] Through the Clinton Foundation, Cipla (along with Aspen Pharmacare) sold triple cocktail therapy for as low as US$140 per patient per year.[19]

Whereas multinational corporations spent up to 35 percent of sales on marketing and administration, Cipla spent only 9 percent of sales on selling its products (Figure 6.1).

There were three main factors responsible for Cipla's cost savings in marketing. First, like all generics companies, Cipla benefited from marketing expenditures by the companies that brought drugs to market and built demand within the global medical community. Second, the message was simple: low-priced drugs treating life-threatening conditions. Third, the firm leveraged social and media networks in the form of activist groups and nonprofit organizations. For example, when the company was ready to offer ARVs at the sensationally low price of US$350 per patient per year, Cipla made the offer directly to global aid organization Médicins Sans Frontières (Doctors Without Borders), and because it was in the organization's interest to drive prices down it helped publicize the offer.[20] The *New York Times* reported the offer on the front page—publicity no marketing budget can buy.

In addition to cost savings due to reduced marketing expenditures, Cipla streamlined its operations to reduce cost at every critical juncture. Rather than segmenting the global market by negotiating prices in each country as its competitors did, Cipla offered a tiered pricing system that led customers to segment themselves. The requirements for the lowest tier were simple: bulk preorders, prepayment, free-on-board shipping, protection against price inflation of raw materials, and indemnity from patent suits. These simple requirements dealt with two additional critical junctures: inventory cost and cash flow. As it received preorders, the firm could buy raw materials and produce its product efficiently, minimizing inventory and waste. With prepayments, the firm could make purchases with cash, eliminating finance charges; it could invest the positive cash flow in company growth; and it could prevent bad debt. With bulk orders planned in advance, manufacturing capacity could be optimized and manufacturing costs minimized. Because orders were purchased free-on-board, buyers took responsibility for shipping and customs, further reducing uncertainty and risk for Cipla.

FIGURE 6.1. SELECTED FINANCIALS FROM MULTINATIONAL PHARMACEUTICAL COMPANIES AND CIPLA, 2004.

Company	Local Currency	Net Sales (Local Currency, Millions)	Marketing and SG&A	R&D	Material and Production Costs	Other Expenses	Net Profit
GlaxoSmithKline	British pounds	20,359	35%	14%	21%	9%	22%
Boehringer Ingelheim	Euros	8,157	n/a	15%	16%	58%	11%
Bristol-Myers Squibb	U.S. dollars	19,360	33%	13%	31%	10%	13%
Merck	U.S. dollars	22,938	32%	17%	22%	4%	25%
MNC average			33%	15%	22%	12%	18%
Cipla	**Rupees**	**23,276**	**9%**	**3%**	**47%**	**19%**	**22%**

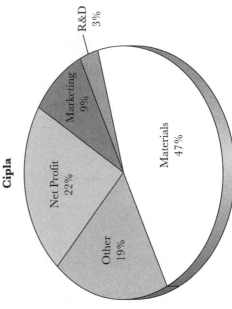

Cipla

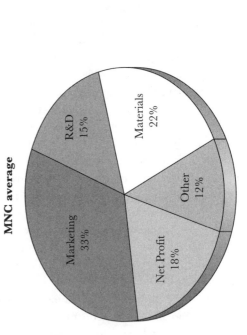

MNC average

Source: Edgar Online, company annual reports, company Websites.

The virtuous cycle of cost reduction could not continue indefinitely, and India's 2005 patent laws were a huge blow to Cipla, the national pharmaceutical industry, and the poor who depended on India's low-cost generic drugs for their survival.

It was unlikely most people in India would have access to new drugs in the future without government intervention: issuing a compulsory license, mandating price caps, or modifying the patent law. Cipla, though lobbying for such intervention, could not wait for a government decision. The company began making low-cost investments in a number of diverse areas: developing its own intellectual property through patents and an R&D partnership in biotherapy, focusing on exports of low-cost off-patent drugs to developed markets (exports were already at 45 percent of sales and growing), and entering joint ventures with foreign firms in India and overseas. In October 2005, the Ugandan health minister announced that Cipla and local firm Quality Chemicals Ltd. had signed a deal to partner with the Ugandan government in building Uganda's first ARV manufacturing facility. Since Uganda was one of the World Trade Organization's designated "least developed nations," it would not be required to adhere to international patent standards until 2016. The Ugandan ARV plant would manufacture new antiretroviral therapies as they became available, distributing them to Uganda's AIDS patients and exporting them to Kenya, Tanzania, Rwanda, and other least-developed nations.

Brazil

The Brazilian government was the first to produce ARVs. When Brazil launched its National AIDS Program in 1992, the nation's HIV prevalence rate was equal to South Africa's, with a typical patient surviving only six months after being diagnosed. By 2005, Brazil's National AIDS Program was the global gold standard for fighting AIDS; it contained the epidemic to a prevalence rate of only 0.7 percent while in South Africa the rate was thirty times higher. The National AIDS Program succeeded largely because it was a product of Brazil's unique political, social, epidemiological, and economic circumstances.

Following an army revolt, from 1965 to 1984 a succession of military regimes ruled Brazil, suppressing individual rights, suspending constitutional protections, and imposing press censorship. During this time, revolutionary movements formed, with activist leaders punished or exiled. In 1985, Brazil elected a civilian president and in 1988 ratified a new constitution declaring health a universal human right. Many government leaders who took office were former activists and union organizers favoring liberal social policy.

Journalists and others embraced their new right to free speech, candidly discussing sexuality in general and homosexuality in particular, and this openness contributed to the success of Brazil's HIV prevention program. One path of prevention was through schools, where students received HIV education and free condoms starting in their early teens. When the school prevention program was instituted, only 5 percent of young people used condoms during their first intercourse; by 2003, that number had increased to 55 percent.[21]

The initial spread of HIV in Brazil, as in many other nations, was among high-risk groups (gay men, sex workers, and intravenous drug users) in metropolitan areas. The concentration of the epidemic was a favorable epidemiological condition increasing the likelihood of containment, and the fact that it had spread among middle- and upper-class, well-educated communities meant the government had to pay attention.

Oddly, Brazil's economic instability was one of the keys to the success of its National AIDS Program. From the mid-1980s to the mid-1990s, the new government was spending much faster than it was collecting taxes, causing hyperinflation of up to 2,000 percent. Government leaders realized currency devaluation would put imported drugs out of reach and made a landmark decision to ensure access to ARVs by investing in local production capability.[22]

Case Study: The National AIDS Program

As the government of Brazil took action against the AIDS crisis, starting with creation of the National AIDS Program in 1992, commitment was complete and unambiguous. The strongest step occurred in 1996, when President Fernando Henrique Cardoso signed a law making ARV treatment free for life to everyone who needed it. The National AIDS Program's prevention practices all centered on understanding the problem and never blaming the person. This customer-centric approach recruited supporters from all the high-risk groups; it even won the support of the Catholic Church in Brazil. Prostitutes' unions were highly active in supporting HIV/AIDS education, meeting regularly with the National AIDS Program directors to help determine policy. The no-blame, human rights–based perspective was so fundamental that in the summer of 2005 the director of the National AIDS Program turned down $40 million of USAID funding on principle because the grant would have required recipients to sign a pledge condemning prostitution, which is legal in Brazil.[23]

By 2001, the National AIDS Program had averted 50 percent of the 1.2 million predicted infections, reduced the hospitalization and mortality rates by 50 percent, and cut mother-to-child transmission by two-thirds.[24] The number of new AIDS cases declined each year, and by 2005, 100 percent of reported HIV patients were under treatment. Ninety-seven percent of the population understood how AIDS was transmitted, and free condoms and free needles were widely available.

In 1992, the state-run pharmaceutical facility Far-Manguinhos started local production of AIDS drugs not covered by Brazilian patent law at that time, and within a year these drugs were distributed at a fraction of the cost of the patented versions. By 2004, Far-Manguinhos manufactured 37 percent of ARVs distributed in Brazil at an average cost savings of 60 percent.[25] The greatest economic advantage of local production, however, was in leveraging price negotiations with pharmaceutical companies. Since the late 1990s, Far-Manguinhos had reverse-engineered all the AIDS drugs available, so that at any time Brazil could declare a national emergency and start full-scale production of these drugs. Drug price negotiations repeatedly made global news as Brazil bargained down patented drug prices by 40–60 percent, a total reduction of 87 percent when combined with Far-Manguinhos–produced medicines (Figure 6.2). Compulsory licensing was a credible threat, but as of 2005 the Brazilian government had never had to follow through.

The miracle of this successful social program was its profitability, both social and economic. The benefits outweighed the costs by every measure, with a $2 billion expenditure generating financial savings of $3.8 billion on reduced hospitalizations and lowered drug prices.[26] Shrewd business management was the foundation of the National AIDS Program's processes and practices, such as maintaining a central database to ensure proper treatment and control inventory, implementing mobile treatment units to reduce hospitalizations, and working with activist groups to spread educational messages and save marketing costs.

FIGURE 6.2. ARV DRUG PRICE REDUCTIONS THROUGH BRAZILIAN NATIONAL AIDS PROGRAM, 1996–2002.

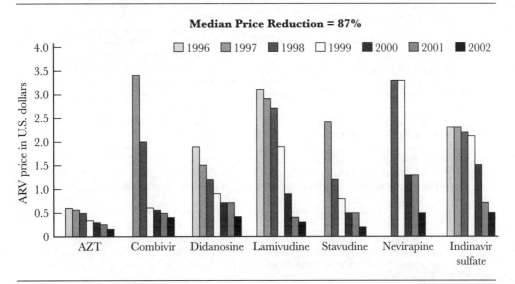

Source: Presentation by Pedro Chequer, director of National AIDS Program, Brazilian Ministry of Health.

A Customer-Centric Marketing Paradigm

From the success patterns of the three organizations we have discussed (Aspen Pharmacare, Cipla, and the Brazilian National AIDS Program), we have developed what we call a customer-centric marketing model. In Table 6.1, we contrast customer-centric methods of distributing generic drugs with traditional methods of distributing patented drugs. The traditional drug company builds market share through physician sales calls, while the customer-centric firm defines the patient as its customer, building market share by creating new markets and empowering new customers to participate

TABLE 6.1. CUSTOMER-CENTRIC MARKETING PARADIGM.

Traditional Marketing: Multinational Pharmaceutical Companies	Customer-Centric Marketing Paradigm: Generic Pharmaceutical Manufacturers
Sales focus • Physician sales calls • Stimulating sales growth by augmenting salesforce	Customer focus • Voice of the customer • Working with patients to identify solutions • Leveraging social networks
Transactions • Short-term monopoly profits, price skimming • Dispensing medicines	Relationships • Long-term, sustainable profits • Creation of infrastructure and programs • Partnerships with competitors
Market-driven • Satisfying current customer needs • Existing high-volume global markets	Market-driven and market-driving • Satisfying current customer needs • Expanding markets
Technology-pushed • High-risk R&D investments • Product development	Market-pulled • Low-risk operational investments • Business processes
Make and sell • Heavy marketing expenditures • High sunk costs, long development cycle	Sense and respond • Reducing controllable uncertainty • Nimble production mechanisms
The "Four Ps" • Premium marketing strategy • Success = winning market share • Marketing decisions in marketing department	Culture, strategy, tactics • Low-cost marketing strategy • Marketing decisions across all functions

in markets. The traditional drug company maximizes transactional short-term profits; the customer-centric firm maximizes long-term profits by building relationships and infrastructure, integrating both upstream and downstream, employing creative promotional tactics, minimizing costs, and reducing uncertainty. Using practices such as these, Aspen Pharmacare, Cipla, and the Brazilian National AIDS Program have been able to optimize their cost structures to earn above-average returns on comparatively low capital investment while saving the lives of the poor.

CHAPTER SEVEN

MEETING UNMET NEEDS AT THE BASE OF THE PYRAMID

Mobile Health Care for India's Poor

Pablo Sánchez, Miguel A. Rodríguez, Joan E. Ricart

If in answer to the question "What are firms for?" we said that one of the main components of any corporate purpose is to "satisfy human needs profitably" or to "create wealth for the company and the people the company serves," most people would agree. At the base of the pyramid (BOP), however, we find companies behaving paradoxically: there are more unsatisfied needs at the BOP than anywhere else, but multinational corporations (MNCs) entering developing countries have generally chosen to tailor existing products to the needs of the rich. The private sector in these countries has failed to offer products or services to the low-income segment, even though this is where most basic needs remain unmet and the majority of the population is to be found.

There are three main explanations for this. First, elite and urban consumers in developing countries are more similar—psychologically closer—to American, European, and Japanese consumers than the impoverished inhabitants of shantytowns and rural areas. Second, there is an institutional deficit in the developing world that makes conventional MNC operations all but impossible.[1] Third, traditional MNC cost structure is taken as a given, so that low-income markets cannot be served profitably because the target customers cannot afford their products and services.[2] In other words, established assumptions and perceptions about low-income markets block entry into these same markets. As Prahalad and Hart (2002) state, the biggest challenge is to change the existing dominant logic of MNC executives so that they start to see low-income markets as a business opportunity.

Because current business models mainly address the needs of premium markets, the basic needs of the world's poor remain largely unsatisfied. In actuality, 80 percent of the world's population is either ignored or inadequately served by the private sector. By sheer size, however, this is a market few enterprises can afford to ignore. Furthermore, from an ethical viewpoint companies are the only social institution with the capability to serve these markets. Thus, they have a duty to design and create sustainable opportunities for the poor to improve their standard of living.

This is a striking irony: the private sector is failing to serve the market segment in which the most needs remain unmet. To resolve this, we analyze the DISHA (Distance Healthcare Advancement) project initiated by Philips India and identify the main requirements of a cost-effective business model for providing essential health services to low-income markets. DISHA's goal is to deliver high-quality, low-cost diagnostics to people who cannot access existing health care systems. This goal crystallized in 2004 when qualitative and quantitative research conducted in sixty Indian villages assessed health-seeking behaviors and needs. The research revealed that people with lower income levels spend a larger proportion of their income on health care than those with higher incomes. A large percentage of those expenditures—some studies suggest up to 80 percent of the total—go to paying high interest (60–120 percent per year) on health care loans, while the rest is absorbed by travel and lost work time. DISHA aims to extend access to primary health care services to approximately 275 million people in India living on between $1,000 and $2,000 a year. In the first stage, DISHA is focusing on maternal and child health, as well as trauma. Current users pay only for diagnostic services (an average of US$1.80) and for medicines purchased. In the second phase of the project, total care (including diagnosis, medicines, teleconsultation, and so on) will cost an average of US$6–7 per user, substantially less than the private health system.

One of the main limitations of our study is that the DISHA project is in the early stages. Although we cannot be sure of its future profitability, DISHA's managers believe there is a clear value proposition and that once the project reaches a larger population it will be profitable.

Key Factors of Business Models in Low-Income Markets

The DISHA case has allowed us to identify three common, interrelated factors that seem especially relevant for implementing innovative new business models in low-income markets: (1) use of new and advanced technologies, (2) development of partnerships, and (3) integration into social networks.

Use of New and Advanced Technology

Contrary to popular belief, we observed that business models for serving the poor tend to be technology-intensive. Moreover, as we have found in cases such as GrupoNueva[3] or Hindustan Lever,[4] the technology used is not simply a downgraded version of traditional solutions from developed markets. For example, Philips addresses rural markets through DISHA by using advanced technology adapted to local infrastructure and customers' needs. The DISHA project is the first mobile telemedicine initiative conceived in India, combining imaging and medical diagnosis with satellite connectivity to offer online consultation. Philips provides diagnostic equipment to customized teleclinical vans (including X-ray equipment, an ultrasound machine, EKG devices, a defibrillator, blood and urine analyzers, and so forth), while ISRO (a government organization) provides connectivity and allocates the required bandwidth on its satellite free of cost. Philips also furnishes telemedicine hardware and software. As a result, even patients residing in remote villages can consult with a doctor through the teleclinical van. Diagnostic tests are conducted in the van itself, and if required a specialist at a referral hospital may be consulted. All necessary patient information is transmitted via satellite. Videoconferencing is available for the specialist to interact with the patient and the onsite doctor.

As the DISHA project shows, when adapted to the local context new technologies can be particularly suitable for satisfying people's basic needs. In this case, DISHA offers accessible and affordable health care, reduces total health care spending, and affords early detection of illness.

In analyzing the benefits of new technologies in poor areas, we observed two other important issues: how technology contributes to sustainable development, and how it enhances connectivity. The number of people reached by the DISHA van is a key indicator of the project's social performance. As regards environmental performance, the medical equipment used conforms with Philips's eco-design standards. In addition, DISHA's use of communication technologies is a clear example of how poor people can gain access to quality health care through a virtual connection. If a physical connection is difficult owing to gaps in existing infrastructure, communication technologies can fill the gap.

Development of Partnerships

Traditionally, strategic partnerships and joint ventures have been used to gain access to new markets and acquire knowledge about local conditions. Indeed, partners can be especially valuable in challenging environments where foreign firms lack certain resources or competencies. Though this is also true for low-income markets, in DISHA's case—as in others such as Patrimonio Hoy (CEMEX[5]), Amanco (GrupoNueva[6]), and

Tetra Pak,[7] we observed that companies overcome infrastructure deficiencies through a *shift from a product delivery system to a total solution delivery system.* Indeed, developing a venture aimed at providing an integral offering is more complex than merely producing and selling a product. It requires successful delivery of the partners' support.

A strategic partnership between Philips, a government agency (ISRO), Asia's largest health care service provider (Apollo Hospitals), and one of India's most respected NGOs (DHAN) has brought DISHA's vision to life. Philips built a customized teleclinical van, complete with diagnostic equipment. ISRO developed a satellite-based telemedicine network to provide specialty health care consultancy to remote populations. Apollo Hospitals Group is a pioneer in the field of telemedicine in India and is credited as the first to set up a rural telemedicine center in the village of Aragonda in Andhra Pradesh. Apollo supplies and trains the doctors and paramedical staff for the teleclinical van, while specialist doctors and operational staff at Apollo's hospitals offer specialized diagnosis and care for patients visiting the van. The DHAN Foundation contributes the vital link to the local community and plays a key role in stimulating community participation in the project. DHAN performs marketing and communication activities in rural communities to raise awareness and build trust in the project. DHAN also furnishes nutrition and hygiene counseling (through home follow-ups) and trains village volunteers to motivate and take part in counseling. This gets the villagers actively involved in the project.

As we observed, this business concept implies seeking the support of partners that can leverage their own competencies and expertise in the project. Indeed, DISHA believes that only by cooperating with highly knowledgeable, complementary partners is it possible to introduce affordable and sustainable solutions tailored to particular living conditions. As DISHA's general manager put it, "This project could not be carried out by any one organization on its own. Neither Philips, nor ISRO, nor Apollo, nor any NGO could do this on its own. We bring the partners together, each with its own competencies, to make the project a success. This is the business model of the future. You simply cannot do everything by yourself."

In fact, DISHA is looking to extend the partnership to include an insurer. DISHA's general manager recognizes that an insurance partner covering rural patients' medical expenses may be needed, to "close the gap in our value chain." Medical insurance is an unknown concept in most rural areas, so insurance firms do not have specific products for this market. Philips is analyzing the costs and proactively seeking such a partner. In the pilot phase, the problem was solved by using the DHAN Foundation's own medical insurance system. After this pilot project is evaluated, the results will be used to build a business model for a health care delivery system that includes the cost of insurance.

Thus alliances are critical in low-income markets because they make it possible to combine the resources and competencies of the partners and develop an integral offering to satisfy the basic needs of the poor. Moreover, the DISHA case confirms the widespread view that it is important to collaborate with both traditional partners (private companies) and nontraditional partners (government agencies, NGOs, local communities[8]) to facilitate access to these markets and fully use their capabilities.

Finally, we observed the prominent role that Philips played in leading and coordinating the partnership. As DISHA's general manager states, this is a source of competitive advantage: "The core competence, I would say, is bringing partners together, and that is going to be tough [for any competitor]."

Accordingly, we can say that *acting as a promoter, leader, and coordinator of partnerships is a sustainable strategic capability that is crucial for entering low-income markets.* It is important to note that information technology can reduce communication and coordination costs in this kind of decentralized system.

Integration into Social Networks

The third factor we observed is Philips's integration into social networks. Hart refers to such integration as a *native capability* that "enables the corporation to become truly embedded—part of the local landscape rather than an alien force that imposes its will from the outside."[9] It involves engaging extensively with local people and customers in order to truly understand their circumstances and bring business solutions that satisfy their primary needs. As we saw earlier, Philips engaged with local groups to understand the basic needs to be addressed and design the most appropriate delivery model.

Traditional literature on emerging markets has emphasized the presence of "institutional voids"[10]—lack of infrastructure, weak institutional systems, absence of market intermediaries, and the like—that constrain firms' activity and growth.[11] Rather than trying to overcome limitations in the environment, Philips crafted its business model to fit the idiosyncratic system of low-income markets, characterized by informal social relationships and interpersonal networks that enhance the value of social capital.

Philips joined with social partners (the DHAN Foundation) to *gain access* to consumers, among other things. The DHAN Foundation has been working for several years with local communities, has legitimacy, and is trusted. Philips relies mainly on DHAN's extensive social network, which ensures that all the rural patients who belong to self-help groups that work with DHAN visit the DISHA teleclinical van. DHAN Foundation members also directly engage the community and train volunteers to build awareness of health and hygiene issues. This prescreening team visits villages to assess those most in need of diagnosis and passes this information on to Philips. On Saturdays, the DISHA team participates in health screening camps run by partner NGOs, further strengthening health promotion. To increase the number of potential patients, Philips is seeking the support of additional NGOs to strengthen the interaction among patients, doctors, and DISHA vehicles. In other words, Philips aims to become more embedded in order to have better access to local communities and reach as many people as possible.

Integration into social networks permits *physical access* to end customers. We also observed that being native was critical to achieving *mental access*. Indeed, as we saw in the cases of CEMEX, Amanco, Hindustan Lever, and Tetra Pak, a corporation embedded into the local culture can gain the trust and legitimacy it needs to interact with customers. In the DISHA project, DHAN's involvement was essential to enabling doctors working in the vehicles to win the trust and faith of rural patients. Ultimately, interaction between consumers and a network of companies and institutions creates a personalized co-creation experience that enhances the value perceived by the consumer.[12]

New Business Models for Low-Income Markets

As our analysis of the DISHA project has shown, to serve low-income markets companies may need to develop innovative business models that radically reduce the traditional MNC cost structure. This can be done through a balanced combination of advanced technology, alliances with traditional and nontraditional partners, and integration into local social networks. As represented in Figure 7.1, these elements combine to produce a business model whose characteristics make it especially valuable in low-income markets.

Indeed, one of the main aims of business models in low-income markets is to foster sustainability, especially social sustainability, while ensuring profitability. As we have seen, use of technology can contribute significantly to this goal. The DISHA project seeks to satisfy one of the primary unsatisfied needs of poor segments: health care assistance. Similarly, and as discussed in Chapter Twenty-Five, Amanco has designed a trickle irrigation system that guarantees year-round water access, reduces the cost of irrigation, and increases the quantity and quality of crops, helping to raise incomes for farmer in Mexico. CEMEX's Patrimonio Hoy project (discussed in Chapter Fourteen) makes housing available and improves housing conditions in poor areas. The integration of these corporations into local social networks has made them more knowledgeable about the real needs of local people.

Becoming socially embedded in the local community is essential to building trust. Some companies operating in low-income markets engage directly with customers to obtain credibility. CEMEX, for example, has established relationships with local leaders and women who promote the Patrimonio Hoy program; some of them are also Patrimonio Hoy customers. Philips chose to partner with a renowned and trusted institution, the DHAN Foundation, which for almost ten years has fostered

FIGURE 7.1. ELEMENTS OF NEW BUSINESS MODELS SERVING LOW-INCOME MARKETS.

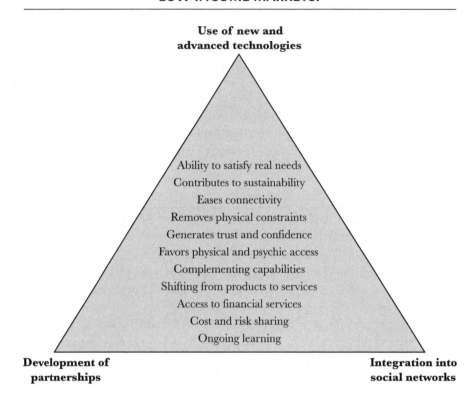

microcredit initiatives and supported agricultural development in rural areas. Embedded ties with local people and institutions give these companies physical and mental access to rural customers.

We also observed that, to address needs at the BOP, most companies develop a business model completely different from their traditional one. This *new model involves offering an integral service rather than a product*. Because this integral service is more complex and requires resources, technologies, or capacities that the corporation may not initially possess, partnerships become crucial to gain access to the necessary competencies. In this context, competitive advantage comes from forming, leading, and managing partnerships. As these processes are path-dependent and based on trust, the results in terms of competitive advantage are highly sustainable.

The need for partnerships and integration into social networks has a further implication. Specifically, we observed a clear *coevolution* of both the business model and the service in response to partners' suggestions. There is ongoing learning in these projects; business models should be flexible enough to permit adaptation, as long as new inputs and know-how are generated.

In summary, besides reducing the cost structure, these three factors—use of new and advanced technologies, development of partnerships, and integration into social networks—enable the corporation to understand cultural, economic, and social contexts and generate the knowledge and trust needed to succeed. This becomes especially relevant for finding solutions that satisfy real needs and offer a clear value proposition to potential customers.

CHAPTER EIGHT

ENERGIZING THE BASE OF THE PYRAMID

Scaling up Successful Business Models to Achieve Universal Electrification

David J. Jhirad, Annie Woollam

Affordable and reliable energy services underpin economic development.[1] Electricity services are vital to connectivity, communications, transport, health care, agricultural outputs, and financial services; greater energy and electricity consumption correlate closely with greater human development (Figure 8.1). In the modern era, no country has experienced a reduction in poverty without a significant increase in energy consumption.[2] Recent analysis confirms that without a dramatic increase in access to energy services around the globe, the United Nations' eight Millennium Development Goals (MDGs) for poverty reduction will not be achieved.[3]

Approximately 2.4 billion people still lack access to modern energy services and are limited to traditional biomass fuels for their cooking and heating needs.[4] Nearly 1.6 billion people lack access to electricity.[5] The vast majority live in sub-Saharan Africa, South Asia, and other regions of the developing world. Without decisive action by governments, civil society, and the private sector to break the vicious circle of energy poverty and human deprivation, the absolute number of people in energy poverty will remain unchanged in the year 2030.[6] This outcome is clearly not in the long-term economic and security interests of wealthy industrialized nations. Taking action to greatly expand energy services is an important step in attacking global poverty and will require political vision and commitment by world leaders, as well as multifaceted innovation on an unprecedented scale.[7] Bringing three billion of the world's people up to Western European electricity consumption standards of approximately 6,000 kilowatt-hours per capita annually will require an additional two

FIGURE 8.1. INCREASED HUMAN DEVELOPMENT INDEX DEMANDS INCREASED PER CAPITA ELECTRICITY CONSUMPTION.

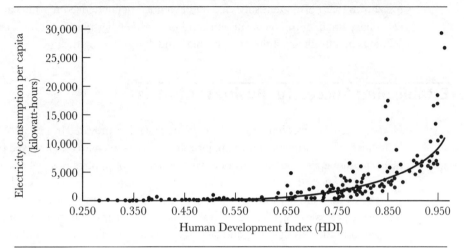

Source: United Nations Development Programme. *Human Development Report 2005*. New York: UNDP, 2005. Statistics database available at http://hdr.undp.org/statistics/.

million megawatts of power capacity, the equivalent of two thousand large power plants.

Expanding Enterprise and the Role of the Private Sector

Central to this innovation is private enterprise, bolstered by sound public policy and good governance. The role of entrepreneurship and innovation has been largely absent in the poverty eradication strategies of governments and multilateral development organizations. To create incentives for these organizations to change, successful business models with the potential for scale-up and financial sustainability are crucial. The thesis of this paper is that successful models exist and can be replicated and scaled up to eradicate global energy poverty.

The International Energy Agency projects that US$16 trillion of investment will be required in the international energy sector over the next twenty-five years, US$9.6 trillion of which will be needed in developing and transition economies.[8] Public funds will be required, but the private sector is critical to mobilizing the capital and technology needed to improve access to electricity services.

Grant funding by governments and international assistance agencies is required to leverage private capital into difficult markets. Furthermore, government policies and measures can create incentives for local and multinational enterprises to enter low-income energy markets. There are, however, significant lessons to be learned. History has shown that permanent subsidies and extended dependence on grants and concessionary finance from governments and donor agencies have inhibited scaleable solutions by subsidizing affluent consumers and marginalizing the poor.[9]

Establishing Successful Business Models

Grid-connected energy infrastructure, and energy services provided by private and public utilities, will continue to play a major role in underserved areas. However, the emphasis in this paper is on enterprises serving businesses or populations that are unlikely to be grid-connected for many decades, whether for financial or institutional reasons.

Distributed energy and power technologies have an important role to play in increasing access to electricity services,[10] especially in rural communities or regions isolated from the existing grid, and lacking transmission, distribution, and fuel transport infrastructure. Distributed systems include diesel units and renewable resources such as solar, biomass, geothermal, or small hydro. Distributed energy technologies are characterized by relatively high investment costs per kilowatt installed. But such systems do not require transmission and distribution infrastructure, and fuel costs are low (or zero in the case of renewable systems). Therefore business models to support dissemination of these environmentally sustainable systems at an affordable price require innovative financing to spread their initial costs over the life of the system. Serving this market through scaling and replicating successful businesses represents a daunting challenge.

This paper analyzes three enterprises that provide electricity services to poor communities. Shell Solar's operations in Sri Lanka and India are part of a large multinational serving the household sector using an individual systems ownership model. DESI Power in India and IDEAAS in Brazil are two local entrepreneurial enterprises serving income-generating purposes, and employing village-ownership and fee-for-service models, respectively.

These enterprises have demonstrated that there is a viable market for energy and electricity services in poor communities, beginning with those at the top of the base of the socioeconomic pyramid (BOP). Here are key characteristics of their successful business models:

- An in-depth understanding of the local market, community, and specific customer needs
- Meeting the financing challenge through low-interest loans and government or donor grants (without financing assistance, the up-front investment cost of some systems is prohibitive for BOP customers)

- Fostering the parallel development of productive, entrepreneurial enterprises that require electricity

Extending these successes to the 1.6 billion people without electricity will require strategic marketing and manufacturing breakthroughs that dramatically reduce the cost and accelerate the global market for solar electric and other distributed power systems. Such breakthroughs are necessary to allow the international distributed power industry to build large-scale, highly efficient manufacturing facilities to produce modular systems at competitive prices and without public subsidies. Modern manufacturing and deployment of low carbon energy systems on a significant scale have the potential to reduce both poverty and carbon emissions.

Shell Solar

Shell Solar operates throughout Asia, but this analysis focuses on their operations in southern India and Sri Lanka.

Technology and Systems

Shell Solar's basic photovoltaic (PV) home system gives the customer either DC or AC power. The average DC and AC systems yield approximately 200 and 500 watt hours per day, respectively. Every system comes with solar panels, a battery, a charge controller to regulate the flow of electricity into and out of the battery, system wiring, installed lights, sockets for appliances, battery storage, and an inverter for AC. Modules are covered by a ten-year warranty, and the deep-cycle batteries are covered for one year. Approximately 50 percent of the cost of the system is the PV module, with the remaining 50 percent in the balance-of-system (BOS), which is dominated by battery cost. The PV modules are manufactured in Shell Solar factories, or by third-party suppliers. Many BOS components such as batteries, cables, and switches are sourced locally.

The Business Model

Shell Solar establishes a direct sales channel to customers supported by a consumer financing package from rural banks or microfinancing entities. Shell Solar also handles maintenance and service assistance on a contractual or fee basis. The business model has required short-term donor and government subsidies to reduce the up-front capital cost of the systems, train local technicians and administrators, and raise public awareness of the benefits of service. The cumulative number of systems sold by Shell Solar by the end 2005 amounted to approximately thirty-five thousand in Sri Lanka and twenty thousand in India. Consumer finance was the vital factor in achieving these numbers.

Consumer Financing

The price of a system averages about US$650, which includes installation and one year of service. The annual amortized costs represent about 25 percent of an average customer's household income over five years. Consumer financing is therefore essential to increasing access to energy services and profitability of energy enterprises.

In Sri Lanka, Shell Solar developed a credit scheme in conjunction with local banks. Initially, there was only one microfinance institution (MFI) offering consumer credit. A Global Environment Facility (GEF) evaluation report concluded that more MFIs were needed to cater to the solar home system (SHS) market.[11] Currently market penetration of SHS in Sri Lanka is about 10 percent.

Grants from the World Bank and GEF were crucial in priming the market for renewable energy distributors such as Shell Solar, reducing the average cost of each system by about 25 percent. The industry in Sri Lanka grew from one hundred units in 1998 to roughly fifteen thousand by 2004. The key to the rapid expansion was Shell Solar's entry into the market with consumer financing partners, and the subsequent entry of many local competitors.

In India, the International Finance Corporation (IFC) extended a partial guarantee to Shell Solar's Indian banking partners to cover a percentage of net losses, and a UNEP grant was used to reduce interest rates. The industry as a whole installed eighteen thousand SHSs under that scheme. Despite these subsidy and finance schemes, sales are still constrained by limited access to consumer finance.

Project Financing

Shell Corporate made equity investments in Shell Solar operations in Sri Lanka and India. In India, the Photovoltaic Market Transformation Initiative, a joint initiative of GEF and the IFC, made a low-interest, working capital loan of US$2 million to expand their network. In 2004, Shell Solar India and Sri Lanka reached breakeven or better, and Shell Solar's Rural Operations division, which also includes the Philippines, Indonesia, and China, recorded growth of 40 percent. As anticipated, sales declined after the incentives were withdrawn, indicating that the market is still immature.

Management, Maintenance, and Marketing

Shell Solar is required to meet Shell Corporate's profitability criteria. Their operations are supported by fifteen local solar centers in Sri Lanka and twenty-five in India, and by the Shell Solar office in Singapore. The ability to acquire and use a functioning product quickly is important to the consumers and Shell uses this network of solar centers to stock product as close to the customer base as possible. Shell Solar has also developed a small pickup truck that is outfitted to exhibit the solar panels and the lights.

Each solar center is staffed by a local operations coordinator and technicians. Extensive training is required in standard operating procedures, inventory, and cash handling controls; sales effectiveness and sales reporting; and installation and servicing. In addition, there is an ongoing need for monitoring and retraining. After the first year of free scheduled maintenance, customers can purchase an annual service contract, but many do not elect to take advantage of this option. Instead, they turn to one of the Shell Solar local solar centers on an as-needed basis.

The key marketing strategy is word-of-mouth, rather than reliance on traditional forms of media. Shell Solar works closely with local leaders to identify customers who can afford to pay, and who serve as opinion leaders.

Risks

A serious risk to business sustainability is that companies have experienced cash flow difficulties resulting from delays in receiving funds from partner banks and from the local governments. The lack of expansion by Shell's consumer finance partners is a major risk, as is the current supply shortage of panels in the global PV market. Risk is managed with the help of the Shell Solar supply chain team. Consumer finance risk is managed through ongoing discussion and coordination with finance partners.

DESI Power

Decentralized Energy Systems India (DESI Power) is a private Indian company that uses biomass gasification in modular distributed units to provide reliable electricity services to communities for lighting, mechanical power, communications, and connectivity. In urban areas, DESI Power delivers reliable electricity service to industry and educational institutions. In rural and semiurban areas, DESI Power works with independent rural power producers (IRPPs) to install plants and build local capacity to operate them, while also fostering enterprises that use electricity services. DESI Power aims to promote growth in the rural economy while building the market for energy services.

Technology and Systems

DESI Power uses a biomass gasification system to generate electricity in gas or gas/diesel engines. Developed by the Combustion Gasification and Propulsion Laboratory at the Indian Institute of Science in Bangalore, the technology was commercialized by NETPRO Renewable Energy, the current licensee of the technology. NETPRO supplies the plant package and the training of plant staff.

Since 1996, DESI Power has installed nine demonstration plants at a total cost of about US$430,000 for plant and equipment. In addition, it has invested about US$200,000 in organizational development, buildup of infrastructure, project development, training and extension services, monitoring, and awareness building.[12]

The Business Model

The business model for IRPPs is a "build-own-transfer" model. Under an agreement with a local partner, DESI Power designs, constructs, and operates a village power station in close collaboration with local individuals and businesses. DESI Power builds the capacity of villagers to operate and maintain the plant with the goal of transferring ownership, technical and management operation, and maintenance to the local partner. DESI Power's EmPower Partnership Program (EmPP) builds the local market for energy services and ensures the sustainability of the plants, by working with local groups to capitalize on the income-generating opportunities offered by a reliable, clean, and affordable energy source (Figure 8.2).

Local partners may be NGOs, panchayats (a village association), cooperative bodies, or microenterprises. Microenterprises include water supply, agricultural processing, small industries, fuel supply and processing, and agroforestry. In addition, all biomass fuel for the gasifier is locally harvested agricultural or plantation residue, thus affording villagers and local businesses a new income stream.

DESI Power sells energy to the village cooperative or local partner, which in turn sells electricity or a particular service to the commercial end user.

Operational Budget

The cost of each project is made up of three parts: microenterprises, energy services, and infrastructure and power plant. The total investment for a 60KW power plant is between US$140,000 and $150,000. This includes acquisition and installation of the power plant (approximately 60 percent of overall cost), microenterprise infrastructure (24 percent), project development (3 percent), and training and microenterprise development (13 percent).

The operating costs of all plants are covered; even at low load factors, the rural plants yield a return on investment of about 7 percent.[13] The average time to profitability has decreased from four years for the early projects to less than two years. Two features of the market and technology have been important in decreasing the time to profitability. First, DESI Power engages in developing the upstream and downstream markets prior to installation of the plant. Second, DESI Power initially installed dual fuel generators in their plants, but cost considerations have led to phasing out diesel engines.

FIGURE 8.2. ORGANIZATIONAL STRUCTURE OF DESI POWER–LOCAL ENTITY PARTNERSHIP.

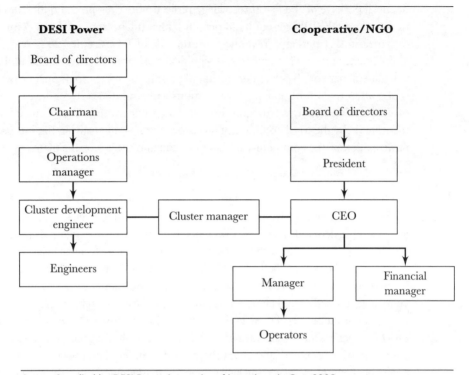

Source: Supplied by DESI Power in a series of interviews in Oct. 2005.

Financing

Plant installation and microenterprise development of the three demonstration projects have been funded by grants. The Dutch government supported the installation of 600KW of biomass gasification power generating capacity in villages. The grant covered approximately 60–70 percent of the plant construction, training, and initial operations and maintenance costs; the remainder was covered by DESI Power, government subsidies, project affiliates, and the local community. A grant from the Shell Foundation supported the initial microenterprise development work in conjunction with implementation of three of the power plants and leveraged more than US$100,000 in investments. Grants will continue to be important to the DESI Power business model to cover the costs of training, capacity building, and extension services. However, DESI Power has come to rely less on grants as other sources of funding materialize, including government support for rural electrification.

DESI Power plans to establish a public–private partnership model under the rural electrification and employment initiatives of the Indian government. The current financial package of the first three village projects under the program includes a mix of local and DESI Power equity (8 percent), investment from the local community organizations (1 percent), revenue from the sale of CO_2 credits (26 percent), and government subsidies (17 percent). A significant private sector Indian bank, ICICI, will make a loan for 48 percent of the initial investment in the program. The program is also attracting grant-making organizations with an interest in replicating models of decentralized energy provision through renewable sources. The financial investment made by the local community has proven crucial in ensuring the interest and participation of the community in the operation and success of the plant.

Risks

DESI Power's financial viability is dependent on maintaining a reliable fuel source and a high level of demand. There are risks inherent in operating in rural markets with poor infrastructure, with credit facilities lacking, and with local people having very basic skills. The main source of livelihood in these villages is agriculture. Because of inefficient farming practices, the availability of agricultural fuels for the biomass gasification process is vulnerable to weather and climate variations, as are farmers' ability to pay for services.

In a parallel effort, DESI Power helps build enterprises based on productive uses of power, including increasing efficiency of agricultural processes. This helps to ensure electricity demand, and DESI Power works with local producers to ensure availability of biomass. However, the lack of a credit market has limited the growth of microenterprise development. DESI Power is building such a market by partnering with a bank to provide credit to new energy-using enterprises in DESI Power communities.

IDEAAS

Founded in 1997, IDEAAS, a not-for-profit based in Porto Alegre, Brazil, supplies electricity to rural communities lacking grid access through installation of PV solar home systems.

Technology and Systems

IDEAAS offers three SHS units. Each delivers 12 volts but with 60, 90, or 120 watts. The basic components of the system are one or more solar panels, a battery, and wiring of the residence. The 60W basic system is installed with four fluorescent lights, as well as an electrical outlet that can power appliances such as a black-and-white television, radio, or cell phone charger. This system can supply ten hours of light per night or three hours of television. The 90W and 120W systems can also support a small water pump (but not a refrigerator).

The Business Model

IDEAAS operates on a fee-for-service model at the top of the BOP. It sells electricity from units installed in individual residences for residential and commercial use but retains ownership of the systems. IDEAAS's Quiron project penetrates deeper into the BOP by investing in productive use of electricity on a customer's property and improving the ability to pay for electricity services. IDEAAS works closely with its for-profit sister organization, Agroelectric System of Appropriate Technology (STA). STA electricians are responsible for systems improvement, as well as manufacture and assembly of some system components. IDEAAS contracts with STA to install and maintain the systems (Figure 8.3).

IDEAAS offers its customers financing to pay the installation fee. The timing and size of each repayment is defined by the customer at the time of installation and is based on ability to pay at different times throughout the year to accommodate seasonal income. The fee-for-service model allows IDEAAS to offer customers lower up-front cost by effectively renting the system. It also creates incentives for IDEAAS to be innovative

FIGURE 8.3. IDEAAS ORGANIZATIONAL STRUCTURE.

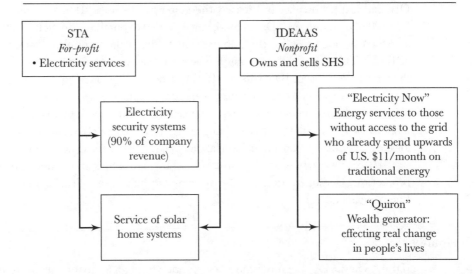

Source: WRI diagram developed through field interviews with IDEAAS, Sept. 2005.

in their design of the systems in order to protect their investment. For example, because IDEAAS is responsible for replacing the battery, which constitutes up to 70 percent of the system cost, much design effort has been put into protecting and extending battery life. Finally, IDEAAS retains the capital in their solar panels and other plant against which to take out loans to invest in more units.

Designing for the Customer

Prior to the trial phase, significant efforts were put into understanding customer needs, abilities, and consumption patterns by surveying IDEAAS's target market. This data was used to determine the price points of the three systems. The survey revealed that families spent at least US$11 on energy each month,[14] which determined the price of the basic system. Customer data also reveal that 90 percent spend less on energy after installation of their solar home system.

On average, a service call costs IDEAAS US$30, about the value of three months of service fees. However, the company found that illiterate customers were not receiving appropriate training and support from the text-based user's manual, and so developed more appropriate communications and teaching tools, significantly reducing service costs. Additionally, payment facilities are conveniently located in areas frequented by customers, such as the electrician's store.

Management, Operations, and Marketing

Originally, STA owned and leased the systems. However, IDEAAS received a US$100,000 grant from a Dutch fund, which it used to purchase 200 SHSs. IDEAAS and STA decided to keep the public grant funds in the nonprofit organization, IDEAAS. This changed the relationship between the two organizations; STA became the service provider for IDEAAS and IDEAAS became the owner of the equipment.

The service contract runs for three years and guarantees a certain wattage and reliable service. If the system breaks down, it is fixed within two days. IDEAAS charges a set monthly fee for providing electricity (ranging from US$10 to $21). Customers are liable for the cost of installation and deinstallation of the system if the contract is canceled.[15]

IDEAAS advertises on key rural radio shows and relies on word-of-mouth for promotion. Demonstrations of the systems are held in an electrician's store in Encruzilhada do Sul.

Finances

IDEAAS and STA operations have been funded through a mixture of direct investment, grants, and loans. Grants are used to build up assets against which traditional loans can be secured. To minimize repayment risk, conditional loans have been used strictly for operational expenses, and traditional loans for investment in collateral assets. Seed capital for the SHS deployed by STA in the trial phase was through a grant from the Solar Development Fund (SDF). SDF also made a conditional loan for market research and development of the business plan. The IDEAAS–STA alliance has taken out approximately US$60,000 in soft and commercial loans, and STA has invested US$45,000 of its own funds in market research. IDEAAS expects to become profitable with installation of four thousand units, which is projected to occur by the end of the fourth year of operations.

Risks

Risks faced by IDEAAS and STA include competition from utilities entering into IDEAAS's current market, default risk, capital mobilization, reliability of partners, and currency risk arising from the need to import solar panels.

Scale-up and Replication of Enterprises Serving Low-Income Communities

A number of business models and technologies have the potential for success in low-income underserved markets, and many have the added benefit of a lowered carbon footprint. To increase market penetration across income levels, these models must be scaled and replicated, and they must incorporate continuous innovation in technology development and deployment.

Scaling up requires three vital elements. First, companies need access to both consumer and project finance, including government and multilateral investments in capacity building in BOP communities. Second, an enabling legal, regulatory, and policy environment is needed. This includes removal of market distortions stemming from preferential government subsidies for competing fuels such as diesel and kerosene, and lifting of import duties that discriminate against new, clean technologies. Third, business and financial institutions must be willing to target unserved communities and engage in market transforming activities to ensure that consumers can pay for energy services.

As evidenced by Shell Solar's success in Sri Lanka, multilaterals can help to develop the low-income energy market with grant programs that create incentives for businesses to enter these markets. Such grants offset the cost of systems and support local financial institutions that make loans for purchase of systems. Extending credit lines to banks and microfinance institutions is also of crucial importance to enable customers to pay for their systems in an affordable manner over time.

Increasing delivery of energy services to BOP communities in developing countries requires a dramatically higher level of private investment in the sector. In replicating and scaling energy enterprises, entrepreneurs in the developing world must surmount two significant limitations: lack of business acumen and experience, and lack of access to capital. To address these deficits in growing the indigenous energy sector, E+Co, a nonprofit public purpose investment company, was established in 1994 to make successful investments in small and medium enterprises providing modern energy services in developing countries. E+Co has proved that coupling provision of capital with business mentoring services is an effective approach to building capacity within a market. As of June 2005, E+Co had US$42.4 million under management and had made 112 debt and equity investments.[16] Repayments were achieving an internal rate of return of 10.2 percent. However, by E+Co's estimates 16,500 entrepreneurial enterprises[17] are needed to deliver modern energy services to eight hundred million people.[18] Additionally, innovative finance options such as Certified Emission Reduction Certificates from the Clean Development Mechanism established under the Kyoto Protocol are needed to help leverage private investment.

Transforming the Market: Changing the Cost Structure of the Distributed Power Generation Industry

Each of the enterprises studied takes an active role in developing the market for electricity services. Shell Solar's market-opening and direct-marketing approach is designed to facilitate deployment of new technology through financial incentives and targeted subsidies. DESI Power and IDEAAS have integrated capacity building services into their business activities. DESI Power has implemented innovative projects that build consumers' capacity to pay for services by expanding income through productive end uses. DESI Power's EmPP program couples power plant implementation with enterprise development to build the commercial market for electricity services. A specific example of a targeted market development initiative is IDEAAS's Quiron project.

The business models analyzed have proved successful in delivering power to tens of thousands of people at the BOP. Extending these successes to the almost two billion people who lack electricity will require strategic marketing and manufacturing breakthroughs that dramatically reduce the cost of distributed power systems.

Using solar PV as an illustration, the strategy involves developing a large-volume, commercially viable global market by a private entity, possibly a foundation, acting as a trusted intermediary between buyers and sellers. A strategy of forward pricing and legally enforceable contracts would enable the international PV industry to build large-scale, highly efficient manufacturing facilities to produce PV systems at competitive prices and without public subsidies. Annual photovoltaic procurements of several times the current world production over a period of several years could allow the international

PV industry to lower installed system cost to below US$2,000 per peak kilowatt. Currently PV systems cost between US$6,000–10,000/KW installed, depending on system size, equipment options, and installation costs. Small systems average US$7 per watt. The average factory price of PV modules is about US$4 per watt, excluding balance-of-system costs, which increase the factory costs by 30–100 percent.

At a price of US$2,000 per peak kilowatt, grid-connected PV generation plants become commercially competitive with peak load diesel or gas turbines. After the anticipated steep and irreversible price drops are achieved, the market should be able to generate further vigorous expansion without additional private sector brokering.

This strategy can be modified appropriately to embrace an entire class of efficient emerging technologies that, because of their flexible, modular, and distributed nature, can be deployed in low- or high-power applications and used in isolated rural markets or modern electric power networks. Some technologies, such as fuel cells, lend themselves well to both stationary and mobile applications with fossil or nonfossil energy sources, as well as to cogeneration of heat and electricity. All these technologies share significant potential for cost reduction from standardization and mass production, and they exhibit superior local and global environmental characteristics. Examples include advanced batteries for electric and hybrid vehicles; biomass conversion and biofuels for transportation; energy-efficient lighting and other devices; fuel cells, gas turbines, and clean fossil systems; hydrogen storage systems; and wind power units.

Conclusions

Our analysis reveals that the market for distributed electricity services at the BOP can be tapped with the right business models deploying modern technology, and that private enterprise can deliver such services profitably with local entrepreneurial talent. Financing, however, remains a challenge. Grant funds from governments and assistance agencies will continue to play an important role in opening the BOP market and fostering growth of the private sector.

The business models studied in this paper are based on realistic, if not conservative, assumptions and good management practices. They are characterized by indepth knowledge of the local market; development of strategic local partnerships has been crucial to their success. Shell Solar, DESI Power, and IDEAAS all demonstrate the need for concurrent development of productive entrepreneurial enterprises that use electricity and create employment and income. They also demonstrate the importance of design flexibility, technology adaptation, training, and mentorship. Building capacity, and transferring operations and management skills to local communities, is an important part of creating new livelihoods and the ability to pay. Analysis by the Global Village Energy Project of UNDP[19] of E+Co's experience with more than one thousand entrepreneurs reinforces these findings, but it also finds that the uncertainty in these markets requires budget planning to allow for unforeseen problems.

Our analysis confirms that scalability requires clear policies and regulatory frameworks that foster incentives and remove disincentives for distributed power systems serving the BOP. Major actions to be taken by governments, as well as by bilateral and multilateral agencies, are to extend lines of credit to allow businesses to enter the market and forge their own partnerships with banks and financing institutions; end market distortions, particularly preferential government subsidies for competing fuels such as diesel and kerosene; phase out all duties on distributed power systems and components; and collaborate strategically to lower costs dramatically and expand markets at an accelerated pace.

CHAPTER NINE

UTILITIES AND THE POOR

A Story from Colombia

Carlos Rufín, Luis Fernando Arboleda

The 1990s witnessed a global wave of reform in network utilities such as electricity, water, and sanitation. In a large number of developing countries, companies providing infrastructure services were privatized and many services deregulated.

These changes have vast implications, not least for the poor. More than 1.2 billion people currently suffer from water scarcity, for example. In the absence of a piped water supply, poor families—particularly women and children—are forced to fetch water from distant and often polluted sources, representing a heavy physical burden and significantly heightened risk of disease. Alternatively, they must buy expensive water from water trucks or bottled sources. Development of network utilities can thus have a large impact on poverty in urban areas[1] where network service provision is most economical. Injecting private capital and competitive market mechanisms into network utilities has the potential to help the poor by lowering the cost of water, thus ensuring cheaper access to one of the essentials of life.

Yet experience, conventional wisdom, and ideology would seem to indicate otherwise. Private ownership of network utilities was almost universally replaced by public

In drafting this paper, we have benefited greatly from extensive discussions with and analytical perspectives of the organizers of and participants in the Inter-American Development Bank's 2004 seminars on Private Utility Supply in a Hostile Environment, particularly Jaime Millán and Luigi Manzetti. The material presented here, although based in part on the final report for the seminars (Manzetti and Rufín, 2004), represents our individual views alone and all errors are ours.

ownership after the Great Depression and Second World War. Most foreign-owned utilities were nationalized and private utilities were generally seen as interested in only serving large-volume, high-paying customers.[2] Conventional wisdom holds that the poor cannot afford to pay for network utility services, although in fact they usually pay significantly higher prices or incur higher costs for alternative sources such as firewood or water brought by truck. Some regard it as immoral to profit from the sale of life's necessities, even if another such necessity—food—is supplied almost exclusively on a for-profit basis.

In developing countries, private utilities face additional challenges. Privately owned network utilities are usually regulated to prevent abuses of monopoly power, since the physical networks needed to deliver service are most efficiently operated by a single entity. Government control over prices and quality levels creates the potential for indirect expropriation, especially in many developing countries where governments can have substantial influence on judges and regulators. As a matter of fact, the latest wave of utility privatization has already met with significant setbacks, particularly in Latin America.[3] In Cochabamba, Bolivia, privatization efforts were met with widespread social mobilization and protest, and they eventually failed. In Argentina, privatization failed in Tucumán and the province of Buenos Aires, and most recently in the city of Buenos Aires even after more than ten years of service and generally positive results.[4] In Colombia, the European operator Suez-Aguas de Barcelona is selling its remaining stake in Aguas de Cartagena and leaving the country.

In view of these challenges, it seems especially important to question whether "bottom of the pyramid" approaches,[5] drawn mostly from consumer goods industries, can be applied to the seemingly intractable problem of private utility provision for the poor. The account that follows—about a water utility in Colombia called Sociedad de Acueducto, Alcantarillado y Aseo de Barranquilla, S.A.E.S.P., or AAA for short—is ground for optimism. It shows that the apparent contradiction between private utility ownership and serving the poor can be addressed through an appropriate choice of company strategy. In fact, AAA's story suggests that, for private network utilities operating in developing countries, serving the base of the pyramid is not just an opportunity but a strategic imperative. A company's "social license" to operate, which is reflected in regulatory decisions with a direct impact on profits, can be maintained only if the needs of a large part of the population are being met.

The Setting

In Colombia, almost 10 million people lack access to piped potable water. According to a 2005 study by Colombia's Ombudsperson Office, 221 of the country's 1,013 municipalities have a "very low-quality" piped water supply. Municipal water utilities, in particular, are plagued by political clientelism, leading to massive theft and non-payment, poor service, overstaffing, and high operating and financial losses. Contracts are manipulated to favor political cronies; companies are overstaffed with political appointees; there is high turnover of employees, mirroring the political cycle; investment is insufficient and prioritized according to political criteria rather than equity or efficiency; and there is widespread failure on the part of government agencies, politicians, and their friends, families, and supporters to pay their water bills. Utility services, especially water and sanitary services, are regarded as an entitlement to be funded by tax revenues rather than user charges. These conditions set in motion a perverse cycle in which poor service creates greater reluctance to pay. Facilities fall into disrepair, the level of service coverage declines, accounting procedures and customer data are inadequate, and customer service is nonexistent.

In response to these limitations, in 1994 the Colombian government opened the supply of utility services to private concessions and created a regulatory regime for utility services. Under this system, utility charges for residential consumers are based on the socioeconomic level of the area, according to a six-tier system in which the top two tiers subsidize the three lowest ones and the fourth tier is charged at the actual cost of service.

One of the companies to undergo privatization under the new legislation was the water utility of the city of Barranquilla, the country's fourth largest with a population of 1.4 million. A twenty-year concession (subsequently extended to 2033) was awarded in 1996 to AAA, a company owned by the municipality, local investors, and a consortium of private and public Spanish companies. AAA's service area corresponds to one of Colombia's most troubled regions, characterized by high poverty (the overall poverty rate is estimated at 60 percent), a large number of refugees from guerrilla warfare with precarious means of subsistence, and great racial and ethnic diversity.

AAA's Initiatives

Initially, the controlling owner of AAA (Spanish utility Agbar) had no intention of—and no clear strategy for—addressing the needs of Barranquilla's poor. As a result, AAA as well as the municipal government were faced by social protests in areas lacking piped water and sanitation. Agbar managers saw no viable solution and decided to sell their stake. In response, AAA's local shareholders managed to convince the local management team to stay on and help find a buyer for Agbar's stake.

AAA's management developed an integrated strategy that combined market mechanisms with strong outreach to political and nongovernmental organizations in the region. The first pillar of the strategy involved a number of new initiatives to meet customer needs and hence willingness to pay, transforming the relationship between the company and consumers. Major investments were made to increase water quality and the number of people with access to water and sanitation. AAA revamped its database and developed appropriate strategies to identify the customers most likely to experience difficulty in paying their bills—mainly the poor. Payment terms and conditions were tailored to the circumstances faced by poor customers. Bills were simplified to facilitate comprehension for semiliterate individuals and to avoid any impression that the company might be trying to deceive consumers. Weekly (or even daily) bill payment was made possible, thus tailoring the collection cycle to the low cash reserves of the poor. The service line was fully subsidized by the government, and the cost of the meter was repaid in thirty-six months, again addressing the inability of the poor to make large cash outlays. Mobile units were created to allow customers to pay without having to travel to distant company offices. Instead of relying on negative incentives for payment such as fines and threats of legal action, AAA used gifts and discounts to ensure timely payment.

The quality of customer service was also prioritized. The company spent heavily on personnel training and quality management systems. Phone hotlines were set up to report malfunctions and complaints. A quality management system was established to analyze customer claims and complaints, and to assess the level of customer satisfaction with service quality in AAA's offices.

Another element of the new customer outreach strategy was a media effort to improve the company's public image. AAA developed a publicity campaign to show that it sold water at a very affordable rate compared to gasoline and soft drinks. It also sought to improve its image through external quality audits, which would permit impartial assessment of the company's service quality. AAA gained three ISO 9001–2000 quality certifications for several processes, including those involved in potable water supply (water intake, treatment, distribution, billing, revenue collection, and customer service) in the city of Barranquilla.

AAA also recognized that the ability to fulfill its social and financial objectives depended on the cooperation and goodwill of other local actors. The company sought to convince these actors that they were all in the same boat. AAA could do well only if customers paid their bills, for which it needed community cooperation and government support. In turn, AAA's financial health would allow it to improve service and invest in the community, thereby reinforcing both customers' willingness to pay and the government's support.

When it came to cooperation with poor communities, the company identified that its first tasks were to better understand the needs of these communities and develop an effective means of communicating with them. To do this, AAA identified institutions and community leaders who could serve as intermediaries between the company and the residents of slum areas. These intermediaries helped the company devise action programs focused on the specific needs of the communities they represented. Next, the company and the intermediaries created community groups to educate people on the value of water service, the importance of paying for it, and the need for policing against fraud. Local subcontractors (usually community-based entrepreneurs) were also hired to overcome the skepticism of local residents about company intentions. These subcontractors not only had good knowledge of the slum areas but were known by slum residents. As a result, they could credibly reassure residents that their task was both to enforce collections by detecting fraud and cutting off delinquent customers and to provide better service and help the community.

AAA invested in community activities to further reinforce the message that it was not just another business but one with a stake in the well-being of the communities it served. AAA sought to fund activities that would directly identify the company as a valid local actor, which would in turn give the company greater local legitimacy and protect it against theft, fraud, and social mobilization against its activities. For instance, AAA supported local sports, an act highly valued by the communities. This support, in turn, gradually built trust and allowed the company to take such steps as installing individual meters for payment (in lieu of a previous flat fee)—a move community members initially feared because they thought it would increase their payments.

AAA also funded educational and social activities at the municipal level, earning the trust of local mayors. Public authorities were engaged by AAA from the outset in order to gain subsidies that would help AAA offer low rates while improving service. An agreement was reached with municipal and federal authorities to extend service to the area where most of Barranquilla's poor lived. Local authorities also conferred legitimacy on AAA's efforts because consumers regarded the authorities as representing the interests of the community. Finally, municipal governments helped resolve land tenure issues and legalize squatters' residency status, the latter a major issue for utilities in any urban slum because slum residents lack legal rights to the land they occupy and local governments are often afraid of conferring de facto rights by formally supplying utility services to these areas.[6]

AAA did not, however, stop using more traditional methods of curbing fraud and nonpayment. The customer database was updated to better identify potential fraud. Meters were better protected against tampering. Corrupt employees were fired and inspections were performed regularly. Of particular interest is how these efforts dovetailed with the push to develop a closer relationship with communities and authorities. Realizing that the extent of fraud and theft also depends on social attitudes toward these activities, AAA launched an educational program to promote self-policing of water facilities and coordinated legal actions against offenders with the police and the municipalities.

Results

These initiatives appreciably improved AAA's performance on a number of counts. First of all, as Figures 9.1 and 9.2 show, quality of service (as measured by a variety of indicators) increased steadily, suggesting improvement in the lives of the poor.

FIGURE 9.1. INDICATORS OF SERVICE QUALITY FOR BARRANQUILLA, 1990–2004.

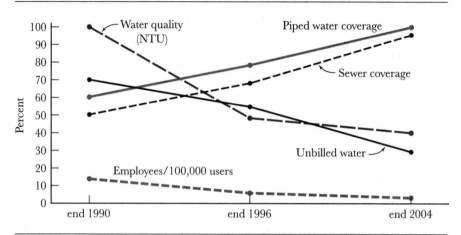

Note: Water quality measures the concentration of impurities. Therefore a lower value indicates a higher level of quality.

Source: AAA.

Coverage is a particularly important indicator in this regard because households without piped water must often purchase water at a much higher cost from water trucks or obtain it from remote or contaminated sources, and lack of access to sewers facilitates the incubation and spread of disease. From 1996 to 2004, AAA increased water supply coverage in Barranquilla from 78 percent to nearly 100 percent, and sewerage coverage from 68 percent to more than 90 percent.

Public opinion polls reflected the improvements in service quality. AAA's own surveys—later confirmed by an independent poll—showed that in 2003, 80 percent of respondents graded the company's service as excellent, and 70 percent described billing procedures as clear and understandable.[7] In Soledad, a nearby town with four hundred thousand inhabitants, local residents demonstrated to request that water and sanitation services be supplied by AAA instead of the inefficient local municipal provider. As a result, in 2001 AAA was awarded a twenty-year concession on water services to Soledad,[8] followed by concessions in the neighboring municipalities of Puerto Colombia and Galapa, and later, an extension to another five additional municipalities in the province. In fact, the current governor of the province has encouraged AAA's expansion as a means of making the province a model for water supply for the rest of the country—in contrast with the failures encountered by Agbar in this same area.

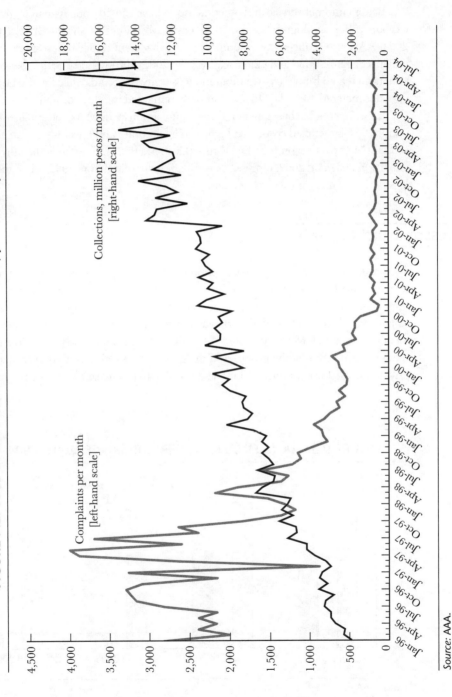

FIGURE 9.2. AAA COLLECTIONS VS. COMPLAINTS, JAN. 1996–JULY 2004.

Complaints per month
[left-hand scale]

Collections, million pesos/month
[right-hand scale]

Source: AAA.

Better customer service and other measures have caused nonpayment to give way to cooperation. As Figure 9.2 shows, revenue collection rose steadily from 1996 to 2004. AAA also reduced the amount of water that went unbilled in response to the initiatives against fraud and pilferage. Over the 2002–2004 period, the number of customers increased from sixty-two thousand to seventy thousand, while the total volume of water metered and billed by the company remained roughly constant.

Improvement in collection and lower fraud also helped AAA's bottom line. Water utilities face large fixed costs, so a higher collection rate and lower losses can have a substantial impact on profitability. Figure 9.3 shows that AAA attained healthy profitability in 2001 and 2002, representing a major turnaround from 1996, when the utility's net profit margin was –34 percent.

Lessons and Caveats

To a large extent, AAA's experience parallels the lessons emerging from current research on the business of reaching the poor. AAA sought to create informal partnerships with poor communities and the government. The partnerships were created and sustained by the benefits they offered to all participants. For governments, the arrangement was a solution to a major source of political mobilization and protest. For AAA, the support of community groups and the government legitimized its existence as a privately owned water utility and made it possible to extend service to the poor with-

FIGURE 9.3. AAA'S FINANCIAL PERFORMANCE, 2001–2004.

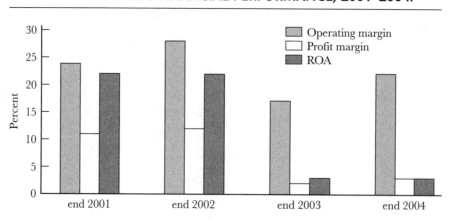

Source: AAA.

out depleting the company's financial resources. For the low-income communities, the partnerships ensured access to the essential resource of potable water, at a lower cost than other forms of supply and under greater hygienic conditions, while at the same time recognizing community members as citizens who also deserve basic services.

Outreach initiatives were matched by innovative measures to meet customer needs and provide superior service, as well as traditional solutions to prevent fraud and abuse. AAA dismissed corrupt employees, installed meters more resistant to tampering, and improved fraud detection. It asked poor customers to pay the legally applicable rate for their consumption, without exception; in exchange, AAA offered the poor better-quality service than any alternatives, sought subsidies to dampen the adverse impact on household budgets, and revamped its commercial policies to address the particular needs of the poor.

To be sure, important problems remain. Legitimacy is still fragile. The company continues to face the need for a sustained campaign of communication with customers about the positive impact that AAA's services bring to the community. Attitudes favorable toward nonpayment and fraud, although abated, are still common. It is clear that attitudes can only change if positive results are perceived over a long period of time. Serving the poor entails long-term commitment, requiring a permanent effort on the part of utility management, as well as development of systems, incentives, and values that reinforce the objective of treating the poor as legitimate customers. Above all, collaboration with municipal authorities has improved, but corruption and political interference in company operations still amount to the number one problem.

Political interference is especially challenging because the company needs subsidies to serve the poor. As Figure 9.3 shows for the years 2003 and 2004, company profitability is by no means guaranteed and varies with the level of subsidization received. AAA receives not only cross-subsidies from better-off consumers but also additional subsidies from the central government to help refugees and slum residents. Even so, the company estimates that current subsidies and rate revenues allow it to furnish extensive (though not universal) service and do not permit carrying out environmental improvements or replacing its asset base.

A basic premise of the BOP framework is that serving the poor can be profitable if the right business model is used to transact with the poor. In fact, companies have been told to "fly under the radar" of "central institutions" and avoid dependence on "national governments, corrupt regimes, and central infrastructure planning."[9] AAA's unequivocal reliance on subsidies as part of its effort to reach the poor suggests either that the BOP's assumptions need to be tempered or that despite its innovative and progressive commitment to serving the poor, AAA is ultimately a flawed example of BOP strategy in practice. We can only speculate as to the answer to this question. But it is clear that for utilities, which are subject to price and quality regulation, engaging national institutions is unavoidable. In addition, the economics of production and distribution may simply limit the range of viable business models, absent major technological change. In the case of other utility services, a specialized physical distribution network is the least-cost means of delivery in densely populated areas.[10]

If there is a possibility of escaping dependence on subsidies in provision of utility services for the urban poor, at present it seems to lie not in eliminating physical networks (although in the case of electricity this is at least a foreseeable possibility) but in innovating *around* the network. To mention just three possibilities, (1) prepayment cards, which have proven so successful for the spread of cell phones, are readily adaptable to electricity supply to help the poor manage their consumption of electricity according to their cash flow; (2) microcredit and, more generally, extension of financial services for the poor can remove a major barrier for access to utility services, namely the up-front cost of service installation (service line, meter, and internal wiring or pipes); and (3) local entrepreneurs can be subcontracted to carry out installation, billing, collection, maintenance, and repair services, possibly leading to a more desirable cost-service ratio for poor consumers. Whether innovation around physical networks can constitute a veritable new business model for utilities, along the lines advocated by the BOP framework, remains to be seen. The BOP framework has much to offer, but it cannot be expected to be a panacea. Greater theoretical and empirical rigor is required to ascertain its coherence and applicability.

CHAPTER TEN

BRINGING NATURAL GAS SERVICE TO POOR AREAS

The Case of Buenos Aires's Moreno District

Marcelo Paladino, Lisandro Blas

Lack of access to basic public services, such as natural gas to heat one's home and cook, is a major problem for the poor in Argentina and other developing countries. Until recently, companies and local governments in Argentina had no way to collaborate effectively to solve the problem of underprovision of public services to poor neighborhoods.[1] Following their privatization or concessioning during the 1990s, local utility companies found themselves facing mounting pressure from government and civil society to serve the poor, most of whom—even if they had access to these basic services—could not afford them. Despite several failed attempts to expand service to the low-income market, Gas Natural BAN, a recently privatized natural gas utility in Buenos Aires, finally succeeded with a model that addressed the social and economic constraints that had rendered past projects unprofitable.[2] In this paper, we present Gas Natural BAN as a unique example of private-public collaboration that has brought natural gas service to a previously unserved, low-income community.

Gas Natural BAN's main partner in this project was Comunidad Organizada ("Organized Community"), a coalition of forty NGOs based in the Moreno district of Buenos Aires. The project was also championed by Fundación Pro Vivienda Social (Social Housing Foundation, or FPVS), Mutual el Colmenar (a local NGO), and FONCAP (a government social development fund). By coordinating and facilitating cooperation among various actors (NGOs, the private and public sectors), Organized Community established a model of social management that successfully leveraged local community involvement and ultimately brought access to natural gas service to four thousand families. The project also produced solid economic results for the gas service provider and offered the company a replicable model for expanding service to other low-income areas. The aim of this paper is to reflect on the initiative's key success factors and the conditions for sustaining and replicating similar efforts elsewhere.

Expanding the Reach of Natural Gas Distribution

In 1991, Argentina's government launched an aggressive privatization program under which Gas del Estado (a former state gas distributor) was split into several business units. Gas Natural BAN was established as a result of this division and became one of the distribution companies for the Buenos Aires province. Following privatization, the company, like other newly privatized utility providers, struggled to comply with legal requirements that it expand its service delivery area to poor neighborhoods. The financial viability of this expansion was hindered by the fact that the company found it difficult to establish service connections, payment conditions, and financing plans that met the needs of low-income customers.

Overview of the Moreno District

Moreno is located in the northwestern region of Buenos Aires province, thirty-seven kilometers to the west of the city; in 2001, it was home to approximately 380,000 residents. During the 1980s, the city suffered a series of social and economic setbacks that led to soaring poverty and unemployment rates. In the early 1990s, 10 percent of households in the Moreno district were living in critically overcrowded conditions; by 2001, this figure had climbed to 40 percent.[3] At the end of 2002, Moreno was one of four districts in greater Buenos Aires where 65 percent of the population lived in poverty.[4]

Transforming the Poor into Customers[5]

Fundación Pro Vivienda Social (FPVS) was created in 1992 by a group of businessmen and scholars committed to addressing social problems. The group's mission was to contribute to solving poverty by improving housing and living conditions for the poor, mainly through provision of microcredit.[6] But the most important result, as one of the founders put it, was that "after ten years of hard work, FPVS earned the trust of people from Moreno."

In January 2001, FPVS partnered with Gas Natural BAN and El Colmenar, an NGO that had been working in the Moreno district for more than fifteen years, on a project to expand gas service into poor areas through a model of community involvement. The proposed project was submitted to a World Bank contest in May 2001 and was chosen from twenty-four hundred applicants as a "model of social management." FPVS and El Colmenar received an award of US$250,000.

In June of that year, these organizations summoned other NGOs and local community organizations to debate strategies for addressing the natural gas problem. In September, FPVS, El Colmenar, and forty community organizations formed a formal coalition that they christened Organized Community (OC). They defined it as "a work space that gathers local organizations, groups and institutions, aiming at strengthening the union and organization between neighbors and improving the quality of life in the Moreno neighborhood."[7] After listening to the demands of area residents, OC concluded that constructing a gas pipeline in the neighborhood would allow residents to switch from costlier alternative fuels to cheaper piped natural gas and thus lead to extensive cost savings (see Table 10.1). In light of these savings, OC recognized that such an infrastructure project was particularly well suited to being self-financed by community members.

OC surveyed almost 80 percent of area households about the amount they would be willing to pay for natural gas service, and how they would finance it. Eighty-three percent of those surveyed reported they were potential users of the new natural gas service. The remaining 17 percent preferred that no gas pipeline be built, mainly because they felt they couldn't afford to pay the construction costs. Through this analysis, it was learned that most residents were willing to pay a monthly installment of ARS$22.75 each for construction of the pipeline.

Financing

At project inception, OC had only a general sense of local residents' willingness to pay for the pipeline and no way to secure their commitment ahead of time. To cope with this financing gap, OC decided to channel existing funds for construction through a trust known as the "Solidarity Pipeline." This trust facilitated a link among residents,

TABLE 10.1. COST OF NATURAL GAS VS. ALTERNATIVES.

Alternative Fuel	Market Price (Pesos)	Equivalent Price for Equivalent Amount of Piped Natural Gas (Pesos)
10 kg LPG cylinder	$25	$3.38
45 kg LPG cylinder	$72	$9.60
1,000 kg of firewood	$14	$6.00
10 liters of kerosene	$12	$1.90
10 kg of coal	$3	$0.80

Source: Fundación Pro Vivienda Social.

FPVS (which contributed its World Bank award), FONCAP (a government loan fund that contributed ARS$2 million, or approximately US$2 million at the time), OC, and Gas Natural BAN, all of which committed partial payment for construction costs. The total cost was to be recovered at the end of construction with payments from area residents who had signed on for service.

Those community members willing to participate signed an adherence contract. Each signatory thus committed to paying his or her part toward the total cost of constructing the gas pipeline. The costs to connect individual houses to the pipeline were not included as part of the agreement; this work would be completed by local contractors and paid for individually by residents. Because having more participants would lessen the cost to each, residents were encouraged to convince their neighbors to take part in the project. With 70 percent of households participating, the initial cost for pipeline construction would be ARS$844 per household. If 80 percent agreed to help shoulder the costs, the price to each would have been just ARS$781; with 90 percent commitment, the price per household would have dropped even further, to ARS$728.

Pipeline Construction

A contractor was hired to build the external and internal gas pipelines. The external pipeline consisted of the main line, or "spine," and the secondary lines bringing service to each block. The first stage involved laying all the pipelines, feeding almost two thousand households. To build the secondary lines, at least 70 percent of the households on each block had to agree to the construction process and become signatories to the trust. The second part of the construction was the internal pipeline, which connected the gas supply directly to the houses. This stage of the project was carried out by the residents themselves, with the help of licensed gas technicians authorized by Gas Natural BAN.

Payment Plan

By October 2004, 77 percent of area residents had selected a four-year payment plan instead of a longer-term option, with monthly payments of ARS$41.50 (about US$14) (Table 10.2). The interest paid through the financing plan belonged to the trust fund and became a sort of "compulsory savings" that would later be used to fund other neighborhood infrastructure projects.

Social and Economic Impacts

The most significant impact of the new pipeline in the Moreno district was that the average monthly expenditure on alternative fuels, typically 13.8 percent of total monthly income, dropped to 3 percent using natural gas, freeing up funds that could

TABLE 10.2. FINANCIAL TERMS (AT 70 PERCENT RATE OF ADHESION).

Number of Months	12	24	48	72	120
Monthly installment fee (in Argentine pesos)	$95.66	$60.49	$41.50	$34.23	$26.73
Total cost	$1,148	$1,452	$1,992	$2.464	$3,207

Source: Fundación Pro Vivienda Social.

be dedicated to other daily necessities. Natural gas also contributed to family security, being a safe fuel, and gave residents a clean, inexpensive way to heat their homes, something that was considered a luxury in the past.

By April 2005, twenty-two hundred local residents had signed the contract to access the external pipelines. This level of participation and satisfaction showed a marked difference from other projects Gas Natural BAN had carried out in two key aspects. First, and most notably, 70 percent of the households signed on, while previous projects achieved only 55 percent participation. The second difference was the speed with which customers were acquired; in the Moreno District it took from one to three years to stabilize the adhesion level, whereas other projects required anywhere from five to eight years to achieve the same.[8]

Lessons for Gas Natural BAN

In January 2005, Salvador Gabarrós, president of Gas Natural BAN, visited the Moreno District and concluded that the project represented a new model for expanding gas services to poor areas. By October 2005, the company was heading up three similar projects in nearby neighborhoods, with a huge expansion planned for the following year using this new community involvement approach.

The Economics of the New System

The results of this project help answer a key question in the field of poverty alleviation: Are community-based infrastructure projects economically feasible, or do they merely build community solidarity? The Moreno district project shows that it is possible to work with this new kind of customer. As it turned out, the real question was not whether low-income customers were willing to pay for natural gas service, or for the pipeline itself. Instead, the challenge was finding a way to build the pipeline at a cost that was economically feasible for both the company and potential clients.

There is very little difference between the length of the investment recovery period for a pipeline expansion in a poor community like the Moreno district and similar expansion in wealthier neighborhoods (Table 10.3). The monthly nonpayment rate in the Moreno district varies between 4–5 percent, a figure similar to the overall company average.

Conclusions

The key to this project's success was intentional community involvement. By allowing the local population to help structure the program, the project leaders were able to create a new level of trust between all involved, generating invaluable social capital.

In addition, the local government considered the project a success because it helped the poor elevate their quality of life and gain access to a recognized service provider, while also enabling the government to reduce the pressure it faced to invest in public infrastructure.

TABLE 10.3. YEARLY AVERAGE CONSUMPTION, COSTS, AND REVENUES: AVERAGE VS. MORENO DISTRICT CUSTOMERS.

	Average Customer	Average Moreno District Customer
Cubic meters consumed during a year	1,066	506
Months to recover the investment	38	43
Costs	*Pesos/year*	*Pesos/year*
Invoicing and collection	4.22	4.22
Maintenance and after-sales services	6.42	6.42
Other expenditures	0	0
TOTAL	10.64	10.64
Revenues		
Fix charge	45.42	45.42
Gas sales (margin)	46.98	22.30
TOTAL	92.40	67.72

Source: Gas Natural BAN.

Finally, this project dispelled some perennial myths about public service expansion into poor areas, showing that:

- In impoverished areas, where there is a notable lack of confidence in the state and other institutions, it is possible to instill a sense of cooperation.
- Projects such as the one described are not only attractive and equitable for poor customers but profitable for the company.
- It is possible to evolve from a "gift and subsidy culture" to one engaging the local community in full involvement. If this is successfully done, the private company, often heavily criticized, can be transformed into an active creator of social capital and cultural change.
- Projects can create conditions that allow the local population to become an active body driving social development in their community.

In conclusion, the commitment of all participants to transparency and projecting a genuine interest in serving people generates trust. In this important way, community involvement can significantly increase social capital as well as the quality of life for people at the bottom of the pyramid.

PART THREE

BUILDING THE BOP VALUE CHAIN

Once low-income consumers satisfy their basic needs for water, foodstuffs, and energy, they begin to dedicate a growing share of their income to nonessentials: processed and packaged foods, personal care products, household improvements, appliances, and electronics. However, for the poor to achieve a higher level of consumption, they must also earn higher income. Business has a role to play in driving this income growth, both as a direct employer and through products and services that boost the productivity of the poor. This section of the book takes the reader from one end of the BOP value chain to the other, starting at the bottom in Chapters Eleven through Fourteen by examining the business models used by three retailers to effectively design, price, market, and distribute consumer goods to the poor. Chapters Fifteen through Seventeen move the analysis up to the level of production and illustrate the power of integrating the poor into global supply chains.

In "Multiahorro: Barrio Store," Wilson A. Jácome, Luis E. Loría, and Luis Reyes Portocarrero profile Ecuadorian retailer TIA's innovative store format targeted at low-income, urban consumers. In response to a currency crisis and shrinking revenues at its mainstream supermarkets, TIA developed the Multiahorro retail format, a low-cost operation uniquely suited to BOP customer preferences for location, product assortment, pricing, and service.

Dwindling market share and plummeting demand for film also spurred Kodak Brazil to shift its gaze from the Brazilian upper classes to the country's mass market.

In "Photography and the Low-Income Classes in Brazil: A Case Study of Kodak," Melchior Dikkers and Paulo Cesar Motta trace the company's powerful turnaround story. Through a series of dramatic organizational and operational transformations, led by a visionary manager who himself had grown up poor, Kodak came to recognize and successfully tap into a latent and unmet demand for cameras and film among Brazil's lower classes.

In Chapter Thirteen, "The Complex Business of Serving the Poor: Insights from Unilever's Project Shakti in India," V. Kasturi Rangan, Dalip Sehgal, and Rohithari Rajan describe how the multinational consumer goods manufacturer refocused its efforts on India's rural poor in the face of growing competition from new market entrants. By training and hiring low-income, community-based saleswomen, the company successfully expanded the reach of its products to an additional sixty thousand rural villages. By relying exclusively on low-income women as their front-line salesforce, Unilever also created a significant source of income for a traditionally marginalized group.

In "Patrimonio Hoy: A Groundbreaking Corporate Program to Alleviate Mexico's Housing Crisis," Arthur Segel, Nadeem Meghji, and Regina García-Cuéllar discuss the social and economic benefits created by Patrimonio Hoy, CEMEX of Mexico's unique self-build housing model for low-income customers. Like Unilever's Project Shakti, one key to the success of the program has been the company's ability to tap the local knowledge and social capital of community "promoters" to sell the company's savings-led housing program. In this case, women make up the primary salesforce, and their deep knowledge of the economic situation and the reliability of their neighbors has proved critical to building a creditworthy customer base.

Although low-income consumers undoubtedly desire affordable products and services, they also need the money to buy such goods. In addition to direct employment of the poor, Chapters Fifteen through Seventeen demonstrate that the private sector can help integrate the poor into the global production system and facilitate market transactions that enable them to get a better return for their efforts.

In "Creating Strong Businesses by Developing and Leveraging the Productive Capacity of the Poor" (Chapter Fifteen), Kapil Marwaha and his coauthors offer examples of three Indian businesses—a major milk cooperative, a snack manufacturer, and an artisan's cooperative—to demonstrate the enormous social and economic value that can be created by giving the poor a chance to partake in the production process.

Ravi Anupindi and S. Sivakumar describe in "ITC's e-Choupal: A Platform Strategy for Rural Transformation" how ITC, a large Indian conglomerate, established a network of five thousand Internet-enabled entry points that gave low-income farmers the market information and infrastructure needed to sell their produce at more competitive prices. As one of the largest buyers of these commodities, ITC itself has benefited because the model reduces costs and improves the quality of the products it sources.

In the final paper of Part Three, Ray Goldberg and Kerry Herman sketch the history of consumer packaged goods giant Nestlé's efforts to create a reliable source of milk supply in "Nestlé's Milk District Model." Because Nestlé's milk is by and large produced by thousands of farmers with small cattle holdings in many developing countries, the company's supply chain efforts have gone far beyond just sourcing. Nestlé has made available the technology, training, and investment to enable small farmers to produce and sell high-quality milk at a competitive price.

CHAPTER ELEVEN

MULTIAHORRO

Barrio Store

Wilson A. Jácome, Luis E. Loría, Luis Reyes Portocarrero

In 1960, the retailer TIA opened its first store in Guayaquil, Ecuador, by using what at the time was an unorthodox strategy: targeting customers in the lower half of the socioeconomic pyramid. By the end of 2005, TIA was operating sixty-three stores incorporating three business models and was the third largest retailer in the country, with estimated annual revenues above US$130 million.

TIA's growth strategy has been driven by a successful business model innovation,[1] Multiahorro, a *barrio* or neighborhood store format, created to better serve bottom-of-the-pyramid (BOP) customers. The Multiahorro stores are located in some of the poorest and most densely populated neighborhoods of Ecuador and seek to offer a limited assortment of goods at the lowest price.

For nearly half a century, TIA has provided quality services, profitably, to the Ecuadorian poor and significantly helped to improve the welfare of the communities it serves in small but important ways.[2] The stores sell basic goods at affordable prices, present clean and hygienic shopping spaces, and offer courteous customer service.

Financial support for this paper came from IDE-Business School and TIA-Ecuador. The authors wish to acknowledge the contribution of constructive comments and excellent discussion with Ignacio Sanabria, Sandro Sgaravatti, Leonardo Pesantes, Alessandro Pensatori, and Paola Meléndez, all with TIA-Ecuador. Additionally, helpful comments and suggestions that significantly contributed to the quality of this paper came from José Aulestia and Ernesto Noboa, both with IDE-Business School.

The Evolution of TIA's Business in Ecuador

TIA's vision is to become the leading retail chain in Ecuador for household, personal, and daily use goods. TIA's brand is widely recognized as a symbol of true customer value and savings, one that contributes to the welfare of Ecuadorian families and the communities it serves. The company offers goods of practical use for families, boasting the best deals and promotions available in the areas where it operates.

The mission of TIA stores can be summarized in three points:

1. To contribute to the welfare of the Ecuadorian households and the communities it serves
2. To increase, year after year, the value of the company
3. To promote the professional growth of its employees[3]

To better serve middle-income (socioeconomic level C in Table 11.1) and lower-income (D1, D2, and E) customers, TIA has developed three contrasting business models.

TIA Stores: The Traditional Model

The traditional model employs thematic events and seasonal promotions in the sale of household consumer goods in cities with a population above thirty thousand. Besides offering a good assortment (between two thousand and four thousand stock keeping units or SKUs) of groceries, perishable goods, and dairy products, other products are imported for special events (Christmas, Mother's Day, Father's Day, Back to School, and so on). The stores offer a variety of imported products, from clothing and toys to small kitchen appliances, pencils, and TV sets. The TIA brand stores have an undisputed reputation for everyday low prices, which are maintained and reinforced with special events and discounts throughout the year. This business model targets

TABLE 11.1. ECUADOR, MONTHLY INCOME PER HOUSEHOLD IN U.S. DOLLARS.

Socioeconomic Level	Urban Area	Rural Area	Percentage of Families
A, B (higher-income)	$2,400/mo. or higher	$1,585/mo.	3
C1 to C3 (middle-income)	$420	$280	25
D1, D2, E (lower-income)	$132	$77	72

Source: TIA Stores (2003).

lower-middle- and lower-income customers. Fifty-one TIA stores use this traditional format and account for approximately 80 percent of the company's total sales.

SUPERTIA: The Supermarket Model

The supermarket model specializes in selling household consumer goods in inner cities with a population of more than one hundred thousand. An everyday low price strategy is buttressed with special events and discounts throughout the year. A full assortment (four thousand to six thousand SKUs) of groceries, perishable goods, meats, and dairy products are offered. This format targets middle- and lower-income customers. Five SUPERTIA stores are responsible for 17 percent of the company's total sales.

Multiahorro: The Barrio Store Model

The Multiahorro model is primarily focused on low-income customers who live in very poor and densely populated neighborhoods with at least twenty thousand inhabitants. This barrio store model applies and promotes a "lowest price around" strategy. A limited basic assortment (about thirteen hundred SKUs) of groceries, perishable goods, and dairy products are offered. Seven Multiahorro stores currently account for 3 percent of total company sales. The barrio store has very strong growth potential, and not only in Ecuador. The model could be replicated in most emerging markets and poor neighborhoods worldwide, even in the most advanced and industrialized national economies. Its main features are presented and analyzed in greater depth here.

The penetration of the supermarket industry as a share of the total food retail industry in Ecuador is approximately 25 percent. In other words, three-quarters of the population buy food in grocery stores, independent small stores, minimarts, and traditional open air markets. TIA viewed this as an important business opportunity, because traditional suppliers to the Ecuadorian poor in large cities, inner cities, and rural areas have usually sold small quantities of basic products at very high prices.[4] In addition, these suppliers have made available a minimal variety of products and quite poor customer service and have not been able to guarantee the quality and freshness of their products.

In 2000, the Ecuadorian economy was dollarized, the local currency was taken out of circulation, and much of the population was impoverished almost overnight. As a consequence, customer loyalty was lost and competition increased. The marketplace became more segmented and supermarkets began carrying nontraditional items. Under these circumstances, it became clear that TIA's strongest growth opportunities were to be found in the rural areas and in the poor neighborhoods of Quito and Guayaquil. Certainly the best opportunity of all lay in cities, thanks to Ecuador's vast rural-urban migration. This phenomenon had nearly inverted the country's demographic proportions: fifty years ago, 71 percent of the population lived in rural areas, compared to 39 percent in 2001.[5]

Customer Profiles

According to information gathered through nationwide market research studies, TIA's typical customer:

- Is a housewife
- Is between twenty and forty years of age
- Departs from home
- Travels to the store using public transportation
- Is a homeowner
- Buys on a weekly basis
- Is aware of promotions, offers, and special discounts

TIA's Financial Results

By the end of 2005, TIA was operating a total of sixty-three establishments, with total annual revenues of US$127 million. Average annual sales for all TIA stores were a little over US$2 million, but there was significant variations in performance among the formats. The average amount a customer spends on each shopping trip ranges between US$5.20 at Multiahorro stores to US$5.06 for traditional format stores and US$5.81 for SUPERTIA stores.

Between 2000 and 2005, the number of TIA stores grew from twenty-eight to sixty-three. During the same period, revenues and net income more than tripled. For this five-year period, the average profit margin was 6.4 percent, the average return on assets was 21.2 percent, and the average return on equity was 63.4 percent.

Multiahorro: The Barrio Store Model

Thanks to their deep understanding of the specific context and circumstances of serving poor customers, TIA's board of directors identified the opportunity to develop a new business format tailored to the needs of customers in the poor neighborhoods of Ecuador's main cities. To design, develop, and implement this business model innovation, TIA assembled a special cross-functional task force and empowered it to function as a skunk works team, which could ignore conventional dogma and produce a breakthrough innovation.[6] In this sense, the Multiahorro barrio store format was designed specifically to target customers from socioeconomic segments D and E of the population, traditionally served by informal markets and small independent neighborhood stores. Multiahorro is currently the only chain of retail stores in Ecuador with this type of business model and value proposition for this market niche. It is now capturing the lion's share of the market in these areas, formerly the province of small mom-and-pop businesses and corner stores.

As of 2005, there were five Multiahorro stores in Guayaquil, one in Quito, and one in Esmeraldas. Results have been overwhelmingly positive, surpassing original projections. Because of this, the company is moving forward with a rapid growth plan. The business plan calls for opening one hundred such stores within a five-year period.

On average, the stores have a surface area of 200 square meters, are replenished daily, and offer a limited assortment of basic goods. Their objective is to have the lowest price for all products offered in the neighborhood, which is defined as a radius of five blocks around the store's location.

In many respects, the stores have had a positive impact on the populations they serve. The main beneficiary of the increased competition introduced by Multiahorro stores is the customer, who is able to buy his or her basket of goods at a lower price. Customers prefer the stores because they offer a low-price alternative to traditional neighborhood stores, coupled with special offers and a clean and safe environment. Additionally, they offer a somewhat larger assortment of products compared to local competitors, and they guarantee the quality and freshness of their products.

Two hundred twenty-three customers were interviewed prior to November 2005 and gave a number of reasons for patronizing Multiahorro: convenient prices (44.6 percent), special offers (21.5 percent), convenient location (21 percent), and product variety (16.7 percent). The same customers, when asked to compare Multiahorro with two of the largest local supermarkets, popular markets, and other small stores, said that Multiahorro's products were the cheapest (37.3 percent; see Table 11.2), their stores were cleanest (21.3 percent), and their product quality (24.1 percent) and assortment (21.8 percent) were better.

Average sales for Multiahorro stores have reached US$75,000 per month. About 20 percent of the products are offered under the house brand, which in turn accounts for 20–30 percent of sales. It is expected that the share of products offered under this private label will rise in the near future, and the margins should grow at least at the same rate.

A key success factor for Multiahorro's business model is its low-cost operation. Only nine employees are required to run a store, and they are trained to perform in all areas of the business. In addition, most store employees are staffed from the local neighborhood.

The physical establishments themselves are rarely owned by Multiahorro and are located in high-traffic areas in very poor and densely populated neighborhoods having few formal employment opportunities. These areas are usually under high threat of theft. In the case of the El Guasmo location in Guayaquil, in operation for more

TABLE 11.2. MULTIAHORRO, UNIT PRICE COMPARISON WITH *BARRIO* STORES.

	Prices (U.S. $)				Multiahorro's Price	Var. %
	Store 1	Store 2	Store 3	Average		
Milk (1 liter)	0.65	0.67	0.60	0.64	0.39	−0.39
Small yogurt	0.50	0.55	0.30	0.45	0.30	−0.33
Chlorine (bottle)	0.75	0.75	0.75	0.75	0.69	−0.08
Chlorine (sachet)	0.15	0.15	0.15	0.15	0.06	−0.60
Detergent (250 g)	0.60	0.50	0.60	0.56	0.33	−0.41
Skin care soap (125 g)	0.40	0.65	0.50	0.52	0.33	−0.36
Diapers (12 units medium)	1.40	2.00	1.50	1.63	1.39	−0.15
Shampoo (200 ml)	1.35	1.50	1.71	1.52	1.19	−0.22
Cooking oil (1 liter)	1.25	1.25	1.30	1.27	1.09	−0.14
Rice (1 lb)	0.22	0.18	0.22	0.21	0.22	0.06
Quaker Oats (250 g)	0.30	0.25	0.35	0.30	0.25	−0.17
Cane sugar (1 lb)	0.30	0.20	0.30	0.27	0.22	−0.17
Noodles (200 g)	0.40	0.40	0.45	0.42	0.19	−0.54
Margarine (1/2 lb)	0.75	0.80	0.75	0.77	0.69	−0.10
Eggs (unit)	0.10	0.08	0.08	0.09	0.07	−0.19
Chicken sausage (8 units)	1.40	1.40	1.40	1.40	1.05	−0.25
Chicken (1 lb)	0.90	0.90	0.85	0.88	0.75	−0.15
TOTAL	$11.42	$12.23	$11.81	$11.81	$9.21	−0.22

Source: Data taken on Oct. 11, 2005, from stores in the Guasmo area of Guayaquil, Ecuador.

than five years, a history of philanthropy and development projects with the local community means the store and its customers have never been robbed or threatened by local violence. This fact is particularly notable when one takes into account the extremely adverse business, social, and political circumstances of both the neighborhood and the country.[7] The location of the stores is selected not only for exposure to potential clients but also with consideration for other social outcomes. For example, a store might be located close to a public school, a church, or a police station, all of which could benefit from Multiahorro's financial support.[8]

Multiahorro, acutely aware of these local needs, donates to and directly collaborates with local civic organizations. In return, the beneficiary is expected to join in local group efforts aimed at improving the neighborhood. Aid given to the local community contributes to developing a sentiment of reciprocity and a feeling on the part of community members that the store and its employees are good neighbors (Figure 11.1). As an added benefit, they receive ongoing feedback and gain access to relevant information that helps them improve their operations[9] and protect them from theft or burglary.

Conclusion

The Multiahorro case study exemplifies how national or international corporations can choose to serve BOP customers and make a real difference in the quality of life of millions of poor people around the world. At the same time, through successful business model innovations, these companies can make a profit, even under adverse business, social, and political circumstances.

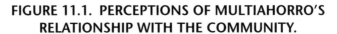

FIGURE 11.1. PERCEPTIONS OF MULTIAHORRO'S RELATIONSHIP WITH THE COMMUNITY.

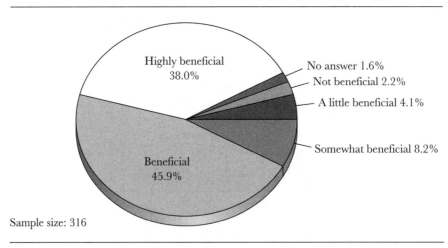

Sample size: 316

CHAPTER TWELVE

PHOTOGRAPHY AND THE LOW-INCOME CLASSES IN BRAZIL

A Case Study of Kodak

Melchior Dikkers, Paulo Cesar Motta

This chapter examines why Kodak Brazil waited until 2004 to target low-income consumers and outlines the company's approach and strategy when it finally did so. The threat of digital photography and a three-year decline in profits and market share created an environment receptive to the unexplored, low-income market. However, to exploit this market segment Kodak had to overcome internal doubt and learn about low-income consumers and their behavior. Once it did finally target the low-income market, Kodak saw its traditional camera sales increase by 60 percent and film sales decline significantly less than those of its competitors—6 percent for Kodak compared to 20 percent for the market.

Low-Income Classes in Brazil

According to the World Bank's 2005 World Development Indicators, Brazil's 2004 population was 178.7 million and income per capita just US$3,090 (US$8,090 adjusted for purchasing power parity). The proportion of the population living below the poverty line (defined as US$2 a day) was 22.4 percent in 2001. Households are

---

This research is based on interviews of seven Kodak employees at their offices in São Paulo, Brazil. The interviews were conducted on four occasions between April 14 and October 3, 2005.

classified according to their purchasing power as falling into one of five categories: A, B, C, D, or E. It is generally understood that classes C and D encompass those whose purchasing power and living standard fall between the upper and middle classes (classes A and B) and the poor (class E). The bottom of the pyramid, classes C, D, and E, comprises three-quarters of Brazil's population, yet it accounts for less than half of total consumption (Table 12.1). If the poor (class E) are excluded, low-income classes account for 60 percent of the population and 38 percent of all consumption.

Penetration rate of consumer durables gives another perspective on Brazil's low-income market. According to Kodak's 2004 research, market penetration of cameras was just 35 percent.

Why Kodak Ignored the Low-Income Market Until 2004

In October 2003, Kodak sent Flavio Gomes on assignment to Brazil as general manager with the mandate to turn around the local operation. Although most aspects of the turnaround were tactical, the new focus on the low-income classes became a pillar of Kodak's strategy in Brazil. When asked whether Kodak had previously ignored the market opportunity the low-income classes represented, Gomes was to the point: "The opportunity has always existed but nothing was ever done about it." Our interviews suggest that Kodak ignored the low-income market for three reasons: (1) local management did not understand the low-income classes sufficiently, (2) Kodak Brazil possessed limited decision rights, and (3) Kodak's headquarters held inadequate performance expectations.

TABLE 12.1. BOTTOM OF THE PYRAMID IN BRAZIL.

Class	E	C,D	C,D,E
Qualitative description	Poor	Low-income	Bottom of pyramid
Percentage of population	16	60	76
Percentage of consumption	4	38	42
Average Income			
US$ per day (PPP)	2.6	8.7	7.4
R$ per month	260	964	812
Income Range			
US$ per day (PPP)	<4	4–18	<18
US$ per year (PPP)	<1,500	1,5000–6500	<6,500
R$ per month	<400	400–2,000	<2,000

Note: US$ income is per person; R$ income (in reais) is per household.

Source: Family Budget Research 2002–03, Brazilian Institute of Geography and Statistics; 2004 World Development Indicators. Analysis: Dikkers and Motta.

Insufficient Understanding of Low-Income Classes

According to Gomes, Kodak's management in Brazil typically originated from classes A and B. As he put it, "The problem starts at university where students, mostly from classes A and B, learn to market to themselves." It is "the elite marketing to the elite." They also learn that advertising targeted at classes A and B serves as aspirational advertising for classes C and D. These conditions made it difficult for Kodak Brazil to understand classes C and D and the potential business opportunity they offer.

Until 2004, Kodak believed that camera penetration in Brazil was 60 percent. Although Kodak did not separate revenue by market segment, the company nonetheless assumed that classes A and B accounted for 80 percent of Kodak's business, implying that classes C and D accounted for only 20 percent.

In 1994, Kodak conducted a study that revealed that half of Brazilian households did not have cameras because they were too expensive. After these results, no further research was conducted. By October 2003, Kodak Brazil had been studying classes C and D for three years yet never implemented a specific marketing strategy for this population. Focus on classes A and B was so entrenched that Kodak continued to ignore classes C and D even after additional market research became available.

Limited Decision Rights

Historically, Kodak's general manager in Brazil enjoyed little autonomy and lacked the flexibility needed to run things differently from how they were done in the United States. Numerous examples illustrate this point: advertising campaigns were produced in the United States and then translated for the local markets; the company lacked local authority to replace Kodak batteries with another brand in order to reduce the cost of a retail camera kit; and it was unable to treat local financing initiatives as a marketing expense because they did not fit Kodak's standard practices.

Inadequate Performance Expectations and Measures

Managers' incentives were largely determined by the performance expectations and measures set by their bosses or company headquarters. Gomes said of his experience in Brazil, "Kodak thinks more about market share than market growth." Since film is Kodak's highest-margin-producing product and also the business with the highest market share, it is understandable that management sees margin and market share as important performance metrics. However, these measures are less useful if the product has not yet reached its market potential. It is often more profitable to grow a market than to increase market share or maintain margins.

Until 2001, Kodak Brazil achieved good financial results by focusing exclusively on classes A and B. Since management was primarily evaluated on the basis of earnings from operations, there was little incentive to grow the market. Yet simple benchmarking within Kodak (comparing Brazil to other developing countries) and within Brazil (comparing cameras to other consumer durables) would have highlighted that the low-income classes in Brazil were being ignored.

What Prompted Kodak to Seize the Opportunity

Our interviews suggest that three factors prompted Kodak Brazil to target the low-income classes in 2004: an adverse competitive context, senior management support for the idea, and awareness of the opportunity.

Poor Results and the Threat Posed by Digital Photography

The threat posed by digital photography lay primarily in elimination of film revenues. Film was not only Kodak's largest source of revenue but also the product with the highest margin and market share. Digital photography also negatively affects printing revenues because photographers can store their photos electronically rather than in print form. In addition to lower revenues, digital photography also threatens Kodak with a lower-margin product mix; margins on digital cameras and printers are lower than on film and printing.

In 2000, Kodak debated the threat posed by digital photography and concluded that although digital cameras would rapidly take over in the developed world, the substitution would take longer in developing countries. Kodak deemed it essential to slow the decline in film revenues as much as possible by selling traditional photography products to the low-income segment in developing countries. Despite these discussions and the studies conducted, Kodak Brazil did not specifically market to classes C and D until October 2003.

The impetus for Kodak to give Gomes the managerial power and freedom he needed to execute a successful turnaround came from three years of poor results. Under pressure to deliver the kind of results expected from a turnaround, he was keen to explore opportunities that had been ignored in the past.

Leadership and Senior Support for the Idea

Flavio Gomes had more power and autonomy than previous general managers, but this difference alone does not explain Kodak Brazil's 2004 turnaround. Gomes, who had grown up poor himself, demonstrated leadership skills and a deep understanding of the low-income classes. In a short period of time, he successfully designed a coherent strategy for targeting the low-income market, obtained sufficient autonomy from headquarters to execute it, and overcame skepticism about the new strategy among his colleagues in Brazil.

The turnaround situation meant Gomes secured privileged access to Kodak's senior management in the United States. For example, six months after taking over as general manager he presented an update on the turnaround to Dan Carp, Kodak's CEO at the time. Support from senior management in the United States was essential in getting Brazil added to a select group of countries (China, India, and Russia) that could continue to invest in marketing traditional photography technologies.

Awareness of the Opportunity

The third factor that prompted Kodak to target the low-income classes was growing awareness that the company was missing out on an important opportunity. Corporations such as Casas Bahia, Unilever, Atlas (a manufacturer of stoves and washing machines), Multibras (Whirlpool's Brazilian subsidiary), McDonald's, and Claro (a mobile phone operator) were having success with low-income consumers. Articles and statistics reporting that classes C and D were growing also reinforced this new interest. Kodak explored this increasingly apparent opportunity with various studies:

- *Benchmarking studies.* Kodak's studies revealed that photography was still relatively underdeveloped in Brazil. Gomes reached this conclusion by comparing (1) camera market penetration in Brazil versus other countries, (2) market penetration of cameras versus other consumer durables, and (3) film usage in Brazil versus in other countries (Table 12.2). The studies showed that camera penetration in Brazil was in fact only 35 percent, rather than the 60 percent penetration estimated previously. It also showed that Brazil's position was lowest in camera penetration (ninth), thereby confirming Gomes's intuition that Kodak Brazil gave market share more attention than growth. Kodak interpreted the poor results in the benchmarking studies as an indication that it was not reaching the low-income classes in Brazil.
- *Best practices studies.* The juxtaposition of the benchmarking studies and the noticeable success of certain companies motivated Kodak to learn from those with experience doing business with the low-income classes. From Casas Bahia, Kodak learned the importance of offering consumer credit and advertising it. Unilever explained how they conduct consumer research and make use of ethnographic studies. They also discussed with Gomes their experience in launching a new product in the poorer northeast region of Brazil.
- *Marketing research.* Kodak reviewed old marketing research and conducted additional studies. Revisiting a usage and attitudes survey from 2001, Kodak estimated

TABLE 12.2. KODAK'S BENCHMARKING STUDIES.

Camera Market Penetration

Malaysia	90%
United States	85%
Argentina	60%
Brazil	35%
China	17%

Market Penetration in Brazil

Television	98%
Refrigerator	85%
Camera	35%
Washing machine	34%
Car	33%

Film Usage[1]

Japan	4
United States	3.5
Europe	1.7
Argentina	1
Brazil	<0.5

Note: [1]Rolls per capita per year.

Source: Kodak research and presentations.

that classes C and D accounted for about 70 percent of film consumption in 2001. These surprising statistics were calculated by applying the burn rate for each class to the population distribution. Although these statistics would increase as classes A and B abandoned traditional photography, digital substitution was low in Brazil at the time. Kodak concluded that, despite its targeting classes A and B, the low-income classes had already become their largest market segment.

• *Consumer research.* Although classes C and D were Kodak's biggest consumers of film, little was known about their consumer behavior or their attitude toward photography. Consumer research and ethnographic studies made Kodak aware of the distinct issues these consumers face. This knowledge was essential for Kodak to develop an effective marketing strategy specific to these customers. For one thing, Kodak discovered that a camera was always on the "shopping list" of those who did not own one, although it often remained at the bottom of the list. In another study, thirty-five people from classes C and D in São Paulo and Recife were given a camera and film. Kodak returned a month later to discuss the participants' photographs and experience. Gomes said that Kodak "saw a lot of emotion during those meetings." Some participants cried and many felt guilty that they did not have photographs of their parents, themselves, or even their children as babies.

Kodak learned from them that monthly payment amounts were more important than overall price and that the preferred monthly payment was R$10 (about US$10 on a PPP—purchasing power parity—basis). Kodak also learned that where consumer credit is not available low-income consumers cope creatively. However, these coping mechanisms often lead to lower aggregate demand. For instance, many borrow a camera for a special occasion, but Kodak research indicated that nonowners take fewer pictures and are sometimes reluctant or even embarrassed to borrow someone else's camera. In Brazil, consumers take one hundred days on average to develop a new roll of film—the longest time span in Latin America. Some ask simply to see the pictures at the store after development because they can't afford to pay. Since Kodak's cheapest film (Kodacolor) is available only in thirty-six exposures, low-income consumers sometimes share a roll of film by getting the photo store to cut off and develop only the exposed frames.

What Kodak Did to Target the Low-Income Market

Once Kodak decided to target the low-income classes, it needed an approach that dealt with employees' lack of understanding about the new market segment. Kodak also needed to ensure that the strategy for low-income classes was coherent with the technological changes taking place in the industry. The marketing strategy, in turn, had to make it easier for low-income consumers to become active photographers. To achieve these objectives, Kodak transformed its organizational culture, adapted its strategy for traditional photography, and developed a marketing strategy specific to the needs of low-income consumers.

Transforming the Organizational Culture

Given the preconceptions about classes C and D and how to market to them, Gomes had to develop an organizational culture that understood the low-income classes and found creative, low-cost ways of doing business with them. Employees learned the culture through anecdotes containing insights into the behavior and attitudes of the low-income market segment. According to Gomes, "The photos [and transcripts from the ethnographic studies] appealed to people's emotions." Many others at Kodak used similar examples or phrases to describe key learnings about classes C and D: "The number one barrier to increasing camera penetration is payment terms"; Kodak "needs to be where our consumer is"; and classes C and D "cannot afford to make a mistake" by purchasing a low-quality camera. Examples were about sharing cameras, sharing film, and the difficulty in using a camera or loading the film.

In less than two years, employees evolved from not mentioning classes C and D to viewing their consumer market in two segments—A and B, and C and D—each with its own distinct strategy. Employees sought to adapt Kodak Brazil's marketing strategy for traditional photography to the needs, tastes, resources, and habits of low-income consumers. Kodak employees also reiterated Gomes's strategy for the low-income classes: reaching them where they shop; adapting payment terms to what they can pay; and reminding them, through advertising, not to lose life's important moments.

Adapting the Strategy for Traditional Photography

Traditional photography was important to Kodak Brazil since it was the largest source of revenue. Kodak realized it could prevent neither the switch to digital photography nor the ensuing decline in traditional revenues. The only option was to offset this decline by marketing to classes C and D. Brazil's classes C and D were appealing for two reasons. First, the low camera-market penetration rate indicated that photography in general had potential to grow. The assumption was that most of this growth would come from the low-income segment. Second, classes C and D, given their lower purchasing power, are more likely to buy a traditional camera and film than a digital camera. Kodak therefore concluded that it would aim to maintain revenues from traditional photography by targeting the low-income segment. Since Kodak's strategy for penetrating the low-income classes relied on traditional photography, it became apparent that traditional photography and the low-income classes were two aspects of one strategy.

Although Kodak had always used "camera seeding" to increase film demand, they needed to take this concept to its extreme in doing business with the low-income segment. The principle of camera seeding is to promote camera ownership, which in turn increases demand for film. Camera seeding at its extreme means that Kodak makes no profit on cameras and considers other camera manufacturers as "partners" in increasing market penetration. As a result, Kodak decided to earn profits solely on film, for two reasons. First, because growth from the low-income classes is driven more by camera penetration than the film burn rate, Kodak was better off trying to sell cameras to nonowners than to convince camera owners to buy more film. Second, Kodak's research showed that the expenditure required to buy a camera was the largest barrier to photography in Brazil. Since expenditure is determined by price and payment terms, Kodak offered consumer credit and reduced the price on its low-end cameras, selling them at cost.

Developing a Specific Marketing Strategy

A marketing strategy specifically designed to target the low-income classes is one that takes into account their needs, attitudes, behavior, tastes, habits, and resources. Until Gomes took over as general manager, Kodak marketed to classes A and B, believing its clients were primarily from the upper and middle classes. Although some initiatives might have attracted or benefited the low-income classes, Kodak had never developed a specific marketing strategy for classes C and D. Gomes stressed the need for a holistic approach rather than isolated initiatives. The marketing strategy for the low-income market was successful because together the various initiatives made photography easier to afford, use, buy, and remember. Without an initiative to address each of the important barriers low-income consumers face, Kodak's strategy would have been much less effective.

Conclusion

This case illustrates why businesses must understand low-income consumers. By not doing so, they risk missing valuable opportunities, whether for growth, innovation, cost-effectiveness, or extending the life cycle of a product. The low-income classes in Brazil gave Kodak an opportunity to grow its consumer base and slow the decline of high-margin film revenues.

This case also suggests the importance of the information needed to understand the low-income classes. Local employees need a detailed, research-based understanding of the low-income classes to design an effective marketing strategy. Senior management, on the other hand, must realize the benefit of doing business with low-income consumers. Only then will they adapt the company's strategy, resources, organizational characteristics, and performance mechanisms to take advantage of the opportunity.

CHAPTER THIRTEEN

THE COMPLEX BUSINESS OF SERVING THE POOR

Insights from Unilever's Project Shakti in India

V. Kasturi Rangan, Dalip Sehgal, Rohithari Rajan

From the time of independence in 1947 until the late 1980s, the Indian economy was heavily regulated. Successive socialist-leaning governments imposed restrictions on the private sector's ability to invest in or expand its business; a "license" from the central government was required for such activity. Moreover, there were strict regulations on foreign ownership and investment in private enterprise. Hindustan Lever Limited (HLL), a subsidiary of the global food giant Unilever, had a stable base of operations throughout this period,[1] and it successfully built a leading position in several categories, notably soaps for personal cleaning and detergents for fabric washing, as well as hydrogenated cooking oil.

In the early 1990s, the Indian economy began to open up. Import restrictions were eased in many sectors and foreign investment was welcomed in several others. The country's GDP grew at a healthy 6 percent over the decade leading up to the turn of the century. In 2003, with an estimated population of nearly one billion people (of which nearly 750 million lived in rural areas), India's per capita income was reported at US$600 (US$2,900 on a purchasing power parity basis). With increasing connections and presence in global markets, the economy was predicted to grow at the same rate, if not faster, through the next decade, leading to quite optimistic projections regarding rapid creation of a sizable middle- and lower-income market. With such an optimistic outlook for the economy, HLL's top management identified rural India as a key source of growth and competitive advantage for the future. They reasoned that although the growth rate in urban markets would soon plateau as competition heated up (from the entry of foreign competitors emboldened by the country's increasingly liberalized economy), rural wealth would continue to grow, as would the market for consumer products.

HLL had historically enjoyed greater reach into rural India than any other consumer goods marketer. However, rivals began to emulate a number of its rural distribution initiatives, and the advantage it enjoyed was clearly short-lived. Rural India was characterized by lack of access, poor logistics, underdeveloped commercial infrastructure, scanty reach of electronic media, and a significantly lower literacy level. Across HLL's categories, per capita consumption in rural India was far below its urban penetration, and brand consciousness was even lower.

In December 2001, the company launched *Shakti*, a Hindi word for "strength" or "empowerment." The ambitious program was aimed beyond the top 250 million urban consumers with whom HLL already had a relationship. Shakti was targeted at serving the next 500 million consumers below the top of the pyramid.

This paper aims first to describe the background of the Shakti initiative and discuss the program itself. We then offer some back-of-the-envelope calculations and projections of the potential economic and social value created by the initiative. We close the paper with lessons learned and our observations on the key challenges faced by private enterprises as they attempt to address the needs of poor consumers.

HLL Background

The company, with sales of US$2.3 billion in 2004 (Rs.110 billion), gained market leadership in a range of product categories and across a broad spectrum of price points in each category. It had a sterling reputation for the quality of its management (for decades, Unilever left the company in the hands of very capable Indian managers) and the astuteness of its business strategy. It was known for many innovative R&D projects and new product introductions in the local market. For example, HLL was the first to introduce the idea of a detergent cake, which made sense for most Indian consumers who did not own a washing machine but rather washed clothes in running tap water. The company showed considerable innovation in locating and developing indigenous sources of fine oils that went into soap manufacture. The company's broad product line, covering nearly a thousand SKUs across twenty or so categories, included detergents, personal products, beverages, and foods. It was the category leader in most of the products and markets it competed in, with an aggregated market share around 40–45 percent. Its leadership position, however, came under steady and serious challenge in the last decade, so much so that in 2004, sales turnover declined for the first time in a decade, albeit by a small percentage (–2 percent). Profits, however, slumped by 29 percent, from US$388 million to US$276 million.

Competition

In the tightly regulated and constrained economic period prior to the early nineties, to some extent HLL enjoyed the incumbent's advantage. Most of the competition came at the lower end, with lower-end products. But as the Indian economy gradually opened, world-class competition emerged at the top end as well. Thus HLL's competition took two broad forms. In the lower price segments, competition came from a large number of informal local players. Each typically operated in a small geography, invested little or nothing in brand building, offered higher trade margins, and sold to consumers at prices considerably lower than those of HLL's brands. In the higher-price segments, competition came from organized global brands, such as Colgate-Palmolive and Procter & Gamble (P&G). Unlike HLL, P&G entered India only after the passing of liberalization laws and then competed fiercely in the hair care, fabric wash, and feminine hygiene categories.[2] Through 2004, HLL and P&G were embroiled in a price war that spread across many product categories.

Sales and Distribution System

Thousands of independent retail and wholesale outlets, rather than a few large chains, characterized the Indian consumer goods market. Nearly seven million outlets in India stocked fast-moving consumer goods. HLL served a million of these outlets—each of which it considered a distinct customer—through a distribution network of seven thousand "stockists." Within the past decade, the company has almost doubled the number of stockists, which in turn secured the company excellent market coverage and an intensive network of retailers in the top hundred thousand towns and villages, reaching 250 million people.

Challenges to Rural Distribution

More than 70 percent of India's one billion people reside in rural villages. Per capita income in rural India is approximately 44 percent of that in urban India, but in terms of aggregate purchasing power rural and urban market demand for consumer goods is more or less equal. In 2005, the approximate market size for the range of products marketed by HLL was approximately $6 billion, with demand equally split between urban and rural markets. If the 750 million rural consumers were to consume products at the same intensity as the urban consumer, then the overall market size would double to nearly $12 billion.

There were three challenges in the way of achieving this potential. The first was the challenge of *reach:* distributing products to India's 638,000 villages was difficult, especially as many were not connected to urban centers by air or rail, and road connectivity was poor. Accessing remote markets, even where feasible, meant additional costs. Since the market potential was low to begin with, appointing a local stockist to service these markets was not a viable option. Moreover, nearly 90 percent of these settlements were populated by fewer than two thousand people (Table 13.1), which made for a low business potential in each market.

The second challenge was *communication*. Rural markets were largely media-dark. Less than a third of rural households owned a radio; fewer than one in five owned a television. A relatively low literacy rate further reduced the effectiveness of print media.

The third challenge was *influence*. Low category penetration and per capita consumption patterns were not going to change dramatically even if product availability improved, or even if the brand proposition were somehow communicated effectively. Consumers would have to change their attitudes and behaviors toward personal hygiene practices. Many of the rural consumers were hardly used to brushing their teeth with toothpaste and a brush. A large proportion washed and scrubbed with naturally and locally available substances rather than with soaps, which were not widely found. Running water was still not present in many villages, and where it was often had to be shared by multiple community members. Water sources themselves—be it from a well, pond, or tap—were frequently contaminated.

HLL's Rural Distribution Strategy

As shown in Figure 13.1, India's consumers can be divided into four approximately equal segments of about 250 million each. The top quarter billion, mainly urban consumers, accounted for about half the market potential. This segment was where most competition for the customers' wallet took place. In spite of the increasing intensity of its rivals, HLL had a strong presence in this market segment, mainly because of its brands and distribution network.

TABLE 13.1. DISTRIBUTION OF VILLAGES IN INDIA.

Population	Number of Villages	Percentage of Total
Fewer than 200	114,267	17.9
200–499	155,123	24.3
500–999	159,400	25.0
1,000–1,999	125,758	19.7
2,000–4,999	69,135	10.8
5,000–9,999	11,618	1.8
10,000 or more	3,064	0.5
Total	638,365	100

Source: Kashyap (2004b).

FIGURE 13.1. STRUCTURE OF HLL'S MARKET REACH IN INDIA.

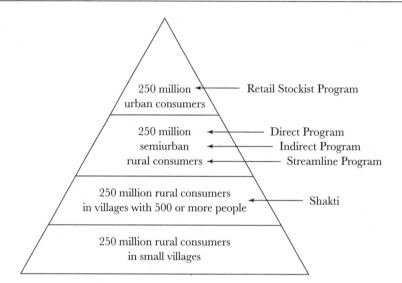

Not wanting to rest on its laurels, the company began a serious effort to serve customers in the second segment through a variety of rural distribution programs in the 1960s. Its approach to rural distribution was governed by the two criteria of accessibility and viability, and a number of initiatives were pioneered to increase reach into these markets. Table 13.2 shows the models HLL employed to overcome challenges in rural distribution.

Project Shakti

Project Shakti was meant to tap into markets that had neither business potential nor market accessibility. Launched in December 2000, it had at the heart of its model the Shakti entrepreneur. A local villager, the Shakti entrepreneur was trained as a door-to-door salesperson, or more accurately a traveling retailer who operated out of her home. The second key component of the model was the arrangement of a microloan for these entrepreneurs. In addition to the Shakti entrepreneurs, HLL also recruited a Shakti *Vani,* or "communicator," who educated rural consumers on health and hygiene and drummed up primary demand for the product category and HLL's brands. The final component of the model was installation of iShakti: Internet-connected computers in the homes of Shakti entrepreneurs to offer educational packages to consumers

TABLE 13.2. HLL'S APPROACH TO RURAL MARKETS ON THE BASIS OF BUSINESS POTENTIAL AND ACCESSIBILITY.

	Low Business Potential	High Business Potential
Inaccessible	*Shakti*	*Streamline:* rural wholesalers used local means of transport such as motorcycles, rickshaws, or even bullock carts to reach rural retailers.
Accessible	*Indirect coverage:* HLL stockists sent out products in a van to sell them to retailers, usually for cash.	*Direct coverage:* HLL appointed a "combined stockist," instead of one for each product line (detergents, personal care, beverages, and food product categories).

Source: Rangan and Rajan (2005).

in the village and also serve as market research pipelines for the company's headquarters. By mid-2005, HLL had appointed and trained about fifteen thousand Shakti entrepreneurs to cover some sixty thousand villages in five states. The Vani program covered about one-third of these villages. Nearly four hundred iShakti Internet-accessible kiosks were set up, mainly in the state of Andhra Pradesh, in collaboration with the state government's A.P. Online initiative. The Shakti target for 2010 is to reach half a million villages through about one hundred thousand entrepreneurs.

The Shakti Entrepreneur

HLL decided to pilot the model with women. This decision was based on a number of factors. Women were the target consumers for the bulk of HLL's products, and underprivileged rural women constituted the most marginalized group in society. They were also more likely to be committed to Project Shakti, since they would surely value the additional income. Also, women were likely to have greater access to the homes of potential consumers. Under the Shakti entrepreneur program, underprivileged rural women were recruited as Shakti entrepreneurs and trained to manage a small business. To manage this network, HLL set up a team of nearly one thousand rural sales personnel (RSP) to visit, select, engage, motivate, and train Shakti entrepreneurs in managing businesses and door-to-door retailing. These RSPs were employees of a third party but were selected, trained, and managed by HLL.

From the outset, HLL chose to partner with self-help groups to extend its rural reach. Various NGOs, multilateral agencies, government bodies, and public sector banks set up self-help groups in rural India; these groups functioned as mutual thrift societies. Ten to fifteen women in a particular village would get together and form a group, which would meet regularly, and each member would contribute a small amount of money to a common pool. Once the pool attained a threshold, the sponsoring agency would step in and offer microcredit to one or more members of the group, to be invested in an approved economic activity.

One of Shakti's core thrusts was to give the project sustaining power by making the added financial income attractive for the Shakti entrepreneur. The company calculated that a household with a per capita income of US$250 (which was the rural average) could substantially increase its income through door-to-door selling of Shakti products. The microloan was arranged to support a monthly sales turnover of about US$225, so that after paying about US$5 for the monthly installment of loan plus interest there would be a net profit of about US$15 per month, or US$180 annually. The company's expectation was that with a hundred thousand entrepreneurs it would be able to reach half a million villages. This would mean additional sales of $250 million, assuming that all the Shakti entrepreneurs worked at full potential. Though the whole program could take five to seven years to roll out, it was also possible that productivity might improve with more brands and products being added to the portfolio.

The Shakti Vani

The Shakti Vani or communication initiative was a health, hygiene, and wellness package targeted at rural communities. A local woman was appointed as a Vani[3] and trained and positioned as an expert on matters relating to personal and community health and hygiene. She would then cover a cluster of villages, organizing school contact programs, self-help group meetings, and village get-togethers to communicate best practices in the areas of personal health and community hygiene. To make her communication more effective, she was given specially developed aids, such as pictorial literature that could be understood by illiterate people and interactive games that would interest her audience while driving home the message.

iShakti

The third intervention was the iShakti community portal, which empowered the rural community by creating access to pertinent information. The computer was inevitably located at the home of the Shakti entrepreneur, so she could invite members of her community to visit her home to gain information and education. Users of the kiosk could access content on education, employment, agriculture, health, grooming, and entertainment. All areas within the iShakti site were accompanied by voice-over in the local language. All content areas also offered users the option of posing e-mail queries if the information they sought was not available on the portal. HLL employed a panel of experts who answered these queries within twenty-four hours.

Potential Economic and Social Value Created by Shakti

At the 2004 sales level of US$227 per entrepreneur per month, Shakti is approximately a US$40 million business. By 2010, HLL aims to have one hundred thousand entrepreneurs, and if the average business size does not change Shakti will hit US$270 million in sales. The company's gross margins have averaged 40–45 percent (the most recent year being 40 percent) and its net margins have averaged 10–15 percent (the most recent being 10 percent), so Shakti is projected to add US$27–$45 million to the bottom line. But this is only a conservative estimate, because rural consumption expenditures and the Shakti entrepreneurs' productivity will no doubt go up after the program reaches maturity.

The critical assumption here is about potential margins. It is doubtful the company can preserve its gross margins, especially if the bulk of the sales are effected in "sachet" sizes (small, individually packaged SKUs of leading brands), which are bound to have a lower margin because of the higher packaging cost per unit. But the lower gross margins would be more than offset by lower sales and distribution costs, which are only incremental to the existing infrastructure in this case. First of all, the cost of RSPs, the salesforce that manages and trains the entrepreneurs, accounted for about 12 percent of sales revenue in 2005. Add to that the estimated 3 percent costs of the Vani and iShakti support programs, and Shakti would have enough head room even if gross margins were only in the 35 percent range. As a matter of fact, Shakti broke even in 2004. The nature of the business development model is such that even though most of these costs vary with sales development, economies of scale have started to kick in, allowing the possibility of a contribution to the bottom line. The challenge lies in growing sales at a much faster rate than overhead.

Another important benefit of the project, and one that is still relatively easy to measure, is the net wealth that Shakti generates among underprivileged rural women. Today, a Shakti entrepreneur's net income is about 7 percent of sales. By 2010, HLL expects this margin to go up to about 10 percent. With a hundred thousand entrepreneurs generating US$270 million in sales, and at 10 percent net margin, this adds up to annual wealth creation of nearly US$27 million. This amount reflects only the margins made from HLL's products. The company fully expects its entrepreneurs will also take on complementary products to fill out their retail product assortment, in which case the net wealth created could be significantly higher than what is afforded them by the HLL product line alone.

It is more difficult to measure the benefits related to Shakti's impact on the community. Undeniably, Shakti creates social value by spreading awareness and adoption of best practices in health and hygiene. It creates income, develops enterprise, and enhances the social status of underprivileged rural women, one of the most marginalized constituents of Indian society. Through iShakti, it aims to provide information on a variety of areas, which in turn creates social value.

All these benefits might be difficult to quantify, but they need to be acknowledged. However, had HLL not decided that Shakti was scalable, this social value might never have been created. There is, in other words, a case for greater involvement by the public and social sectors. In a situation where initiatives such as Shakti cannot be scaled up owing to business viability constraints, it is imperative that the public or social sector step in to shoulder some of the costs, thereby making the project viable for the private sector and ensuring that social value is maximized.

In Shakti's case, there is in fact already much evidence to demonstrate its crucial dependence on the external infrastructure support afforded to it in the state of Andhra Pradesh, where a forward-looking state government subsidized investment in Internet-ready computer installations. For the same reason, it cooperated in providing Vani communicators access to its public schools to impart health and hygiene information (and, by the way, brand messages too). The state government of Andhra Pradesh saw this as an opportunity to build public infrastructure with private capital. Of course, this sort of arrangement creates its own sets of challenges for a private investor such as HLL. It rightly has to worry about competitors taking a free ride on the primary demand created by its innovative Vani communication program, and even more important be concerned with losing its most assiduously cultivated retail channel—the Shakti entrepreneur—to competition. Nevertheless, in HLL's case having the leading market share has given comfort that even after competition follows the company to rural markets, it will still be the primary beneficiary.

Lessons Learned and Challenges Ahead

The initial success of the Shakti initiative allows us to draw several conclusions.

The Viability of the Commercial Model

The most critical determinant of success in a BOP intervention is akin to the "moment of truth" that all businesses face. Here, the moment of truth is the viability or health of the "last mile." Most BOP consumers (even the urban poor in isolated slums) are relatively inaccessible. Very often, a regular distribution or communication medium is extended through a last mile to cover these consumers. This could take the form of an additional rural distributor or a van that goes into slums and plays television advertisements. In the case of the Shakti model, the last mile is the Shakti entrepreneur, and the moment of truth is the income she earns. The entire Shakti intervention eventually depends on a barely literate, economically disadvantaged, and often socially repressed woman. Unless Shakti fundamentally changes her life, it is not bound to work.

A typical Shakti entrepreneur earns approximately US$15 per month. Thus the first challenge is to appoint the *right* entrepreneur—someone for whom such an income is significant. HLL worked with women from families living below the poverty line, and for these families Shakti usually significantly improved household income, from 50 percent to 100 percent.

Since the consumption level of low-income consumers tends to be lower, the business potential in BOP markets, in the short run, is lower than that in urban markets of comparable population. This affects not only the business generated for the organization but also the viability of the last mile. The solution lies in product-line breadth and depth. HLL enjoys a huge advantage because it offers entrepreneurs a portfolio of more than forty-five brand franchises, including some of the largest, most trusted consumer brands in India. For organizations that do not have the benefit of starting out with such a comprehensive portfolio, the solution lies in partnership. Thus other products—whether foodstuffs, agricultural implements, or financial services—could be clubbed with the company's personal care products.

The Importance of Being Customer-Led

For most organizations, BOP consumers are relatively inaccessible, which makes creating product availability the biggest challenge. Distribution is a big challenge and a necessary prerequisite to building brands, but it cannot work in isolation. Shakti's objectives went beyond distributing HLL's products in rural markets. It had to design products and systems to address customer needs. In addition to enhancing HLL's direct reach, Shakti forms a unique channel of one-to-one brand endorsement as well as community education. Moreover, Shakti does not work alone; it is backed by HLL's packaging and price-point innovations in the form of sachets as well as brands specifically targeted at low-income consumers. In other words, a company entering the BOP should be ready to accept market feedback and design products and services that are appropriate for the markets it chooses to serve. Simply taking the same product through rural channels will not serve the purpose.

The Significance of Partnership

Designing a successful and sustainable BOP initiative takes multiple iterations, much time, and significant investment. The Shakti model went through a number of iterations even before its first pilot in 2000. After the basic model went beyond pilot phase in the state of Andhra Pradesh, it was still not clear that the model could be rolled out across the country. India's states differ widely in cultural diversity, political environment, availability of microcredit, and basic infrastructure. This mattered because the model was critically dependent on microfinance institutions and NGOs to help identify self-help groups and Shakti entrepreneurs.

If the objective is to create a business model, partnership is an obvious route. But for a BOP business initiative to truly battle poverty, it is imperative that nonbusiness sectors also tap into the partnership opportunity. Shakti has created a broad pipeline that can be used for much more than distribution of HLL's products. HLL recognizes this; it has partnerships with more than 350 NGOs across the country and works closely with a number of state and central government agencies. Shakti entrepreneurs, Vanis, and iShakti kiosks form a vast network that can influence development in the most remote communities. NGOs attempting rural communication on health, for instance, could vastly enhance their impact by using the Vani network.

Private sector organizations often create infrastructure where this is not their role, but the social value of their efforts is not optimized unless the government and the NGO sector partner with them. It is often too expensive for the private investor to undertake development of public infrastructure if there is no guarantee of monopoly control to recoup the investment. Consortia of private developers, especially if they have complementary interests (or even competitive interests), would benefit much from such cooperation. After all, it is this bridge that will provide the infrastructure to the development of future markets. The question is, Who motivates these partners to come together, and at what cost and incentives? It is our belief that governments have a responsibility in encouraging and catalyzing formation of such groups in the interests of their citizens.

The Challenge of Sustainability

Earlier in this paper, we projected a potential revenue gain from Shakti of about US$270 million for the company by 2010. Netting out trade margins and taxes, it would still mean additional revenues of about US$200 million, and at current Shakti margins of 15 percent this represents an incremental income of about US$30 million. Realistically, a world-class business like HLL would be about a US$3.5 billion company operation with net margins of about US$350 million (assuming current levels of activity) by 2010. Shakti could well contribute nearly 10 percent of that net income. Thus sustainability and scale go hand in hand. That is, if Shakti hits revenue and margin goals, it will be an important part of HLL's portfolio, ensuring for itself a sustained growth model. Shakti could take off with the right investments and become an important part of the firm's portfolio of business activities, not only in contributing to the bottom line but also in development of a unique channel capability, which gives it an edge over large national and global competitors. Even more important, Shakti has the potential to make a fundamental contribution to enhancing the wealth and quality of life of the rural poor even as it delivers a key strategic advantage to the company.

CHAPTER FOURTEEN

PATRIMONIO HOY

A Groundbreaking Corporate Program to Alleviate Mexico's Housing Crisis

Arthur I. Segel, Nadeem Meghji, Regina García-Cuéllar

In December 1999, CEMEX, a leading global building solutions company based in Mexico, launched Patrimonio Hoy (PH), a sales, distribution, and savings program intended to serve Mexico's large self-construction housing market. CEMEX created the program with the dual purpose of alleviating Mexico's housing crisis and creating value for the company. Patrimonio Hoy has proved to be a tremendous success, reaching more than one hundred thousand Mexican families during its six years of operation and aiming to reach more than one million by 2009. This paper discusses the program's role in promoting social and economic development in low-income Mexican communities while creating profits and growth for CEMEX. It also discusses some key challenges CEMEX has overcome in conducting business with this traditionally underserved customer segment.

Housing in Mexico

Mexico has one of the worst housing shortages in the world. There is a need for 1.5 million new homes annually, though only 500,000 are built each year.[1] At the time CEMEX launched PH, 40 percent of cement consumption in Mexico came from the

This paper has benefited from "Patrimonio Hoy," by Arthur Segel, Michael Chu, and Gustavo Herrero, Harvard Business School case no. 9-805-064, Harvard Business School Publishing, Boston.

self-built, low-income segment[2]; one-third of all new homes in Mexico were informally constructed. Typically, these homes had only one room, which served as the kitchen, living room, and bedroom for the entire family (on average consisting of four to six people).[3] These rooms often lacked a proper roof, leading to significant leakage during the rainy season. Most did not have access to sewage facilities and fewer than half had access to telephone service.

Inefficiency in the Self-Built Housing Segment

Despite the prevalence of self-built homes, the self-construction process in Mexico was slow and inefficient. The purchasing and construction process was often delayed because few low-income individuals had the capital to purchase all the needed materials at one time. Moreover, these individuals had neither the savings habits nor the access to credit to make the purchases. As a result, the materials were bought at irregular intervals and in varying amounts. Additionally, individual families did not have the expert knowledge to properly construct a house, thereby slowing the construction process and leading to lower-quality homes. The result was that it took an average of five years to build an individual room.

Patrimonio Hoy (PH)

Created in 1998, PH allows low-income families to obtain access to services, cement, and other building materials on credit through a well-planned savings program. Through PH, CEMEX helps organize its customers into groups of three families and requires that each family contribute US$13 per week for seven cycles of ten weeks. Within each ten-week cycle, CEMEX provides access to ten weeks' worth of building materials and services after only two weeks of payment. The families collectively pay off their debt during the remaining eight weeks. Within each weekly payment, US$11.50 is the direct payment for materials and US$1.50 is the participation fee. As an added benefit, CEMEX gives families architectural consulting and warehousing services.

CEMEX hires local promoters to generate sales and monitor the program within their assigned areas. The individuals are typically townspeople with well-established personal networks. Promoters conduct house visits and interview potential customers to evaluate creditworthiness. Currently, PH has sixty-two offices in twenty-nine cities (Figure 14.1). The program has served more than a hundred thousand families since its inception in 1998 and has loaned out construction materials valued at $42 million— enough to build 650,000 square meters of rooms. Its customers have been able to

FIGURE 14.1. GEOGRAPHICAL PRESENCE AND PATRIMONIO HOY'S GROWTH.

State	City	Number of Cells
Veracruz	Córdoba	1
	Orizaba	1
	Veracruz	5
	Jalapa	2
Jalisco	Guadalajara	8
Mexico City	Ecatepec	4
	Toluca	3
Guanajuato	León	4
	Irapuato	1
	Celaya	1
Oaxaca	Oaxaca	4
	Salina Cruz	1
	Tehuantepec	1
Michoacán	Morelia	3
	Uruapan	1
Puebla	Puebla	4
Chiapas	Tapachula	1
	Tuxtla Gutierrez	1
	San Cristobal	1
Nuevo León	Monterrey	3
Querétaro	Querétaro	2
Morelos	Cuernavaca	2
Aguascalientes	Aguascalientes	1
Hidalgo	Pachuca	1
Nayarit	Tepic	1
San Luis Potosi	San Luis	1
Tabasco	Villahermosa	1
Tamaulipas	Reynosa	1
Zacatecas	Zacatecas	1

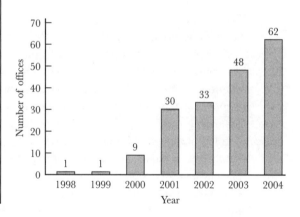

Source: CEMEX.

decrease the average time for room construction from five years to just over one year, while decreasing the cost of construction by approximately 20 percent.[4] CEMEX plans to expand the program to one million customers by 2009 and hopes to eventually reach a large portion of the sixteen million self-built homes in Mexico.

Value to Key Stakeholders

PH's employees, customers, and distributors all derive significant value from the program.

Value to Promoters

PH currently employs more than five hundred promoters and has employed some one thousand over the past five years, of which more than 98 percent are women. This is particularly significant because women constitute only 35 percent of the Mexican workforce.[5] Promoters work part-time and earn an average of US$200 per month, which is significant compared with the average family's income of US$320 per month in the communities served by the program.[6] This income has allowed many promoters to become PH customers themselves, and in some cases to start their own businesses. Rosenda Rodriguez, a promoter for five years, said, "Before I worked for PH, I was just a housewife. Now, I am earning my own money and recently started my own grocery business."[7] Furthermore, PH conducts weekly training for promoters in sales, communications, and relationship management. By attaining valuable skills and income-earning potential, these women have increased agency over their financial destiny.

PH has increased promoters' self-confidence and elevated their role within the family. Teresa Pinedo, a promoter for five years, said, "My husband didn't want me to become a customer, so I became a promoter without asking him and now I earn my own money which I use for the program." Gema Lopez, also a promoter for five years, said, "As a promoter, I feel more confident as a woman to speak in front of people in my community."

Value to Customers

Customers also benefit from PH in a number of ways.

Access to Credit. Prior to PH, many of these customers lacked access to formal credit because they did not have a legal title over their home. In addition, the Mexican mortgage market—like similar markets in many developing countries—was unsophisticated and shallow. In emerging markets alone, the amount of "dead capital" locked up in extralegal housing currently exceeds US$9.3 trillion.[8] Traditionally, the primary source of savings for many low-income families in Mexico was the *tanda* system.[9] However, families often used only 15 percent of their funds for investment, with the remainder spent on consumption.[10] Customers also accessed credit through local money lenders, who charged excessive interest rates.

CEMEX used the existing tanda savings system as a basis to create a new model for providing credit. Through PH, CEMEX uses social capital ("social networks and the norms of reciprocity and trustworthiness that arise from them"[11]) as opposed to traditional collateral to extend credit. Specifically, the families that form a group are jointly accountable for repayment. If one of the families fails to contribute, no other family receives its materials for that week and the defaulting family loses social standing in the community. Mutual accountability encourages families to evaluate one another's credit risk prior to forming groups, preventing less reliable individuals from participating.

This model of social capital as a source of collateral is not new; the Grameen Bank and many other microfinance organizations use it to lend to the poor. However, unlike those institutions PH uses this model to sell a product, as opposed to simply lending money.

CEMEX also relies on other incentives to encourage repayment and thus mitigate credit risk. Promoters are gatekeepers who decide whether a family qualifies for the program. They are compensated on the basis of the number of clients they enroll and their tenure in the program. Hence, promoters have incentives not only to find families willing to join PH but also to ensure that participating families continue to pay once enrolled. Moreover, PH offers incentives to reliable clients, such as access to better credit terms and recommendation letters for other credit suppliers and institutions.

Improved Service. In addition to the increased construction speed and quality, PH customers also receive a higher-quality product and better customer service. Traditionally, some wholesalers and retailers manipulated their poor customers by overstating the amount of materials needed for a given project. Furthermore, delivery of construction materials was unreliable and often delayed. To avoid these problems, CEMEX selected the most reputable distributors and implemented rigorous control systems. In fact, if a distributor is late in delivering materials, it must give the customer a free bag of cement.

Improved Living Conditions. Through PH, customers are able to expand their home and improve their living conditions. Also, because of the architectural services provided, home quality and structural integrity is better. For example, Veronica Oropeza, along with her family of eleven, used to share a single room with a dirt floor. During the rainy season in Monterrey, her home would flood, causing knee-high mud. Now, through the program, she has built an elevated cement floor that eliminates the flooding problem. Additionally, her school-aged children have more space to study at home, improving their educational opportunities.

Increased Net Worth. Customers of the program enjoy direct economic benefits associated with having a larger, higher-quality house built in less time. The market value of an additional room built through PH is MXN$19,800, whereas the market value of a traditionally made room is approximately MXN$16,300. Given that the time and cost for construction are lower, customers in PH experience an annual return of 27 percent on their investment, in contrast to the −1.1 percent return realized through the traditional building process.[12] This increase in the family's net worth is important, since most of these families have no other form of savings.

Improved Savings Habits and Greater Investment in the Future. PH has changed the mind-set of its participants, giving them the discipline to save and showing them the benefits of investing in the future. Most families did not save a significant amount prior to participating in PH. For example, Lourdes Victoriano said, "I needed more space but did not have the discipline to save money. PH gave me the discipline I needed and has shown me the value of saving." Ninety-seven percent of those surveyed stated that their participation in PH has increased the importance they place on saving, and 83 percent said they plan to increase the amount they save in the future.

Increased Entrepreneurship and Income. As a result of the program, PH customers have been able to start or expand small businesses since they now have increased living space. According to our survey, approximately 24 percent of the families served by PH operate some form of small business from their home. However, for most of these families, it is a challenge to run a business because of space constraints. For example, prior to PH, Carina Ortiz used to sell and cook food on the street corner. Running a business from her home was not an option because her family of seven shared a single room with a cardboard roof. Through PH, Ortiz built a room where she has opened a small grocery store generating monthly sales of MXN$6,000. In fact, 33 percent of the 160 customers surveyed indicated that their improved living conditions and additional space have increased their ability to conduct business activities from their home, and 69 percent stated that their family income has increased after joining PH. In most cases, it is the woman who operates the individual business while the husband has a salaried job; thus women enjoy greater economic independence and agency.

Increased Confidence and Agency. As a result of their increased productivity, savings, and net worth, customers have changed mind-sets and feel a greater sense of control and self-esteem. Jacoba, a customer of three years, said, "Our family feels very content because we have savings, preparing us for surprises that the future might hold."

In fact, 93 percent of customers surveyed said they believed they had more control over their future; 75 percent stated they felt more respected in the community as a result of increasing the size and quality of their home. According to Héctor Ureta, director of self-construction of CEMEX Mexico, customers of the program have come to expect more out of themselves and society than before they joined.

Value to Distributors

CEMEX decided to partner with local distributors to serve its self-construction consumers. PH distributors are local merchants, selected on the basis of quality, geographical reach, and delivery capacity. Since they generally serve CEMEX's commercial business, they have an incentive to also perform well in this market. According to Ureta, "For [CEMEX] to distribute materials directly to each of these homes would imply enormous costs in terms of logistics and time spent getting to know the communities. [Distributors] bring to the table knowledge of the communities and the know-how of the construction-materials home delivery."

Distributors have increased and stabilized their sales through the program and strengthened their relationships with CEMEX. The average distributor reports monthly sales of US$13,900, with one-third attributable to PH. Overall, profit margins on cement and materials are approximately 15 percent.[13] Additionally, because distributors have access to PH customers, they are able to cross-sell other building products. Alicia Guerrero, a PH distributor, commented, "We feel good about PH, because we sell more, our credit risk is lower, and the margins are similar to our other sales."

Benefits for CEMEX

For CEMEX, the PH program has meant a boost in sales and profitability as well as an improved national and international corporate image.

Increased Sales and Profitability

According to Juan Castro, CEMEX's marketing vice president, PH has garnered organizational credibility because it is profitable and self-sustaining; it is not intended to be mere charity. PH broke even for the first time in 2003 and is currently generating steady profits. In 2004, the program's net profits before taxes were MXN$13.9 million, or approximately US$1.3 million.

To reach one million clients by 2009, PH has to grow 55.5 percent every year.[14] With this many clients, PH would generate US$23.8 million in profits in 2009 (see Table 14.1). Even in such a scenario, PH remains a minor component of CEMEX Mexico's overall business, constituting only 1.4 percent of forecasted CEMEX Mexico

TABLE 14.1. PATRIMONIO HOY: PROFITABILITY PROJECTIONS.

Assumptions

Weekly cost to program members	$11.50
PH membership fee	$1.50
Cost of construction materials	$10.00
Distributor discount[a]	7%
Gross contribution to PH (membership fee + distributor discount)	$2.20
Annual growth rate for active clients	55.5%
Number of weeks per year	52
Promoters' wage per month	$70
Number of existing offices as of 12/31/03	48
Yearly cost of promoters	$403,200
Yearly cost of 48 existing offices	$2,814,196
Yearly cost of each new office	$35,500
Yearly central administration overhead costs	$782,604
Annual growth of overhead costs (10% of customer growth)	5.55%
Number of promoters per office	10
Number of clients per new office	950

TABLE 14.1. continued

Profitability of PH Program	2005	2006	2007	2008	2009	With 5 million clients
Accumulated number of families in the program[b]	171,050	265,983	413,603	643,153	1,000,103	5,000,000
Number of active families in program[c]	111,840	173,912	270,433	420,523	653,913	3,269,231
Average number of paying families[d]	65,788	102,301	159,078	247,367	384,655	1,923,077
Number of full-paying clients served per office	675	707	741	777	850	900
Number of offices	83	120	178	269	410	2,027
Membership fee	$~.50	$1.50	$1.50	$1.50	$1.50	$1.50
Construction materials	$10.00	$10.00	$10.00	$10.00	$10.00	$10.00
Program fee revenue	$5,131,500	$7,979,483	$12,408,095	$19,294,588	$30,003,085	$150,000,000
Distributor spread revenue	$2,394,700	$3,723,759	$5,790,444	$9,004,141	$14,001,439	$70,000,000
Gross revenues	$7,526,200	$11,703,241	$18,198,540	$28,298,729	$44,004,524	$220,000,000
Operating costs of offices	$4,061,370	$5,368,890	$7,429,575	$10,664,199	$15,663,512	$73,062,228
Wages to promoters	$698,424	$1,007,691	$1,495,290	$2,260,666	$3,443,601	$17,025,270
Overhead cost	$871,384	$920,273	$971,348	$1,025,258	$1,082,160	$826,039
Total operating expenses	$5,632,178	$7,296,855	$9,896,213	$13,950,123	$20,189,273	$90,913,537
Income before taxes	$1,894,022	$4,406,386	$8,302,327	$14,348,606	$23,815,251	$129,086,463

Notes: [a] Distributors give PH a 7% discount on materials. This enters as part of PH's revenues.

[b] The number of accumulated families in the program is the total number of families that have enrolled in PH during its history.

[c] The number of active families in the program is the total number of families that were served by PH during that year, on average 65.4% of accumulated clients.

[d] This is the equivalent number of families that paid the 52 weeks of the year. This figure is different from the number of active families because not all active families pay fees all year round. On average, 58.8% of active families pay every week of the year.

Source: CEMEX.

sales for that year. On the other hand, if PH were to reach five million clients by 2009, the program would generate around US$129 million in profits in that year and likely constitute a much larger share of CEMEX's overall business. However, if one includes the additional profit stream generated from cement sales through PH, the program begins to appear much more profitable. Including profits generated from cement, the program's net income would be US$43.7 million if it reaches one million clients by 2009. If PH reaches five million customers by 2009, the program's net income would be US$228.5 million, more than one-third of CEMEX Mexico's 2004 net income. This demonstrates the significant potential for the program to eventually make a large contribution to the firm's overall profitability.

Because of PH, CEMEX not only has a larger share of the low-income market but has encouraged increased consumption in this market as well. Families build rooms faster than before, and they purchase more cement. The average customer builds roughly three rooms through PH. The program is currently growing at more than 50 percent per year, resulting in cement sales of approximately sixty thousand tons in 2004, an increase of forty-eight thousand over the previous level.[15] CEMEX's top thirty commercial customers purchase an average of forty-eight thousand tons per year, which means PH generates sales equivalent to those of a large commercial customer.[16] Additionally, many families served by PH have at least one commercial construction worker or mason at home. CEMEX believes that by showcasing its brand and effectively serving these individuals, it generates future business.

Finally, PH brings to CEMEX revenue diversification in its Mexican operations. During the 1994 Mexican crisis, the company's domestic sales plummeted by 50 percent, but sales in the self-built segment dropped only 10–20 percent.[17] The lower volatility in this segment was extremely attractive to CEMEX and was a key impetus for the creation of PH.

Improved Corporate Image

PH has also strengthened CEMEX's reputation as a socially responsible firm. According to CEMEX's Castro, "PH is a key part of the corporate mission of providing construction solutions to improve the standard of living in Mexico and has improved CEMEX's overall image." CEMEX reports that it has seen increased interest from a number of socially responsible investment funds, and that the program has recently received significant attention from stock analysts. CEMEX also claims that it received highly positive feedback from its large commercial customers. According to Bob Willard, a leading expert on the business value of corporate sustainability strategies, "Loyal customers are attracted to the company as much as the product. Company values matter as much as product features."[18]

However, CEMEX recognizes that there is even greater potential for the firm to publicize the program. In 2003, CEMEX conducted interviews with external and internal stakeholders to better understand how the company was perceived. According to the survey, only a small percentage of those surveyed knew about CEMEX's various social projects. Yet most of them said it would improve their perception of the firm if they were aware of such projects, demonstrating the significant potential for CEMEX to improve its overall image through PH.[19]

Costs for CEMEX

Although PH has created significant economic value and set the stage for long-term growth, CEMEX confronts several risks in pursuing this program: credit, inflation, and operational risk.

Through PH, CEMEX increases its exposure to credit risk because low-income customers cannot put up personal assets as collateral, and they lack credit history. Additionally, transaction costs are high relative to loan value, thanks to the lack of information about customers and small loan sizes. Thus traditional financial institutions have avoided serving this market. The total mortgage portfolio in Mexico in 2004 was US$65 billion, or 6 percent of Mexico's housing stock, versus 44 percent in the United States.[20] Despite these risks, PH has achieved an impressive repayment rate above 99 percent.

By freezing prices over the cycle, CEMEX also exposes itself to inflation risk. Although inflation stabilized to 4.9 percent between 2001 and 2004, Mexico has experienced significant inflation in recent decades—with the rate as high as 52 percent in 1995 during the currency devaluation crisis.[21] CEMEX also faces operational challenges in scaling this highly decentralized cash business. CEMEX establishes offices in each community it operates, hiring ten promoters, one architect, and one or two full-time employees. There are challenges in recruiting and training local personnel along with creating monitoring and control systems to ensure proper accounting and standardized operations. According to Ureta, "We are striving to turn PH into the equivalent of McDonald's" in terms of consistency of operations between offices. Furthermore, given the high transaction costs of serving this segment, CEMEX is constantly seeking to increase efficiency in order to effectively scale this business to one million customers by 2009 and expand the program internationally.

Interest Rate Charged

The implied interest rate that CEMEX charges PH customers is difficult to calculate because the program fees include the cost of money as well as a variety of services. According to Ureta, "Our rates fare out well versus those charged by microfinance institutions, but even that is not a fair comparison: we provide much more than just credit to buy materials, we help our customers convert their scarce cash into livable assets more efficiently, we give them technical assistance, we freeze prices for them, we store the materials for them in a safe warehouse, and we are there to provide them with advice on all their needs."

One calculation of this implied interest rate results in a nominal interest rate of more than 100 percent per annum. This is calculated by assuming a weekly US$1.50 interest payment over ten weeks and a weekly principal payment of US$11.50 for eight weeks (loans are effective after customers pay down two installments). Although this rate is seemingly high, it is comparable to what is charged by most microfinance institutions serving a similar market. The high rate is explained by the transaction costs associated with serving this market, especially as a percentage of loan value, and the fact that there is limited public information about these customers, making it hard to evaluate risk.

According to CEMEX, the implied rate is much lower because only 27 percent of the membership fee constitutes the financial payment for the program while the remaining 73 percent is used to cover costs. From these assumptions, the annual implied nominal interest rate is well below that of typical microfinance institutions.

Conclusion

As PH's customers and promoters attest, having a comfortable home allows them to start businesses, give their children better educational opportunity, and feel more confident about their future. Furthermore, it creates employment and entrepreneurial opportunities for women in these communities, thereby enhancing their social status and individual agency. Yet, unlike a traditional corporate social responsibility project, PH is a profitable and sustainable venture. The low-income customer segment in Mexico has been traditionally ignored because it is perceived as unprofitable and risky. PH demonstrates, however, that serving this segment can be profitable and that, even though there are unique risks involved in conducting business with this segment, they can be mitigated through serious commitment to engaging customers and addressing their particular needs and values. PH's ability to help low-income Mexican families while improving its own bottom line is a compelling model for other multinational businesses seeking to generate corporate value while improving the lives of some of the world's neediest families.

CHAPTER FIFTEEN

CREATING STRONG BUSINESSES BY DEVELOPING AND LEVERAGING THE PRODUCTIVE CAPACITY OF THE POOR

Kapil Marwaha, Anil B. Kulkarni,
Jipan K. Mukhopadhyay, S. Sivakumar

In this paper we reason that unprecedented economic and social value can be created by a self-reinforcing process whereby business invests to develop the productive capacity of the poor and then leverages this capacity as an input to strengthen business competitiveness and growth. We illustrate this proposition with the help of case studies and show that the economic and social value created accordingly is far greater than what may be achieved by merely selling goods or services to the poor.

Selling to the Poor vs. Developing and Leveraging Their Productive Capacity

According to some recent propositions, businesses that increase the capacity of the poor to consume by providing affordable and easy access to goods and services tap into a new, enormous, and viable market. Claims have been made that when the poor are treated as consumers, they can reap the benefits of respect, choice, and self-esteem—and also climb out of poverty. However, as the pragmatic analysis of this paper shows, these propositions may appear intuitive but their veracity is as yet unproven.

Increasing the Poor's Capacity to Consume

The rich have a high capacity to consume. This is not simply due to the lower unit costs they face, but also because of their higher level of income. Conversely, the poor have a low capacity to consume; again, this is not simply because they face high unit costs[1] but rather because they earn a *low level of income*. We make this point because, at the end of the day, the tiny amount of "consumer surplus" captured by the poor on their daily survival budget of $1 or $2 hardly makes them a feasible and sustainable market for companies. Changes in income, however, can have a powerful effect. According to India's National Council of Applied Economic Research, when agricultural output (and therefore income) is high, sales of consumer durables are also high.[2] Thus any attempt to grow the poor's capacity to consume must focus on increasing their income.[3]

Climbing out of Poverty

Poverty is the severe condition of economic deprivation suffered as a result of being unable to sufficiently realize the economic potential of one's own talents and efforts. In the case studies that follow—all of which describe business models with a strong poverty reduction focus—we observed that the productive capacity of the poor was first organized, developed, and harnessed by an external catalyst in order to produce wealth. Notably, current engagements of "selling to the poor" are often a case of selling essentially to those *low-income* individuals who are already above the clutches of poverty. Businesses should not operate under the mistaken belief that servicing this segment is equivalent to true poverty reduction.

The Model

Our model describes a self-reinforcing process whereby business invests to develop the productive capacity of the poor, leverages such capacity to strengthen business competitiveness, and drives growth—creating a sound business model capable of creating unprecedented economic and social value. The model offers an efficient value chain as well as a higher scale of operations for business on the one hand, and reduction of poverty and economic dualities in society on the other.

These are the essential requirements of this model:

• The productive capacities of the poor are organized, developed, and leveraged as inputs to business.
• Such processes contribute to creation of commercial value for business.

- This commercial value yields economic surplus; that is, the commercial value exceeds all costs involved in its creation and strengthens competitiveness or business growth.

- The poor are remunerated in a fair manner for the goods and services they provide.

Through such a process, the poor become an important part of the definition of business, to the benefit of both parties. We elaborate on this after presenting profiles of three enterprises on which our research is based.

Gujarat Cooperative Milk Marketing Federation (GCMMF)

GCMMF is India's largest food product marketing organization. It is a state-level apex body of milk cooperatives in Gujarat that aims to ensure fair returns for low-income farmers and also high-quality products at reasonable prices to consumers. Table 15.1 features data on GCMMF's membership, production, and sales.

GCMMF's products—milk and a range of milk products—are marketed under the Amul brand. Development programs offered by the cooperative on topics such as breeding improvement, cleanliness, and leadership, coupled with milk processing and procurement, ensure that the Amul range of products are market leaders imposing stiff competition on even well-known multinationals that operate in this sector in India.

Shri Mahila Griha Udyog Lijjat Papad (SMGULP)

SMGULP is an organization that has acted as a catalyst in empowering poor urban women across India for the last four decades. Based on Gandhian business principles,[4] SMGULP today has more than forty thousand women members (workers) in sixty-two branches and forty divisions across thirteen Indian states. SMGULP's main product is a thin, round, savory snack called *papad*, production of which is the major activity of its members.

TABLE 15.1. GCMMF'S PROFILE.

No. of producer members:	2.42 million (largely subsistence farmers)
No. of village societies:	11,615
Milk collection (total 2004–05):	2.08 billion liters
Milk collection (daily average 2004–05):	5.71 million liters
Annual sales (2004–05):	US$645 million (US$3.2 billion by purchasing power parity)
Distribution network:	3,000+ dealers, 500,000+ retailers

Source: Company interviews.

SEWA Trade Facilitation Centre (STFC)

Promoted by the Self-Employed Women's Association (SEWA) and established in 2003, STFC is a company owned by about thirty-five hundred poor women artisans pursuing craft activities in drought-affected and disaster-prone districts in Gujarat, India. These artisans are the shareholders and owners of the company and the suppliers of traditional hand-embroidered products. STFC converts their traditional skill set into a major income-generating activity that proves to be an effective disaster mitigation tool. STFC delivers a range of support programs to the artisans, including marketing and product development support, quality standardization, access to capital, and state-of-the-art technology.

Key Learnings

Our research of these enterprises has afforded us several insights.

First, regarding essential requirements, the cases we have outlined all meet the four requirements of our model. These companies *organize, develop, and leverage the poor's productive capacity as a key input to their business.* The productive capacity of the poor is latent. Without the assistance of external agents, it is improbable that they will organize and develop their productive capacity. The organizations covered in our study all served as external catalysts, organizing and developing that productive capacity, which they then leveraged into a business model.

GCMMF's origins can be traced to the work of a handful of individuals who organized farmers and strengthened their productive capacity. Today GCMMF is a highly successful business that has as its underpinning 2.4 million farmers hailing largely from a subsistence farming background. The productive capacity of the farmers continues to be developed through a series of training programs.

Similarly, SMGULP has organized, developed, and leveraged the skills of more than forty thousand poor urban women. STFC has organized thirty-five hundred poor artisans and delivers integrated support solutions (product development, quality standardization, information systems, market support, and access to capital) to enable them to convert their traditional skills into the business mainstream.

These three examples also meet a second essential requirement because they *create direct commercial value* by harnessing the productive capacity of the poor. The latest annual turnover figures for GCMMF, SMGULP, and STFC are Rs.29 billion, Rs.3 billion and Rs.15 million, respectively (US$3.2 billion, $300 million, and $1.5 million by purchasing power parity), with exports to several countries.

These ventures also meet the model's third requirement because they *yield economic surplus* and use the productive capacity of the poor to strengthen their competitiveness and bolster growth. The commercial value this creates yields economic surplus; that is, the value exceeds the costs involved in its creation, and the processes used help to address the key constraints that limit productivity, innovation, growth, and competitiveness. This results in an economically feasible—in fact, competitively superior—value chain.

Financial soundness and profitable operations have seen GCMMF and SMGULP grow through the decades. A good deal of GCMMF's competitiveness can be attributed to creating quality inputs: basic inputs such as milk, culminating in advanced inputs including technology, training, and academic institutions.

Finally, the examples studied all *remunerate the poor in a fair manner.* Apart from being right conduct, remunerating the poor in a fair manner is a sound business practice to ensure scale and sustainability. Unlike dairy farmers in less successful dairy units,[5] GCMMF's members receive prompt payment at market prices for the milk supplied. Similarly, every member of SMGULP earns wages according to the labor she contributes. STFC's stated vision is to strengthen the capacity of women artisans with a view to provide them economic security.

Fair remuneration helps the poor liberate themselves from the stranglehold of poverty and elevate their social status. A World Bank report, "India: The Dairy Revolution," highlights the beneficial effects of higher income in relieving the worst aspects of poverty.[6] This report also discusses the impact of higher income on such specific dimensions of poverty as emancipation of poor women and education of poor children. Women in most Indian villages have a confined social role (much to their detriment). Noting that the social and productive impact of women's dairy cooperative societies is dramatic, the report points out that participation in income-earning activities gives women social endorsement to meet outside the home, develop leadership skills, and take business responsibility, thereby significantly changing the socially constructed pattern by which women lead their lives.[7] Noting that "for the very poor, education seems to be nearly as important as being able to buy enough to eat,"[8] the report also points out that "for the poorer villages, [the additional] milk income meant the difference between going to primary school and not being able to attend."[9]

It has been STFC's experience that the poor artisans' increased income has brought down rural migration by as much as 80 percent. We also noted through our field study of STFC how the income earned by the women constituted the main source of household income, thereby enlisting the indirect support of their husbands in their work—a groundbreaking attitudinal shift.

The case studies demonstrate that business models containing these essential requirements can create significant economic value while simultaneously catalyzing social development by alleviating poverty (Table 15.2).

It is pertinent to note that these essential requirements form the model's core prerequisites. The absence of one or more of the essential requirements in an initiative renders the initiative weak in its endeavor to create sustainable economic and social

TABLE 15.2. PROFILE AND BENEFITS OF THREE INDIAN ENTERPRISES.

	GCMMF	SMGULP	STFC
Structure	Cooperative	Cooperative	Company
Size of initiative	Large	Medium	Small
Focus area	Rural	Urban	Rural
Employees	Farmers	Women workers	Women artisans
Business benefits (impact on competitiveness)	Higher input volume; higher input quality	Lower input costs; higher input quality	Higher input quality
Social benefits	Increases productivity and income; includes empowerment of women	Increases productivity and income; empowerment of women	Increases productivity and income; empowerment of women

value. For example, many corporate social responsibility (CSR) initiatives are not designed for leveraging inputs to business (the first essential requirement); nor do they create economic surplus (the third essential requirement). Consequently, even companies with award-winning CSR programs limit their investment in CSR initiatives to (for example) 0.5 or 1 percent of net profits while, notably, no such limits are put on investment in business strategies that offer sufficient economic returns.

Conclusion

In closing, we must note that visionary leadership and empowered employees constitute the critical underpinnings of this model. All the enterprises we studied were established and run by committed leadership with a vision to fruitfully engage the poor through creative administrative mechanisms that strengthen the business value chain. Such leadership recognizes the important role of building capacity among the poor. The exuberance and commitment of the employees at the enterprises we visited was apparent and an obvious contributor to business success. Besides creating a successful business model, leaders must also win the trust of the poor. Without this critical ingredient, long-term business success is not possible.

CHAPTER SIXTEEN

ITC'S e-CHOUPAL

A Platform Strategy for Rural Transformation

Ravi Anupindi, S. Sivakumar

With a national GDP of US$2.6 trillion (based on PPP[1]) in 2002 supporting a population of about 1.03 billion, India is the seventh largest economy in the world. Twenty-four percent of GDP is derived from agriculture, and India's agriculture economy—measured in terms of arable land, diverse agro-ecological zones, and status as one of the top three producers of several major crops—also occupies a significant position in global agriculture and is potentially a food factory to the world.

These strong aggregate statistics, however, belie the plight of the rural Indian farmer, approximately 25 percent of whom live below the poverty line. Although agriculture comprises a quarter of the overall national economy, close to seven hundred million people, or 70 percent of the population, who live in rural areas depend on it. Indian agriculture is characterized by three fundamental features: *fragmentation, dispersion,* and *heterogeneity.* Fragmentation is implied by the size of land holdings, which average 1.5 hectares (3.7 acres). This lack of scale adversely affects the production efficiency, productivity, and quality of their produce and decreases their bargaining power. India's rural population is highly dispersed and made up of six hundred thousand villages with low population density averaging three hundred persons per square

This document would not have been possible without assistance from several people at ITC. In particular, we wish to thank Rajnikant Rai, Shailendra Tyagi, M. Srinivasa Rao, C. V. Sarma, and Abhijit Roy of ITC-IBD along with Ashesh Ambasta of ITC Corporate for their time and patience in numerous discussions on various initiatives as well as comments on earlier drafts of the paper.

kilometer. The geographical dispersion has an adverse impact on the connectivity—both physical and informational—between farms and markets. Finally, there is significant *heterogeneity* in Indian farming, relating to both type of farmer and type of crop. Heterogeneity among farmers exists in terms of their investment and risk-taking capacity, knowledge level, size of holdings, soil and rainfall conditions, cash flow needs, and so on. Heterogeneity is perhaps an asset, but it also poses a significant challenge in delivering customized solutions for productivity improvement, especially in the face of fragmentation and geographic dispersion.

The implications of these characteristics for farm productivity are further exacerbated by the lack of adequate *infrastructure*—physical (road connectivity, teledensity), social (health, education), and institutional (access to credit and risk management tools)—in the rural areas. The poor state of the physical infrastructure increases the cost of the physical and information flows between the farmer and the market. For example, problems with roads mean that an estimated 20–30 percent of produce is wasted because of inability to reach marketing and processing centers.[2] Inadequate social infrastructure, particularly in education and social security, limits the ability of the farmer to implement best practices and invest in productivity improvement. An unsatisfactory health infrastructure sucks away whatever little earning he has toward meeting essential health care expenses. Finally, the weak institutional infrastructure shifts the risk inherent in agribusiness to the party (the small and marginal farmer) least capable of bearing it. The gaps in physical and institutional infrastructure are partially compensated by the existence of multiple intermediaries in the farm-to-market supply chain. These intermediaries, though delivering critical value at low cost, also extract a significant share of the profits from the supply chain and thus leave little for the small farmer.

The result is that weak infrastructure combined with the characteristics of fragmentation, heterogeneity, and dispersion exacerbate the asymmetry of interactions between the farmer and the intermediaries, leading to a vicious circle of low equilibrium. Small holdings and dependence on monsoon rains reduce the farmer's risk-taking capacity, leading to lower-than-required investment and poor productivity. Coupled with the weak market orientation of these supply chains, the resulting value added is low, ultimately leaving scant margins for the farmer.

Past governmental efforts have focused on building unbundled institutions (auction yards, agricultural extension services, agro-inputs, credit, and the like) as alternatives to the exploitative cycle of dependency spun by the traditional intermediary. The effectiveness of these institutions has been hampered by the challenges of the rural reality outlined here. The government definitely has a critical role to play, but we believe that private companies can build a profitable business model out of streamlining the broken value chain and bringing the poor closer to the markets. Profits can be captured from the very process of streamlining the value chains, which in turn resource the creation of market infrastructure. Better market infrastructure can then be leveraged by the company to provide a host of products and services to rural consumers, increasing shareholder value through serving society. In this paper, we describe a case study of an Indian company in just such an endeavor.

The ITC Group (www.itcportal.com) is one of India's largest private sector companies, with market capitalization of approximately US$13 billion and annual sales of US$3 billion. ITC has a diversified presence in cigarettes, hotels, paperboard and specialty papers, packaging, agribusiness, branded apparel, packaged foods and confectionery, greeting cards, and other fast-moving consumer goods (FMCG). The International Business Division (IBD) of ITC, started in 1990, exports agricultural commodities such as soybean meal, rice, wheat and wheat products, lentils, shrimp, fruit pulps, and coffee. As a buyer of agricultural commodities, ITC-IBD faced the consequences of an inefficient farm-to-market supply chain. Increased competition in commodities as India liberalized its economy coupled with low margins made it imperative for ITC-IBD to rethink how it could create a sustainable competitive advantage in the farm-to-market supply chain of which it was only a part. With a mandate to grow its agribusiness, in 2000 ITC-IBD (hereafter referred to as ITC) embarked on an initiative known as *e-Choupal* to reengineer the procurement value chain using information and communication technology. The experiment has been extremely successful for ITC; as of 2005 the network consisted of more than five thousand e-Choupals and 127 hubs operating in six states of India for procurement of soybeans, wheat, shrimp, coffee, and spices.

In this paper we explain how the e-Choupal infrastructure has been architected as a business *platform* through which a host of products and services are provided, linking the local farmer to global markets. We first articulate the key elements of the platform. Subsequently, we illustrate the power of the platform using examples from soybean and wheat procurement and identifying economic and social benefits for various stakeholders. We conclude with discussion of how the platform has been leveraged in distribution and retail of products and services and its fit within the overall business strategy of the ITC Group.

e-Choupal as a Platform

The e-Choupal business platform consists of three layers, each at a different level of geographic aggregation. Each layer is characterized by three key elements that correspond to (1) the infrastructure (physical or organizational) through which transactions take place, (2) the entity (person or organization) orchestrating the transaction(s), and (3) the geographical coverage of the layer. Together, the three layers and three elements constitute a *3 × 3 infrastructure* for the platform.

The first layer consists of the village-level kiosks with Internet access (or *e-Choupal*), managed by an ITC-trained local farmer (called a *sanchalak*) and located within walking distance (one to five kilometers) of each target farmer. The relatively sparse population density in rural India justified location of one e-Choupal per cluster of five villages. Instead of building a separate infrastructure to host the kiosk, ITC decided to place it in the home of the sanchalak. The second layer consists of a bricks-and-mortar infrastructure (called hubs) managed by a traditional intermediary who has local knowledge and skills (called a *samyojak* in his new role) and is within tractor-riding distance (ten to thirty kilometers) of the target farmer. Since the infrastructure was initiated to facilitate procurement, it was decided that the hub should be located at a distance similar to those for other channels available to the farmer. Finally, the third layer consists of a network of companies (consumers of farmers' produce and providers of products and services to the farmers and other rural consumers) orchestrated by ITC, fostering a pan-Indian presence.

Together this three-layered infrastructure allows ITC to provide a complete end-to-end solution to satisfy the needs of both farmers and consumers at the village and global levels. The platform is illustrated in Figure 16.1. The 3×3 infrastructure operates on these key business principles:

• *Information and knowledge are free.* Any villager can walk up to the e-Choupal operated by the sanchalak and seek information and knowledge without having to pay for it.

• *Freedom of choice in transactions.* After accessing information at the e-Choupal, farmers are free to transact through any of the various channels including the one supplied by ITC. From the perspective of the farmer, freedom to transact is liberating and affords dignity. From ITC's perspective, a farmer's choice ensures the ongoing pressure to provide a compelling value proposition.

FIGURE 16.1. THE e-CHOUPAL PLATFORM.

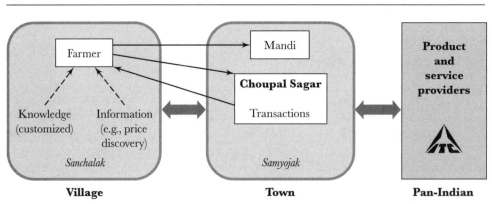

- *Transaction-based income stream for the sanchalak and samyojak.* Both the sanchalak and the samyojak earn revenues (through commissions) that are based on the transactions (purchasing or sales) they generate.

Procurement Value Chain

We illustrate the power of the e-Choupal platform using the procurement value chain for soybean and wheat. The farm-to-market supply chain for soybean and wheat, both before and after e-Choupal intervention, are quite similar. Therefore we illustrate reengineering of the procurement value chain using soybean first.[3] Subsequently, we discuss some unique issues and challenges in the wheat value chain.

Soybean Value Chain

The size of the soybean (popularly known as the "miracle bean") market in India is more than US$1.2 billion. Production of soybean in the country has been growing at the rate of 5.6 percent over the last ten years. Aggregate production is increasing, but the yield rate (averaging 870 kilograms per hectare) is still only one-third of the yield rate in the United States and Brazil.

Traditional Model. An Indian farmer typically has several channels to sell soybeans, but today close to 80 percent of the beans are sold through *mandis,* or regulated (spot) markets. The physical infrastructure of a mandi is provided by the government; the actual trading is done by private parties. The mandi prices also serve as a guide to other channels of trade.

Postharvest, a farmer typically likes to sell his crop quickly to pay off debts and prepare for the next season. With little reliable information regarding prevailing prices, the farmer transports the produce in bulk, covering an average distance of ten to thirty kilometers to the mandi. Once there, he engages a commission agent (CA),[4] who displays the produce in a heap in the mandi yard. The produce is then visually inspected and auctioned, typically using a straight auction monitored by a government-appointed agent. Following auction, the beans are manually bagged, weighed, and loaded on the buyer's vehicle. In an ideal situation, the farmer should get full payment for his produce. In reality, at many small mandis the CA often spreads the full payment over a number of days, forcing the poor farmer to make multiple trips to town.

As a buyer, ITC engages its own CA at a mandi. Typically, ITC would authorize its CA every day to buy a certain quantity at a price not to exceed a maximum limit. The produce is then transported to a processing plant or a warehouse.

Although the mandi is a fair price discovery mechanism in the context of fragmentation, dispersion, and heterogeneity, there are several inefficiencies in this traditional supply chain. From the farmer's perspective, they include (1) price discovery occurring too late for him to backtrack, (2) significant delays in the process that are due to peak-season congestion, (3) unscientific quality assessment and consequently payment rarely commensurate with quality, (4) handling losses, and (5) no guarantee of immediate full payment. In addition, the process also extracts a psychological toll on the farmer as he depends on the traders and CAs for (financial) assistance in other activities and cannot risk alienating them. Further, given the farmer's relative level of education, there is asymmetry in social standing between the farmer and the traders or CAs. ITC, as a buyer, also faced several challenges, including (1) higher ultimate cost of procurement owing to inefficiency of flows, (2) inability to capture same-day price fluctuations on account of lack of visibility in real-time transactions, (3) no guarantee of quality produce, and (4) lack of impact on the production cycle. By placing himself right in the middle of the flow between the farmer and ITC, the agent extracted rents from both parties.

e-Choupal Platform. Using the e-Choupal platform, the reengineered process works as follows. First, ITC offers up-to-date information regarding mandi prices on the e-Choupal Web portal. It also announces a procurement price for direct purchase at its hub. Now a farmer obtains price information before leaving his village. Should he choose to sell to ITC directly, the sanchalak gives the farmer a *parchi* (note) including his name, village, quality of produce, and the conditional price quote, authorizing the farmer to go to the e-Choupal procurement hub. At the hub, the farmer's produce undergoes a scientific inspection for quality and is weighed electronically. At each of these stages, the farmer is given appropriate documentation. Once the transaction is complete, the farmer is paid cash in full.

Overall, the reengineered supply chain reduces several nonvalue-added tasks, thereby improving efficiency of procurement. The contrast between the traditional channel and the e-Choupal platform is highlighted in Table 16.1.

TABLE 16.1. COMPARISON OF TRADITIONAL AND e-CHOUPAL PLATFORM MODELS OF PROCUREMENT.

	Traditional	e-Choupal Platform
Price discovery	Mandi	Village
Quality inspection	Visual	Scientific
Weighing	Manual (w/ material loss)	Automatic (no material loss)
Choice	Effectively none (only mandi)	At least two (ITC hub and mandi)
Prices	Unpredictable (mandi is a spot market)	One channel (ITC hub) with fixed price
Sell-to-cash cycle	1-2 days	3-4 hours
Distance traveled to sell	10-30 kms	10-30 kms
Labor and handling	More	Less

Benefits. Procurement via the e-Choupal platform offered several economic benefits to the farmer, ITC, and the CA. Table 16.2 shows the cost savings for the farmer as well as ITC.

The farmer benefits from *reduced transaction costs, better service,* and *superior decision making through choice.* For soybean procurement, for example, a farmer's cost has decreased on average by 50–60 percent primarily through cost-avoidance in terms of elimination of commissions, cost of handling, and other losses. Better service is a measure of quality; the "sale-to-cash" cycle for the farmer, measured as the time taken to complete the sale (from the time of arrival at the location of sale, whether hub or mandi, until the farmer gets 100 percent cash for his produce), has been significantly reduced. This cuts the farmer's selling expenses (avoided costs of board and lodging at the mandi location). Finally, since price discovery now occurs in the village, the farmer has a choice regarding where to sell (hub or mandi) as well as when (now or later). Monetarily, the value of this choice is already captured by the previous two metrics of reduced transaction cost as well as superior service. Furthermore, the availability of a competitive e-Choupal channel puts the farmer in a position to sell at a better price in other channels as well.[5]

The immediate benefit to ITC is improvement in procurement efficiency for soybeans. ITC has, on average, reduced its costs by 25–30 percent. Further, having a direct and cheaper source of commodities allows ITC to increase its revenue base by offering commodity services such as customer-specific structured offers based on lot size, delivery point, storage, pricing, quality segregation, credit, and the like, which were not possible when procurement was restricted to the mandis. In the last three years, ITC's turnover from soybeans has increased by approximately 60 percent. Finally, by buying from a farmer, ITC is the first company to put money in the farmer's pocket—more money than he ever got before—while treating him with dignity.[6] This power of buying with dignity is enormous for brand building.

Regarding benefits to the CA, obviously their role in procurement of commodities for ITC through the mandis has diminished. Given his local knowledge and

TABLE 16.2. THE e-CHOUPAL PROCUREMENT ADVANTAGE.[a]

Transaction	Mandi Supply Chain		e-Choupal Model	
	Farmer	ITC	Farmer	ITC
Freight	120	120	120	0
Labor and handling	50	40	0	40
Commission	150	100	0	50
Handling loss	50		0	
Bagging		75		75
Cash disbursement costs				50
Total costs (for each stage)	370	335	120	215
Total costs for the chain	705		335	

Note[(a)] All prices in rupees per metric ton.

resourcefulness, however, the CA was co-opted by ITC—as a *samyojak*—to provide several logistics services needed at the hubs in the e-Choupal network. The samyojak played a critical role in activities such as facility management, furnishing labor resources, buying and selling some of the goods for distribution, and thus earning commissions. Consequently, ITC gave the CAs an opportunity to expand their role from trader to service provider through the e-Choupal platform.

The Web portal in addition also acted as a knowledge delivery mechanism. It possessed information on best practices, localized weather information, general statistics on commodity production and consumption, links to commodity markets, discussion groups, and more. Such knowledge increases the awareness of the farmer, allowing him to be a more productive citizen.

The Wheat Supply Chain

Wheat is the most widely grown and consumed grain cereal in the world. With annual production of 65–75 million tons, India is the second largest producer in the world after China, accounting for 12 percent of world wheat production in 1999–2001.[7] Wheat production in India has increased almost tenfold in the last five decades and accounts for approximately 35 percent of India's total food grain production, a remarkable achievement made possible by the "green revolution."[8] In parallel, the government of India developed a system of institutions with the objective of supporting, controlling, and stabilizing grain prices and seeking to ensure basic food availability at reasonable prices to consumers.

Traditional Model. Given the importance of wheat in the Indian diet, about 70 percent is consumed locally or sold to the government for public distribution. The rest is available for private trade, which either goes to retail trade as grain or is sold to the flour mill industry. This industry supplies to bakeries, agro-industries, and restaurants, as well as retail.

A large fraction of the grain for private trade moves through the mandi system, a channel whose inefficiencies for the farmer as well as ITC we have already identified. An additional important issue is "quality loss" in the traditional wheat supply chain. There are several varieties of wheat, each with its own quality level, produced in India. The traditional mandi infrastructure, however, permits neither scientific analysis of the various quality levels nor proper segregated storage. Consequently, the grain released in the market is of one "aggregate" fair–average-quality (FAQ) variety. Often the traders would blend high-quality wheat with a lower quality and sell the mix at the price of FAQ wheat, pocketing the differential. Furthermore, the compensation a farmer receives is rarely commensurate with the quality of wheat he supplies.

e-Choupal Platform. In addition to efficiency gains of the type described earlier for soybean procurement, in wheat ITC saw opportunities to leverage the e-Choupal to compete on variety. On the demand side, there was sufficient evidence that lack of high-quality wheat stunted the growth of many domestic wheat-based agro-industries such as bakeries, biscuit manufacturers, and so on. ITC's internal research as well as independent research confirmed the potential for variety in wheat production and distribution to increase revenues significantly. Consequently, ITC invested in segregation and identity preservation infrastructure at its hubs, which included storage systems and testing equipment as well as manpower training and variety-based pricing mechanisms. Now when the farmer comes to sell wheat directly to ITC at its hub the produce is segregated into lots depending on the quality and variety of wheat determined after scientific analysis; the farmer is then compensated accordingly.

Benefits. Economic benefits similar to what was described for soybeans also accrue in wheat procurement. There are several additional benefits.

The farmer now gets payment commensurate with the quality of wheat he produces. In the long run, farmers will respond to the incentives and increase production of higher-quality grains, improving the overall quality of the produce in India.

Wheat procurement via the e-Choupal platform has allowed ITC to differentiate itself by competing on variety, increasing its market share to about 10 percent of the volume available for private trade. The segregation capability benefits external as well as internal customers. For the former, ITC becomes the supplier of choice. Internally, ITC's Foods Division,[9] which entered into branded and packaged foods in 2002, is able to leverage the e-Choupal procurement network to source high-quality wheat and produce better products without sacrificing efficiency. This capability has allowed the division to compete effectively in the branded foods market. In particular, ITC's Aashirvaad brand of wheat flour became a market leader within the short span of two years since launch. The superior sourcing capability also allowed it to innovate and offer better products at cheaper prices.

Over time, ITC has expanded the network for procurement of coffee, shrimp, spices, and so forth, adapting the hub infrastructure appropriately and deriving similar benefits for all stakeholders. The e-Choupal platform has also allowed ITC to change the dimensions of competition in agribusiness—which traditionally was treated as a commodity business—to include quality, variety, and commodity-based services.[10]

Conclusion

Although the e-Choupal platform was initiated to facilitate more efficient and effective procurement, the connectivity—both physical and informational—between the farmer and the market that it facilitated has allowed ITC to use it for (reverse flow) distribution of goods and services from the market to the farmer. For example, the platform has been leveraged to reengineer the agro-inputs value chain to give the farmer better-quality inputs with customized knowledge of its usage while benefiting the manufacturer with increased market penetration and better information about its ultimate customer to assist in new product development. To facilitate distribution, the hub operations were expanded to include a retail front called Choupal Sagar. Similarly, the platform is being used to deliver financial services presently focused on insurance. Finally, the infrastructure of the platform has allowed effective implementation of capacity-building initiatives, including water and moisture conservation, livestock development, and so on. ITC expects to capture the benefits of these capacity improvement projects through its procurement, distribution, and retail activities.[11]

The e-Choupal platform architecture is a 3 × 3 infrastructure operating on three key business principles. The resultant network organization has several important characteristics. It allows *community empowerment* through real-time information and customized knowledge. With freedom of choice and local management, it facilitates development of *community-responsive grassroots organization*. The system maintains *efficiency* through the competition inherent in choice. It overcomes the challenges of the rural landscape through virtual aggregation, giving it the *power of scale.* By collaborating with appropriate providers of products and services, it also delivers the *benefits of specialization.* Finally, with anchor business support by ITC—the network orchestrator—the platform provides an *increasing returns ecosystem.* Thus the 3 × 3 architecture, in conjunction with the three business principles, effectively deals with rural India's three fundamental characteristics while side-stepping the three infrastructural inadequacies, thereby creating a universal business platform. In the process, ITC creates a "virtuous cycle" through increased incomes and trust building, and it captures the latent value in rural India's dormant markets.

The e-Choupal effort is central to the success of ITC's International Business Division, but it also has had a significant effect on ITC's overall business strategy in terms of having an impact on other ITC businesses leveraging the e-Choupal channel as a source of supply as well as providing market access for their products and services.

Over the next seven to ten years, ITC's vision is to create a network of twenty thousand e-Choupals and more than seven hundred Choupal Sagars (expanded hubs with retail and other services) entailing investment of nearly US$1.15 billion, thereby extending coverage to one hundred thousand villages—representing one-sixth of rural India.

√ good

CHAPTER SEVENTEEN

NESTLÉ'S MILK DISTRICT MODEL

Economic Development for a Value-Added Food Chain and Improved Nutrition

Ray A. Goldberg, Kerry Herman

What people pay for consuming food and what people are paid for producing food are political questions as well as economic issues. Violent swings in food prices put pressure on those least able to adjust to change: the poor, small-scale farmer and the low-income consumer. As a result, the private sector has an important role to play in improving the efficacy of the food system as it responds to consumer health, nutrition, and economic development needs in a socially and environmentally responsive manner.

Since its inception, the Nestlé Company has recognized this responsibility. Its milk district model, discussed in this paper, has given small-scale producers and landless laborers the opportunity to become part of the economic system. It has done so in a manner that developed local leadership; local research; and local grading, storage, and distribution systems while cooperating and partnering with local, regional, and national governmental authorities. It has also done so to respond to the growing nutritional needs of the countries in which it is involved.

This paper is an excerpt from "Nestlé's Milk District Model: Economic Development for a Value-Added Food Chain and Improved Nutrition," HBS case no. 9-406–906, Boston: Harvard Business School Publishing, 2005.

The Nestlé Milk District Model

The world's largest milk company, Nestlé holds a leadership role in the global dairy system and has a long history of building supply chains by working with producers directly or through farmer cooperatives and governmental institutions. The company has consistently built food systems that contribute positively to the financial well-being of producers, the nutritional needs of consumers, and the economic development of many countries around the world.

Nestlé's successes have been due in no small measure to being an engine of rural development through its milk district model, and to the care the company has taken with its supply chain—something increasingly valued by consumers in the wake of various food safety and security concerns and rising public interest in health and nutrition. Most recently, Nestlé's milk districts in Pakistan, Brazil, Mexico, Chile, India, and China, among other nations, reported substantial positive results. In 2004 in Pakistan, for example, Nestlé purchased close to 253,000 tons of fresh milk, up from almost 145,000 tons in 1998. More important, the number of farmers selling milk to Nestlé in Pakistan rose from 104,000 to more than 130,000 in that same time. In Brazil, Nestlé's milk producers almost doubled their daily output from 1989 to 2004, going from 405 liter to 978 liters per day. From 1980 to 2004, Nestlé's total yearly intake in India increased by a factor of five, from about 50 million kilograms to almost 250 million kilograms. In China, milk sales per farmer increased by 30 percent from 2002 to 2005, and farmers were receiving an average of US$300 a month—twelve times the national average farm income in that country.

Nestlé S.A.

Founded in 1866 in Switzerland, Nestlé has grown from a small company producing powdered milk and cereal products for infants into a global food company feeding much of the world's population. Increasing diversity and fragmentation of world markets called for local sourcing to ensure the freshness, quality, and competitive costs of Nestlé's products. By the end of World War II, Nestlé was more decentralized; its traditional manufacturing center—Europe—was replaced by a dispersed distribution system as import restrictions and local sourcing became a highly important factor in local manufacturing. Nestlé began establishing factories in developing countries as early as 1921 in Araras, Brazil; then in other countries in Latin America; and later around the globe. Postwar, the company focused on a diversified policy within each food sector in order to meet consumers' needs. New products were added as growth accelerated and companies were acquired.

Through the 1990s, as trade barriers fell and world economic markets developed into integrated trading areas, Nestlé was well positioned to serve new markets opened in Central and Eastern Europe, Africa, China, Brazil, Chile, and other Latin American countries, while maintaining its leadership role in India, Pakistan, and other markets. By 2005, Nestlé had sales of $68 billion, with five hundred factories in eighty-three countries and 247,000 employees around the world.

Nestlé and Global Dairy

There are few genuinely global players in the dairy products market, and only four (Nestlé, Danone, Fonterra, and Parmalat) with representation in every region. The geographic fragmentation of the market is underlined by the global importance of companies such as the U.S. manufacturer Dean Foods and the Japanese players Morinaga Milk Industry, Meiji Dairies, and Snow Brand Milk, despite the fact that they register significant sales only in their native regions. Other major players are India's Gujarat (Amul Dairy) and China's Bright Dairy. Cooperatives play a major role in the dairy system in both the developed and developing world.

By 2000, there were several prominent changes taking place in the developing world's dairy system. Farmers themselves were building successful institutions and powerful cooperatives, such as Gujarat and Fonterra. To hold on to its position, Nestlé needed to maintain its leadership role and continue to develop partnerships with such institutions where and when appropriate. Consistently, Nestlé went to local farmers within their factory regions to establish a steady and secure supply of fresh milk that improved the long-term viability of the farming community and fostered new opportunities for those outside the commercial system. Procurement needs and issues of food safety, quality, and national priorities drove this strategy.

Nestlé set up one of its first milk districts outside of Europe in the 1930s, in Ocotlan, Mexico; by 2004, Nestlé had adapted its milk district model across a range of regions, among them many Latin American countries, the Caribbean, much of Asia, and also Africa. As conditions in emerging markets became more competitive, Nestlé looked for better, more economical, and more efficient ways to manage the supply chain and maintain product standards.

Competitive conditions often necessitated setting up collection centers and factories in more remote rural regions in these countries, where a low-cost production system relying on grassland or crop residue for fodder made the district economically and socially viable. This meant Nestlé frequently worked in remote areas where conditions were undeveloped; prior to its arrival the local population was frequently partially or completely excluded from the national and global market. Once a milk district was built, these constituents often reaped benefits far beyond selling and producing milk: access to veterinary expertise, infrastructure, training, grading systems, quality and safety controls, and a fair and transparent pricing and marketing system, as well as a financial support system. For most regions, more than 90 percent of the total cost of milk delivered at the factory gate was paid to farmers. The total rural economy benefited from the milk district model in improving all related activities and the transfer of knowledge to the producer, the producer's family, and the community at large.

Setting up a Milk District

In its simplest terms, setting up a milk district involved negotiating agreements with farmers for twice-daily collection of their milk, installing chilling centers in the larger communes and collection points in the villages or adapting existing collection infrastructure, arranging transportation from collection centers to the district's factory, and implementing a program to improve milk quality. Selection of a location was based on an in-depth analysis and was informed by several factors:

- Present milk production quantities and production potential of the area, according to available fodder resources, agricultural land, and farmers' interest in dairy.
- Present milk production costs and milk prices in the area were also factored in. This excluded many higher-cost areas near cities, where the raw milk market was very competitive and often occupied by companies producing fresh milk products with high margins.
- The income farmers could earn from fresh milk versus the income from alternative (that is, not supplementary) crops was taken into account.
- Present milk collection systems (if any), the presence of competitors, current milk quality, and potential to achieve the required quality were also assessed.

The Nutritional Impact. Creating a greatly expanded dairy industry through the Nestlé milk districts not only benefited milk farmers and their families but also had a significant impact on the nutrition of the country. Milk and milk products play an essential role in consumer nutrition, serving as an important source of energy, protein, calcium, magnesium, and phosphorus, as well as many essential vitamins and trace minerals. Milk contains a good quantity of protein, and the nutritional quality of its protein is first-rate. It furnishes the eight essential amino acids as well as many others.[1] Milk protein carries a high amount of lysine, which makes it the ideal complement to cereals notoriously low in this essential amino acid and which frequently forms the basis of most developing-world diets.

Procurement at Nestlé: Applying the Milk District Model. In 2004, Nestlé spent $2.2 billion for fresh milk alone,[2] either with farmers or third parties. Nestlé purchased raw dairy materials from three sources: semiprocessed milk solids such as powders, fresh milk from farmers, or fresh milk from third parties. Nestlé's sourcing principles guided relations with farmers and explicitly emphasized sustainability and good environmental practices.

Safe, high-quality food products were Nestlé's chief priority, and direct procurement made traceability easier. To ensure quality, Nestlé had an assurance plan with training and manuals detailing good farm practices for each district. Farms were audited regularly to ensure requirements were followed. Nestlé continuously extended technical support to farmers to reach certain quality or competitive standards, and testing was ongoing at the collection and cooling centers.

With fresh milk, food safety was a primary concern. To ensure a secure and economical supply, direct procurement was sometimes the best answer. Procuring directly from farmers had advantages and disadvantages. Direct access to the farmer could better regulate quality and stabilize the supply and cost of the product, but it was less flexible because Nestlé had to buy the entire quantity offered by the farmers.

The company therefore worked to have stable business relationships with its farmers. Surplus supplies presented less of a challenge for Nestlé than they did for the farmer. The expense of buying up surplus in the springtime was countered by the security of a steady supply at a stable price throughout the entire year, especially when milk production was sparse. For the farmers, the predictability of a regular monthly payment from Nestlé was an important element too.

By the end of 2004, Nestlé had approximately 290,000 dairy farmers supplying Nestlé factories directly. Of those, approximately 130,000 were in Pakistan, 70,000 in India, 30,000 in China, 12,000 in Morocco, 2,000 in Uzbekistan, 9,000 in Sri Lanka, 3,500 in Peru, and 3,500 in Panama. Almost all suppliers in the countries mentioned were small-scale producers. In 2004, small-scale producers (producing less than fifty liters a day) delivered an estimated 33 percent of Nestlé's fresh milk supply in 2004, while large-scale producers (producing more than four thousand liters a day) supplied less than about 15 percent. The balance was supplied by medium-scale producers.

Wow!

Building Capacity. To help get a district started, Nestlé brought in several expatriates to run a new factory. Unlike other companies, it also cultivated local resources so that almost all countries today have 100 percent local leadership. Expatriates were often from an earlier first-wave country, where the milk district model was already in place. First-wave milk district expatriates had more credibility with the local farmers and factory workers and allowed the company to expand in new geographical areas and rely on skills from people developed in the first generation of the model. Over the years, Nestlé developed local people by sending them from one country to another, transferring knowledge and best practices; eventually most returned to their home country.

One main bottleneck to the model was ensuring that Nestlé had enough experienced milk district expatriates to keep up with growth in developing countries.

Encouraging Sustainable Production. Both Nestlé and their farmers worked continuously to maintain environmental balance and sustainable farming practices as they introduced and grew dairy activities. In some regions, training was developed in partnership with local universities. In Brazil, for example, Nestlé (through Dairy Partners Americas) conducted the Dairy Farming Development Program, offering training to college students attending programs in veterinary medicine, agronomy, animal husbandry, dairy product technology, food engineering, and land surveying courses. In India, an innovative project was conducted to produce biogas from manure and other wastes, for use in the production of energy.

Some of Nestlé's milk district regions were not based on grassland or pasture fodder. Instead they relied on residues from local crops—especially corn stalk in China. In these instances, cows were not in the field grazing, and therefore managing their waste was a concern. To address this, Nestlé partnered with local universities and the Swiss College of Agriculture to identify methods for milk district farmers to counter the potential imbalance of nitrogen and improve their productivity by recycling cow manure as fertilizer. Although this meant an additional investment in storage, transport, and spreading of manure, as well as export of 85 percent of the manure to crop farms, both the local environment and the farmer's overall situation were improved.

Economic Benefits. Nestlé's activities in a milk district generated considerable income, for both the farmer and the community. According to Hans Jöhr, Nestlé's corporate head of agriculture, "Once you start to operate a factory in a region, the farmers see this is not a development project like those that a government might finance, where you come in for one, two or three years, and then leave when the project is over. If we are setting up a factory, we're there to stay for tens of years; you have to justify the investments to your shareholders. It is a very strong message to send to the local communities, and it says that we are really going to buy local raw materials."

From 2001 to 2004, milk sales per farmer increased by 30 percent, and the milk supply experienced an overall improvement in quantity, composition, and bacteriological quality. Nutrition, health, and income indicators all improved substantially in each region.

Conclusion

Jöhr described the role Nestlé played across the many regions where it operated:

In fact, building milk districts is not the core business or core competence of Nestlé. But there is a need to set them up, and then one day farmers will be able to organize themselves and form organizations such as a breeder's association of the region, and so on. Once we have built these capacities, then capable and skilled local people will take care of that and will continue to do that. We are trying to put in some incentives there, to help build that capacity in order to make sure that later on people can be self-responsible for carrying on these activities. And these activities should definitely have a positive impact on productivity increases and quality assurance and food safety issues, which is a benefit for us at Nestlé. And once it's established we can move out and really concentrate on what we are good at: that's developing finished products and R&D of new ones.

To continue its growth in the developing world, Nestlé's milk district model will have to find ways to function in less productive dairy systems, ways that are based on grasslands or other sustainable fodder. Although milk yields are lower and farther removed from urban centers, the cost-effectiveness of the milk production can remain competitive against milk powder imports from dairy powerhouses such as New Zealand. Nestlé CEO Peter Brabeck-Letmathe recognizes that Nestlé is looked to as a leader in helping the food system improve the position of low-income producers and low-income consumers through their own activities and through partnerships with cooperatives and public and private institutions. He is concerned to leverage the company's experience in countries such as Pakistan, India, Brazil, and China to maintain a leadership position in the global food system, consistent with its strategy as a wellness company and a partner in improving the food system for the benefit of all participants and the consumers it serves.

PART FOUR

BUSINESS AND LEADERSHIP MODELS

Consumer insight is critical to business success in penetrating the base of the pyramid. The chapters in Part Four highlight successful business models that are customer-centric and leverage the poor's social capital. However, equally important is the value system of the corporation seeking to reach out to the poor, and the depth of commitment to this value system among employees at all levels.

Drawing on eleven case studies in Latin America, James Austin and his coauthors, in "Building New Business Value Chains with Low-Income Sectors in Latin America," conclude that mainstream corporations must overcome four common challenges in addressing base-of-the-pyramid consumers: bridging cultural gaps, understanding low-income consumers, developing creative solutions to make products and services affordable, and building new low-cost value chains (especially new distribution systems) to reach the poor economically. Austin and colleagues emphasize leveraging partnerships and engaging the community in the production and consumption process as crucial ways to keep costs down in the interest of affordability.

Yet, as Gerardo Ablaza and the coauthors of Chapter Nineteen point out in "Viable Business Models to Serve Low-Income Consumers: Lessons from the Philippines," marketers can adapt their programs to the base of the pyramid and generate sales without necessarily having a positive social impact on the poor communities in which they operate. They cite the positive example of Manila Water in the Philippines, which offered new options to poor communities: collective installation of water spigots (each serving multiple households) and collective billing (allowing group insurance coverage of each installation). As a result, community spirit increased and delivery costs were lowered as community members became agents of the company, watching out for unauthorized persons tapping the water supply.

Closing this section, Rosabeth Moss Kanter's "When Giants Discover the Disadvantaged" highlights the importance of sustained leadership on the part of top management in explaining how private sector corporations can succeed in serving the poor. Drawing on two examples from the financial services sector, she notes that it is not sufficient to simply adapt a business model, product design, or service delivery system to the special demands of the poor segment of the market. The values and culture of the corporation, especially a climate of entrepreneurship and social responsibility, are critical to motivating employees at all levels to take the segment seriously.

CHAPTER EIGHTEEN

BUILDING NEW BUSINESS VALUE CHAINS WITH LOW-INCOME SECTORS IN LATIN AMERICA

James E. Austin, Patricia Márquez, Ezequiel Reficco, Gabriel Berger, Cristina Fedato, Rosa Maria Fischer, Juliano Flores, Henry Gómez-Samper, Francisco A. Leguizamón, Gerardo Lozano Fernández, Andrea M. Prado

Business engagement with the poor is fraught with challenge. Yet building new business value chains with low-income sectors also holds significant potential for generating returns to companies as well as benefits to society. This paper presents initial findings of research currently under way at member schools of the Social Enterprise Knowledge Network (SEKN).[1] Our objective is to focus on the distinct economic roles of low-income consumers, suppliers, and business partners for a select number of companies drawn from across Latin America. Three research questions are addressed: What leads companies to engage low-income groups? What are the key challenges faced, and what management practices do they employ to overcome them? What has been the social and economic impact of these engagements?

Our field-based studies of eleven cases reveal considerable diversity among low-income groups and how companies and poor communities can pursue promising opportunities through innovative engagement. Table 18.1 lists the cases, shows the nature of the link between the company and low-income sector, and notes whether the poor are largely urban, rural, or semirural dwellers. The companies in our sample run the gamut of three public utility providers (Aguas Argentinas, AA; Gas Natural BAN; and AES-Electricidad de Caracas, AES-EDC); CEMEX, which sells building materials to low-income groups in Mexico; Costa Rica's CSU-CCA Group, a food processor and supermarket operator; Brazil's Orsa (a pulp and paper mill) and Natura (a cosmetics manufacturer); Colombia's Sucromiles, which developed a powder calcium citrate supplement for the poor; the U.S. firm Starbucks, which sources coffee from subsistence growers in rural communities in Chiapas, Mexico; the

TABLE 18.1. CASES REVIEWED.

Cases	Initiative with Low-Income Sector	Scope	Role of Low-Income Sector	Need Met
Aguas Argentinas	Drinking water and sewage in Buenos Aires low-income neighborhoods	Urban, local	Consumers	Drinking water
Gas Natural BAN (Argentina)	Providing natural gas to low-income community Cuartel V in Buenos Aires province	Urban, local	Consumers	Natural gas
AES-Electricidad de Caracas (Venezuela)	Barrio Eléctrico: prepaid electric system in a 300-family shantytown Cero Maraña: dealing with illegal connections in shantytowns of Caracas	Urban, local	Consumers	Electric energy
CSU-CCA Group (Central America)	Sourcing fruit from farmers in Costa Rica, Honduras, and Nicaragua	Rural	Suppliers	Income, technical training
CEMEX (Mexico)	Patrimonio Hoy: innovative housing services and construction program Construmex: construction program for Mexican immigrants to United States who want to build homes in their country of origin	Urban, rural	Consumers	Housing
Orsa (Brazil)	Sustainable initiatives of furniture making and manioc flour	Rural, local	Suppliers	Income, capacity building
Natura (Brazil)	Sourcing chestnut oil and other natural products from community coops	Rural, local	Suppliers	Income
Posada Amazonas (Peru)	Eco-lodge created in partnership between Rain Forest Expeditions and native community	Rural, local	Business partners	Income, capacity building
Sucromiles S.A. (Colombia)	Provide calcium citrate supplement to low-income consumers	National	Consumers	Health, malnutrition
Starbucks	Sourcing coffee from farmers in Chiapas	Rural, local	Suppliers	Income, capacity building
Monsanto	Serving poor, small-holder farmers in Mexico and all over world	Rural	Consumers	Income, capacity building, assistance

Peruvian lodge Posada Amazonas, a business partnership between an eco-tourism company and the indigenous community Ese'aja; and the agribusiness company Monsanto, working with nonprofit organizations to find new ways to serve small farmers.

Despite the disparities among the cases chosen, all these bottom-of-the-pyramid businesses had to overcome the same set of challenges: (1) overcoming cultural gaps, (2) relating to low-income sectors, (3) dealing with financial dimensions, and (4) building value chains.

Overcoming Cultural Gaps

Companies must be prepared to overcome a variety of cultural, social, geographic, and emotional cleavages that so often split Latin American society. The poverty level in some countries is as high as 80 percent, with significant rates of unemployment and informal economic activity. Profound differences exist between the educated middle-class and upper-class groups who are linked to an increasingly global economy and those left behind in rural as well as urban communities. The outcome of these cleavages is mutual misunderstanding,[2] which not only separates top management from middle managers and employees but also influences organizational attitudes toward the economically deprived.

Transcending Worldviews

Prejudice and stereotypes can lead businesses to think of low-income sectors only in terms of traditional, low-value functions. That was indeed the case of the eco-lodge Posada Amazonas, where Rainforest Expeditions' (RFE) young Peruvian engineers and their indigenous partners held quite divergent worldviews. RFE was initially focused on the community's assets, seeking to lease access rights to their lands. Over time, they began to view the community as a source of labor, gradually employing community members as workers. Finally, the company began to see the community as a partner and created a fifty-fifty joint venture with them. A successful, yet complex, partnership has evolved between RFE and the Ese'aja community. Widely differing attitudes on work practices among groups, stemming from altogether dissimilar lifestyles, pose an unrelenting daily test to the enterprises' development.

Electricidad de Caracas (EDC) in Venezuela, founded by members of the local patrician elite at the start of the twentieth century, traditionally targeted clients from the middle and upper classes. Even though the inhabitants of Caracas's burgeoning slums had been stealing energy from the company's power lines for years, EDC never thought to look at the slum dwellers as potential customers. So how does a company break out of its traditional mind-set to incorporate the poor? In this case, a takeover by the international company AES in 2000, coupled with poor financial results, led to a bottom-up revision of EDC's business model and an initiative to turn free-riding power users into paying customers.

Interestingly enough, the idea of targeting the low-income sector did not originate from top management. It was first raised by a group of technical staff members who had been with the company several years and lived right next to the city's poor communities. Eventually, management agreed to launch a pilot program to which workers could sign up voluntarily, outside their paid time. Encouraged by the results, the company committed to two initiatives: "Barrio eléctrico" (Electric Neighborhood) and "Cero marañas" (Zero Illegal Connections). The former was a pilot project to bring prepaid electrification to a low-income community. The latter was a process of eliminating illegally connected lines while encouraging neighbors to pay for their energy through an educational campaign highlighting the benefits of doing so.

The case of the CSU-CCA Group also shows the need for both parties to adjust their worldview. Nicaraguan farmers were accustomed to growing simple monocultures of beans or corn. About a third of them dropped out of the company's initiative because of the difficulty of adjusting to the new discipline and the demands of horticulture. They often misunderstood the instructions of the Costa Rican agriculture technicians, who were used to working with growers with a higher level of education and experience in horticulture.

Organizational Culture

As seen in these instances, culture can create inadvertent bias in the organizational context that must be changed in order to incorporate the poor.

At the time it was acquired by AES, EDC's corporate culture mirrored the values of the engineers who ran the company and the technicians it employed. Results were measured by kilowatt-hours produced or number of meters installed, not in terms of customer satisfaction. The fact that the company was a public utility with a monopoly on service also conspired against the creation of momentum inside the company to serve the poor. Over time, however, this attitude began to change thanks to both the pressure to generate revenues and the growing influence of those employees who were advocates for poor customers.

In Argentina, when AA management decided to begin addressing the poor's demand for water, the company first had to transform employee attitudes and approaches to serving the poor. To address this challenge, a Department of Sustainable Development was created that in turn trained twenty-five hundred employees on the difficulties low-income communities face and on best practices for constructive interaction with these communities.

In summary, overcoming individual and organizational cultural gaps is essential to developing business with low-income sectors. Myths and stereotypes about the poor—about their needs, aspirations, and lifestyles—are not confined to the psychological mind-set of individuals and groups but are also embedded in organizational culture. A company must sometimes significantly alter its management and operating structure in order to foster a new culture that enables business engagement with the poor.

Relating to Low-Income Sectors

Business engagement with low-income sectors entails generating insights, weighing strategies, and building relationships. One early challenge is building the capacity to obtain and interpret relevant information about low-income communities. Once these steps are under way, difficulties may be faced in overcoming mistrust and establishing fruitful communication.

Getting to Know Them

Standard consumer research rarely offers reliable information about poor consumers. Store audits, for example, may not survey retail outlets in low-income communities. The absence of useful knowledge about economically deprived people often deters companies from viewing them as potential customers, suppliers, or partners.

In the case of AES-EDC, where employees from the company played a key role in conveying information about slum dwellers and *barrio* dynamics, its blue-collar workforce pushed the idea in the periodic *cara a cara* (face-to-face) meetings with senior management. Once the idea got the go-ahead, this engineering-minded company innovated by hiring social workers and sociologists to document the traits and needs of the potential customers. For AES-EDC, this discovery process was lengthy—and sometimes dangerous. For example, when the company made its first attempt to explore the idea of using a prepaid energy card by surveying poor customers, its employees were received at the entry point of the barrio by a posse with drawn guns.

A company undertaking social initiatives can learn about low-income consumers on its own or through alliances with social welfare organizations. For instance, both Orsa and Natura in Brazil were previously engaged in social projects with local communities through NGO partnerships and had learned from the experience. For Starbucks, an alliance with Conservation International (CI) enabled it to understand how to work with outlying coffee growers to improve their product and meet company standards. CI had a team of three full-time and several part-time agricultural extensionists who visited coffee growers, lent assistance, and monitored results.

To understand low-income customers, companies need a solid understanding of previous market dynamics. In other words, they must ask how the poor engaged in business transactions and economic life before they arrived. This is critical to determining whether a business can bring a superior value proposition to the low-income consumer. In Argentina, Gas Natural BAN, thanks to its close relationship with the social housing foundation FPVS, learned how poor consumers met their energy needs without access to piped gas. Purchasing canisters of liquid gas cost consumers five times as much as direct service from BAN would, but the high cost of connecting and converting to natural gas (which entailed an outlay that could run as high as US$1,000) was an insurmountable barrier for these cash-starved potential clients.

In cases such as Starbucks and the CSU-CCA Group, where the poor serve as suppliers, it was critical to understand the existing market dynamics. As Michael Quinlan, CI's leader of the Chiapas project, observed, "Farmers are great economists: 'a day doing what I know, I feed my family. A day trying a new way, I might not.'" Thus if the company does not design mechanisms to reduce risk and generate immediate rewards, the new relationship might not prosper. Starbucks offered significant premiums over the prevailing market price to give farmers the incentive to adopt the practices needed to produce high-quality and environmentally sustainable coffee. Similarly, the CSU-CCA Group paid small farmers immediately upon receipt of fruits and vegetables, as opposed to the longer time frame it typically used with larger companies.

Using Partners

Having relevant knowledge about the poor and their needs is just the first step toward engaging them in business. Companies also face a lack of partners that can serve as intermediaries between them and the poor. The poor live in places and under conditions (economic, social, legal) that are often foreign to companies accustomed to serving mainstream markets. How do you approach that world? How do you talk to people in your target market if their language and everyday dynamics are different from yours? How do you nurture relationships? Companies surveyed resorted to insiders and NGOs, through whom they built a link to the community and from whom they could obtain specialized skills. These strategic cross-sector alliances appear to be very important as a bridge-building vehicle.

Following the lead of its own technical staff, AES-EDC decided to initiate a dialogue with local barrio leaders and request an informal "license to operate"—a step that yielded positive results. Eventually the company experimented by letting the community regulate energy use itself, through local leaders. These leaders (very often female) have come to play the role of account executive for the company, coordinating use of collective power meters with the prerogative of collecting payments and disconnecting those who fall behind.

Most of the companies in our sample worked through social development agencies, advocacy groups, community-based organizations, and government offices to establish trust with these new customers. For instance, Monsanto possessed little knowledge of or access to Mexico's small farmers. Consequently, it partnered with the Mexican Foundation for Rural Development, which had been working with small farmers throughout the country for decades to improve their productivity and standard of living. The foundation brought customer knowledge and credibility to the partnership; Monsanto brought new technology and financial assistance. This combination created a new distribution channel and system tailored to the low-income farmers' special needs and circumstances.

Partnerships with local leaders and independent organizations enabled businesses in our sample to achieve their objective of establishing ties with poor communities. However, as previous research has shown, cross-sector partnering is far from risk-free.[3] The CSU-CCA case illustrates this point: working with Nicaraguan NGOs diminished the overall efficacy of the enterprise, through delays caused by unnecessary bureaucratic procedures.

Governing the Relationship

Any initiative dealing with the impoverished is likely to involve multiple stakeholders. C. K. Prahalad acknowledges that working at the bottom of the pyramid will always involve co-creation of wealth on the part of different actors,[4] but he does not venture much into the specific challenges posed by doing so. Without proper governance arrangements, business engagement with low-income sectors is likely to fail, or never get off the ground.

In a broad sense, the concept of governance refers to the administrative processes and systems by which any enterprise actually works. In the context of doing business with low-income sectors, it entails tackling a number of relevant questions: How to make decisions effectively? How to establish fruitful partnerships with diverse small units? How to secure long-term commitments from them? In other words, how to articulate effectively and dynamically the interests of all relevant stakeholders? This is particularly important in initiatives where there is an essential asymmetry between the parties. In the corporate world, governance refers to the hierarchical relation between principal and agent, which develops in the context of a stable institutional framework. By contrast, business initiatives with low-income sectors are often governed through an ad hoc regime that emerges from a flat and unstable coalition. From our research, a particularly salient challenge for the poor is organizing themselves to become effective partners.

The experience of Starbucks in Mexico exemplifies the challenge of creating ad hoc institutional arrangements that can be leveraged to overcome the fragmented nature of the poor.[5] To reach the volume that Starbucks required for meeting its procurement needs, it had to aggregate the production of thousands of small-scale producers. This could not be done one-by-one, because negotiating with so many farmers would have imposed prohibitively high governing costs. Starbucks needed fewer interlocutors with whom to negotiate and reach agreements, establishing long-term commitments for both parties. "So we decided that the best way for those small farmers to be organized was to work through a business partner of ours," says Dennis McCray, manager of business practices for Starbucks.[6] "Essentially what we were saying was, 'If you want to sell to us directly you have to actually use an intermediary.' And so they created their cooperatives."

Organizing the poor in cooperatives is a widespread practice in our case sample, the importance of which should not be underestimated because it requires a unique vision of project management. The feasibility of doing so in some cases was considered a make-or-break factor by the private sector when it came to venturing into this market. Consider the experiences of Orsa and Natura, two socially minded private Brazilian companies that sought to turn the country's biodiversity into a source of economic, environmental, and social wealth.

Since 2003, Orsa Florestal has been engaged in development of sustainable forestry and agriculture with the communities of the Vale do Jarí. The experience has shown mixed results. A history of failed cooperatives in the region, coupled with a deeply ingrained culture of individualism and geographical dispersion of the farmers, conspired against the company's efforts to organize them into cooperatives. Farmers have demanded that Orsa Florestal buy their production individually, which pushes the governing and transaction costs of the initiative upward. Moreover, Orsa Florestal is finding it close to impossible to align more than five hundred individual farmers behind company strategy, or to change the way they do things.

The experience of Natura, on the other hand, has evolved in the opposite direction. Its Ekos product line is made from plant and vegetable oils traditionally used by indigenous communities. The company chose to launch a pilot project in the community of Iratapurú, based mainly on the area's environmental wealth and the expressed willingness of the community's farmers to organize around cooperatives. Natura identified leaders within the community and encouraged them to adopt transparent resource allocation practices, as well as other institutional arrangements that allowed effective self-regulation. Despite its strengths, the cooperative-based model is far from a panacea. Making decisions with a plethora of cooperatives can be a daunting task. As noted earlier, their operating culture does not always fit well in a business environment, and they are after all social organizations as much as productive ones; thus they tend to be riddled with interpersonal rivalries.

Natura's experience also serves to highlight another key governance issue: the need to prevent opportunism and opacity. In this case, Natura brought to the partnership an outside civil society organization, IMAFLORA (Instituto de Manejo e Certificação Florestal e Agricola), which eased the engagement by certifying that production met certain environmental and social standards. Despite the asymmetry between partners, IMAFLORA's participation guaranteed that the business was run in a socially responsible and profitable way.

Managing the Financial Dimension

If not tackled creatively, financial constraints become a critical factor in doing business with low-income sectors. Although the financial challenges of engaging the poor goes beyond simply overcoming insufficient purchasing power, the experiences of several companies in our study show that innovative payment schemes can go a long way in firming up a good business relationship.

Overcoming Insufficient Purchasing Power

Lack of disposable income or suitable collateral to guarantee loans or purchases on credit shuts out low-income sectors from traditional markets. To deal with this short-coming, several companies in our study designed arrangements that entailed group backing and peer pressure as a means for member families to benefit. One such arrangement has long been used by microlenders, where group members guarantee each other's loan; other payment schemes tap in-kind support. According to a CEMEX Patrimonio Hoy promoter, "Poor people lack economic capital, but they draw on social capital. When they come into the program, they mortgage their identity." Payment schemes offered to low-income groups by Starbucks, CSU-CCA, Gas Natural BAN, and AES-EDC were all positively received.

Companies must look for new ways to recover costs and generate a return. Initially, for example, AES-EDC proposed a prepaid energy card that was lauded by the pilot barrio community where it was tested but has yet to be approved by regulatory authorities. At the same time, the practice of prepaying for cellular phone services is widespread among the poor in Venezuela. In some cases, AES-EDC also targeted groups as clients through collective meters. All the group members were collectively responsible vis-à-vis the company, and one among them would serve as an account executive for the whole group. This individual would be in charge of tracking payment and eventually disconnecting those who fell behind on payments.

To build waterworks in poor communities, AA overcame its customers' economic limitations by allowing them to contribute labor. Installation costs represented a significant barrier to expanding service to low-income consumers, and labor accounted for as much as 50 percent of the total. Once the installment-cost barrier was overcome,

AA undertook a survey to determine the service rates that it could realistically offer customers in poor communities.

Sucromiles's Tricaltone product is an example of product innovation to reach poor children, pregnant women, and elderly individuals who have little access to milk. Tablet production is expensive because of the costs of starch and a special coating. To reduce costs, the company produced Tricaltone as a water-soluble powder packed in a can with a measuring spoon. The product's price is less than half that of any other calcium source in Colombia.

A Different Kind of Business Investment

Several of our cases show that companies doing business with the poor have to invest—on their own or in partnership—to develop potential consumers or business partners. Business ventures may be combined with philanthropic or other social initiatives, often defying their previous business logic and time frame.

For Monsanto, fulfilling its vision for "abundant food and a healthy environment" meant implementing a strategy that would reach beyond the normal bounds of commercial agribusiness and have an impact on the world's resource-poor and subsistence farmers. In their small-holder farmer program, the company recognized a potential business opportunity in the untapped market of the roughly seven hundred million small farmers who work half of the world's one billion hectares of farm land. However, given the precarious situation faced by these farmers, the company was fully aware that the program was a long-term investment involving philanthropic initiatives (such as employee voluntarism and microcredit programs) that ran in parallel with its commercial sales and technical assistance activities.

But companies do not have to face the financial burden of inadequate infrastructure on their own. The social value created by such ventures can open the doors for development agencies and social investors. For RFE, building an eco-lodge in the Amazonian rain forest posed a substantial financial challenge. Banks and financial institutions did not think the project was worth the investment, so RFE turned to international development finance institutions. The Peru-Canada Fund eventually decided to support the initiative, offering US$250,000 over a three-year agreement for infrastructure and furnishing. Similarly, the CSU-CCA Group had the support of international aid agencies for its Nicaragua program, which was the work of a cross-sector alliance. This was also the case with Gas Natural BAN's initiative. The Fondo de Capital Social provided US$3 million in financing and the World Bank gave a $250,000 innovation award to the partner NGO for carrying out the project.

Governments can also contribute to developing business with low-income sectors. The CSU-CCA Group had support from the Costa Rican Ministry of Agriculture and the Ministry of Health for education campaigns that raised product quality and eased the work for all involved. Coordinating efforts with the government was a successful experience; the group is planning to replicate it in the other Central American countries where it operates.

Unfortunately, our sample shows that working with regulatory agencies also entails some risk; relations between regulatory agencies and utilities are often politically charged. In Argentina, AA established a discounted rate, but at the end of 2001 the government did not permit the company to raise its fees in response to the economic crisis. In 2005, the company faced a US$600 million debt. In Venezuela, owing to delays in government approval, AES-EDC has been stalled in efforts to launch its prepaid system.

Building New Value Chains

Serving the poor successfully requires putting in place new value chains that cater to the specific characteristics of the group. Low-income markets are often characterized by low margins and high volume. Thus reaching this market most often implies creating innovative schemes that take into account the obstacles facing low-income people and successfully circumventing those obstacles.

The poor tend to live in remote or hard-to-access places. Reaching low-income sectors implies developing new distribution networks able to reach them, but at the same time keeping fixed costs low to make the enterprise viable. AA created whole new systems for billing and collection as well as construction that directly involve the poor in servicing low-income neighborhoods. Gas Natural BAN created an even more complex new value chain with operating functions shared by the company, a local NGO, the community, and financing agencies.

Construction of a new value chain often requires organizational flexibility to generate structures and develop practices so that the poor can effectively engage with the commercial channel. Starbucks lacked staff skilled in organizing communities into cooperatives and providing direct technical assistance. CI carried out these functions and Starbucks helped to ensure quality standards, created corresponding price incentives, and distributed the coffee into the high-value specialty market.

Participatory systems play a central role in developing these new value chains. AA brought together a variety of community actors, among them NGOs, the regulatory agency, and municipal officials. The approach was highly participatory in the diagnostic and prescriptive areas. For example, they abandoned their typical billing system, which relied on the postal service, and instead had local community organizations deliver bills and collect payments in person. The company also ran consumer education programs about the importance and careful use of water resources.

Gas Natural BAN also used a participatory approach, though one that was even more elaborate and formal because of the somewhat greater complexities of natural gas distribution systems. The NGO FPVS became the financial manager of a new community-established organization that directed construction of the natural gas networks. The company contributed to FPVS to help build the network, provided the gas, and created a billing system. In turn, the municipality has furnished the necessary construction authorizations, and a financial institution is making construction loans.

Sucromiles does not sell calcium powder directly to the poor but instead sells it to the Transcend Foundation, which then sells Tricaltone to companies that fortify their products with calcium and sells them door-to-door, and through a specialized consumer distributor.

In building new value chains, it makes sense to think of the philanthropic and business investments as complementary. The philanthropic expenditures are part of the process of developing supplier and consumer markets, which involves removing market imperfections. The temporal dimension is important: market development is a long-run investment process rather than a quick transaction.

A close look at the companies in our sample brings into question Prahalad's assertion that MNCs—with their global reach, extensive knowledge, and deep pockets—are in a particularly privileged position to engage with low-income segments.[7] Although the strengths that Monsanto and Starbucks bring to bear are undeniable, our research suggests that medium-size firms (such as Orsa or Natura in Brazil) and even small ones (such as Rainforest Expeditions, in Peru) can also make substantial contributions. What they lack in scale they can compensate for with flexibility, capacity to innovate, and boldness.

Assessing Economic and Social Value

The cases we have studied yield significant evidence that business engagement with the poor can simultaneously generate private profits and a better society.

AES-EDC not only tapped a new market but also tackled the long-standing practice of massive electrical free-riding, which had been considered undesirable but unavoidable. The problem is far from solved, but the trend has begun to reverse, and the prospects are encouraging.

For the community, electrical service has become safer and more reliable. In the past, the poor who depended on illegal connections periodically had to pay an informal supplier the cost of reconnecting to the system and new wiring, while also sustaining the cost of replacing burned-out appliances. At the same time, illegal connections were extremely unsafe, with high-voltage cables hanging low and unprotected. Moreover, AES-EDC's services, which now light up previously dark streets, have brought an enhanced sense of public safety to the Caracas slums.

Starbucks' project in Chiapas, which pays coffee farmers US$1.20 per pound (compared to the prevailing market price of US$.48), has raised incomes by 40 percent. Furthermore, because they now practice more environmentally friendly farming techniques, more natural habitat is being protected and river pollution has been reduced. Additionally, the increase in socially differentiated quality coffees has generated greater customer satisfaction and profitable sales for the company. The Mexican pilot project has been successfully expanded to Costa Rica, Colombia, and Guatemala and constituted the basis for formulating a radically different set of coffee purchasing guidelines incorporating environmental, social, and economic criteria for all the company's procurement operations.

The CSU-CCA Group supplier development program has significantly transformed the productivity and output quality of Costa Rica's small and medium farmers, and it is trying to do the same with Honduran and Nicaraguan small-holders. As a mass retailer, the group is in the position of having a transformative effect on supply chains and is using that power to generate social value for small farmers while simultaneously strengthening its supplier system—a step critical in making better products available to the consumer. For the farmers, the project has increased the value-added of their products, improved their capacity to export, and eliminated intermediaries.

AA's program was evaluated by a local university, which found that the company's water services brought a positive economic benefit to families and the community. Almost eighteen thousand people have gained access to water services through the program. Another even larger group of existing users benefits from service improvements.

For RFE, the fact that its eco-lodge was a community-owned venture became a differentiating feature and a source of competitive advantage in the eco-tourism market. Posada Amazonas could charge up to 40 percent more than others in the region and led its category in sales volume (10–15 percent more than its immediate follower). The business financially benefited both the company and the community as joint venture partners. It also fostered an environmental benefit, by preserving the rain forest as a productive asset. The community was able to increase its skill base through the management and technical training received from its business partner.

Tentative Conclusions

There are a number of possible lessons emerging from our research.

• *The opportunities are real and realizable.* The private sector has much to gain from taking a fresh look at low-income sectors, trying to identify the barriers that prevent them from accessing traditional markets, and then putting in place innovative schemes that take into account the specificities of the segment.

- *The poor must be key building blocks in new value chains.* Building new value chains can be enhanced by integrating the poor into decision making and management. When companies see them as active agents and partners rather than passive recipients, considerable latent organizational power and capacity is unleashed. These new value chains will often require companies to invest in training to build the poor's capacity to fulfill new value-adding functions.

- *Company workers can be leaders in entering the low-income sector.* A company's lower ranks may be better placed to develop empathy and understanding of the needs of those at the base of the pyramid. Even the best-intentioned senior leadership may be simply too removed from the realities of the poor to see what could be obvious to others. Senior leaders, however, play an important role in creating an enabling environment for such initiatives to prosper.

- *Social sector organizations can be powerful partners.* In accessing low-income sectors, the leverage of existing social organizations, networks, and practices proved highly effective. They served as bridging vehicles to facilitate the interface between the businesses and the disadvantaged groups. They brought along cultural understanding and credibility, as well as specific knowledge and skills that companies lacked. There are, however, great challenges in developing relationships with these new partners.

- *Access requires new delivery systems.* Access is a key, but only a starting point. Distributing goods or services to economically deprived populations or procuring inputs from them is usually challenging, because they often live in areas that are remote, hard to get to, or violent. To meet this challenge, companies must put in place specifically designed systems that take into account the living patterns of this segment.

- *Organizational culture must achieve compatibility with new clients.* At times, to serve low-income sectors a company's culture must be changed. Accessing the poor may require thinking out of the box.

- *Innovative and tailored business models are needed.* Serving the poor requires new business models that account for their specific characteristics and offer superior value propositions: innovation in products and brands, pricing and payment, distribution channels, and alliances.

Our examination of these Latin American experiences shows important opportunities for business to productively engage with low-income groups. Despite the challenges involved, the results reveal that if companies integrate the poor into new value chains, such ventures can unleash their productive potential and create significant business and social value.

skimmed

CHAPTER NINETEEN

VIABLE BUSINESS MODELS TO SERVE LOW-INCOME CONSUMERS

Lessons from the Philippines

Gerardo C. Ablaza Jr., Antonino T. Aquino, Christopher Beshouri, Kristine Romano, Jaime Augusto Zobel de Ayala II

This paper seeks to understand the business models of firms whose core business is *delivery of products or services to low-income segments, including the poor.* We want to know what it takes to profitably run a business that serves these segments and to determine if there are common, exportable principles and key success factors for companies operating in other industries and geographies. We are especially interested in businesses focused on core products and services—such as water, electricity, banking, and telephony—that can have a significant *developmental impact* on the communities where they operate.

Our motivation is threefold. First, low-income communities in the aggregate represent an enormous revenue pool. Second, private sector capital and skills are critical in developing infrastructure and institutions such as telecom, water, and banking, but investors need compelling examples that this can be done profitably in low-income areas. Third, finding breakthrough business models can have enormous developmental impact. For instance, effective water provision generates price and income effects; cheaper water leads to more income for other things and can raise the quality of life. Reliable telecom services can improve farmers' access to markets, ease the costly consequences of bad roads, and even allow safe transfer of funds. There are also positive

This paper has benefited from the generous input of many of our colleagues, including Blums Pineda, Jeff Tarayao, and Bryan Patrick Lim of Globe Telecom; Vicky Garchitorena of Ayala Corporation; Sherisa Nuesa and Glo DeCastro of Manila Water; and Joval Pantangco, Kendrick Chua, and Kristine Darang of McKinsey and Company.

207

spillover effects from these businesses in terms of creating viable community groups, raising awareness and education, and promoting a culture of entrepreneurship.

Scope of Inquiry and Approach

We focus on industries where expectations of profitability in serving low-income groups are low and developmental impact is expected to be high (Figure 19.1). In the first part of the paper, we develop a basic framework to understand the key characteristics businesses must contend with in serving low-income consumers. Some of them are familiar in type (for example, income level) but distinct in form (day laborers with little disposable income). Others are unique (culture, geography) to a low-income demographic.

In the second part of the paper, using a case from the Philippines, we examine how a business adapted its approach to reflect the characteristics of the low-income segment, including critical environmental factors. We look closely at community-based solutions and how our subject firm used them to address the unique characteristics encountered in serving low-income consumers. We derive broad exportable principles at work in these community-based solutions.

FIGURE 19.1. FOCUS ON BUSINESSES PERCEIVED AS UNPROFITABLE BUT WITH HIGH "DEVELOPMENTAL" EXTERNALITIES.

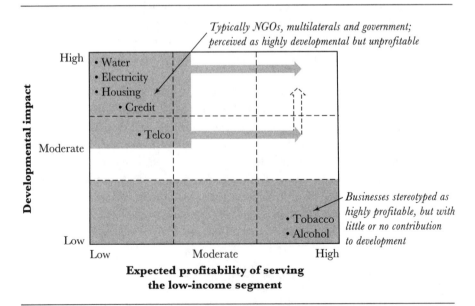

Lastly, we place the findings in the context of the corporate social responsibility (CSR) dialogue and consider how firms may be underestimating the value and impact of community-based initiatives on strategy and operations.

Three Key Insights from Our Work

Three common findings emerged from our analysis. First, success in serving low-income consumers requires developing distinctive customer insight and tailoring the business model to fit those characteristics. Tailoring the business model actually lowered operating costs and led to product innovations that had application beyond this segment. "Tailoring the business model" may sound straightforward, but it can take businesses some time to become aware of key characteristics and translate their understanding into actionable business models.

Second, community-based agents—individuals or groups drawn from the communities themselves—are needed to help businesses align incentives and promote the partnerships required to overcome the unique challenges of serving the low-income segment. This model works for a range of challenges, including principal-agent problems, such as those arising from low disposable income, asymmetric information, and cultural characteristics. They also foster a web of relationships and support structures at the micromarket level that can be used to deliver complementary or adjacent products.

Third, even though businesses may be engaged in what appears to be corporate social responsibility initiatives, these activities are actually central to the viability of the businesses in two ways. First, such activities are a unique instrument for resolving significant business model challenges, such as bill collection and infrastructure security. Second, they also positively affect the condition of low-income groups, helping businesses forestall adverse actions such as nationalization and subsidized pricing. In this respect, the community-based activities are not a by-product of a desire to do good, but actually an operational and strategic requirement. For the company we examine in this paper, the broad implication is quite clear: addressing social issues is not merely adjacent to strategy, but central to it.

Developing Business Models to Serve Low-Income Consumers

In many emerging markets, finding profitable ways to serve low-income segments is a huge revenue opportunity. There are at least ten fast-growing but low-income economies that represent new markets for successful players. Together they represent about half the world's population and nearly US$15 trillion in income.[1] Focusing on these markets is critical to long-term growth. In the Philippines, the bottom 90 percent of all households earns an average of US$600 per month, yet represents 60 percent of the country's purchasing power. Scale-based businesses must find ways to serve these segments simply to be viable.

A Framework for Understanding Characteristics of the Low-Income Segment

The low-income segment has important characteristics that raise the cost of doing business. Some are common to any business but grow more acute as income falls. Other characteristics are unique in that they arise precisely because of the demographics, culture, and geography of low-income markets. These characteristics pose challenges to business viability and can raise the costs of doing business (Table 19.1). Here we describe these challenges and their business model implications.

The relatively low purchasing power of low-income consumers gives rise to several challenges. The first is an *acquisition challenge:* that of bringing a consumer into the market. Mobile phone handsets represent a significant initial outlay for potential telecommunications subscribers. In the Philippines, a handset priced at Ph.P. 3,000 can easily be 15–25 percent of the income of an average D- or E-class consumer.

Informational problems add to the challenge of initial entry and sustaining demand over time. Information is vital to assessing the creditworthiness of potential customers, and crucial in provision of services involving a "postpaid" model. *"Parceling" challenges* arise from the low absolute level of income, which limits the quantity that can be purchased at any one time. Businesses need innovative methods (such as sachet marketing) to deliver products and services in parcels that match the limited daily cash flow of this buying segment.

If businesses do pursue the postpaid model, they have to contend with *collection challenges.* This is complicated at the bottom of the pyramid by simple logistical realities such as locating and contacting consumers who are delinquent. Pursuing delinquency can also be costly (and dangerous) to personnel. Collection problems drive high eligibility standards, which reinforce acquisition challenges. *Infrastructure*—quality of roads, effectiveness of the postal system, questionable cold chains—can inhibit delivery, making it harder and costlier to support production and distribution into geographies where many low-income consumers reside.

Income, information, and infrastructure challenges are familiar in all business activity, albeit in a less acute form. In working with low-income groups, there are also some unique characteristics that must be dealt with. One has to do with *security and environment:* rural and urban poor environments are conducive to social action and resistance. Per capita income is low, services tend to be weak, there is typically minimal government support and high unemployment. This creates considerable stresses in low-income communities. Political and social groups target such areas, which makes it difficult to enforce contracts and puts assets at risk.

TABLE 19.1. UNIQUE AND COMMON CHALLENGES IN SERVING LOW-INCOME GROUPS THAT MUST BE OVERCOME.

Challenges	Definition	Implication	Example
Common			
• Acquisition			
– Affordability	• Initial expenditures to access service may be onerous	• Standard eligibility requirements can reduce size of the servicable market yet not add expected screening value	• Telco (post-paid): Initial provision requires relatively high income level
– Information	• Information problems that make it difficult to assess customer creditworthiness		• Water: Connection to piped water requires a legal land title, which low-income households may lack
• Parceling	• Constraints on the amount of product that can be purchased at any one time	• Typical size or amount of single unit of product can inhibit product purchase	• FMCGs: Consumers with hand-to-mouth subsistence can only afford a day's worth of goods
• Collection	• Logistical costs of collecting customer payments, especially if product or service has already been rendered	• Post-paid models expose the business to higher credit risk, more instances of default and increased collections cost	• Public utilities (water, electricity): Provider encounters difficulties in collection oftentimes resulting in suspension of service
• Infrastructure	• Lack of basic facilities and services to support creation and/or distribution of goods	• Increased cost of inputs and delivery for businesses • Higher transactions costs for the consumer	• Roads: Lack of farm-to-market roads inhibits ability to reach and to service the poor • Lack of "last mile" infrastructure prevents water distribution
Unique			
• Security and environment	• Threat of vandalism or sabotage to business facilities and infrastructure due to class action	• Location of business facilities in poor environments are more prone to class action or resistance	• Logging and mining facilities: Indigenous groups enforce payment of "revolutionary taxes" under threat of damage to physical assets or people
• Education/culture	• Cultural and educational characteristics that form strong beliefs for or against a product or business	• Selling side: Stereotypes about low-income groups by well-educated, well-paid individuals in businesses may be inaccurate • Buying side: Low education levels or popular belief may lead to misguided purchase decisions	• Loan sharks: Superior sources of credit require paperwork and environment unappealing to consumers with limited reading or writing skills
• "Maslow"	• Feeling of entitlement to most basic needs, such as water, food, and electricity	• Nonfulfillment of the poor's basic needs may lead to theft or pilferage	• Electricity: Illegal tapping of electricity is justified by a feeling of entitlement to what is perceived as a public good

Firms seeking to expand their business into low-income segments also need to deal with an *educational* issue of the target segment that can directly constrain demand. Many low-income consumers use pricier services than those available from established businesses (as an example, illegal money lenders). However, consumers do not fully appreciate the implications of some of these consumption choices due to their limited access to information and education.

The issue may be *cultural*—on the buying and the selling sides. A poor individual with unique purchasing habits and preferences may have concerns about interacting with proprietors in traditional ways. On the selling side, many big businesses consist of well-educated, well-paid individuals accustomed to interacting with other professionals and businesspeople.

Culture has another aspect. The sense of community is stronger among lower-income groups, making it necessary to consider the segment collectively. Poor communities, especially in the countryside, are often organized around a few dominant individuals who exert significant influence on the community. They may be political figures or prominent business leaders to whom the community feels a sense of indebtedness and loyalty. Because of their influence, they serve as gatekeepers to the community. Businesses that wish to reach underprivileged communities must first connect with the gatekeepers.

A final characteristic has to do with beliefs of the consuming public. Economic classes struggling to fulfill basic needs may view some products and services as an entitlement. They may see water, for example, as critical to their own hygiene and the health of their children and thus view their access to it as a right, not a matter of affordability. We call this the "Maslow" effect.[2] For companies, it means consumers will secure services through whatever means available, including illegal connections to water mains or electricity lines. Of course, this can also put in jeopardy long-term provision of services. It is a hard problem to solve. Households need to take a long-term view, but liquidity needs are high among poor households, implying a high discount rate on future streams of benefit or income. Extending their horizon to consider a long-term stream of benefits requires considerable effort.

The extent of these characteristics varies from one business to another. For telephony and water, collections and infrastructure are important issues. The Maslovian challenges, however, appear more acute in water than telephony, and security and environment are more challenging in telephony than in water.

These characteristics create challenging obstacles to reaching and penetrating low-income segments and thus can raise the cost of doing business. Solutions typically involve a departure from business models used with higher-income segments. Firms need approaches designed to fit particular characteristics of low-income segments.

Businesses in Action: Tailoring the Business Model to Serve Low-Income Segments

We examine Manila Water Company (MWC), a business owned by the Ayala Corporation in the Philippines and engaged in water distribution services, to draw lessons on working with low-income consumers.[3] Ninety percent of MWC's customer base is residential, and more than half consists of middle- to low-income customers. It is important to establish that MWC has done well against objective measures of performance, and relative to peers. In 2004, it returned 16 percent on capital employed, the best among a set of peer companies in Asia. Revenue growth has also been strong, nearly doubling over the last three years.

Manila Water

In 1995, the Philippine government divided the Manila metropolitan area into East and West Zones, each to be run by a separate water concessionaire for twenty-five years. MWC won the concession to run the East Zone, originally as a joint venture among Ayala Corporation, U.S.-based Bechtel Enterprises, and United Utilities.[4] The partners inherited a largely dilapidated network and faced political uncertainty surrounding the arbitration process and the regulatory regime.

From the very beginning, MWC confronted significant challenges. Only two-thirds of the franchise area had water service. Water pressure was erratic; barely one-fourth of the population had twenty-four-hour water service. As much as 65 percent of the water that left the treatment plant was "nonrevenue water" (NRW)—water not billed because of leakage through holes in pipes, illegal connections, or measurement problems due to faulty meters. Collections also were largely ineffective, and the organization was overstaffed and had low productivity.

Low-Income Consumers as a Long-Run Strategic Priority

In assessing its strategy in 1997, MWC management focused on two main issues. The first was the huge NRW problem. Part of this was due to pilferage and part to wastage arising from weak infrastructure. The concession required the company to drive NRW down over time, with penalties if it did not meet targets and premiums if targets were exceeded. Solving the wastage portion of NRW was also critical to expansion; with a limited water supply, stemming leakage was critical to expanding consumer and geographic coverage over time.

Management also identified a second, subtler concern: the absence of effective and quality service to the low-income segment. Before the 1997 privatization, the government required residents to show proof of land ownership before granting a water connection. Yet many poor residents belong to "informal settlements," from which proof of ownership of property is not possible. As such, they had to purchase water from vendors who charged up to ten times as much as the cost of piped water for every cubic meter of water delivered. As a consequence, the low-income segment was a major source of pilferage, accounting for 20–30 percent of the total. These illegal connections also caused damage to pipelines and other infrastructure, increasing capital expenditures and reducing service quality down the line.

Even for those low-income residents who were able to present a legal title, water service was unacceptable. Until then, they had the least priority in terms of capital investment. This left them with dilapidated infrastructure and consequently the worst service quality in the franchise area.

MWC and Ayala Corporation also saw the failure to serve the low-income segment as increasing the risk of adverse government intervention in the long run. The absence of clean, safe water has direct economic and quality-of-life consequences, putting at risk the health and productivity of low-income communities. If such conditions were to persist, management reasoned, MWC would put itself in jeopardy of renationalization or aggressive price subsidies. This is a genuine threat in countries such as the Philippines and Indonesia, where the poor make up a large part of the population and there is a history of price supports on basic services.

At the same time, MWC saw advantages in prioritizing low-income areas. It would solve the huge NRW problem. It would allow MWC to meet regulatory targets on its billed volume and customer base cost-effectively; the cost of connecting the poor communities, which are located in the network's central distribution system, was lower than that of connecting areas in the East Zone, where new primary pipelines had to be laid.

In the end, MWC determined that delivery of service to low-income consumers must be a strategic priority, and in fact, was a strategic necessity. From a commercial perspective, better service to low-income areas would help reduce systems losses and make the business viable. From a social perspective, it would promote economic development by delivering tangible benefits such as proper service delivery and hygiene, and improved livelihood opportunities, while helping inoculate MWC from adverse regulatory or government actions. In taking this strategic decision, the Ayala Corporation and its partners were attempting to strike the right balance between their own direct interests in securing required returns from the business and their wider interests (and felt obligation) to promote economic development. Neither set of interests could predominate in strategic and operational decisions. But neither could be neglected if MWC was to be truly sustainable in the long run.

Operational Challenges and Business Model Adaptations

To deliver on its strategic plans, MWC had to deal with three urgent operational challenges. First, most households did not have proper water facilities (faucets or toilets) or in-house piping installed. Installation could cost as much as US$130, or 50–60 percent of household monthly income. Second, piped-in water is a postpaid product, but low-income users tend not to save, have significant cash flow issues, and want to consume frequently in smaller parcels, all of which lead to the familiar collections problem. A third problem, arising from education and cultural issues, is that despite the dramatic improvement in their quality of life from having running water many poor perceived it to be more expensive than the bulk water sold by vendors and carried in by can.

MWC devised a game-changing scheme that overcame the acquisition-and-collections challenges: the option of collective installation and collective billing. Consumers choose from three options: one meter per household; one meter for three or four households; and a bulk water meter serving up to forty or fifty households. In the latter two schemes, the connection fee of Ph.P. 6,500 per household is reduced by as much as 60 percent, as costs are shared across multiple households. Submeters are used to measure water usage in each household, and everyone on the "group meter" takes responsibility for payment of the total bill.

The collective billing scheme has proved incredibly powerful. Not only has it helped lower access costs but it also effectively gives the service provider "group insurance coverage" on bill payment. Individual households provide this insurance by assuming liability for the full extent of the services consumed. These billing regimes shift responsibility for monitoring and enforcing payment to neighbors, who are in the best position to do so (because of information and leverage) and who have the most to lose from failure to pay. This scheme also provides a form of "social insurance" to the members of the collective. If one household has cash flow problems in a given month, the other members of the collective help cover the shortfall. Thus the collective is also a low-cost mechanism for pooling funds to manage the natural risk of cash flow problems that arise in low-income communities.

Most communities have opted for collective billing. About 30 percent of the urban poor bill through these mechanisms; the collection efficiency in communities that use it is 100 percent. Consumers recognize the savings in collective installation, as they share the cost of at least some of the infrastructure (pipes, main meter) and installation. Consumers also recognize that sustained service provision depends on the actions of others. Given close proximity to one another, tied households can observe day-to-day actions, shape behaviors, and impose sanctions.

MWC also offers installment payment schemes for the initial installation costs if the consumer does not want collective billing. In some instances, the local government units subsidize a portion of the cost. Multilateral funding agencies, notably the Asian Development Bank, have also offered programs to help in this area.

Additional challenges remained for MWC, including security, cultural challenges, and Maslovian issues. Solutions to these challenges required the business to solve a fundamental "principal-agent" problem. In the next section, we discuss the nature of the principal-agent problem and illustrate how MWC is resolving it by tapping into a powerful community dynamic.

Community-Based Agents to Align Incentives

Despite its business model adaptations and considerable progress, MWC continued to experience substantial pilferage. With hundreds of kilometers of pipes, the company knew it could not protect its assets through the traditional means of security guards, police protection, and enclosures.

To protect its assets, MWC needed the help of local communities—and not just the mayors, *barangay* (village or neighborhood) captains, and school principals but also residents themselves. Residents are best able to monitor developments on the ground and shape and influence the behavior of their neighbors. In this respect, the solution to challenges was to be found inside the community, and the task of business was to determine how to harness this capability.

A Unique Principal-Agent Problem

We can view this challenge as a fundamental principal-agent problem that exists between the businesses and the local communities. The communities (the agents) have much more ability than MWC (the principal) to take actions that will benefit the company or prevent those that will hurt it. For example, the community is in a better position to control negative externalities such as service disruption arising from individual decisions not to pay. Key leaders have hard-to-replicate information on what is taking place in communities, and they can shape people's views and govern or sanction behaviors. No amount of expense will position MWC better than community leaders or residents in terms of information or influencing ability. Therefore, working with leaders and elevating community awareness around the economic and social role of the company in people's lives becomes the key instrument for resolving the principal-agent problem.

Tapping into Micromarket Dynamics

Figure 19.2 is a simplified example of the complex dynamics taking place in communities; it illustrates how community partnerships can help solve principal-agent problems. There is both a commercial dynamic and a corresponding community dynamic.

FIGURE 19.2. MAPPING THE INTERNAL DYNAMICS
OF THE LOCAL ECOSYSTEM.

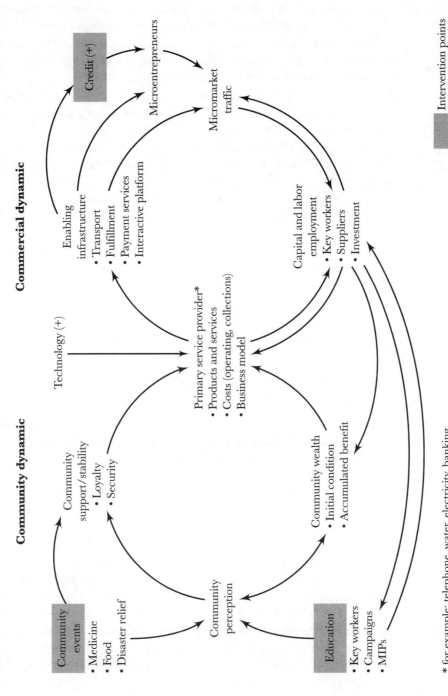

Community dynamic

Commercial dynamic

Community events
• Medicine
• Food
• Disaster relief

Community support/stability
• Loyalty
• Security

Technology (+)

Enabling infrastructure
• Transport
• Fulfillment
• Payment services
• Interactive platform

Credit (+)

Microentrepreneurs

Micromarket traffic

Primary service provider*
• Products and services
• Costs (operating, collections)
• Business model

Community perception

Community wealth
• Initial condition
• Accumulated benefit

Capital and labor employment
• Key workers
• Suppliers
• Investment

Education
• Key workers
• Campaigns
• MIPs

Intervention points

* for example: telephone, water, electricity, banking

Consider first the commercial dynamic. By providing more affordable water service to an area, MWC positively affects purchasing power and demand. It also promotes employment, both directly through its own hiring and through jobs and investment taking place in product and service supplier networks. Water services also have an indirect development impact within the commercial dynamic, freeing up time previously dedicated to hauling water that can now be applied to more productive activities. Overall price and income effects, as well as taxes paid, drive the local micromarket economic traffic.

The commercial dynamic interacts with a reinforcing community dynamic. Employment generates community wealth, which helps sustain demand. It also strengthens community perceptions of MWC that directly influence the degree and stability of community support. Community support provides the critical mechanism for addressing a host of issues: security, leakage, cultural gaps.

Positive community dynamics can be reinforced (or negative dynamics reversed) with "circuit breakers" such as education and community activities. Education raises awareness of the quality-of-life impact of water. Education and skills training converts MWC into a "livelihood partner" by helping residents upgrade human capital, which can help the unemployed secure jobs. Community events tie companies and communities together around important social occasions (religious festivals, local holidays, celebrations) and inject funds for food, health, and leisure activities.

Manila Water: Aligning the Community Through a Broad Program of Benefits

As with all Ayala companies, MWC was already active in a number of ad hoc social initiatives—community, livelihood, and sanitation programs—although they were scattered throughout the organization. Through these initiatives, relationships in a number of barangays were developed by various parts of the organization.

For MWC, however, getting involved in the community was essential to success, not a matter of social motivation. Although the ongoing *Tubig Para sa Barangay* (Water for the Community) program helped resolve billing issues and educate customers on the value of piped water, challenges remained. For one, there was the Maslow phenomenon described earlier: because water is a basic need, low-income consumers have felt a sense of entitlement to the service, justifying their illegal connection. Many have also simply lacked the income to pay in the first place. For another, because MWC is a public utility provider it has to work closely with local governments to lay pipelines and build proper infrastructure in public areas. Some businesses resort to extralegal solutions to secure local government support; MWC as a matter of principle does not do so, believing they are inherently unstable in the long run.

To address livelihood issues and win cooperation from local authorities, MWC opted for another route: delivering a package of benefits to local communities beyond water and supporting the development projects of local leaders. In this respect, MWC was repositioning itself as a livelihood partner, extending to the communities a "livelihood bundle." The more value at stake the community has in MWC (or any company), the more likely it is that communities will take action in support of the business.

MWC designed a three-pronged development package for Manila's low-income residents: (1) water provision, (2) livelihood support, and (3) sanitation and sewerage. Some of these initiatives strengthen the commercial dynamic associated with MWC, while others reinforce the community dynamic.

On the first prong, MWC developed an umbrella program, Caring for Health and Safety, to bring affordable and clean water supply to public schools, hospitals, and public markets in the East Zone of Metro Manila.

MWC also launched a livelihood program, called Livelihood for the Community. Under this program, and in partnership with Bank of the Philippine Islands, MWC makes small loans available to organized groups to operate microenterprises such as street stalls and food services. MWC's "Suki Partners" vendor management program also made jobs available to more than fifteen thousand people. The program taps the services of small-scale entrepreneurs in the East Zone. Some operate as couriers delivering MWC's bills; others operate as contractors laying water pipelines. MWC is also putting together a program to address sanitation needs of low-income residents under its Sanitation for the Community program.

By pursuing this three-pronged program, MWC is seeking to establish solid partnerships with communities, and to heighten the economic and social benefits that MWC delivers. By expanding communities' stake in the business's viability, MWC is able to enlist their support in monitoring water connections, protecting the infrastructure, and ensuring timely billing.

Exportable Learnings

Three common observations can be drawn from MWC's experiences on the use of commercial forces and community-based agents to make businesses viable.

First, the communities are in a better position than the company to resolve issues that potentially lead to nonservice. Communities possess information and have the moral authority and leverage of proximity to monitor behavior and impose sanctions whenever individual actions compromise benefits to the community.

Second, deliberate investment in education and communication was necessary to resolve the principal-agent problem. These investments were the key to making communities aware of the value at stake that would be put in jeopardy if unique challenges could not be resolved.

Third, although education and communication were critical to raising awareness, MWC had to extend the set of economic benefits beyond the direct impact of its core services to embed and solidify its role in the communities. This has meant extending water provision to other key users (hospitals, schools) as well as fostering additional economic opportunities through livelihood programs.

CSR and Serving Low-Income Consumers

Traditionally, corporations have taken up and promoted social activities out of a sense of obligation and commitment to their wider community. However, many of these activities have been adjacent to the core activity of the firms sponsoring them. The objective within the broader corporate social responsibility movement is to link social initiatives more integrally with the core strategy and operations of businesses. That is, social activities would move along a spectrum from being "cause-oriented" (volunteerism, donations) to "strategy-oriented" (part of the essential operations or strategic priorities of business).

The intent is desirable, but the full movement from left to right along this spectrum requires a fundamental transformation in the motivation behind social initiatives. It might be said that although activities to the left are motivated by the desire to "do good," activities on the right are driven by the objective to "do well." Firms locate themselves on the left side of the spectrum because there is a natural limit on the amount of money profit-seeking firms can invest in social causes without putting their own viability at risk. Firms move toward the right only if one or both of two conditions apply: (1) they are pursuing a commercial venture that directly targets low-income areas, or (2) there are social issues at play that put a firm's strategy at risk. In the former case, the discussion is around developing viable business models that can profitably serve low-income areas. In the latter case, the discussion must be around incorporating into an existing business model social concerns that may alter the competitive landscape. Both can be present as well, as in the case of Manila Water. But at least one of these conditions is necessary for social considerations to become core to strategy.

At the same time, we would argue that businesses—to their own detriment—do not always recognize when social issues are in fact central to their strategy, and thus they underinvest in corresponding social initiatives. There are two common reasons. First, firms often neglect to recognize emerging topics or trends in the social sphere that could directly threaten their core business. Social issues can be a force shaping a firm's competitive environment, and firms need to address and respond to these forces. Yet many firms do not anticipate these issues, putting them at risk of adverse regulatory or social actions that would constrain their strategic independence (such as setting of nutritional requirements for fast food companies) or hold them financially responsible for consequences of their neglect (as with legal rulings against McDonald's). These issues feed into fundamental drivers of corporate performance and can pose a threat to the core strategy or operations.[5] Firms need to consider how to mitigate these threats.

Second, firms do not always see the potential for social initiatives to help improve performance. Social initiatives can help them tap into huge potential revenue pools or resolve thorny operational issues.

MWC's actions respond implicitly to social issues as a competitive force and harness them to resolve operational issues. With respect to social issues, the company is highly profitable in a country with a large poor population and a weak government fiscal situation. Not surprisingly, it is frequently the target of new tax schemes or other efforts to transfer wealth. It can also be difficult to secure reasonable regulatory rulings.

MWC's community-based activity has paid a unique dividend on the regulatory side. In 2002, MWC and regulators met to discuss a tariff increase. Such events attract NGOs and civil society organizations that typically resist proposed rate hikes. In this case, something extraordinary happened: ninety barangay captains and community leaders showed up to express their support for MWC's request. Each captain spoke to the commission, expressing appreciation for the positive impact of MWC on their community. They told stories of how residents used to begin their trek at midnight to bring water back to their household by dawn, of new jobs and entrepreneurial activity, of support for special needs and projects. To a person, they supported MWC's petition for a tariff increase.

For these local leaders, MWC was an essential partner in their livelihood and quality of life, and they were prepared to stand by the company to ensure it was treated fairly. In this case, social initiatives translated into critical and vocal community support, constituting a powerful counterbalance to regulatory or legislative actions to cap prices, mandate infrastructure spending, or interfere with operational decisions.

As has been shown, MWC also used social initiatives to resolve collections problems, manage NRW, and protect its assets. These initiatives to engage and align community support helped to resolve critical operational challenges and contributed directly to performance.

Conclusion

Serving the bottom of the pyramid profitably poses distinctive challenges. The experience of Manila Water demonstrates that businesses can serve low-income segments profitably. We believe business models that are designed with the distinct characteristics of the low-income segment in mind and that leverage the community aggressively are able to achieve a competitive rate of return while also delivering an important developmental impact in the marketplace. This case is also an important contribution to the broader CSR dialogue. It helps establish that firms cannot be expected to build CSR into their strategies without a compelling proposition for doing so. At the same time, when responding to social issues companies should not overlook the positive contribution that doing so can make to performance.

CHAPTER TWENTY

WHEN GIANTS DISCOVER THE DISADVANTAGED

Managerial Challenges and Success Factors in Building Capacity to Serve Underserved Markets

Rosabeth Moss Kanter

Companies, especially large ones, are increasingly aware that there is a significant potential market at the bottom of the pyramid (BOP). This paper draws from case studies of inner city banking in the United States and Brazil to illustrate managerial dilemmas surrounding the entry of established companies into underserved markets, and how companies can successfully resolve them.

Entering into new ventures that target this underserved population can be risky, which is a primary reason many have been hesitant to pursue such opportunities. Companies that choose to enter into transactional relationships in this market group, however, are discovering additional links in the value chain. Successful companies tend to display several similar characteristics: an entrepreneurial outlook toward exploring new markets and ventures, top leadership that sets and drives the vision, a strong internal culture that facilitates readiness to explore BOP markets, processes that help guide and evaluate new ventures, and willingness and patience to find ventures that are consistent with the company's existing values.

The author wishes to thank Research Associate Ryan Raffaelli for his excellent contributions.

First Community Bank[1]

First Community Bank (FCB) began as BankBoston's venture to serve poor inner city markets (becoming Fleet Community Banking after Fleet acquired BankBoston, and now part of Bank of America's community banking group). FCB was created in response to pressure from activists for banks in the region to improve their compliance with the Community Reinvestment Act. Doing so would also garner favorable ratings that would influence authorities in approving acquisitions.

BankBoston (BKB) traced its origins to 1784 and later became known as one of the two leaders in high-tech financing (Bank of America was the other). In its 1990 three-year strategic plan, BKB named "New England preeminence" and "community reinvestment" as two of its top ten objectives. BKB's studies, however, found that its operating efficiency was low among banks. Some of this was due to location (Northeast banks were generally high-cost operations thanks to the costs of real estate, wages, energy, and the like); BKB also had internal inefficiencies. Thus every expense was scrutinized, more favorable supplier contracts were initiated, and products were rationalized and treated as commodities.

External pressure also encouraged BKB to explore new market opportunities. A 1989 report by the Federal Reserve in Boston showed a large racial disparity in mortgage lending by Boston banks between 1981 and 1987. The problem was attributed to bank practices such as lack of branches and automated teller machines in minority neighborhoods and inadequate minority hiring. To address the problem and meet the legal obligations put forth under the Community Reinvestment Act (CRA) of 1977, BankBoston created Boston First Banking to meet the needs of underserved urban minority communities. Gail Snowden was appointed to head Boston First Banking when it opened in March 1990 as a network of seven urban branches.

Snowden did not want to do charity banking. Instead, she wanted to treat the market with respect, developing a real business that would generate profits for BKB. She established a profit-driven community lending operation and separated CRA compliance, public relations, and philanthropy from the business functions. CRA activities would thus be "mainstreamed" throughout the bank via specialized products and an emphasis on real estate lending in low- and moderate-income areas.

In 1991, Boston First Banking was renamed First Community Bank. After two years of focus on individual retail customers, FCB turned its attention to business and economic development lending. FCB created layers of financing necessary for riskier deals and for start-up businesses whose owners might not have personal assets for collateral. Community development officers (CDOs) spearheaded day-to-day outreach efforts, securing in-depth knowledge of areas where First Community Bank conducted its business and where its customers and employees lived and worked. Each CDO focused on specific ethnic and linguistic minority populations in the marketplace and was an active liaison to customers. The CDOs' ties to particular cultures and multi-lingual capabilities differentiated them from their counterparts in other urban banking institutions. Every FCB officer attended community events as a core part of the job, and branches routinely performed community service.

FCB's structure was almost unique in BankBoston: it was not a separate bank but a separate marketing and administrative unit within the framework of a conventional retail bank. Only private banking for affluent customers had a similar approach. Branches had large external signs for BankBoston, with First Community Bank occupying a smaller line underneath. Although Snowden was held to the same standards as any other business manager, she was given the flexibility to be measured on the performance of the whole branch system, not each individual branch, and of the entire product line, not each individual product or account.

FCB's three-hundred-person staff was about 49 percent minority. Attracting talented bankers got easier every year. It was important to Snowden that FCB staff members work as a team and play many roles; the organization was known for great camaraderie and acceptance of diversity. Snowden was recognized for her passion and had a reputation for being good to her people. She was not hierarchical and sought many opinions.

By 1993, BankBoston was awarded the highest CRA rating, an "outstanding," by the Office of the Comptroller of the Currency—the first major bank in Massachusetts to receive this rating. Building on the success and the lessons of its $6 billion credit initiative, BKB launched a totally reorganized and reenergized Small Business Banking Division and committed an additional $150 million to the First Step Mortgage program, making significant progress in increasing mortgage lending to minority applicants.

FCB reached its profitability target in 1994, earning $4.1 million on revenues of $20.7 million; it could now claim victory in the quest to prove that it was not a charity but a business. At the same time, FCB benefited from the interest of socially responsible investors. After the 1993 outstanding CRA rating, about $50 million poured into BankBoston. The City of Boston, for example, deposited $5 million; Brown University and the Calvert Fund bought $100,000 certificates of deposit (CDs), and the National Council of Churches acquired $25,000 CDs. Routed through FCB, such deposits helped less-profitable branches achieve better results.

ABN AMRO Real[2]

In Brazil, a nation with more than a quarter of the population living on less than two dollars a day, ABN AMRO Real decided to emphasize corporate social and environmental responsibility as a central part of the bank's brand, after a global Dutch bank acquired Banco Real in 1998. Under the leadership of CEO Fabio Barbosa, a

Brazilian native, the bank undertook a set of initiatives to create brand differentiation after the merger. There was also awareness of pressure from NGOs for banks to become more socially and environmentally responsible. This led to actions such as socioenvironmental screening for credit analysis, environmentally focused products (such as a loan for converting cars to emit fewer greenhouse gases), microfinance for poor entrepreneurs in the *favelas* (shanty towns) in major cities, an "ethical" mutual fund, socioenvironmental tests for suppliers, internal reduction of waste and recycling, and a major commitment to workforce diversity and diversity training.

Microcredit was among the first areas the bank tackled under its new mission. ABN AMRO Real formed Real Microcredito in partnership with ACCION International to furnish microfinance in poor neighborhoods in São Paulo. The Real Microcredito joint venture was formed in 2002 and had twenty-two employees. ABN AMRO Real owned 80 percent of Real Microcredito, while ACCION International—which took responsibility for technical support, and whose costs were mostly covered by a US$750,000 donation from the U.S. Agency for International Development (USAID)—owned the rest.

Real Microcredito was viewed by the bank as an opportunity to tap a new market while doing good, especially given intensive competition for more affluent customers. The program was led by Executive Director Maria Luiza de Oliveira Pinto.

Microcredit required a new sales channel. Professionals were sought who had previous experience in commercial credit evaluation and often lived near, or in places similar to, the areas they served. New products and methods of credit analysis and approval were required, as well as new communication strategies. The first experience with microlending was in the Heliópolis favela, the largest low-income community in São Paulo and Brazil's second largest. The initial communication and outreach work included banners and sound cars, as well as brochures. To overcome skepticism, multiple visits involving personalized service were required. Clients needed to guarantee their income individually or through solidarity groups, in which peers served as one another's guarantors.

Real Microcredito's analyses showed that nearly 70 percent of its prospects were listed in the Credit Protection Service (CPS) or Serasa, two credit information agencies. The company decided to bend its rules to make lending feasible. By 2005, 52 percent of fifteen hundred credit applications had been approved. The average loan amount was R$1,350; the average term was seven months (paid monthly). A portfolio of about 14,000 active clients was required for sustainability, since every credit agent had an average of 185 active clients. Expanding the service to other areas in São Paulo was difficult. Many clients did not have the capability to manage the growth of their business. Interest rates were considered high, at 2–3.5 percent per month, according to some clients. Still, the default rate was only 4 percent, compared to a 7 percent rate for banks in general. Real Microcredito forecasted portfolio growth of approximately R$20 million in 2005, if expanding to other areas in São Paulo and Rio de Janeiro.

Since its merger with ABN AMRO, the Brazilian subsidiary has been able to report stellar results. Traditional measures of financial performance were important, and the bank met high standards. Net profit doubled from 2000 to 2004, and return on equity was at least 15 percent each year. By 2004, ABN AMRO Real was the fourth-largest nongovernment bank in Brazil (the third major market for its Dutch parent after the Netherlands and the United States), and number 15 on the list of Brazil's most-admired companies (up from number 153 in 2003). ABN AMRO Real entered 2005 with 1,890 branches and facilities, 28,571 employees, and 9.2 million customers. It furnished 10 percent of the revenues and 7 percent of the profits for ABN AMRO worldwide.

In short, both of these cases describe a successful venture that produces financial value for the company and meets the needs of poor communities. Their experiences illuminate the extra steps required for established companies to achieve this success. This is made clear by a look at the typical challenges such ventures face.

Challenges

Any new venture in an established company is fraught with predictable managerial challenges. Because the venture is new and hence unproven, it requires patient capital and funding flexibility, draining cash rather than throwing it off. It cannot be held to the same performance requirements or measured in the same way as mainstream businesses. It requires intensely committed staff who stay in place rather than rotate through the career structures of the mainstream business, and it requires organizational flexibility to modify policies and procedures that are suitable for the mainstream businesses but less so for a venture that is inherently different. There is often resentment from those in the mainstream businesses toward the new venture unit, and their skepticism or antagonism can undermine it. In underserved or underdeveloped markets, these common challenges are exacerbated by others that reflect characteristics of poor communities and their interactions with the more affluent society surrounding them (which established companies often represent). These issues—transaction size and efficiency, complexity, and distrust—are faced especially by companies offering services such as banking and retailing.

Financial Issues: Transaction Size and Efficiency

Poor consumers are more likely than their wealthier counterparts to engage in a large number of small transactions, but fixed costs per transaction can limit the margin on sales. Metrics used in the mainstream businesses are often inadequate to capture the value inherent in serving this kind of market. Processes applied to mainstream businesses to increase efficiency and margin, such as substituting technology for human interaction, might be difficult to introduce in poor communities because they lack technological infrastructure.

At FCB, Snowden was not measured using the same metrics as her mainstream colleagues, but she was still responsible for meeting bottom-line targets. This flexibility allowed her nascent group to adjust its practices during start-up; it did not remove the need to track and measure performance. However, FCB's approach required more time with each customer, additional resources to sponsor community activities, and greater attention to the unique requirements of each new customer. Initially, these actions cut across the bank's activities, reduced per-transaction efficiencies, required alternative cost management techniques, and were more expensive. Meanwhile, its mainstream counterparts were developing new ways to increase efficiencies via automated teller machines and online banking.

In Brazil's favelas, the country's low literacy rate, high crime, and environmental deficiencies posed an even greater threat to potential customers than to those served by the mainstream business. Poor transportation networks and bureaucracy were notorious for raising costs for ordinary citizens as well as for businesses. In São Paulo, transportation cost consumed one-fifth of a poor person's income, and more than 2.5 hours a day in commuting time.

ABN AMRO Real's leaders believed that redefining the vision and goals to better suit new targets and measures was an important step in helping new programs prove their value to the parent bank. After the acquisition, CEO Barbosa took advantage of the postmerger integration period (often filled with turmoil) to redefine how the bank would measure value. This process helped employees, customers, stockholders, and even its parent bank, ABN AMRO, better understand how the new vision would require nontraditional measures that could facilitate greater efficiencies and new markets. For example, the microcredit program was able to approve smaller, riskier loans for a new client base because the bank developed a specialized credit analysis process to evaluate potential clients. Nonetheless, the program required an explicit decision on the part of leaders to use additional resources to attract new customers.

Operations Issues: Complexity

Poor consumers and communities sometimes differ not only quantitatively (in wealth and income) but also qualitatively from those served by mainstream businesses: they speak different languages, have insufficient knowledge about products and services, are less educated (and more likely to have literacy problems), face residential instability, have little access to transportation, and so on. Companies try to reduce complexity in their mainstream businesses in the interest of efficiency. Serving poor consumers might increase complexity as well as require provision of additional auxiliary services simply to make it possible for poor consumers to access the products or services the company is trying to sell. According to BKB's director of government and community affairs, the credit needs of the inner city could not be met with "product wrinkles" alone (not even new products with favorable rates) but would require a comprehensive approach, including extra time to educate customers.

ABN AMRO Real's leaders decided the bank would be customer-focused, stressing relationships rather than transactions. Steps toward the customer focus goal included increasing decision-making autonomy so branches could solve small problems on the spot, reviewing communications with customers, and encouraging dialogue across areas inside the bank.

Relationship Issues: Mutual Distrust

Potential consumers in an underserved market are often culturally different from employees in large companies (in race or ethnicity) and suspicious of big companies. At the same time, company employees may be skeptical about the market potential and reliability of the underserved, have concerns about personal safety in unfamiliar neighborhoods, or hold inappropriate stereotypes about the population.

Real Microcredito's analyses showed that nearly 70 percent of its prospects were to be found in the Credit Protection Service (CPS) or Serasa, two credit information agencies. When credit agents at ABN AMRO Real initially visited the favelas, they were surprised by the lack of trust for bankers. One credit agent noted, "I never imagined it would be so difficult to lend money in a shantytown. It was really difficult to get these people to trust me." Customer skepticism was coupled with fear on the part of bank employees that entering the new areas could be dangerous.

Solutions

An established company must undergo an internal change process if it is to build the capability to serve the poor, and do so effectively (for poor consumers) and profitably (for the company). First Community Bank and ABN AMRO Real succeeded in building ventures to serve the poor by using some or all of these managerial solutions:

- Passionate, committed leadership able to champion the value of the venture and high-level sponsorship
- Additional strategic impetus to develop the venture
- A managerial structure that insulates the new venture from mainstream pressures
- Alliances with external intermediary organizations
- Investment in community development and community service, including education
- Expanded metrics and innovative ways to assess the value of customers
- Recruitment of staff who understand the community and its culture
- Diversity training for employees

- Allowing variation and associating it with innovation
- Widespread internal communication about the purpose and needs of the new venture
- Career desirability of assignments in the unit

The two banks discussed in this paper were able to find success with BOP programs because they implemented these solutions well.

Passionate Leadership

It is important that a new venture be led by committed champions who bring their passion to the venture, and that those champions have strong sponsorship from the CEO and senior executives.

Parent company CEO Chad Gifford believed strongly in the vision for FCB and championed it publicly. Snowden also benefited from surrounding herself with other internal champions, such as Ira Jackson and Jeff Zinsmeyer, who had experience in community banking. This cadre of support, from above and within FCB, gave her the strength she needed to push FCB's vision. FCB used many programs, systems, and practices common to the rest of BKB but also recognized that at times it would need specialized approaches to reach this unique market. Over time, FCB's distinctive style led to its own culture. For example, because Snowden liked to spend a lot of time getting input and buy-in, many teams were asked to operate without a designated leader— an unusual approach in the hierarchical banking world. Other employees were attracted to the culture and vision of FCB.

At ABN AMRO, Maria Luiza de Oliveira Pinto was given considerable leeway by Barbosa to promote and create markets that could be tied to the "bank of value" vision. The CEO never missed an opportunity to communicate the importance of the bank's values and how programs like the microcredit initiative would create value for the bank's stakeholders.

New Intermediaries

To support the effort of combining value and values, ABN AMRO Real partnered with numerous NGOs, including Friends of the Earth, Greenpeace, Ethos Institute, and the World Bank, asking them to assess progress or provide training for bank staff. The bank's microcredit initiative was a joint venture with another NGO, ACCION International. ABN AMRO Real was chosen by the World Bank to administer a large loan pool for development projects, a first for Brazil.

FCB created community development officers (CDOs) to oversee outreach activities that focused on specific populations in the marketplace, and to serve as liaison to customers. CDOs became actively involved in the community as a first step in alleviating mistrust and preconceptions about banks among the community. Because of their hands-on involvement, CDOs better understood the unique needs and challenges facing their new customers. With this information, they could customize FCB's services to better suit their customers' needs.

Diversity Programs

Because the BOP community is generally unlike mainstream customers in language, race, and other elements associated with economic disadvantage, building effective relationships requires training staff to overcome bias and grow more understanding of differences. Diversity programs also help the whole organization mirror the population while surrounding the venture with a receptive, tolerant culture.

ABN AMRO recognized that their employees were not representative of the Brazilian population. Only 10 percent were African Brazilian, only 9 percent of managerial positions were held by women (all of them white), and a mere 10 percent of employees were over forty-five years of age. The disabled population was close to zero, though a 1991 nondiscrimination law required larger employers to have the physically challenged constitute 5 percent of their staff.

Bank leaders saw diversity as a potential competitive advantage, attracting a broad segment of the population that was poorly served in other companies as well as stimulating employee creativity. A diversity program was launched in 2001 with appointment of a committee. Diversity goals were communicated through written material, lunch seminars, and videotapes, but with few results. Leaders recognized a sensitive issue involving personal values and so added support to integrate diversity within the bank.

At FCB, employees were encouraged to embrace the diversity of their customers as a way of differentiating themselves from competitors. Examples abounded of extra services extended to individuals at FCB branches, including translation of documents by multilingual staff, explanation of customs to newly arrived immigrants, and advice on how to pick a neighborhood or find a good school. This increased time per banking transaction but made FCB part of the fabric of the community.

Innovation

New ventures inevitably must innovate because mainstream approaches by definition do not apply to the new market (which is one reason it is underserved). This is much easier in an environment that is actively encouraging and views the new venture as producing innovation with applications throughout the rest of the company.

The culture that fostered FCB's ability to attract new customers also helped them find ways of tackling the perennial problems that confront the mainstream business. One FCB executive stated, "We are responsible for an unusually high amount of market innovation. First Step products are now bankwide; kids in the suburbs use them to buy their first home. Our brochures in foreign languages are stocked widely; we were one of the first to use a person of color in bank advertising. We're always looking for different ways to do things." FCB's organization structure made it easier for Snowden and her team to champion new ideas.

Communication

Openness to learning is another enabler related to innovation. ABN AMRO fostered open dialogue within and outside the bank, unusual in a region that was still shaking off the legacy of an authoritarian past. The company's social responsibility theme, "banco de valor" (bank of value), was adopted after open brainstorming by the executive team, sharpened by a self-assessment based on NGO guidelines, and refined through educational sessions for nearly two thousand managers and employees. The bank went public with its commitment, and Barbosa acted as a role model for transparency. When he received a letter from a disgruntled customer who questioned the bank's discussion of making capitalism more humane and inclusive in light of high interest rates, he invited her to headquarters. A partial transcript of their conversation was later published in a bank report, *Human and Economic Values, Together.*

Conclusions

As these examples show, successful BOP ventures are surrounded by a values-based culture, numerous enabling structures, and strong leadership. From them, two broad conclusions can be drawn. First, for a multiunit business to effectively transition to serving the bottom of the pyramid, an internal change process guided by vision and values is often necessary. Leadership matters and is essential for the organizational flexibility needed to make the venture succeed.

Second, it is impossible to make the business case for BOP ventures without including an element of corporate social responsibility. A culture that is value-based, not just numbers-based, is a helpful ingredient in ensuring that a new venture serving the poor can succeed.

The Corporate Values Approach

Emerging market opportunities lead companies toward new markets and customers. Companies using a rational market demand approach (Figure 20.1) to evaluate the risk and return of launching a new BOP venture incorrectly assume that "if we build it, they will come." They believe a market exists without additional effort on their part. But this kind of purely economic analysis misses many aspects of what is required to reach populations that have been left out of the economic mainstream. This approach ignores altogether the challenges of managing ventures that differ from existing lines of business.

Successful companies recognize that new BOP markets require more than traditional evaluation techniques. When companies choose to explore new BOP opportunities, a corporate values approach (Figure 20.2) is required to effectively manage downside risk and increase the likelihood of success.

FIGURE 20.1. RATIONAL MARKET DEMAND APPROACH.

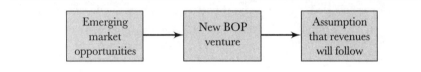

FIGURE 20.2. CORPORATE VALUES APPROACH.

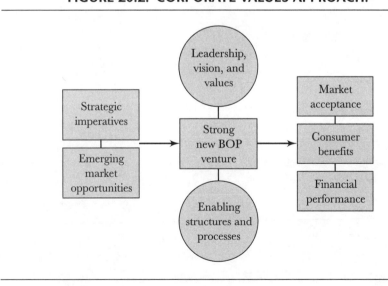

My research suggests that successful companies place significant emphasis on leadership, vision, and values, and they also develop appropriate enabling structures and processes to support the venture. As we evaluate the success of this chapter's two featured banks, it is clear that both companies benefited from top executive support as well as new structures and processes that enabled the ventures to grow outside the confines of the mainstream business. In addition to market opportunities, model companies also capitalize on new strategic imperatives. As a result, strong new BOP ventures are accepted by the market and yield financial gains and consumer benefits.

ABN AMRO Real and FCB's successes were not happenstance. As more companies in various industries attempt to develop tools to approach BOP customers, they find they cannot create value without leadership from the top. In addition, successful companies are careful about whom they choose as partners and customers. They pursue ventures that align with the company's vision and values. Once they make a decision to undertake a BOP venture, they make adequate resources available and develop specialized structures and processes to support the new concept. These factors typically contribute to greater likelihood of success—and ultimately create sustainable value for the company and the new BOP market segment.

PART FIVE

THE ROLE OF GOVERNMENT AND CIVIL SOCIETY

To reach profitability at the base of the pyramid, companies often rely on government, civil society groups, and local entrepreneurs to lower the costs of doing business, access key customer groups, and build legitimacy and goodwill.

In some cases, government regulation creates incentives for businesses to engage in activities with strong social benefits. In Chapter Twenty-One, "The Role of Financial Institutions in Revitalizing Low-Income Neighborhoods," Carolyn Welch and Ann Scoffier describe how U.S. legislation (including the Community Reinvestment Act and Regulation Y under the Bank Holding Company Act) spurred the banking sector to dramatically increase its investment in low-income communities. The chapter looks at the example of City *First* Bank, a for-profit, mission-driven entity that has benefited from a potent combination of regulatory support and patient investors to create a financing pool for small business development and low-income housing.

Doug Guthrie and Michael McQuarrie also investigate the impact of regulation on the U.S. low-income housing market in Chapter Twenty-Two, "Houses for the Poor and New Business for Banks," but argue that the social benefits derived by regulation are sometimes more the outcome of accidental loopholes than strategic intent. They trace the recent surge in investment in low-income housing to the Low-Income Housing Tax Credit, which the authors view as one of the greatest boons to corporate America. Interestingly, they argue that the legislation unintentionally altered the risk profile for corporate investment in low-income housing by giving companies a double tax break, thereby spurring a high level of profit-driven activity directed at urban renewal.

Government regulation itself can be a powerful driver for change, but sometimes the mere threat of regulation is enough to drive business innovation in poor markets. In "The South African Financial Sector Charter," R. S. Tucker, Thomas Mondschean, and Bruce Scott describe how the South African government's Black Business Empowerment (BEE) initiative—the aim of which is to engage more blacks in business management and ownership—has catalyzed voluntary social commitment in certain industries. The authors detail the successful efforts of the South African financial services sector to self-regulate its operations in order to meet a range of BEE social and economic objectives, thus preempting formal regulation.

Chapters Twenty-Four through Twenty-Seven delve into the contributions made by civil society groups and local entrepreneurs as both catalysts of and partners in BOP ventures. As bridge builders, gatekeepers, and knowledge depositories, civil society actors can deliver crucial access, market intelligence, and legitimacy to their business partners.

In "How Social Entrepreneurs Enable Human, Social, and Economic Development," Christian Seelos and Johanna Mair analyze Sekem, an Egyptian agricultural firm and social enterprise dedicated to adding economic, social, and cultural value to Egyptian society. Founded by an entrepreneur with a powerful vision of holistic economic development, Sekem illustrates the role entrepreneurship can play in developing countries to fill the void left by inefficient government and institutional structures.

Long-term commercial partnerships between large companies and social enterprises have the potential to create mutual value and ensure deeper social impact than can either working alone. This is the argument made by Valeria Budinich, Kimberly Manno Reott, and Stéphanie Schmidt in "Hybrid Value Chains: Social Innovations and Development of the Small Farmer Irrigation Market in Mexico." The chapter describes a pilot project conducted by two social entrepreneurs and Amanco, Latin America's leading water system company, to deliver irrigation systems to small-scale farmers in Mexico. The authors explore the multiple needs of small farmers and the market opportunity for companies, and discuss why the current value chains serving large farmers are unlikely to be transferable to small, low-income farmers without the assistance of civil society partners.

In Chapter Twenty-Six, "Entrepreneurship and Poverty Alleviation in South Africa," Frederick Ahwireng-Obeng and Mthuli Ncube argue that reducing South African poverty requires business to strengthen and expand its relationship with BOP entrepreneurs. The authors demonstrate their argument with a case study of South African Breweries, which has developed a series of profit-driven programs to stimulate entrepreneurship throughout its value chain.

Linda Hill and Maria Farkas close Part Five with "A Gentler Capitalism: Black Business Leadership in the New South Africa." This chapter traces the career of Irene Charnley, a black South African born at the bottom of the pyramid who now sits at the top, working in an operations role at Johnnic Group. An architect of a new way of doing business in South Africa, Charnley worked to expand cell phone service to poor South Africans and other African nations, while she also fought tirelessly for affirmative action in her own company. This case discusses the question of how business leaders and entrepreneurs can push companies internally to make business decisions that are economically sound and benefit the poor.

CHAPTER TWENTY-ONE

THE ROLE OF FINANCIAL INSTITUTIONS IN REVITALIZING LOW-INCOME NEIGHBORHOODS

Carolyn Welch, Ann Scoffier

For more than three decades, policy makers, regulators, and community advocates in the United States have sought to engage banks and bank holding companies in helping to address the vexing economic and social challenges that beset lower-income communities. Many of these efforts have been aimed at encouraging banks to apply their business strategies to serve markets traditionally underserved for a variety of reasons, including a history of discrimination and a perceived absence of profit opportunities.[1] These policy strategies are predicated on the fact that communities need ready access to capital in order to foster investment and development, and ultimately to become self-sustaining and prosperous. Implicit in the policies is the idea that, with innovative approaches, underserved markets can represent viable business opportunities for financial institutions, and access to credit can unleash the energy and talent of low-income community entrepreneurs.

One piece of regulation recognizes the vital role that banking institutions play in the economic viability of lower-income communities. In January 1995, the Federal Reserve Board of Governors issued a revised interpretation of Regulation Y, the regulation that implements the Bank Holding Company Act, which expanded the scope of community development activities permissible by bank holding companies

The views expressed are those of the authors and do not reflect the position of the Federal Reserve Board of Governors or City *First* Bank of D.C., N.A. This paper does not represent a supervisory assessment or endorsement of City *First* Bank of D.C., N.A., its parent company, or any of its affiliates.

and recognized that "bank holding companies possess a unique combination of financial and managerial resources making them particularly suited for a meaningful and substantial role in remedying our social ills."[2]

This provision encourages bank holding companies to make equity and debt investments in organizations and initiatives that promote the economic rehabilitation and development of low-income areas.[3] Initiatives include real estate development activities, such as affordable housing and commercial business, which primarily benefit low- and moderate-income communities and residents through access to housing, jobs, and services. Similar authority enables banks to invest in activities that primarily benefit low- and moderate-income communities and their residents.[4] These and other regulations such as the Community Reinvestment Act recognize the catalytic role that financial institutions play in promoting economic development and providing financial access and capacity building in economically distressed communities.[5]

Over the past three decades, these policy-based strategies and their incentives have stimulated a variety of business responses by the banking industry. Many financial institutions have established subsidiaries, known as community development corporations, to engage directly in community partnerships for economic development. Regulation has prompted large banks to make direct investment in independent community development entities and intermediaries. To be poised to respond to such investment and lending opportunities, larger banking organizations often establish separate departments that specialize in identifying viable investment and lending opportunities, and structuring project financing that uses leveraged funding and tax credit programs to enhance the financial viability of the transactions.

Public-Private Partnerships

Public policy has evolved to recognize the limits of one-dimensional strategies in revitalizing economically distressed communities. As a result, multifaceted, public-private collaborations have become vital to addressing market gaps in lower-income neighborhoods. Community economic development initiatives are typically funded through collaboration among many players: government, philanthropy, nonprofit organizations, faith-based organizations, and businesses. This expansive base of partners has furthered the public dialogue on both the interests of and appropriate roles for the various entities involved in revitalizing and stabilizing low-income communities. Current community economic development policy centers on the premise that the public sector should serve as a catalyst for revitalization by (1) creating incentives that attract private sector investment for redevelopment while (2) supporting local organizations and leaders in defining the vision for the community and implementing corresponding programs and projects.

Community Leadership

Decades of policy and funding experimentation have demonstrated the essential role that local leaders must play in driving redevelopment efforts in lower-income communities. With their intimate knowledge of the market and vision for development, community-based leaders have essential knowledge and can most effectively identify the market gaps and mobilize resident support of redevelopment projects.[6]

In response to a lack of banking presence in their neighborhoods, community leaders and activists throughout the country have established a broad base of community development corporations that provide a range of local redevelopment services, from funding to technical assistance and social services. Many of these organizations offer credit to support small entrepreneurs and affordable housing developers, increasing access to asset accumulation for lower-income populations. In some cases, local leaders have endeavored to offer full-service banking to their communities, often in response to both real and perceived gaps in financial services in their market. From this void has emerged community development financial institutions (CDFIs). These mission-driven banks, thrifts, loan pools, and venture capital funds promote community development and focus their efforts on stimulating the local economy, creating jobs, and improving the quality of life in low-income neighborhoods. With this mission, an institution's viability pivots on its capacity to be innovative in every aspect of its business, from capitalizing its operations, underwriting and servicing loans, and attracting investors to designing retail products that respond to the financial services needs of its community.

This paper explores the business strategy of a CDFI bank located in the U.S. capital, City *First* Bank of D.C. This institution, opened in November 1998, was founded by a group of community leaders who believed that their underserved neighborhood could be revitalized only through the presence of a local community bank. With this determination, the founders appealed to both the economic sensibilities and civic responsibilities of local and national partners to establish City *First* Bank of D.C., whose market consists primarily of low- and moderate-income neighborhoods with an overall poverty level of 19 percent.[7] The institution's managers have been strategic and unconventional in executing the bank's business plan. Further, the model illustrates how a low-income community can be empowered through use of policy and business strategies that tap local leadership, public and private sector institutions, and federal bank regulatory agencies.

The Origins of City *First* Bank of D.C.

As Washington, D.C., emerged from a recession in the mid-1990s, a group of concerned citizens established a nonprofit organization to analyze the local market to determine the credit and capital needed to stimulate economic development in the community. A stagnant economy, bank consolidation, and bank failures had contributed to a void in access to credit that local small businesses needed to sustain and grow their operations. To demonstrate the demand for small business loans in the community, a nonprofit organization, Community First, Inc., became a certified lender under the U.S. Small Business Administration's 504 loan program, which grew into a $10 million operation in a five-year period. This demonstration project lent insight into the broader demand for financial services in the community, leading to creation of a community bank that could provide the full complement of necessary credit and deposit services.

Capitalizing City *First* Bank of D.C.

To assemble the approximately $9.4 million required to capitalize City *First* Bank and its bank holding company, CFBanc Corporation, organizers appealed to the interests of a range of private and public institutions with a vested interest in revitalizing the bank's target market. With motivations including business development, regulatory incentive, mission fulfillment, and public relations, these local and national investors committed to being passive partners and patient investors in the bank.

The primary investor of the bank holding company is a nonprofit organization, City *First* Enterprises, Inc. (f/k/a CFBanc Holdings, Inc.), which amassed its 48 percent stake in the bank holding company through funding from the U.S. Department of Housing and Urban Development, a federal agency with the mission "to increase homeownership, support community development and increase access to affordable housing free from discrimination."[8] This funding was supplemented with a $1 million grant from the District of Columbia's Department of Housing and Community Development, an agency charged with furthering community economic and affordable housing development in the city's low- and moderate-income neighborhoods.

The next largest stakeholder in the bank holding company is Georgetown University, making a $1 million grant consistent with the institution's community service and investment interests.[9] University officials recognize that an investment in a community development bank promotes a vital community, critical to the stability and viability of Georgetown University.[10]

Additional mission-oriented funding, nearly $2 million, was secured from the National Community Investment Fund (NCIF)[11] and Fannie Mae Corporation, a government-sponsored enterprise with the statutory obligation to "take affirmative steps to assist primary lenders to make housing credit available in areas with concentrations of low-income and minority families. . . ."[12]

A group of six large bank investors and one national mortgage lending company supplied an additional $1.4 million in equity to capitalize the bank. These institutions recognized that a community development bank could more effectively meet the market demands of the lower-income, low-volume communities of Washington, D.C. In addition, banks receive favorable recognition from their regulators under the Community Reinvestment Act for investments in City *First* Bank, in fulfillment of the statutory objective that "regulated financial institutions have continuing and affirmative obligation to help meet the credit needs of the local communities in which they are chartered."[13]

The bank's deposit portfolio is essential to the capitalization of its lending program. Approximately 40 percent of the deposit base is the result of concerted efforts to attract large, stable institutional depositors, such as public authorities, foundations, nonprofits, churches, faith-based and nonfaith-based social service agencies, and companies for whom corporate citizenship is an important part of their vision. Nonetheless, City *First* Bank must be competitive on rate and service in order to retain these accounts.

In raising institutional deposits, City *First* Bank has taken advantage of two programs: a public-sector local program and a private-sector national program. Through the District of Columbia's Local, Small, Disadvantaged Business Enterprise (LSDBE) Program, a relationship with City *First* Bank rewards businesses who are competing for city contracts with extra points in the competitive bidding process. Because institutional depositors' investment policies typically require that the bank collateralize or otherwise insure deposits, the bank participates in the Certificate of Deposit Account Registry Service (CDARS), which enables member banks to obtain federal insurance on large deposits (up to $25 million), allowing banks to attract large, stable deposits.[14]

Developing Business Lines Responsive to Local Market Credit Needs

With its community development mission, City *First* Bank management recognized that redevelopment of the economically distressed neighborhoods in its service area would require unique products and lenders to implement the strategy of broader revitalization led through the development of micromarkets. With this, lines of business naturally developed around the market's primary agents of community economic development: small businesses, affordable housing redevelopers, and nonprofit community organizations such as churches, charter schools, and community development corporations. Generally, these segments are underserved by traditional financial institutions because their unique characteristics do not lend themselves to standardized bank products or processes. Accordingly, the bank's business strategy revolves around four fundamental tenets:

1. *Market specialists.* To serve its niche market of small entrepreneurs, nascent real estate developers, and nonprofit directors, the bank employs lenders who possess a high degree of market expertise and can meet the demands of its resource-intensive clientele. Intimate knowledge of the market allows lenders to structure credit consistent with the pace of a specific business in a particular neighborhood.

2. *Flexible underwriting.* Because its customers' credit and business experience are often limited or unfavorable, management recognized that standardized credit scoring techniques would not be a viable approach to loan underwriting. Therefore the bank's underwriters evaluate the viability of the business, the reasonableness of the credit request in the context of the lenders' market, and the capacity of the borrower to meet the terms of the loan agreement rather than relying on a computer-generated score. This credit assessment process also ensures that credit is structured to achieve success for both the borrower (through repayment) and for the community (through completion and sustainability of the project).

3. *Unique, responsive products.* Although resource-intensive, the extensive market and borrower intelligence of City *First* Bank lenders enable creative and responsive product development and provider differentiation. For example, traditional creditors typically offer separate loans for acquisition, construction, and permanent financing to borrowers seeking to renovate residential housing, which can increase the cost of credit through the loan processing fees assessed at each stage of financing. Further, the borrower may have to seek another lender during the process because a creditor may not offer all of the various types of credit that the project requires. To distinguish itself in the market, City *First* Bank has combined these various loans into one product, enabling affordable housing renovators to obtain all of their financing at one institution. Similarly, this approach to product development has extended to the bank's other clientele as well, with City *First* Bank distinguishing itself as an exclusive creditor among local charter schools, houses of worship, and nonprofit social service organizations.

4. *Loan servicing and credit oversight.* As with the other aspects of the bank's credit process, loan servicing and oversight is resource-intensive, with the lenders furnishing extensive technical assistance to borrowers to ensure that the business is meeting its targets and obligations. Necessarily, the bank retains all loan servicing responsibilities in order to preserve its close client relationship, maintain its presence within the community, and cultivate new business through the community networks.

Financial Performance

Since opening in late 1998, City *First* Bank has demonstrated impressive growth (Figure 21.1), originating $170 million in loans (with $66 million loans outstanding in 2004) and increasing its deposit base by 1,200 percent in the six-year period. With nearly $105 million in assets by year-end 2004, the bank earned $1.3 million and reported a 1.59 percent return on assets (ROA). The average ROA for the banking industry was 1.36 percent for 2004.[15]

In addition, City *First* Bank experiences lower-than-average default and delinquency rates on its loans, which it attributes to a high-touch approach to loan serving and the extensive technical assistance offered to borrowers. For 2004, the bank reported a rate of 0.1 percent of net charge-offs to average loans, as compared to the industry average of 0.67 percent.[16]

The bank has a comprehensive approach to risk management. In addition to rigorous monitoring and oversight strategies, management maintains higher-than-average loan loss reserves, executive management is highly involved in credit decisions, and the board of directors plays an active role in credit and loss mitigation policy development.

FIGURE 21.1. FINANCIAL RESULTS, 1998–2004.

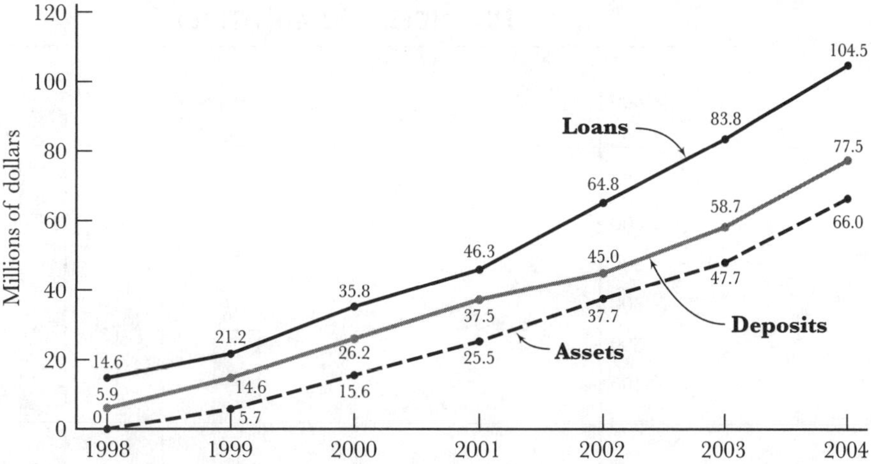

Source: City *First* Bank of D.C.

Community Impact

As a mission-driven institution, the impact of City *First* Bank's banking activities is critical, but measurement of impact and success is a vexing challenge for the community development industry. The metrics necessary to establish causality between the discrete activities of one institution and the larger economic condition of a community are not available. Therefore attribution of direct community impacts is limited to the direct relationships that the bank has with its clients. Discussion of City *First* Bank's community impact centers on creation of affordable housing units, businesses, and jobs resulting directly from the bank's lending activities.

Within the bank's first five years of operation, it has steadily increased its portfolio of loans to redevelop affordable housing units (Figure 21.2). As of year-end 2004, the bank has directly financed redevelopment of more than seventeen hundred affordable housing units, growing this line of business by 145 times over the period.

In addition, through its lending activities to small businesses and entrepreneurs in the community, nearly eighteen hundred jobs have been created or retained (Figure 21.3).

These financing activities have had a direct impact on the personal wealth of local housing developers and entrepreneurs in the market, contributing to increased net worth for these borrowers. Community residents have also benefited from the

FIGURE 21.2. AFFORDABLE HOUSING UNITS FINANCED (CUMULATIVE).

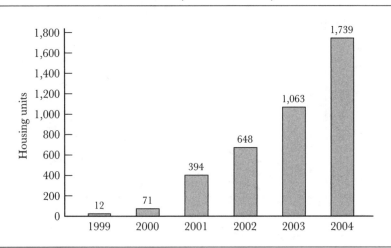

Source: City *First* Bank of D.C.

FIGURE 21.3. JOBS CREATED OR RETAINED (CUMULATIVE).

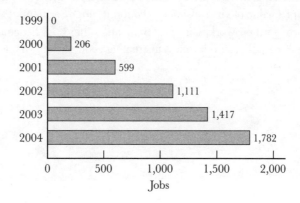

Source: City *First* Bank of D.C.

success of local business owners. For example, City *First* Bank's financing of a job training enterprise resulted in bringing computer technology training to 150 residents, with 60 students placed in positions within the community. Another financing arrangement to a tenant association enabled renters of a thirty-nine-unit apartment building to become homeowners through conversion of the residence to condominiums.

Replicating the City *First* Bank Business Model

These observations of City *First* Bank's strategies, performance, and impact demonstrate both desired public policy and practical outcomes when banking regulation, public-private partnerships, and community leadership converge. With its multiple institutional investors, strategic collaborations, and niche market approach to its business, the bank represents a dynamic model for enabling and funding community economic development.

City *First* Bank offers community developers and policymakers a rich case study for exploring the intersection of public and private interests in redevelopment of low-income communities and strategies for serving their residents. This community development bank also permits insight into policy mechanisms that present meaningful incentives to for-profit organizations to give low-income populations access to competitive financial services.

The origins and operations of City *First* Bank underscore the merit of rebuilding a community from within, tapping local leaders to impart the vision and facilitate implementation and empowering entrepreneurs and residents through access to credit, asset building tools, and employment opportunities. Further, the response of investors, institutional depositors, and business partners to City *First* Bank also demonstrates the market value of the mission of economic empowerment of low-income populations. Through their work, City *First* Bank and other CDFIs demonstrate the interdependence of policy and business in creating economically viable markets that yield both financial and social returns.

CHAPTER TWENTY-TWO

HOUSES FOR THE POOR AND NEW BUSINESS FOR BANKS

Creating a Market for Affordable Housing

Doug Guthrie, Michael McQuarrie

In the 1970s, America's cities were in deep crisis. Decaying housing projects, deindustrialization, and municipal budget crises left many cities in a state of abandonment and disarray. Cities such as Cleveland experienced bankruptcy and the subsequent collapse of municipal government.[1] Because of redlining—the practice of denying or increasing the cost of banking services to residents of certain areas—banks were singled out as one of the key culprits in the decline of urban centers. However, in the three decades since the turmoil of the mid-1970s, banks have built a new business around aggressively pursuing the market for low-income housing.

Community development banking is now a lucrative business in major banks across the country. To take one example, in 1999 Bank of America, which holds the oldest bank-owned community development corporation in the country, pledged $750 *billion* over a 10-year period to community development initiatives,[2] the vast majority of which would take place in low-income housing in urban areas—the very same areas that banks systematically disregarded in the 1970s. As Figure 22.1 shows, the greater part of these resources—nearly 80 percent, or more than $86 billion in the first five years—has gone to affordable housing. This is not charity; it is clearly a market in which U.S. banks are making money by serving the poor. Indeed, in the Bank of

Research for this paper was funded through a grant from the Ford Foundation, with additional support provided by the Social Science Research Council. Direct correspondence to Doug Guthrie, Department of Management and Organization, Stern School of Business, New York University, New York, NY 10012; doug.guthrie@nyu.edu.

FIGURE 22.1. BANK OF AMERICA'S LENDING AND INVESTMENT IN COMMUNITY ECONOMIC DEVELOPMENT, 1999–2004.

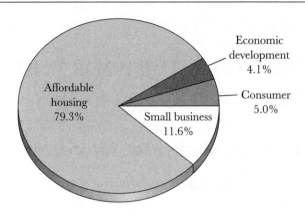

Source: Bank of America.

America case, in 2002 the community development banking division posted revenues of $160 million and operating profits of $60 million.[3]

How was this market created? Policy makers and scholars often point to the federal legislation of the 1970s as a turning point: the Equal Credit Opportunity Act of 1974, the Home Mortgage Disclosure Act of 1975, and the Community Reinvestment Act (CRA) of 1977 are widely credited with the transformation of banking presence in urban centers.[4] Though necessary, these federal acts alone were insufficient stimulants for bank involvement in low-income housing markets, and it is a mistake to see them as successful in their aims. Indeed, the key piece of legislation—the catalyst that gave creation of an inner-city housing market serious momentum—was a small provision in the Tax Reform Act of 1986, the Low-Income Housing Tax Credit (LIHTC). We argue that it is actually the synergistic relationship between the CRA and the LIHTC that transformed bank practices in pursuit of the low-income housing market.[5] The history of this legislation illuminates how legislators, corporations, and institutional entrepreneurs came together to create a market that legislators on their own failed to shape. The LIHTC was the catalyst that brought banks, corporations, community developers, and local governments together to build the market for low-income housing.[6]

Making Banks Accountable

That many cities were in deep crisis by the early 1970s was clear to virtually all observers of urban life in the United States.[7] In the post–Civil Rights era, there was also growing recognition that many housing policies were shaped by a racism that undergirded the very institutions that dealt with housing development, from banks to the Department of Housing and Urban Development in the federal government. "Redlining" practices by banks became one of the hottest issues of the time, and community activists began to pressure legislators to do something about the issue.[8] The Fair Housing Act (1968), the Equal Credit Opportunity Act (1974), the Home Mortgage Disclosure Act (HMDA) (1975), and the Community Reinvestment Act (CRA) (1977) were all results of this pressure.[9] HMDA and the CRA are often viewed as going hand-in-hand, as the former forced banks to report their lending practices while the latter articulated standards by which banks should manage their lending.

There are two parts to the CRA. First, lenders are required to serve the local communities in which they do business. Second, in serving those communities, they must serve the entire community, including low- and middle-income constituencies.[10] Under the CRA, lending institutions are required to (1) provide fair access to credit and deposit services (for example, ensure that local communities have access to local branches or ATMs), (2) ensure that citizens have access to a public CRA record, and (3) guarantee that banks are involved in the local communities they are required to serve. The agencies that assess bank practices in the area of the CRA are the Federal Reserve Board, the Office of the Comptroller, the Federal Deposit Insurance Corporation, and the Office of Thrift Supervision. Individual bank establishments are rated on a scale of 1 to 4 (1 = outstanding, 2 = satisfactory, 3 = needs to improve, 4 = substantial noncompliance).[11] What amounts to the real teeth in the CRA lies in the fact that bank mergers are contingent on approval from the federal government. Thus, if a given bank seeks to acquire a second bank, one of the criteria on which banks are assessed is their adherence to the CRA.

Many scholars view the CRA as largely responsible for turning America's urban crisis around; this is a misreading of the legislative history and of legislation's immediate impact. Indeed, its actual effect in the 1970s and early 1980s was relatively small. Banks generally became involved in low-income communities through grants and charitable donations to local nonprofit organizations—they changed their behavior enough to get CRA credit—but the legislation did nothing to change the logic of their lending practices. Because urban areas were still considered high-risk, for the most part, banks chose not to change their lending practices with respect to high-risk urban areas.

In 1981, as part of the Economic Recovery Act, Congress attempted a new change in the tax code that would give individuals incentives to invest in low-income housing—just as corporations are allowed to write-off taxes against the "passive losses" tied to the depreciating value of their assets, individuals were allowed to take passive losses against the depreciating value of low-income property.[12] By the mid-1980s, however, many in Congress recognized the host of problems that were associated with this provision. First of all, though the passive-loss provision encouraged private ownership of low-income housing, it was actually contributing to urban blight; because the provision hinged on depreciating value, the incentives were for individuals to intentionally allow newly purchased properties to become run-down (the more depreciation in the value, the greater the write-off). However, unlike corporations, which need to protect the quality of their assets, the new landlords of low-income housing had no incentive to raise property values. Second, many wealthy individuals were finding ways to avoid taxes entirely, simply through investment in run-down property.[13]

In 1986, Congress passed a major overhaul of the federal tax code, the Tax Reform Act of 1986. The act included a small provision that would have major implications for the development of low-income housing while producing a windfall for corporations: the Low-Income Housing Tax Credit (LIHTC). Although the LIHTC is often cited as an instance of bipartisan cooperation that led to an effective system of privatizing a public good, the reality is that the LIHTC was not originally intended for corporations. Yet social entrepreneurs figured out a way to make the LIHTC extremely beneficial for the corporate and banking community, thereby creating an attractive business opportunity for them and at the same time serving the poor of America's cities. The LIHTC's history suggests that social entrepreneurs can derive significant value by using legislation to create business opportunities that benefit both the corporate sector as well as low-income communities.

Congress passed the LIHTC as part of an effort to close the passive-loss loophole, which, as was described earlier, had become lucrative for wealthy individuals. Congress clearly and explicitly acknowledged at the time that creating the LIHTC required closing the passive-loss loophole; there was widespread agreement that investors should not get a double dip with both passive losses and tax credits, which are dollar-for-dollar write-offs against tax liability. It is crucial to reemphasize here that the LIHTC was originally intended for *individuals*. In the entire record of the Ninety-Ninth Congress, there is no mention of corporations as intended beneficiaries of the tax credits. Indeed, the entire debate over whether to eliminate passive losses centered on how to move rich people away from investments that rely on depreciation to those that would use the tax credit. At the time, the consensus among people in the community development industry was that the legislation would not help them much.

However, in early 1987, a group of people involved in community development in Cleveland realized that corporations were much better suited for investing in the LIHTC than individuals, for a variety of reasons. They saw something in the legislation that others did not: corporate tax liability is much greater than individual liability, so the potential pool of cash that could be channeled into low-income housing was much greater. More important, although Congress had eliminated passive losses for individuals, the shelters still existed for corporations (corporations have long held the benefit of passive-loss write-offs against depreciation of assets). The innovation was that, if they could create an intermediary organization to manage the properties, low-income housing could be counted as a corporate asset. This meant companies could double-dip by buying tax credits *and* writing off passive losses against future depreciation of low-income property. By itself, the LIHTC offered no more than an even tradeoff with paying taxes to the government, and corporations had little incentive to participate. But once passive losses were added, the deals were irresistible. Joe Hagan, the current president of the National Equity Fund and the broker of the first corporate LIHTC deal, estimated that many of the early packages he put together yielded an additional 15 percent return for corporations in unpaid taxes over the following decade. Rather than simply pay taxes, corporations could take their tax liability, "invest" it in low-income housing, and generate significant extra income. With beneficiaries on both ends of the political spectrum, powerful lobbies quickly formed to protect the LIHTC. By the late 1980s, this political mistake would become one of the key engines of urban revitalization in the United States, giving rise to a whole new industry of community developers and related financiers. It also became one of the most significant vehicles for corporate welfare, guaranteeing it an entrenched place in the federal tax code. In short, since 1986 the LIHTC has become the primary driver behind the flow of resources into inner-city housing project development, accounting for more than $5 billion in corporate dollars invested in low-income housing. It is important to note, however, that the figure of $5 billion only scratches the surface of what the LIHTC actually means in terms of the flow of resources. As Figure 22.2 shows, in the past Section 8 New Construction Projects were built almost fully on government direct allocations. The LIHTC acts as initial financing that then leverages other sources—usually constituting somewhere between 15 and 30 percent of the total financing of a low-income housing development project—in order to make the financing by commercial institutions more attractive. As a result, the resources here offer financing that attracts financiers—namely, banks and developers—that heretofore had little to do with low-income development projects.

In an LIHTC deal, the IRS allocates tax credits to the states at a rate of $1.80 per person in the state population. State housing agencies then distribute the credits to developers on the basis of a point system that reflects the priorities of state government. Syndicators such as the National Equity Fund sell the credits to corporations, often at a discount, and developers use the resulting capital to erect low-income housing units. The credits usually fund 30–70 percent of a property's development costs, with the rest of the capital coming from other sources (bank loans, government housing bonds, private money). Banks usually furnish capital in the form of purchased credits and credit. Finally, the flow of resources across the system is considerably liquid, because LIHTCs can be resold on the secondary market as mortgage-backed securities. Through the secondary market, Fannie Mae has become the largest holder of LIHTCs in the country. Figure 22.3 shows the flow of resources across the organizations that populate this new organizational field.

FIGURE 22.2. FEDERALLY SUBSIDIZED AND LIHTC MULTIFAMILY HOUSING UNITS, 1970–2000.

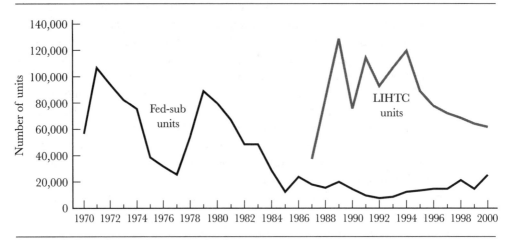

Source: U.S. Census Bureau, Current Housing Reports.

By the time the tax credit was up for renewal in 1989 (Congress had attached a sunset clause), the emerging LIHTC industry was enjoying significant momentum, and powerful interest groups—from corporations to nonprofit developers to the members of Congress who represented them—arose to protect it. The LIHTC soon acquired strong bipartisan support in Congress. Conservatives who pushed for the double tax break for wealthy individuals found they had unwittingly appeased a much wealthier and more powerful constituency: the corporate community. At this point, the debate over passive losses quickly fell away, as Republicans realized they had gotten even more than they initially asked for in their desire to reinstate the passive-loss provision. Congressional Democrats realized that, in an era of declining budgets for HUD, the tax credits, which uncorked a growing flood of resources into urban housing projects, were perhaps the best they could hope for.

Subsequent changes in the industry and legislation came quickly. The LIHTC became a catalyst that allowed community development organizations such as the Local Initiative Support Corporation (LISC) and the Enterprise Foundation to situate themselves at the center of local development deals, giving them an institutional power they never held before. In 1987, both of these organizations founded new subsidiaries, respectively the National Equity Fund (NEF) and the Enterprise Social Investment Corporation (ESIC), which syndicated tax credits and managed the resulting funds. In addition, with new funding sources flowing into the industry, LISC and the Enterprise Foundation began to work with banks as well as corporations in structuring deals.

FIGURE 22.3. LIHTC REGIME.

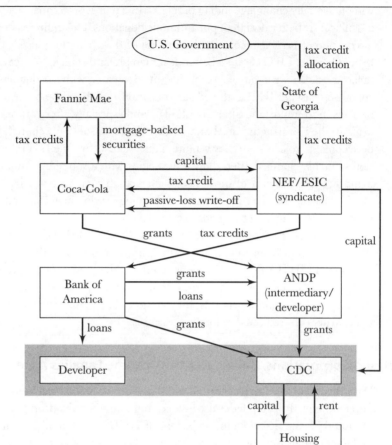

The Implications for Banks

Once intermediary organizations such as NEF and ESIC were in place to manage low-income properties, for corporations the financial benefits attached to buying the credits made participation in the LIHTC program a relatively simple calculus. But large banks began to get involved in inner-city development as well, and the benefit for banks became perhaps even greater. First, as C-corporations large banks were eligible for the same double-dip benefits (credit plus passive-loss write-off) of the LIHTC. Second, because banks had been under pressure since 1977 to direct their business to the inner cities in which they operated as a way to combat redlining, the purchase of LIHTCs became yet another way in which banks could improve their CRA ratings without actually changing lending practices. In a pair-wise comparison, LIHTCs are a significantly better deal than philanthropic donations. Philanthropic donations yield a reduction of taxable income in the amount of the philanthropic gift. Even without the double-dip, LIHTCs are a better deal than philanthropic gifts because they are a dollar-for-dollar write-off of taxable income. However, with the double-dip the benefit of purchasing LIHTCs immediately outstripped philanthropic activity. Third, and perhaps most important, after the LIHTC (and especially after corporations started using it) the risk structure for banks in the inner city suddenly shifted. If inner-city development projects were risky ventures in the years before the LIHTC, the risk equation suddenly changed after 1986. This begins with a subtle but important change in the incentive structure of the development deals that emerged in this period.[14] Once the risk structure of inner-city low-income housing development changed, banks began to see the inner city as a tremendous opportunity.

Because of the synergy between the CRA and the LIHTC, banks actually had the most to gain from this new system. They could realize the same benefits of investing in LIHTCs that corporations could, but they could also improve their CRA ratings. Finally, and most important, with the changing risk structure and the gentrification of these neighborhoods, they could at last realize the value of being the underwriters of credit in developing these areas.

Benefiting Corporations, Banks, and Low-Income Families Alike

With the LIHTC, Congress found a mechanism to privatize low-income housing development. By 1986, federally funded, multifamily units dropped below twenty thousand for the first time in the history of HUD; by 1988, nearly all low-income multifamily units were being funded by the LIHTC. This shift marked a fundamental moment of institutional change, though not only because it represented a transformation of the funding and development of a public good. Government resources in the form of tax credits leveraged other resources, allowing actors in this newly emerging field to create a common pool of funds and a common set of goals. But "privatization" does not really define this process, because it implies a transfer of public expenditures to private hands. Instead, this process represents a basic transformation of fund generation and governance for housing policy. More important, this was one of the early experiments in the trend toward removing the federal government from housing development and management. The LIHTC has become the primary driver behind the flow of resources into inner-city housing construction, accounting for more than $5 billion in corporate investments.

The history of the low-income housing tax credit is a story not only of the unintended consequences of government action but also of the role of social entrepreneurship in creating business opportunities for corporations and banks to deliver services to low-income families. Government creates opportunities, and social entrepreneurs use them to forge new models of action. In 1986, the tax credit was little more than an attempt to deal with the political bombshell that tax shelters for wealthy individuals had become. But it brought unanticipated applications, fundamentally changing the flow of resources in community development and constituting it as a new organizational field. Social entrepreneurs seized on this opening to produce a new model of resource allocation in support of a much-needed public good. The LIHTC was a tipping point of sorts, bringing corporations and commercial banks into community development in an unprecedented way. Today, the LIHTC is backed by a vigorous community development industry that has radically transformed how low-income housing is funded and built in urban areas throughout the country.

Let's look at a concrete example: the African American neighborhood of Mt. Pleasant, which is located next door to the affluent Shaker Heights area in Cleveland. In 1992, construction workers began building fifty new single-family homes in Mt. Pleasant. The dwellings marked the first time LIHTCs were used in Mt. Pleasant. Instead of concentrating the subsidized homes in one part of Mt. Pleasant, developers spread them out over roughly forty blocks, building on vacant lots between existing homes (a technique known as "in-fill" construction). The results soon began to transform Mt. Pleasant. A strip shopping mall was built in 1995. Drug stores began to pop up. Home prices began to rise. Residents took more pride in the area. The local city councilwoman began holding contests for best lawn and most beautifully decorated balcony. Families could lease the three-bedroom, one-and-a-half-bathroom houses for $350 a month, with an option to buy after fifteen years. The lion's share of the new homes were targeted for parts of Mt. Pleasant that were the most deteriorated, but community developers deliberately avoided clustering the dwellings together. Success bred success. Once local banks realized that tax-credit-financed housing was making Mt. Pleasant stabler, they became more comfortable about making construction loans there, adding to the stock of new homes. The fifty-unit Mt. Pleasant Homes project gave way to a second fifty-unit Mt. Pleasant Homes II project (followed in 1997 by the Mt. Pleasant Homes III project). Tax credits combined with historic rehabilitation credits helped finance the conversion of a one-time girl's school, Notre Dame Academy, into seventy-three apartments for seniors. Since the 1986 advent of the low-income housing tax credit program, more than five thousand units have been built in Cleveland.[15]

Assessing the Policy

We need to be cautious about using the LIHTC as a model for public policy. First, the tax credits represent a massive windfall for corporations and banks. Under the current system, corporations and banks receive both tax credits and passive loss write-offs that

Congress has placed out of bounds for individuals. The LIHTC is also one of many mechanisms allowing corporations to become ever less linked to the welfare state.[16] Linking the development of a public good to the logic of the market has costs as well. For example, developers of LIHTC properties have incentives to keep them at the high end of the low-income category—defined as up to 60 percent of local median income—so they can extract the highest rents possible. Fifty percent of median income is certainly low-income, but it is a position that is occupied by the working poor. If the LIHTC replaces all federally funded new construction, then who will build housing for the truly poor? When we posed such a question to a city official in Atlanta, he simply shrugged and said, "Good question. We do worry about what this is doing to the truly poor."

The LIHTC was not a simple case of privatization. Local governments, nonprofit community builders, corporations, and commercial banks came together, each with its own set of interests, in partnerships that have transformed some cities in the last decade and a half. Moreover, these partnerships have empowered local nonprofit and community groups in a way that was not possible before. They have not only brought about a more direct flow of resources for community groups but have put nonprofits at the table with corporate and financial institutions.

These mechanisms are part of a new era of corporate social investment. Though corporations and banks are less moved by the "responsibility" element in the much-touted concept of "corporate social responsibility," they *are* moved by incentives that add up on the accounting side of things. If they can achieve a positive balance sheet while helping to develop a public good, so much the better.

The CRA alone did not have the impact many hoped or thought it would in transforming corporate and banking accountability in inner-city low-income housing development. But coupled with the properties of the LIHTC, corporations and banks were uniquely positioned to benefit from a set of incentives that would help them create an entirely new and lucrative market for low-income housing. Through this mechanism, banks realize the benefits of a new set of markets, and low-income families realize the benefits of rejuvenated low-income urban areas.

CHAPTER TWENTY-THREE

THE SOUTH AFRICAN FINANCIAL SECTOR CHARTER

A Supplementary Market Framework to Achieve Affirmative Action

R. S. Tucker, Thomas S. Mondschean, Bruce R. Scott

This paper reports on a program designed to increase black participation in the South African financial system.[1] The Financial Sector Charter is a comprehensive ten-year plan to encourage, among other things, greater black ownership of financial institutions, a higher proportion of black employment at all skill levels in South African financial firms, a higher level of procurement from black-owned and -operated companies, and increased access to financial services.

There are three elements to the plan that make the charter, in our opinion, unique among other attempts around the world to open up financial systems to the poor and underserved. First, the agreement incorporates a market-driven incentive plan that rewards firms for meeting the targets embodied in the charter, in contrast to other programs that mandate a minimum level that must be achieved to avoid penalties. Second, the charter is more comprehensive (in terms of both the number of areas and the degree of specificity in which improvement in black participation is encouraged) than any other programs we are aware of. Third, the agreement was negotiated between representatives of the South African firms in the financial services industries and representatives of black professional groups that participate or wish to participate in the financial system. This last point is important because in the long run it means the participants have truly agreed to the terms; they accept the spirit as well as the letter of the charter and have achieved a measure of mutual understanding and trust through the negotiation process.

The Context

The need for a new approach arose in large part because little progress was made in dismantling the legacy of the apartheid system following the formal regime change in 1994. Apartheid was a legal system of racial separation and repression that ensured the dominance of whites throughout the economy as well as the political bodies. The repression took many forms, among them a migratory labor system; separate educational systems by race; prohibition of any black rising to the level of supervisor or above in the workplace, trading for his own account outside the Bantustans (lands set aside for black occupation), or owning property outside the Bantustans; and prohibition of any person residing in a "group area" not reserved for people of that race, as well as forced removal of people who were doing so.

The era of formal white political domination ended in 1994 when Nelson Mandela was elected president, the African National Congress (ANC) won a clear majority in Parliament, and both proceeded to form South Africa's first democratically elected government. After decades of oppression at the hands of the white minority, it would not have been surprising for the new government to take forcible action to redistribute wealth and power as well as prosecute and punish key supporters of apartheid. Instead, the government established a Truth and Reconciliation Commission to encourage disclosure and healing, and President Mandela took the lead in assuring key white leaders of their welcome to the new South Africa. This peaceful transfer of power was nothing short of miraculous, and a triumph for all concerned.

At that time, the ruling party included a strong Communist component as well as a powerful and well-organized labor movement. These two key pillars of political support were soon called on to abandon their notions of nationalization, expansionary budgets, and income redistribution in favor of a liberal trade policy, restrictive monetary policy, strong fiscal policy (facilitated by reducing the military budget), and sweeping educational reforms designed to unify the school systems. The willingness of the new regime to forgo long-standing policy goals in favor of policies to promote macroeconomic stability, lower inflation, and market liberalization was a remarkable transformation for a party that had just taken power for the first time, following decades of active and at times brutal subjugation.

However, recovery of the South African economy was less than miraculous. Real GDP per capita barely increased between 1994 and 1999, and only by 1.4 percent per year from 1999 to 2003, though inflation was successfully tamed. Though this performance was better than in preceding years, real incomes in 2000 were about what they had been at the height of the raw materials boom in 1975 and again in 1981. The government's policies were less successful in reducing the black-white income gap. Table 23.1 shows that the average white household earned about 4.5 times as much as its black counterpart in 1995, and by 2000 this ratio was up to six times. Adjusted

TABLE 23.1. MEDIAN HOUSEHOLD INCOME BY ETHNIC GROUPING (IN RANDS).

Ethnic Group (Percentage of Population)	1995 (Current Prices)	2000 (Current Prices)	Percentage Change in Nominal Terms	Percentage Change in Real Terms
African/black (77)	23,000	26,000	13.0	–18.2
Colored (9)	32,000	51,000	59.4	15.4
Indian/Asian (3)	71,000	85,000	19.7	–13.3
White (11)	103,000	158,000	53.4	11.1
Total	37,000	45,000	21.6	–11.9

Source: Statistics South Africa, *Earning and Spending in South Africa,* 2002. The percentage of the country's 1996 population is shown in parentheses. From 1995 to 2000, the consumer price index in South Africa rose by 38 percent. According to the report, the top 20 percent of households earned 65 percent of total income in 2000. The bottom 20 percent of households earned 1.6 percent of total income in 2000.

for inflation, median income for black families fell by 18.2 percent in real terms over these same years while median income for whites rose 11 percent.

Thus, in spite of its new regime, South Africa continued to have one of the most unequal income distributions in the world. In 2000, the 80th percentile of the income distribution earned 17.8 times the level earned by a household at the 20th percentile. Blacks were enjoying their first real successes in the political realm, but they experienced much less improvement in economic terms.

Business as Usual Leads to Pressures for Change

Although abandonment of apartheid in favor of a black majority government was peaceful, it seemed to legitimize the status quo. The business community settled back into doing "legitimate" business as usual. In fact, the level of energy to do something about the economic and social plight of the majority of the population seemed, if anything, to decline, which was due in no small measure to the strong parliamentary majority of the new government. The general attitude of business seemed to be to let the democratically elected government take responsibility for planning the societal transformation while they tended to their own business affairs. White firms recognized that they were going to be increasingly dependent on black political power exercised through government, so they attempted to legitimize themselves by taking on "elite" black partners who might or might not have real power within the firm—a strategy that could amount to tokenism. This response was of grave concern to black professionals, who recognized that they could essentially be bypassed in the new system as they were in its predecessor.

It was in this context that the Black Business Council, a group comprising twenty-one professional and business organizations, grew concerned that the fruits of economic progress were not being widely disseminated within the black community. As a result, the council established a Black Economic Empowerment (BEE) Commission to develop ideas and proposals that would promote broader access for nonwhites to the benefits of the South African economy. The commission issued a report calling for mandatory, broad-based black economic empowerment (BBBEE).

To encourage greater black participation in the economy, the government passed several laws, including the Skills Development Act of 1998, the Employment Equity Act of 1998, the Skills Development Levies Act of 1999, and the Preferential Procurement Policy Act of 2000. In 1999, the government also announced its plans to introduce legislation based on the U.S. Community Reinvestment Act that would impose certain obligations on banks, such as investment in low-income communities in their areas. In 2000, the Home Loan Disclosure Act was passed as the first component of this platform.

Along with these initiatives, there was public pressure to accelerate the pace of reform. In October 2000, the South African Communist Party (SACP) launched a "Red October" campaign against the banks, demanding access for all to the banking system. The relationship between government and the private sector (and banks in particular) deteriorated as government felt the pressure from its own low-income constituency and received little assistance from the private sector in addressing it.

Early in 2002, the government announced that it was prepared to pass legislation that would compel firms to adopt BBBEE programs or suffer consequences in their transactions with government. The Department of Trade and Industry established a BEE Unit with a mandate to promulgate charters for the various sectors of the economy. Once these charters were promulgated, government agencies would be obliged, when calling for tenders, to take into account the BBBEE credentials of would-be suppliers. As much as 30 percent of the weighting conducted in considering a tender might be based on those BBBEE credentials. Potential suppliers to or supplicants of government would be rated on the extent to which their purchases were from black-empowered suppliers. This meant that business-to-business transactions were likely to force most, if not all, large firms to adopt similar BBBEE programs or risk being shut out of public sector business.

The first government-initiated charter was the Liquid Fuels Industry Charter, followed fairly closely by the Mining Sector Charter in mid-2002. These two initiatives were a wake-up call to the business community, and perhaps to government, as well as to the potential power of the proposed regulatory changes. Mistakes were made in the early phases of the latter attempt, including a leak of an early draft of the charter. In a very short space of time, many billions of rand were wiped off the market capitalization of the sector. The adverse market reaction was primarily attributable to a provision in the draft that if a company did not achieve the extremely high targets, its mining licenses might not be renewed. Once the BBBEE decision was announced, it became clear that if the banking industry did not do something proactively, then government would intervene and impose obligations on its sector as well. The debacle following the leak of information about high targets in the mining sector also carried a powerful warning. The financial sector, which was much more susceptible to loss of confidence, could not afford to land in the same predicament.

The Financial Sector Embraces the Concept of Proactive Negotiation[2]

After mass marches in August 2002 by the South African Communist Party (SACP) on the offices of the Banking Council, and faced with an upcoming Financial Sector Summit on August 20, the staff of the Banking Council argued that the industry was at a crossroads. Either an adversarial relationship typified by animosity and negative legislation would be entrenched or a constructive partnership between government and the banking sector would be established, and the decision of which road to choose must be made quickly—or it would be made for them. The board of directors of the Banking Council chose the constructive path, concluding that the industry had no alternative but to move onto the knife edge between making the maximum sustainable contribution to reconstruction and development of the country and simultaneously maintaining the strength and stability of the financial services industries.

It was agreed that the appropriate occasion to signal this commitment would be a speech by Derek Cooper, chairman of Standard Bank Group and Liberty Group, on behalf of the financial sector at the government's Financial Sector Summit on August 20, 2002, in which he stated: "I represent the financial sector, comprising banks, the life offices and short-term insurers. . . . We are fully aware of the need for economic empowerment of all the people of this wonderful country. It would be futile to believe that there can be prosperity for some, without there being a reasonable level of prosperity for most. . . . Today is, for us, a watershed. All four constituencies have effectively been involved in putting together a framework agreement which signifies a new beginning. The next step is to use this framework agreement as the first input for developing the financial sector charter."

As a direct consequence of the Financial Sector Summit and the commitment given by the industry, the cabinet suspended the initiative to introduce CRA-like legislation, and the Home Loan Disclosure Act was never brought into force. The suspension was dependent on government being satisfied that implementation of the Financial Sector Charter would produce the results it intended to achieve by way of the CRA-like legislation.

Following the Financial Sector Summit, the Banking Council was authorized by the board to engage the Association of Black Securities and Investment Professionals

(ABSIP) to discuss formulation of a Financial Sector Charter. An immediate issue was to figure out who had standing to represent the various parties that were affected, and in what framework such negotiations should be conducted. The two sides in this negotiation were characterized by asymmetry. The financial services sector was made up of a small number of large firms (for example, four large commercial banks), and their interests were represented by their CEOs and communicated through the usual hierarchies. The smaller banks, foreign banks, and insurance companies were seen as likely to follow their lead.

In contrast, ABSIP was mandated by numerous black business and professional organizations to represent them in the negotiation of the charter. However, ABSIP represented black professionals (interested primarily in black representation at the management level and in training and development) as well as black businessmen and entrepreneurs (interested primarily in provisions for ownership transfer, procurement from BEE companies, and enterprise development). ABSIP representatives were also in the tough position of having to engage their own bosses in the financial sector and holding the line of the black constituencies that they represented without the benefit of a hierarchy to enforce any eventual decisions.

When the ABSIP and Banking Council representatives regathered, it was agreed that participation in the process and in the charter itself should, at all times, be voluntary. It was also agreed that the only sanctions for noncompliance with the charter should be lower ratings in the government's procurement processes and reputational risk from being seen not to be contributing to BEE. When the targets came up for discussion, it was also agreed that they should be achievable and should be *targets*, not undertakings or obligations. With the benefit of hindsight, it seems clear that the proactive and voluntary nature of the initiative lay at the heart of resolving these potentially contentious issues. As a consequence, the parties came to see each other as partners in a joint venture to create a supplementary market framework for recognizing achievement of progress in affirmative action. Competitive pressures would reward the speed as well as magnitude of change, instead of regulatory pressure for minimal compliance to meet deadlines. All parties were committed to finding solutions and had a sound platform for engaging with each other. In a year of negotiations, there was never a walk-out despite a range of problematic and contentious issues.

By January 2003, the other sectors, including the life offices, short-term insurers, collective investment schemes, fund managers, and foreign-owned banks, had been pulled into the process. There was real competitive pressure on all the financial institutions to engage in the agreement lest they lose out on subsequent business-to-business deals.

One week after the first meeting of the negotiating council, a core group of representatives from ABSIP and the Banking Council met with the minister of finance. Representatives of the Economic Policy Unit of the Presidency, the Department of Trade and Industry, and the National Treasury were also at the meeting. The minister impressed on ABSIP and Banking Council representatives the importance of access to banking services and of human resource development as key pillars of the Financial Sector Charter. He deemphasized ownership transfer and stressed that the parties to the process would not be allowed to "play around" with the stability of the financial sector. By its own decision, the government insisted that this was a voluntary initiative and that it would not intervene in the negotiation; most important, it would not under any circumstances participate in determining the targets. The minister also insisted that the process must result in a charter that went to government, and that government would take responsibility for bringing in the other stakeholders, particularly the labor and community constituencies. This decision assisted the negotiators in containing the number of people and divergence of opinions around the table; it proved important once the composition of the Charter Council came up for discussion.

After several months of discussion, the parties were able to reach agreement. The charter was signed by ten trade associations and ABSIP in a public ceremony chaired by the minister of finance on October 17, 2003. The full cabinet of the South African government met and gave its blessing to the charter the night before (while voicing some concerns, particularly about the apparently low targets for black female representation at various levels of management). The minister of finance gave his blessing by chairing the proceedings but held his position that this was a voluntary initiative on the part of the industry, and that it was inappropriate for him to be a party to it. One could be cynical and suggest that he was reserving his right to condemn it if it didn't work, and support government intervention without embarrassment. But this was not what happened. Instead, the minister has been a key public supporter of the charter, holding it out as a model and opposing any suggestion that the government or anyone else should be allowed to intervene in changing the terms or increasing the targets.

What was accomplished? A voluntary agreement was reached by the various stakeholders in the financial services sector to adopt a BBBEE charter under the auspices of legislation that enabled government to compel the public sector to take BBBEE performance into account in awarding tenders of goods and services to government. The agreement had four levers to induce compliance. First, the charter was formally binding on the state in its evaluation of vendors, but not formally binding on firms in their own business-to-business transactions. Second, the firms in the financial sector agreed that all private sector firms should use the scoring system set up in the agreement to evaluate their transactions within the financial services sector. Third, any firm that chose not to comply with this voluntary agreement could expect to suffer a considerable reputational loss from the unfavorable publicity that such an action would be likely to occasion. Fourth, there was also the risk that a withdrawal might induce the government to impose new regulations on the sector.

Overview of the Financial Sector Charter[3]

The charter is implemented through the calculation of a BEE score, and from that score a grade of A through E. There are six basic areas in which firms can accumulate points: human resource development (20 percent), procurement (15 percent), access to financial services (18 percent), empowerment financing (22 percent), ownership and control (22 percent), and corporate social investment (3 percent). A Charter Council was established to interpret charter provisions when necessary, receive and audit reports, monitor progress, and undertake reviews of progress against the charter objectives. The council is composed of representatives of government, labor, industry, and the broad-based community. The resulting extension of the market framework for the financial services sector is shown schematically in Figure 23.1.

FIGURE 23.1. SOUTH AFRICAN FINANCIAL SECTOR CHARTER.

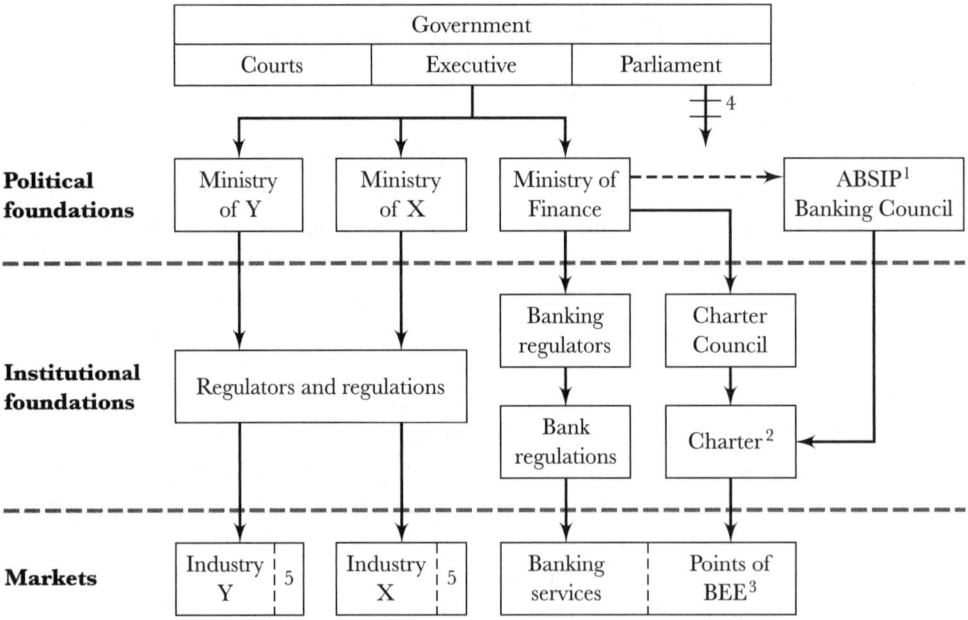

Notes: [1] Temporary political authority implicitly authorized by the South African government.

[2] Supplementary regulations to reflect public purpose (BEE): employment of blacks, services to blacks and the poor, outside purchases, lending to blacks, black equity ownership.

[3] Government and industry backing for supplementary regulations, permits, deposits, tax breaks, business-to-business, reputation.

[4] Mandatory regulations withdrawn.

[5] Mandatory BEE.

Human Resource Development

The human resource development area of the charter is divided into two parts: employment equity and skills development. Management employees are divided into three levels based on salary. Firms receive points for meeting the target for the proportion of black employees in each category, with separate targets for male and female employees.

The second part is skills development, which has two components. First, firms that spend 1.5 percent of their payroll on education and training of nonwhite employees receive 3 points. The second component of skills development is to implement an internship program for unemployed high school graduates.

Procurement

The procurement targets require a financial firm to use the BEE credentials of its suppliers to compute its own BEE scores. The targets specify that by 2008, 50 percent of the value of procurement by financial institutions will be from black-empowered or black companies (or companies with an average BEE score of B or better) and 70 percent by 2014.[4] Although the procurement section determines only 15 percent of a firm's total BEE score, in many ways this is the most important component of the charter because it practically guarantees that financial firms will need to take their BEE scores seriously. In the case of a commercial bank, for example, bank interest and noninterest charges are part of the procurement cost of all their business customers. If a bank has a BEE score that gives them a grade of C, then any business customer of that bank can count only 75 percent of the spending it does with a bank as meeting the procurement standard. This will have the effect of lowering a business's BEE score and make it less desirable as a candidate for government contracts, or even to do business with other firms.

Access to Financial Services

The provisions of the charter that are designed to encourage effective access to financial services for low-income people make up 18 percent of an institution's total BEE score. The specific provisions necessary to score points depend on the type of financial firm. Firms also receive 2 points for spending a minimum of 0.2 percent of their operating profits on consumer education.

One area in which the banking industry has already begun to implement reforms is in basic savings and transaction facilities. Four major banks (ABSA, FNB, Nedbank, and Standard) and the postal savings bank have expanded access to electronic banking services by (1) increasing the number of branches, ATMs, and other service points; (2) allowing equal access to all the banks' ATMs without additional fees; and (3) coming together to offer a basic savings and transaction product known as the "Mzansi" account. This account allows customers to make deposits and withdrawals very cheaply at any ATM machine in the country, and with no administrative fees. The account was first introduced in October 2004. As of May 15, 2005, more than one million accounts have been opened, and 91.3 percent of these accounts are held by previously unbanked clients with their chosen institution.[5] In his budget address to Parliament on February 23, 2005, the minister of finance announced removal of a tax on debit card usage to further reduce the cost of these services.

In addition to providing basic deposit services, banks are also committed to increasing lending to lower-income people. There are targets for loan origination by commercial banks in low-income housing, agriculture, and lending to small and medium enterprises (SMEs) owned by nonwhites.

Empowerment Financing

There are two sets of empowerment financing targets. First, the "charter commits the sector to providing more than R73.5 billion of development finance over the next five years. This includes R25 billion of infrastructure finance; R5 billion of funding for small business; R1.5 billion for rural development; and R42 billion for low-cost housing."[6] This represents 17 percent of an institution's BEE score. Though the banks can meet their share of these investments by originating loans, the empowerment financing targets are for every financial institution that takes savings or investments (defined as "designated investments") from the public (treating even risk insurance as a designated investment) but exclude investments by one financial institution in another (to avoid double counting). The share of the target for each institution is determined by its share of the total designated investments in all financial institutions. For the financial sector as a whole, the empowerment financing target is 3.5 percent of the designated investments.

The second empowerment financing target is to supply resources for BEE equity deals. This represents 5 percent of an institution's BEE score. A common example of a BEE transaction is money lent to a group of black investors to purchase a stake in a firm (analogous to buying stock on margin). The loan might be for ten or fifteen years, it is collateralized by equity, and the dividends from the stock partially offset the interest on the loan. Foreign banks are especially keen to do these deals because in return for exemption from the black ownership targets they need to offer BEE financing instead. Most of the large financial firms now have BEE deals in place to put a portion of their equity into nonwhite hands, but there are a number of small- and medium-sized firms that still need to do this over the next few years.

Ownership and Control

According to the charter, each financial institution has a target of a minimum black ownership of 25 percent by 2010 (14 percent of the total BEE score). A minimum of 10 percent of the target must be satisfied by direct ownership by black people. The remaining 15 percent can be direct or indirect, though firms receive bonus points if some of the remaining 15 percent is also directly owned by blacks.

The issue of what to do about foreign financial firms operating in South Africa was hotly negotiated. Since most foreign-owned banks operate abroad through branches and not wholly owned subsidiaries and typically do not allow foreign ownership if they do have subsidiaries, an alternative means of compliance needed to be developed. The solution was to allow foreign financial institutions to count additional BEE transaction financing, so long as 25 percent of it was in the financial sector.[7] This has actually been a boon to foreign institutions. Much of corporate South Africa has to become BEE compliant, so BEE investment banking deals have become a lucrative source of business in the past two years.

The other provisions under this section of the charter have to do with black participation on corporate boards of directors (3 BEE points) and as corporate executives (5 points). By 2008, one-third of all board members must be black (11 percent of the board members should be black women) and one-quarter of the executives must be black (4 percent must be black women).

Corporate Social Investment

Each financial institution has a target of directing 0.5 percent of its annual posttax operating profit to corporate social investment projects. "Corporate social investment projects are to be aimed primarily toward black groups, communities and individuals that have a strong developmental approach and contribute toward transformation," the charter says. Examples are educational support and training programs, youth development programs, conservation projects, job creation initiatives, arts and culture programs, and youth sports programs.

Conclusions

South Africa still faces serious problems of economic growth, underemployment, and unequal income distribution. Trickle-down economics could take decades to satisfactorily address the legacy of apartheid in a slow or even modest-growth economy. The charter, however, is likely to facilitate improvement in distribution of opportunities and incomes, in particular by forcing firms to quickly make room for more blacks in their managerial ranks. At the same time, it should be recognized that slow growth makes affirmative action a nearly zero-sum game. Some whites will have to be retrenched to open opportunities for blacks. As this proceeds across the economy, white flight is likely to continue, with a loss of skills and university graduates in particular. Thus it should also be recognized that the charter's targets are not without their costs and risks. Ten years is a short time in which to transform the managerial ranks of South Africa's financial sector. Unless the financial sector makes provision for accelerated training of its black personnel, it is surely at risk of promoting some underqualified personnel, with the prospect of managerial mistakes and therefore costs.

If successful, the South African Charter approach will lead to very different and positive results than would a trickle-down strategy, results that should be apparent in less than a decade. Indeed, if the charter's current targets are achieved, the result will be radically unlike the employment gains achieved for blacks in the United States even allowing for their much higher proportion in the South African labor force. However, it should be noted that this reduction in inequality, if it materializes, will not have been achieved because it was the primary objective. It will have been achieved as a by-product of correcting for South Africa's legacy of racism. This distinction is not unimportant.

CHAPTER TWENTY-FOUR

HOW SOCIAL ENTREPRENEURS ENABLE HUMAN, SOCIAL, AND ECONOMIC DEVELOPMENT

Christian Seelos, Johanna Mair

The world's forecasted failure to achieve the UN Millennium Development Goals by 2015 paints a bleak picture for the more than two billion people who live in desperate poverty. Thus governments, multilateral institutions, and nongovernmental organizations (NGOs) continue their search for a recipe for global economic growth. Much of the economic growth and innovation found in free market societies has been credited to entrepreneurial activities.[1] Entrepreneurship, however, is sensitive to context and to the existence of economic reward systems. One necessary condition for growth is that innovation and entrepreneurial activities result in products and services that create value above input costs. Because many input costs—such as provision of infrastructure or legal institutions—are picked up by society in developed countries, the entrepreneur is able to capture a larger part of the value created. Where markets are too inefficient to cater to specific social needs, the government is expected to provide necessary services, as with the welfare system or basic education.

In many poor countries, neither governments nor markets cater to even the most basic needs of their citizens.[2] This indicates the existence of structural and behavioral barriers to growth and development in poor countries. Several authors have suggested

This paper was prepared with the support of the European Academy of Business in Society (EABIS), as part of its Research, Education, and Training Partnership Programme on Corporate Responsibility. The Programme has been made possible by the financial support of EABIS's founding corporate partners, IBM, Johnson & Johnson, Microsoft, Shell, and Unilever.

that current models of economic development underestimate the importance of "social capability" as a prerequisite for growth.[3] This capability builds on human capital, norms of behavior and social organization, and institutionalized property and contract rights, as well as adequate physical capital to enable people to productively participate in economic activities. In this paper, we investigate whether the related phenomenon of social entrepreneurship[4] holds important insights into how entrepreneurs overcome hurdles to economic development in poor countries. We seek to learn from the case of Sekem, an Egyptian organization that aims to create integrated economic, social, and cultural development.

Sekem—A Holistic Vision for Development[5]

Sekem aims to "meet the challenge of the time by contributing towards the all-encompassing development of man, community, and the earth."[6] This mission is an aspiration that has guided its founder, Ibrahim Abouleish, for the last twenty-seven years. After many years abroad, he returned to visit his home country of Egypt in the 1970s. Shocked by the country's widespread poverty and compelled to "heal the land and the people,"[7] Abouleish resolved to change the situation through enterprise. This was the beginning of an initiative that earned him the "Alternative Nobel Prize" in 2003 for creating the "blueprint of the healthy corporation of the twenty-first century."[8]

Building a Business from the Vision

In 1977, Abouleish left his career as a manager and researcher in the pharmaceutical industry in Austria to purchase some untouched desert land sixty kilometers northeast of Cairo. He wanted to prove that the desert could be reclaimed to produce healthy food and natural medicines in an environmentally friendly way. To succeed, he had to overcome numerous hurdles, including securing property rights from the government; negotiating with the local Bedouin population, who had begun to settle nearby; pacifying rural communities that adopted a hostile attitude toward the "intruder"; and battling the Egyptian army when it occupied his land.

Sekem's first three years were devoted to developing basic infrastructure: electricity, roads, houses, irrigation systems, and a sewer system. Abouleish planted 120,000 trees to secure the area from frequent sandstorms. Fertile soil was built through composting, using the dung of forty cows that were a gift from friends in Austria. Finally, cultivation began on a small scale in accordance with international organic standards. Sekem's first shipment of medicinal products arrived in the United States in 1981, followed by a successful entry into the local Egyptian market two years later. Sekem expanded steadily thereafter both domestically and internationally through its four subsidiaries: Isis (established in 1985) packaged and distributed organic cereals, oils, spices, condiments, and a variety of herbs and teas; Atos (1986) was a joint venture producing phytopharmaceutical products; Libra (1988) coordinated organic production and packaged and exported fresh produce to Europe; and Conytex (1990) manufactured organic cotton textile products.

Broadening Impact

By 1990, Sekem's success prompted the Egyptian government to task the organization with development of an organic cultivation method for cotton. Cotton was Egypt's most important cash crop; it was also a magnet for countless insidious pests, making it one of the world's most pesticide-intensive crops. In close cooperation with scientists, farmers, consultants, and consumers, Sekem established use of pheromones to control cotton insects. The results were so convincing that the Egyptian authorities officially promoted the methodology, eventually reducing the use of pesticides in Egyptian cotton fields to less than 10 percent of that of previous years. By 1999, these methods were applied to nearly 80 percent of the entire Egyptian cotton crop.

An important prerequisite for success was changing attitudes toward organic agriculture within Egypt. This included transforming the deep skepticism of farmers, gaining the trust and support of public authorities, and raising awareness among customers. In 1990, the Center for Organic Agriculture in Egypt (COAE) was jointly established by Demeter, a German organic certification network, the Swiss-based Institut für Marktökologie, and Sekem as an independent inspection and certification body to ensure quality control in line with international standards for organic production. In 1992, COAE was appointed by the Ministry of Agriculture as a private inspection body, responsible for inspecting and issuing organic products to the European Union. From COAE's early activities grew the Egyptian Biodynamic Association (EBDA), a nonprofit organization under the Sekem umbrella and an important body in promoting the organic agriculture movement in Egypt as well as providing training, research, and advisory services.

The International Association of Partnership (IAP) was founded in 1997 by Sekem and eight business partners, most of them European, to foster dynamic interaction among farmers, producers, and traders. The IAP partners developed new forms of cooperation based on:

- Exchange of market information, joint strategic planning, marketing, and joint financing concepts
- Development of a code of ethics as a basis for a modern fair trade model

- Development of a contractual basis and an arbitration concept to improve cooperation
- Development of new association concepts that clarified the roles of traders, producers, farmers, and consumers, including property, asset management, and ownership issues

Embracing Culture and Community

In 1984, Sekem established the Egyptian Society for Cultural Development (SCD) in order to reach beyond its commercial activities in pursuit of Abouleish's goals of contributing to "the comprehensive development of Egyptian society" and to realizing "Egypt's unique contribution to global development." At the core of SCD was emphasis on cultivating moral and cultural awareness as a basis for improving living standards.

Education and Training. SCD set up a private kindergarten, primary and secondary schools, an adult training center, and a special needs education program for all the children of the employees and the neighboring community. Teachers were trained in modern pedagogical concepts to enable them to exceed the government standards set for recognized schools, and programs were specifically designed for the particular needs of the community. For example, many poor families depended on income from their children's labor. In response, a special education program was set up so that these children could do light work on the farm in the morning (such as picking chamomile) and then participate in a special educational curriculum in the afternoon.

Medical Center. Originally opened in 1996 for the Sekem community, the medical center was soon providing comprehensive basic health care services to approximately thirty thousand people from the surrounding villages as well.

Academy for Applied Arts and Sciences. The Academy for Applied Arts and Sciences was established in 2000 to promote scientific research that served the needs of Egyptian society and to strengthen the links between development-oriented researchers and development practitioners. It was active in the areas of medicine and pharmacy services, organic agriculture, sustainable economics, and the arts. It also organized a number of cultural events that encouraged the participation of all employees.

Sekem also established the Cooperative of Sekem Employees (CSE) to ensure that the democratic rights and values of workers were adequately implemented and to educate all members of the Sekem community about taking responsibility for society.

Sekem Today

By 2003, all economic activities were under the umbrella of Sekem Holding, comprising six autonomous companies, all with unique brands. The company had revenues of LE (Egyptian pounds) 76.2 million (about US$13 million) and aimed to achieve LE 200 million by 2006. Sekem also started to plan for establishment of Sekem University in Cairo in 2006 to further its educational mission. Sekem's success may continue to have a strong effect on the entire region; high-level delegates from neighboring countries are knocking at its door, asking to implement the Sekem model in their own countries.

Concepts and Theory Building

Sekem had to overcome a series of hurdles to defining and enacting its value creation models. The nature of those hurdles is typical of many poor-country contexts. They include a lack of supply chains from which to secure inputs; inadequate general infrastructure, institutionalized rights (such as contracts), human capital, technology, and knowledge; and deficient health care and other social services.

Dimensions of Value Creation

Sekem explicitly sought to create value in the economic (jobs, income, taxes), social (health services, education, social inclusion and self-esteem), and cultural (music, reading, expression of creativity) spheres. It effectively institutionalized new norms in a number of areas (human rights, labor rights, reduced pesticide use, fair trade, and others) and established various institutions (medical center, academy, schools, COAE, CSE) over time. Moreover, the case illustrates how these various dimensions of value creation are interwoven and are necessary to enable broad-scale development and growth.

The Meaning of "Entrepreneurial"

Sekem represents a fascinating case to rethink the defining characteristics of entrepreneurship—resourcefulness, opportunity recognition, innovation, and creativity. For example, the case permits interesting insights on the notion of resourcefulness. Across the phases of Sekem's life cycle, the organization was able to configure its limited resources in ways that allowed it to develop unique capabilities. Also interesting in this context is Sekem's value network, which enabled it to secure essential resources. Another striking characteristic of Sekem was its ability to recognize and pursue emerging opportunities in the absence of a detailed plan of action. Indeed, Abouleish began with almost no resources but with a solid knowledge base, which he used systematically. He had limited capital, could not rely on existing infrastructure, could not count on support from local partners (except for his family), and had no patents or products. But he possessed specific knowledge (pharmacology) and a propensity for scientific inquiry and systematic problem solving. Furthermore, he could draw from his knowledge of the local context.

From the beginning, Abouleish adopted an opportunistic approach, cooperating closely with a number of individuals and partner organizations to access and build necessary resources. Partnering was crucial in building processes, facilities, and trust. In the case of the COAE and EBDA, Sekem was instrumental in establishing national organizations where none had previously existed. In other cases, Sekem formed strategic partnerships with international businesses.

Sekem succeeded in building an institutional infrastructure that allowed creation of a multibusiness firm; thus the firm and the infrastructure or network have a symbiotic and reinforcing relationship (see Figure 24.1; the six commercial entities of the Sekem Holding lie at the center, enabling but also depending on the various Sekem institutions that organize the economic, social, and cultural spheres).

A Focus on Outcomes from a Development Perspective

As we've seen, areas of contribution by social entrepreneurs in sustainable development can be operationalized on three levels: the basic needs of individuals, those of groups of communities, and those of future generations.[9] Sekem catered to the very

FIGURE 24.1. THE SEKEM NETWORK.

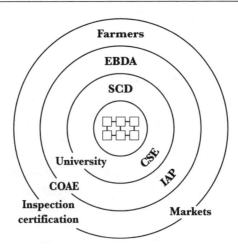

basic needs of thousands of individuals. It also created formal institutions and institutionalized efficient norms and rules for cooperation within communities to everyone's benefit. Furthermore, Sekem addressed the need for choice among future generations. By pioneering organic agriculture in Egypt, it helped maintain the quality of the land as an important resource for the future. Table 24.1 lists some of the elements created by Sekem that contribute to sustainable development.

Reducing poverty and many of its symptoms has become the overarching goal of sustainable development efforts. However, three decades of experience with aid, foreign investment, and policy reforms have produced more stories of failure than of success.[10] For many decades, economic theory assumed that the relative backwardness of poor countries would drive them to "catch up" with richer ones. Unfortunately, this did not happen for many of the poorest countries. Aid and investment—in diverse forms ranging from general capital investment, adjustment loans, and provision of fully equipped factories to more direct efforts such as large-scale education or birth control—did not achieve substantive gains in many poor countries.

Sekem points to a model of how development might be enacted. A growing number of innovative entrepreneurs, often referred to as social entrepreneurs, have shown that it is possible to create and serve markets in developing countries. They create social and economic value by offering products and services that address the most fundamental human and social needs. By scaling up and diversifying, many social entrepreneurs have developed their innovative models into viable businesses. In doing so, they contribute to the economic development of poor countries and the creation of a solid customer base for future markets. Inclusive models developed by social entrepreneurs have the potential for fast global penetration because of the huge latent demand waiting to be served. Furthermore, initiatives such as Sekem create a positive development spiral in which social and economic aspects reinforce themselves.

TABLE 24.1. SEKEM'S CONTRIBUTION TO SUSTAINABLE DEVELOPMENT.

Basic Needs	Institutions	Future Generations
• Education	• Employee contracts	• Healing the land
• Inclusion of disabled people	• Health and safety standards	• More land available
• Dealing with child labor	• Norms and rules (fair play, CSE, IPA)	• Maintain resources
• Medical care	• Formal institutions (COAE, EBDA, SCD)	• Pesticide reduction
• Jobs	• Female participation in economic life	
• Medicine		
• Food		

Discussion

The insights from this example of social entrepreneurship are valuable in the sense that Sekem emphasizes a multistage model of development and poverty eradication. People at various levels of poverty have divergent needs. Understanding that poverty is a symptom rather than a natural state helps to transform the poor into resources by creating human (education, health, and so on) and social capital by organizing them in new ways and changing norms and behaviors. For development organizations, this insight is relevant because it demonstrates that development need not be a linear outcome from isolated inputs delivered by salaried development employees. The fact that social entrepreneurs have direct ownership for development outcomes—and also the ability to experiment and learn in a local context—might point to essential success factors.

For corporations, this insight could be important on several fronts. First, the traditional bottom-of-the-pyramid approach primarily sees the poor as potential customers and less as resources for value creation models. Furthermore, it may be necessary to first invest in building the social capabilities the poor need to participate in economic life before economic growth and large-scale consumption of corporate products and services can occur. Supporting social entrepreneurs and building relationships to bring their initiatives to scale might help speed up this process. Corporations could thus play an important role in long-term development processes. Whereas social entrepreneurs concentrate on formation of social capabilities, companies could extend this to formation of economic capabilities, and indeed commercial activities.

CHAPTER TWENTY-FIVE

HYBRID VALUE CHAINS

Social Innovations and Development of the Small Farmer Irrigation Market in Mexico

Valeria Budinich, Kimberly Manno Reott, Stéphanie Schmidt

Valeria Budinich, Kimberly Manno Reott, Stéphanie Schmidt

B usinesses, particularly those whose products and services address such basic human needs as water, housing, and health, can enter low-income markets more effectively and with deeper social impact through partnership with innovative citizen sector organizations (CSOs). CSOs can scale their social impact significantly if they learn to leverage the infrastructure and resources of large businesses.

The Hybrid Value Chain (HVC) model described here is systemically transforming the relationships between the business and citizen sectors on the basis of mutual economic and social value creation. At the core of this new approach is the assumption that many social innovations are relevant to businesses pioneering the base of the pyramid (BOP) and that the social entrepreneurs[1] who have developed these innovations are natural partners for these businesses. This implies that succeeding at the BOP requires inventing a new form of doing business and an unprecedented level of business-social congruence. It is important to note that HVC partnerships are distinct from typical philanthropic-corporate social responsibility collaborations. Instead, they are based on profits for all partners to ensure long-term sustainability, and on the premise that companies and social entrepreneurs can interact as equals.

We start by highlighting the recent growth of the citizen sector and introduce principles emerging from the work of social entrepreneurs serving low-income families through market-driven approaches. This sets the stage for presenting an initiative that we are currently piloting to deliver irrigation systems to small farmers in Mexico—a case that illustrates the nature of an HVC and its benefits for the actors involved. Conceived and facilitated by Ashoka,[2] this experience is the result of a partnership between two social entrepreneurs and Amanco, one of the leading water system companies in Latin America. Though based initially in Mexico, the model has the potential to rapidly expand to other countries.

We conclude by summarizing the challenges ahead and Ashoka's strategy to enable business and CSOs to establish HVC partnerships, with the ultimate goal of integrating millions of low-income citizens into the global economy in a way that recognizes and fulfills their economic rights as both producers and consumers.

Principles Emerging from the Work of Social Entrepreneurs

The last three decades have seen the emergence of millions of CSOs around the world.[3] Many have developed more experience than businesses—especially large businesses—in delivering products and services to low-income consumers and producers. In addition, social entrepreneurship as a global phenomenon has sparked an extensive array of diverse social networks—many invisible to the uneducated eye.[4] These social networks constitute the early stages of an infrastructure that specializes in serving the poor, one that could be leveraged by businesses as they enter these new markets.

The three basic principles described here are based on Ashoka's experience distilling the main principles[5] emerging from the work of social entrepreneurs advancing market-based social innovations. Each stems from recognition of the three main factors that make it challenging for businesses to target low-income markets: (1) the limited individual purchasing power of potential clients; (2) the complexity of a high-volume business founded on small individual transactions; and (3) poor understanding of the human and social capital of low-income communities. The most successful social entrepreneurs have creatively addressed these factors and developed scalable solutions.

1. *Principle one:* design products and services that tap into the wealth of the poor. Companies must transform the poor's apparent scarcity of means into multiple opportunities by capitalizing on the resources already available to low-income communities.

2. *Principle two:* radically change the logic behind your business model. Success in reaching scale requires rethinking each step of the value chain, from production and distribution to pricing, promotion, and delivery to end consumers.

3. *Principle three:* leverage the power of communities as both consumers and producers. Companies should intervene in a way that contributes to increasing the income of small producers and microentrepreneurs, thus having the synergistic effect of increasing demand for goods and services on the part of low-income families.

These principles represent new standards that are meant to inspire and guide future initiatives. As social entrepreneurs continue scaling up their social innovations, they become valuable partners for companies. But as we describe in the next section, it is necessary to develop a new framework to foster business-social partnerships that carefully balance social impact and profit-making goals.

Developing the Small-Scale Farmer Irrigation Market in Mexico

There are more than a million small Mexican farmers with less than four hectares of land who currently live in poverty because of a lack of physical and financial access to productive technologies such as irrigation systems. They are underserved by irrigation companies and by financial institutions, neither of which currently see them as a profitable market. If those farmers close to a water source could afford commercial irrigation solutions, the market for irrigation system would be as large as US$2 billion in Mexico alone.

These small farmers typically raise a combination of subsistence and cash crops. They struggle to access markets beyond their immediate locale. In addition, they rely on inefficient irrigation methods such as field flooding, hoses with holes, and manual labor. These methods are also significantly wasteful and damaging to the environment.[6]

Access to irrigation technology could dramatically change the lives of small farmers by doubling or even tripling their income, depending on the crops and the location. Moreover, irrigation could enable farmers to plant higher-value crops and time their production for optimal market prices.

Comparison of Irrigation Market Segments

Current business models for irrigation technologies cannot be easily adapted to reach smaller-scale farmers in Mexico because of fundamental differences in the needs and requirements of these segments (see Table 25.1). Although specific to the Mexico case, the scenario described in the table is applicable across the developing world.

One key factor is the current cost structure of distributors, whose margins mainly come from the tailored solutions they design for large farms. In contrast, small farmers need cheaper and more standardized solutions. Even if Amanco's current distributors were equipped to make this shift, right now they have no relationship with small farmers and therefore would need to learn about this new market. Also critical is the need to consider the complete value chain for agricultural production, including financing and commercialization, if demand is to be unlocked. Nevertheless, these value-added services are generally beyond the core competencies of current service providers in the irrigation sector.

TABLE 25.1. HOW MARKET SEGMENTS ARE CURRENTLY SERVED ALONG THE VALUE CHAIN.

Irrigation Subsector Value Chain Steps	Medium and Large Farmers (Market Segment Currently Served by Amanco)	Small Farmer or BOP Market Segment
Product development	• State-of-the-art solutions designed for large farmers readily available and affordable	• Most solutions available in the market are not affordable or are not designed to address small farmers' needs • Reliance on "makeshift" solutions (e.g., widespread use of plastic hoses or water channels dug by hand)
Production	• Highly efficient and productive manufacturing facilities	• High relative cost of technology inputs given the type of homemade solutions
Distribution and logistics	• Network of 200 specialized value-added resellers providing customized irrigation solutions fitting the specific conditions of each farmer's terrain	• Distribution channels are informal and highly inefficient • Inputs are bought through small local retailers; prices are high because of numerous intermediaries
Sales and marketing	• Purchasing decisions are made on the basis of technical specifications, not price • Marketing materials used are highly technical	• Purchasing decision requires first persuading the farmer that she can have a more profitable farm • Need for tailored marketing materials focusing beyond technology
Financing	• When needed, financing is secured directly by clients through local commercial banks	• Conditions of financial institutions or approval process is too complex and costly; a financial "broker" is needed
Marketing of agricultural production	• Clients are well informed about market conditions and maintain direct relations with potential buyers	• Clients are dispersed and require an intermediary that aggregates production and creates market linkages

Note: Some value-added steps were omitted in order to simplify the analysis. For instance, no reference is made here to agricultural inputs and farm management practices.

Designing Hybrid Value Chains That Serve Small Farmers

Given the sizeable irrigation market opportunity and its potential social impact, an increasing number of companies are interested in the BOP market. However, it is clear that creating economic and social value in this market requires a new way of doing business. Such an approach combines the core competencies of irrigation companies and social entrepreneurs who can provide the required value-added services at lower cost.

Ashoka is currently piloting this new type of partnership in Mexico in collaboration with Amanco, a leading company in water systems in Latin America, and two Ashoka Fellows—Arturo Garcia and Juan Jose Consejo—who already work with large networks of small farmers.

This convergence of agendas and resources is creating a novel model for companies to enter BOP markets and for CSOs to achieve greater social impact. A new type of win-win-win partnership, the HVC model draws on each sector's relative strengths (including technology, investment capacity, or logistics for the business sector, and deep understanding of low-income consumers; grassroots networks in rural areas; experience of introducing social change; and perhaps most important, the ability to mobilize local players to offer comprehensive solutions for the citizen sector).

As shown in Table 25.2, by leveraging the social networks of social entrepreneurs in farming communities Amanco can enter the small farmer market faster and more cost-efficiently while strengthening its positioning as an innovator in the corporate responsibility space. For Garcia, who has been looking for ways to advance the sustainability of farmer cooperatives in his home state of Guerrero, irrigation systems and value-added services such as access to markets can help him reach this goal. For Consejo, whose passion is water conservation, irrigation systems offer small farmers an environmentally friendly alternative for watering their crops. Additionally, the commissions on sales that both CSOs receive can be used to expand delivery of complementary services by their organizations. Amanco has committed to grant participating social entrepreneurs wholesale prices equivalent to those of their top distributors. Part of this discount is passed on to final clients (the farmers); the remaining discount supports operating costs and will generate a profit for the CSO once sufficient scale is reached.

Although Ashoka and its partners are still in the development stage of this new business model, they have already made great strides in building a foundation for success. The overall target for the first year of the pilot implementation is US$1 million in sales by the end of June 2006. The project's main accomplishments to date include eleven demonstration plots installed at key locations to allow potential clients to see firsthand the benefits of irrigation systems, 35 hectares of irrigation sold and installed, and a significant sales pipeline of 465 hectares for which quotes are available, along

TABLE 25.2. EXPLAINING THE AMANCO/ASHOKA HYBRID VALUE CHAIN PARTNERSHIP.

	Background	Role	Deal
Small-scale farmer (becomes an empowered consumer and increases her income significantly)	• Over one million small farmers with less than 4 hectares could benefit in Mexico alone • Major opportunity to increase productivity and reduce rural poverty	• Learn about credit opportunities for investment in farm; provide required documents • Make purchase decision and pay 10 percent of costs up-front in cash	• Access to irrigation systems at fair price plus value-added services such as financing, commercialization, and technical assistance • Doubled or tripled incomes
Amanco (water distribution company opens an underserved market)	• Leading Latin American company providing water solutions • Part of GrupoNueva conglomerate; 2004 revenue US$1.3 billion • Chairman mandate that 10 percent of revenues come from BOP by 2008	• Product and technical training • Pricing and quotations • Marketing support (e.g., materials)	• New rural distribution channel for serving small farmers profitably • US$1 million in sales during the pilot phase
Social entrepreneurs (serve small farmers while creating sustainable sources of revenue)	• Arturo Garcia; Network of Self-Managed Sustainable Farmers (RASA); dedicated to increasing economic power of small farmers in coastal Guerrero area • Juan Jose Consejo; Oaxacan Institute for Nature and Society (INSO); dedicated to water conservation in Oaxaca area	• Sales and promotion (aggregating demand) • Technical support to farmers • Leveraging government financing • Partnerships with crop-purchasing companies and trainers in organic farming	• Larger social impact and commissions to be invested in other programs that require subsidies • 35 percent discount on list price creates commissions
Ashoka (acts as a business or social broker)	• Global organization dedicated to creating a globally integrated and competitive citizen sector • 1,700 social entrepreneurs (Ashoka Fellows) in global network	• Facilitates Amanco and social entrepreneurs' partnership • Barrier remover, problem solver • Systematizes learnings	• Contributes to accelerated social change • 1.5 percent commission on total sales of each new rural distributor for three years

with 1,000 hectares in the design stage. Availability of pro-forma quotes has helped mobilize more than half a million U.S. dollars in Mexican government financing[7] through a combination of rural credit financial institutions and subsidies for irrigation. In addition, three strategic alliances have been formed to support sales of the additional crops produced.

Lessons Learned in Building Hybrid Value Chains

Building an HVC is not simple, as Ashoka's irrigation initiative in Mexico demonstrates. The process is also not linear but iterative, with many overlapping steps and multiple lessons learned. In this paper, we use a three-stage process to describe the evolution of the partnership and key lessons learned so far.

Stage One: Engagement of Amanco and Social Entrepreneurs

This first stage focused on securing commitment from both the company and the social entrepreneurs to participate in the HVC partnership. From the perspective of the company, it starts by recognizing, at the highest management level, that there is a profitable market in the BOP and that social entrepreneurs have a valuable role to play. From the social entrepreneurs' perspective, the starting point is the realization that their social initiative can achieve higher impact and become sustainable by partnering with a private company. Once the initial buy-in occurs, both partners are ready to focus on the multiple innovations required along the value chain.

In Amanco's case, the relationship with Ashoka began in 2003 through a conversation between Ashoka chairman and founder Bill Drayton and Stephan Schmidheiny, the founder of GrupoNueva (Amanco's parent conglomerate), who was initiating the process of integrating the company's vision and values with its philanthropic activities.

The process of finding, selecting, and engaging the social partners started with determining the key selection criteria: access to large groups of small farmers, organizational capability, geographic location, openness to innovation, and fit with the organizational mission. Critical to this process was a series of meetings and field visits that enabled the social entrepreneurs and company representatives to get to know each other.

The most important lesson learned in this stage was the need to intricately link the products sold (irrigation systems) with the mission of the social entrepreneurs. A corollary to this lesson is recognition that an HVC is not right for all social entrepreneurs and that there is a steep learning curve for most organizations. External financial and specialized human resources as well as appropriate systems and work processes are required. In addition to management support, Ashoka made soft loans to Garcia and Consejo for the launch period because they did not qualify for small business loans owing to their lack of collateral and inability to meet other stringent lending requirements.

Stage Two: Building Trust, Common Goals, and Vision for Partnership

The building of trust and a common goal and vision has been an ongoing process. It started with development of a joint implementation plan and a letter of intent outlining the "business deal" along with the terms that were the basis for the HVC partnership (see Table 25.2).

But beyond the legal and business requirements, the critical learning in this stage involves the necessary *mind-shift* for all partners. An HVC partnership requires that the partners view not only each other but themselves differently. This happens organically, but it can be facilitated through a few factors:

- Involvement of an outside facilitator to accelerate the trust-building process
- Systematic reflection on key learnings, achievements, and bottlenecks
- Evaluation measurements that are periodically revisited
- External mandates and incentives that create pressure to perform

Ironically, the fact that Amanco had a strong corporate social responsibility program led to some initial reluctance on the part of the local Amanco team to embrace a commercial approach such as HVC. However, the arrival of Francisco de la Torre as Amanco's new CEO accelerated the process of mobilizing the resources needed.

Today, Amanco Mexico has a full-time director to oversee the pilot and an irrigation installer based in Guerrero; this has accelerated the pace of implementation.

Other lessons learned include the importance of a company team leader reporting directly to the CEO, as well as human resources that can focus exclusively on the new business model, rather than being subject to the pressures of traditional business. Finally, in hindsight there is also a need to realize that any kind of innovation requires time to reach critical mass and capture the interest of key players in the company.

Stage Three: Development and Testing of the Business Model

The third stage constitutes the core of the HVC innovation process and involves tactical building and simultaneous testing of the business model. As such, it has entailed a significant amount of operational learning for all parties involved.

When the Amanco technical team visited small farmers, they immediately started to think about adapting their traditional offers to the specifics of this market and significantly lowered the cost per hectare in the process. Through ideas such as standardizing components and shared pumps, they have been able to cut the cost per hectare in half without sacrificing quality. In addition, new offerings such as greenhouses are being developed that are based on small farmers' needs.

Although we initially envisioned the social entrepreneur's role as a distributor specialized in small farmers with a focus on demand aggregation and financial resources mobilization, our collective understanding of what the role would entail greatly underestimated the amount of effort required. For instance, the original financing plan included a 10 percent in-cash contribution from the farmer coupled with a 50 percent government subsidy and a 40 percent federal government agricultural loan. In practice, however, it has required a Herculean effort to secure the government monies. This created an additional challenge to the pilots' progress. Garcia solved this major stumbling block by partnering with Isabel Cruz, an Ashoka Fellow specializing in rural finance, to establish a local financial intermediary. Consejo opted for focusing on lower-price solutions to be less dependent on access to credit.

Path Forward: Scaling up Impact

In 2006, Ashoka's focus is to achieve significant success on the HVC pilot program. One of the key steps in scaling up these efforts at the national level is to identify and train a selective number of CSOs. This means adapting Ashoka's search and selection process[8] for leading social entrepreneurs to the specific requirements of the HVC partnerships. Another complementary approach will be to analyze the potential of a microfranchise model to scale up Garcia's and Consejo's current operations.

By contrast, because the ultimate long-term goal of the initiative is not only the success of these pilots in Mexico but widespread adoption of HVCs in various sectors, it is essential to develop the ability to capture new learnings, compare them across industries, and share them with all the necessary actors.

The work of C. K. Prahalad and Stuart Hart is increasingly capturing the attention of companies around the world, but it is still necessary to translate these concepts into a long-term win-win-win for CSOs. Widespread skepticism prevails among CSOs about the claim that the entrance of companies in these markets will by itself contribute to poverty alleviation. There is also skepticism in business circles about how rapidly CSOs will be able to translate their skills into effective resources in a for-profit market development context. But most actors involved in BOP endeavors agree that a concerted effort on the part of both sectors, as well as government, is needed to ensure that access to products and services results in positive social change for millions of people.

Ashoka's strategy is based on the assumption that a win-win-win scenario makes this type of impact possible. Achieving this scenario at a significant scale to shape the emergence of an inclusive global economy requires a profound change in the roles of low-income individuals, CSOs, and businesses. Once key actors go through the mind-shift needed to realize how attractive this new market opportunity is, competition and commitment to social change will continue to advance the most effective people, businesses, and social institutions. An essential element in this process—not yet in place—is the emergence of leading investors willing to offer the range of for-profit and nonprofit capital sources needed for HVCs to spread.

CHAPTER TWENTY-SIX

ENTREPRENEURSHIP AND POVERTY ALLEVIATION IN SOUTH AFRICA

Frederick Ahwireng-Obeng, Mthuli Ncube

South Africa exhibits a unique case of socially engineered, intergenerationally transmitted, large-scale chronic poverty. The poor are distributed unevenly among the races, with the black population bearing the brunt of worsening inequality. The historical antecedent to this situation included deliberate stripping of the black population of all their assets and exclusion from mainstream economic activity. Although these entitlements were restored when the country achieved political independence in 1994, the majority of blacks today still lack the opportunity to empower themselves and achieve the security necessary to escape from poverty.

The South African government is determined to transform society by redressing inequality and alleviating poverty, largely through fiscal transfers and basic service provision. Its efforts are, however, paralyzed by capacity constraints and poor service provision. On the other hand, the well-developed, white-dominated, and growing private sector is seeking to expand its domestic market in the face of increasing global competition.

We argue in this paper that a business solution to the South African poverty problem is possible. Business will have to review, reorient, strengthen, and expand its somewhat disconnected relationship with the bottom of the pyramid (BOP) in innovative and entrepreneurial ways that do not compromise the commercial motive of private business but at the same time transmit vital assets to, and develop them for, the poor. The entrepreneurial approach to poverty alleviation can be mutually beneficial, affording innovation, cost-reduction, and increased revenue for business while transmitting to the poor the entrepreneurial building blocks needed to enhance and sustain their capability to access resources and meet their basic needs.

We demonstrate this proposition with the case study of South African Breweries (now SAB Miller), which has developed commercially profitable programs that stimulate entrepreneurship and thus alleviate poverty among previously disadvantaged persons.

The policy implication of this paper is that poverty alleviation strategies can be effective and sustainable if they incorporate private sector approaches that promote entrepreneurial development within the target population.

South Africa's Poverty Profile

Through the policies of apartheid and colonialism, poverty in South Africa was transmitted from one generation to another, each persistently lacking the opportunity to accumulate assets. At the community level, there was a deficit of infrastructure and basic assets (physical and human-made). This persistent constraint on opportunity, capability, and security has continued to manifest itself in a vicious cycle of poverty characterized by low levels of productivity, income, savings, and investment.

This paper argues that entrepreneurship can be employed effectively as an instrument for alleviating this poverty. The country has a well-developed private business sector with historical links to the poor, but entrepreneurial activity among the adult population (particularly its majority black population) is comparatively low. For years under apartheid, this population was deliberately excluded from mainstream entrepreneurial activity and deprived of essential entrepreneurial assets—financial, human capital, social, cultural, and political. The challenge for the private sector is to engage with the poor in new and innovative ways that not only serve the profit motive but also develop and transmit entrepreneurial assets to the poor.

Linking Entrepreneurship and Poverty Alleviation

The ultimate goal of economic development is to build sufficient assets and create wealth. Entrepreneurship creates and also distributes wealth and income, as well as political power, within societies cost-effectively and improves social welfare by harnessing previously overlooked, dormant talents.[1]

Given that entrepreneurs are the engines of individual and community wealth creation,[2] a central challenge is to develop a critical mass of such entrepreneurs to play this role. However, the quality and productivity of these individuals' entrepreneurial capital also determines their capacity to create wealth. Three broad components of entrepreneurial capital can be identified as: human capital; social, cultural, and political capital; and financial, material, and natural capital.

We take the view that the various innovative ways in which business interacts with the BOP sector are by definition entrepreneurial in the Schumpeterian sense.[3] These innovations transfer components of entrepreneurial capital to the poor, thereby creating opportunity for action, empowering participation, enhancing security, and improving the capabilities that bring about poverty-reversing outcomes.

We can compare this process with intergenerational transmission of household assets (capital). Table 26.1 shows that household assets transmitted from parent to child to influence the child's future poverty status are the same assets that constitute entrepreneurial capital. This suggests a strong positive correlation between acquisition of

TABLE 26.1. INTERGENERATIONAL TRANSMISSION OF POVERTY-RELATED CAPITAL FROM PARENT TO CHILD.

What Is Transmitted?	How Is It Transmitted?
Financial, material, and environmental capital	
• Cash	• Insurance, pensions
• Land	• Inheritance, bequests, dispossession
• Livestock	• Gifts and loans
• Housing and other buildings	• Dowry, bride wealth
• Other productive or nonproductive physical assets (e.g., rickshaw, plough, sewing machine, television)	• Environmental conservation or degradation
• Common property resources	• Labor bondage
• Debt (negative financial capital)	
Human capital	
• Educational qualifications, knowledge, skills, coping and survival strategies	• Socialization
• Good mental and physical health	• Investment of time and capital in care
• Disease impairment	• Investment of time and capital in education and training
• Intelligence	• Investment of time and capital in health and nutrition
	• Contagion, mother-to-child transmission of disease
	• Genetic inheritance
Social, cultural, and political capital	
• Traditions, institutions, norms of entitlement, and value system	• Socialization
• Position of community (i.e., family)	• Kinship
	• Locality

Source: Hulme and Shepherd (2003).

entrepreneurial capital and enhancement of economic status. For example, a child who inherits debt from a parent may be held in labor bondage as a means of repayment and so be subjected to continued poverty. By contrast, investment of time and money in education and training transmits human capital (knowledge, skills, coping and survival strategies) to improve one's economic status.

The productivity of entrepreneurial capital and its transformational impact—or the extent of its poverty alleviating outcomes—depends on the quality of transmission, experiential transmission being the highest level of economic offering.[4]

An example illustrates this. Providing affordable products and services to poor communities, or extending the distribution outreach of existing products, reduces barriers to access and promotes consumption per capita. Similarly, building supplier relationships and other business linkages with local small and medium enterprises creates economic opportunities for employment generation. Furnishing credit, equity, and other forms of financial capital also reduces vulnerability and enhances security. Furthermore, supporting transfer of appropriate product and process technologies requires training, mentoring, capacity building, and information sharing, which promotes and enhances entrepreneurial capabilities in a given community. Above all, the mere involvement of poor people in a participatory process is empowering. Indeed, their participation enables social bonding and helps to bridge cultural and political gaps, promoting opportunities for a more effective mobilization of other forms of entrepreneurial capital.

Case Study: South African Breweries

South African Breweries (SAB), a beer and beverage producer, has developed a program called SAB KickStart to stimulate entrepreneurship among the poor, who support and buttress its core business. The program covers procurement, distribution, and general entrepreneurial activities.

SAB embarked on an aggressive black economic empowerment campaign during the 1980s in an effort to place a considerable portion of its business with black suppliers. The campaign attempted to alleviate historical inequalities and foster skills and training for disadvantaged individuals.

By the 2004 financial year, SAB contracted with fifteen hundred businesses run by previously disadvantaged people. The total value of these contracts was R730 million. SAB's target for the 2005 financial year was R895 million, which grew to reach R938 million, or 17.3 percent of total local procurement.

In its procurement, outsourcing, and contract-awarding activities, SAB favors those companies that have demonstrated a tangible commitment to black economic empowerment (BEE) principles. SAB's definition of a BEE company is consistent with the South African government's definition as outlined in the Black Economic Empowerment Act of 2003. The BEE Act and its principles seek to make available business opportunities for previously disadvantaged persons who are majority black. A particularly successful feature has been the deliberate linking of SAB KickStart program recipients to SAB's commercial department. Those entrepreneurs who have become successful through an SAB social investment program are then given the opportunity to supply to SAB so as to make their businesses even more sustainable.

SAB makes these special procurement guidelines available to all suppliers. Ownership and control of vendors, as well as broad-based societal empowerment impacts, are considered. Here are some concrete examples of entrepreneurs who have successfully developed enterprises and livelihoods as a result of the SAB program.

Example one: B. Langton Construction Company. Bernie Langton founded her construction company when she identified an opportunity to build pallets for a major paper company for which she was doing construction work. She delivered her first pallets in 1996 and has never looked back. In 1998, she began supplying to SAB and since then her volume to SAB has grown by a factor of twelve. She is now one of SAB's largest pallet suppliers.

Pallet design and specification are critical, because they must be reused many times. Design innovations have been introduced over the years, and B. Langton Construction has continued to deliver top-quality pallets, supplied to all of SAB's breweries. In the process, Langton's business has grown from twelve employees to eighty-one.

Example two: MCG Industries. MCG Industries is a BEE company that supplies SAB with tops for glass bottles and plastic crates for returnable 750ml bottles. Quality is essential, because the bottle tops play an important aesthetic and branding role, ensuring the beer stays fresh and does not lose flavor or carbonation. Similarly, for the returnable crates quality is crucial in withstanding sometimes tough operating conditions and multiple usage. The product supplied by MCG has either been of equal quality or in some cases exceeded that of its competitors.

SAB's relationship with MCG started in the 1980s and has now grown into a multimillion rand relationship. Neelin Naidoo, managing director of MCG, says that MCG and SAB enjoy a healthy business relationship, anchored in sound and equally challenging business principles, underpinned by a high level of mutual respect and trust.

Example three: Taverner Training. SAB has been pressing for formalization of retailers who remain unlicensed. To assist businesses that have become licensed, in 2003 SAB rolled out its taverner program. That year, the program trained 759 business owners, followed by 913 in 2004. This innovative program teaches business skills to a growing number of licensed taverns and has enjoyed significant success. Those taverners who underwent SAB-facilitated training have reported impressive and sustainable improvement in their business:

- Their average monthly sales increased by 30 percent.
- Debt decreased by 28 percent.
- Stock increased by 37 percent.
- Their savings and investments grew 40 percent, which means they can now begin to fund their own expansion.

On the basis of this success, SAB has since stepped up this key program. In the 2006 fiscal year, the company will invest R18 million in taverner training.

Example four: The SAB Owner-Driver Program. A key component of SAB's success is its logistics network and distribution capabilities. It is one of only a few companies that can deliver its products to any area in South Africa within a very short space of time.

The SAB Owner-Driver program was introduced in 1987 to enable company employees to become independent businesspeople. This empowerment program was designed to ensure a high level of customer service and productivity. Since inception, well over R2 billion has been invested in this broad-based empowerment project.

Today, 248 owner-drivers account for 54 percent of all SAB's deliveries. Each driver in turn employs a crew of at least four people. As a result, this R200 million per annum project has fostered at least a thousand jobs and created 250 independent, sustainable businesses. Each truck belonging to an owner-driver is worth about R700,000.

Conclusion

In this case study, we have attempted to show how entrepreneurial assets are being transmitted and also highlighted the benefits to entrepreneurs, communities, and the businesses themselves. The SAB programs on procurement and taverner training and its owner-driver initiative are creating business opportunity, economic empowerment, and economic security for entrepreneurs while developing their essential entrepreneurial capabilities. SAB benefits from these programs through increased revenues, cost reduction and efficiency, and promotion of innovation. The community also benefits from SAB's program through employment creation and the promotion of societal equity.

CHAPTER TWENTY-SEVEN

A GENTLER CAPITALISM

Black Business Leadership in the New South Africa

Linda A. Hill, Maria Farkas

The long walk is not yet over. The prize of a better life has yet to be won.

PRESIDENT NELSON MANDELA'S REMARKS AT HIS FINAL STATE OF THE UNION ADDRESS

In most countries, efforts to alleviate poverty and inequality focus on the government and not-for-profit sectors. But in post-apartheid South Africa, the influx of blacks into business in South Africa has brought into sharp relief the dual roles of business as an economic and a social entity.[1] The country is embroiled in a debate about the role of business in addressing social ills.[2] This is the story of the efforts of one businessperson, Irene Charnley, to do her part in closing the gap between the rich and poor in her country. But to appreciate her story, you must understand her history and her context.

Many of the black business leaders in South Africa were activists during the struggle against apartheid, holding leadership positions in organizations such as the African National Congress (ANC) and the union movement.[3] Following the end of apartheid, some, like Charnley, joined corporate South Africa. Others became entrepreneurs, forming investment holding companies and operating companies.[4]

South Africa's income distribution is one of the most inequitable in the world.[5] The level of inequality has remained relatively unchanged since the days of apartheid. A notable decline in interracial inequality has been matched by intraracial inequality, especially within the majority African population. Some of the country's blacks have prospered through participation in the formal economy, while many others have

We would like to thank Emily Stecker and Rakesh Khurana for feedback on drafts of this article.

fallen farther behind.[6] However, many of those blacks who have prospered—members of an emerging black business elite—are dedicated to discovering new ways of doing business. They are asking normative questions about the means and ends of business in their effort to construct a new social order.

Irene Charnley is a member of this emerging class of black businesspeople who aspire to be architects of a new South Africa. She has become a champion of black economic empowerment (BEE), a movement aimed at integrating blacks into the mainstream economy. She believes that business should play a proactive role in creating economic opportunity for those traditionally at the bottom of the pyramid.

Charnley started life at the bottom of the social and economic pyramid and now finds herself at the top. Although she represents a distinct minority in her country, a black[7] woman director and business executive in corporate South Africa, Charnley is not alone. The number of emerging black business leaders is growing. She and others in her cohort are attempting to establish a "gentler capitalism" in their young democracy, one committed to improving the lives and livelihood of the poor and marginalized in South Africa.[8]

Of course, theory is one thing, implementation another. This paper briefly describes the BEE movement, in particular the work of the Black Economic Empowerment Commission (BEECom), an umbrella body representing eleven black business organizations, of which Charnley was a commissioner. BEECom was formed as a vehicle for black people to craft their own vision for BEE. Irene Charnley and her fellow commissioners did not believe that market forces alone could rectify the structural inequality found in South Africa. Instead, they contended that each sector of society had a role to play in building the future South Africa, including new black business leaders. We then focus on Charnley's role as a change agent, determined to improve the prospects of the previously disadvantaged in her company. The cornerstone of her leadership approach is advancement of marginalized groups through employment, skills transference, and leadership development. We conclude by identifying some of the key questions raised by the natural experiment under way in South Africa of using business as a tool for ameliorating societal inequalities.

Black Economic Empowerment

Nelson Mandela was elected president in 1994 with 63 percent of the vote in the country's first free elections, on a campaign slogan of "A Better Life for All." After decades of white-only rule in which a minority (11 percent) of the population controlled virtually all of the country's wealth came the promise of economic opportunity for all. The South African economy was once again opened to the outside world, but with the end of apartheid and the associated trade embargos and sanctions many companies were ill-prepared to compete in a global economy with its demand for efficiency and innovation. Apartheid left South Africa with a destitute black population with little or no capital or education, an unraveling social fabric, and a business sector owned and run almost completely by whites. In response, the ANC adopted policies to broaden the economic participation of blacks within the constraints of a free market economy.[9] They passed laws such as the Employment Equity Act 1998, which required South African companies with more than fifty employees to formulate, report, and implement concrete measures to increase previously disadvantaged group representation.

To avoid government intervention, English- and Afrikaner-owned corporations responded to the new political climate by participating proactively in what was termed black economic empowerment. BEE consisted of a number of initiatives to increase the participation of previously disadvantaged individuals (including blacks, women, and the disabled) in the formal economy through company ownership and management. Incentives were introduced to reward those businesses that voluntarily participated in BEE. Most notably, several government agencies altered their procurement and licensing requirements to favor companies with blacks in ownership or management positions.

Black Economic Empowerment Commission

As the BEE process unfolded, critics questioned whether the measures adopted were simply making a handful of black people very rich while creating the illusion of black participation.[10] As high unemployment and poverty persisted in black communities, the efficacy of voluntary BEE programs was hotly debated and the call for more aggressive government action gained strength.[11] In May 1998, the Black Economic Empowerment Commission (BEECom) was created under the auspices of the Black Business Council (BBC), an umbrella body representing eleven black business organizations. BEECom's ambition was to develop an integrated socioeconomic program aimed at "redressing the imbalances of the past by seeking to substantially and equitably transfer and confer the ownership, management and control of South Africa's financial and economic resources to the majority of its citizens."[12]

The commission conducted extensive research and consultation with the government, unions, and "established business." In its final report, the commission asserted that unless black people participated more broadly and substantively, the South African economy could never achieve sustained economic growth. In short, the commission argued that meeting the needs of the poor and marginalized was the right thing to do not just from an ethical standpoint but also from an economic one. They argued that the country's prospects were directly linked to prospects for those at the bottom of the pyramid—a radical thought for businesspeople.

A Gentler Capitalist in Action[13]

Irene Charnley grew up in Elsies River, an Afrikaans-speaking, colored area[14] outside of Cape Town. Her father was murdered when she was young, and her mother, a domestic worker, raised Charnley and her two siblings. Like most blacks in South Africa, Charnley and her family lived in poverty. In 1982, she was one of a select group of black South Africans to receive a scholarship to attend university in the United Kingdom. After earning a diploma in graphic arts and reproduction from the London College of Printing, she returned to South Africa. On discovering she was being paid less than her white counterparts in her first graphic arts position, she quit and joined the National Union of Mineworkers (NUM) as a graphic designer for their fledgling newspaper. Soon, with the encouragement of NUM General Secretary Cyril Ramaphosa, she became a key union negotiator. Over time, she came to serve as a trustee on several of the NUM's pensions and provident fund boards.

Charnley's unexpected introduction to a business career came through the NUM, which in 1996 joined with other black investors in the National Empowerment Consortium (NEC) to purchase from Anglo American Corporation of South Africa (Anglo)[15] a 34.9 percent interest in Johnnic, a passive holding company with varying stakes in breweries, pharmaceuticals, foods, media, entertainment, and telecommunications. This BEE deal was one of the most important in the first wave of black empowerment because of Anglo's prominence (it was South Africa's largest company, employing 130,000 people) and the lucrative assets it divested. After leading the negotiations with Anglo for the NUM, Charnley was asked to serve as one of NEC's ten nonexecutive directors on the fifteen-member board at Johnnic. Her mandate was to protect the NUM investment, in large measure made up of mineworkers' pensions, in Johnnic. Along with her mentor Ramaphosa, who was the chairperson of the board, Charnley found herself for the first time sitting on the same side of the table as management.

During her tenure at Johnnic, Charnley played a key role in transforming the passive holding company into an active corporate center with lucrative interests in media and telecommunications. From her first meetings on the Johnnic board, she grew increasingly concerned about what she saw as Johnnic's lack of strategic direction and limited involvement with its investments.

Charnley decided that if she wanted to have an impact, she needed to focus her efforts. To the surprise of many of her peers, she resigned from the boards of most of the union retirement funds on which she sat and concentrated her efforts on Johnnic. In August 1997, she was appointed by Ramaphosa and NEC as an executive in charge of strategy and new business development. She hoped that, as a member of executive management, she would be in a position to protect the NUM investment by helping the company develop and execute a solid strategic plan. Charnley observed:

When I joined Johnnic, the first black person and the first woman, they expected me to occupy an office, attend board meetings, and just be happy because I got a good paycheck. But, in our society, there was no way I was going to do that because you just don't earn money if you don't deliver. It's unethical. We were the first generation of black people who had been successful. It was important for us to ensure that while we were forming a black middle class, we still had a social conscience. I knew that I was in Johnnic for a purpose.

Over time, Charnley transitioned from her position as a nonexecutive board member to an executive in charge of strategy and new business development. Her biggest move was divesting profitable but mature assets to purchase the telecommunications firm MTN. By January 1999, Johnnic effectively controlled just under 50 percent of MTN, making it the majority shareholder. Given their significant stake in MTN, the Johnnic board decided that Charnley would assume a new position: executive director of telecommunications, charged with ensuring the health of MTN.

The Transformation of MTN

MTN was founded in 1992 by two white South African entrepreneurs. From the moment the first cellular network went live in 1994, South Africans eagerly adopted the new technology. Initial projections estimated a subscriber base of 225,000 after five years, but MTN alone had 2.5 million subscribers after that time period. By the time Johnnic consolidated its position as the majority shareholder in January 1999, MTN was a company at a crossroads. Revenues continued to grow, but the sustainability of its strategy was in question. MTN's core market, which consisted mainly of white consumers and businesses, was almost saturated. The company pursued alternative avenues of growth, including international expansion. In addition, like many high-growth entrepreneurial ventures, the company's structures, systems, and processes were in need of rationalization and upgrading.

As required by the government, MTN established an employment equity plan in 1998. To prepare the document, MTN developed targets for each racial group in every department and at all levels of management. The company modified the targets where necessary to create space for whites to still be hired and promoted. MTN was morally and strategically concerned about being perceived as a stable employer for all racial groups. There was a shortage of skilled information technology (IT) workers; in the late 1990s, developed economies around the world were importing IT professionals from countries such as India and South Africa. Foreign jobs were particularly attractive to young, white workers who were unsure of their prospects at home.

In the first months in her new position, Charnley immersed herself in the MTN organization, freely contacting and talking with staff throughout the organization about a range of topics from the very tactical to the strategic. Many MTN executives were surprised by the depth and style of Charnley's engagement with the organization. Some took time to grow accustomed to her take-charge, no-nonsense style while others immediately respected it. But many people—even some of those uncomfortable with her hands-on style—acknowledged that if change was to happen quickly, then her approach was probably necessary. As one executive remarked, "With our structure, a lot of things didn't happen in this company without people putting their fingers in."

As Charnley developed a sense of MTN's operations and culture and felt that progress was being made, she became less involved in operational issues and focused her attention on what she saw as three interrelated strategic priorities for MTN. First, the company's core South African market was maturing; new growth areas needed to be identified and developed. Second, MTN needed to accelerate its expansion into Africa. Third, the company needed to embrace BEE and bring more black people in at all levels. Although approximately 50 percent of MTN's employees were black, less than a quarter of the managers and almost none of the senior team were black. For the purposes of this chapter, we focus on Charnley's efforts with regard to the third priority.

Selecting, Retaining, and Developing Black Talent

To Charnley, the empowerment situation at MTN required swift and decisive action— for both business and social reasons. "BEE was simply the right thing to do to address inequities of the past in addition to being a clear strategic and business imperative," she explained. When she became involved in MTN, the entire executive team (with the exception of one colored man) was white, and more than 80 percent of all senior managers were white.

With the endorsement of her fellow board members, Charnley insisted that black candidates be considered in the candidate pool whenever openings in professional and managerial positions arose. These moves often met with resistance; various concerns were expressed. Some contended that previously disadvantaged job candidates did not have as much experience as white candidates. In response, Charnley reminded the staff that 95 percent of them had not previously worked in the telecommunications industry. Another concern was that among the relatively small pool of skilled black professionals in South Africa, there were simply too few candidates to fuel the revolutionary change in staffing at the company that Charnley seemed to desire. Many proposed that MTN bring in black hires at lower levels and develop them; as they rose in the ranks, the racial profile of the company would be transformed. Charnley was skeptical of the efficacy of this suggestion. Before Johnnic became MTN's majority shareholder, she knew, black management had been hired but rarely promoted. Most left because they saw no opportunity for advancement.

Charnley soon concluded she could not wait for everyone's buy-in to move ahead with the BEE agenda. She instructed executives to begin hiring the previously disadvantaged into senior positions. She believed that the only way to win over the MTN staff was to put the hires in place. Once they performed, they would build credibility with their peers. Charnley knew that it would not be enough to simply hire black employees into MTN. During the months she had been at the company, she had heard of too many examples of racism, both overt and subtle. Charnley resolved that she would do all she could to ensure that new black executives would not be isolated. To that end, she began meeting with them each week to learn how she could best support them. Felleng Molusi, one of Charnley's black senior hires, reflected:

> It is one thing to recruit people, put them in a position and then sit at Johnnic. But, Irene was here every day and you knew you could rely on her support when things got tough. With all the political games, that was important. In a lot of South African organizations, black people were put in key positions and then not given the requisite support. With Irene's backing, at least one was able to operate effectively in an often hostile environment. There were many white people who were willing to support change, but there were an equal number who were resistant, and you never knew who was who.

Charnley explained why she felt the weekly meetings were necessary: "There were black people in the organization whose confidence had been completely destroyed. People withheld information. People wanted them to fail. They were undermined around every corner. You had to be strong to put up with that stuff. And the black employees knew they could stand up and challenge things because they had the support of the board. They knew that I was there to monitor, police, and make sure that things happened."

In her meetings with black hires, Charnley did not simply affirm her support for them. She held high standards for them and made her expectations clear: "I said to people, 'You have to work extra hard, and if you're a woman you have to work even harder. When people sleep, you work. You have to be the best. People must respect you. And they must be oblivious to color because of what you deliver. When you don't deliver, they say black people are incompetent. We've had good black people who have quit because they couldn't take the pressure.'"

To speed up the process of BEE at MTN, Charnley decided to overhaul the company's executive bonus system (historically, bonuses were indexed principally to annual profit). In addition to incorporating stretch targets and emphasizing the importance of key strategic objectives, the new bonus structure would index a portion of the bonuses of the senior managers at MTN to their employment equity targets. Charnley and the human resource director proposed that 45 percent of the bonus be based on achieving financial stretch targets, 35 percent on achieving ten strategic objectives, and 20 percent on achieving employment and procurement equity targets. Charnley did not think senior management would like any part of the bonus overhaul, but she knew there would be special consternation about the employment equity targets.

Whites were beginning to fear for the security of their jobs. One white manager shared his dilemma: "I had employees coming to me, begging me to tell them whether they had a future with the company now that it was an empowerment company. They had a right to know, and I wanted to tell them. But, the truth was that I didn't know. A lot of it depended on whether or not we kept growing." At any South African company, racial tensions of some magnitude were to be expected. But some white executives worried that Charnley's approach might have exacerbated them. As one individual explained, some perceived that black employees had disproportionate access to Charnley:

> Five or ten powerful black executives got together in a clique. Cliques happened all over the company, but it was easier to identify a black clique. I understood why these cliques were there. They made sense in some way, but eventually they were used to gain power. It was a challenge for someone like Irene to deal with. If she was not seen to be outside of both cliques, then there was a problem. And there was a perception in the company that the opposite was true. It's dangerous to see that certain people, by virtue of their race, may have access to Irene that a white person may not. Because, as soon as you have one of the most powerful board members involved in an us-against-the-rest-of-management situation, there is serious trouble for the company. I think Irene had real challenges because she was very powerful to MTN then.

Charnley realized the tensions her approach was creating: "The whites here thought we were moving much too quickly. We couldn't hire the black people we wanted because they thought we were doing 'too little, too late.' And I needed to constantly intervene to make sure the black people we had hired had the space to get their work done. And yet, the only way to keep growing was to keep moving on empowerment. It was difficult balancing all these competing claims."

Assessing Impact

In December 2003, Charnley left her position as executive director at Johnnic Group to take the executive position of commercial director at MTN. During the three years of her appointment as ED of telecommunications for Johnnic, Charnley pressed

MTN to think more strategically about its future growth. She pushed MTN to pay attention to the black market in South Africa, aggressively expand into foreign markets, and capitalize on synergies with Johnnic's other subsidiaries. By 2003, MTN was present in Nigeria, Cameroon, Uganda, Rwanda, and Swaziland, and those operations yielded 36 percent of revenue and 46 percent of EBITDA. Subscribers grew from 2.3 million in 2000 to 8.9 million in December 2003. MTN's share price climbed steadily from 10 rand per share in the autumn of 2002 to 30 rand per share in December 2003.

By 2000, there were five black executives in top management, including the managing director for South African operations, and the company was recruiting a black executive to head up MTN International. Furthermore, out of a total of five group-wide executive directors at MTN, two were black men, one was a black woman, one was a white woman, and one was a white man. Phuthuma Nhleko, an African man, was now CEO. As MTN's commercial director, Charnley led a management "buy-in" of an 18.7 percent stake of MTN Group. The shares were to be allocated to all employees, with 57.2 percent of the shares going to 200 managers and the remaining 42.8 percent going to the staff of 2,153. Because 65 percent of the beneficiaries of the scheme would be black, Nhleko considered the deal to be a "milestone for black economic empowerment." In 2002 and 2003, Charnley was named to *Fortune*'s Global Most Powerful Women in Business list.

The initial path that Charnley and Johnnic took was representative of the one taken by black business leaders in South African corporations. They started off the decade engaging in empowerment deals largely dictated to them by white business. These deals gave black business leaders a foot in the door and capital gains if the stock market cooperated, but they did not offer real opportunities to demand or craft change in how corporate South Africa worked. Charnley soon recognized this reality and began to negotiate for a more active role in Johnnic. She moved from an advisory position on the board to an executive position within management while remaining accountable to the wishes of her shareholders in the union. The shift allowed Charnley to implement rather than just recommend. With this power of implementation, she played a pivotal role in reshaping Johnnic into an active company whose day-to-day operational activities had real consequences for South Africans—and among many other things, to create a context at MTN for black hires to flourish.

Very few of the early empowerment companies established in the mid-1990s were able to exert the kind of control that resulted in change in corporate practices. Whatever the analysis, most observers agree that NEC and Johnnic did not fall prey to as many of the problems as others ran into. Charnley and her company won many accolades for their efforts, including numerous BEE awards.[16] They created real change in one of South Africa's most prominent companies, something few have been able to do.

Key Questions

Charnley's actions were not without controversy, and indeed raise many questions. Few would question her commitment to a vision of business as a catalyst for social change *as well as* a value creator for shareholders. Still, we must ask: Who has benefited from her efforts? Will the actions of Charnley and her like-minded colleagues from BEECom lead to broader, more sustainable change in the economic prospects of those who were previously disadvantaged?[17]

In the MTN Employment Equity Plan,[18] the company establishes its own criteria for the success of its employment equity/affirmative action initiative—equality of opportunity that results in improved business performance: "It is important for the organization to understand that Employment Equity/Affirmative Action cannot be a vision in itself. Affirmative action is a vehicle, a means towards an end, and that end is Equity. The ultimate vision is that of an organization where employees from whatever background will have the opportunity to realize their full potential, thereby enhancing the business objectives of the organization. An Equity vision can only be a driving force for change if all stakeholders help define it."[19]

Charnley has concluded that she must help MTN find a way to operate in the space where ethical behavior meets profitable behavior. Defining this space, which Lynn Sharpe Paine calls the "zone of acceptability," is a necessary first step in enabling business to act as a tool of poverty alleviation.[20]

As should be clear from Charnley's example, locating the area where ethical and economic soundness overlap and then operating within it is delicate work; a "gentler capitalism" is hard work. Did Charnley stray beyond the boundaries? Many believe BEE adds cost to corporations and compromises their competitive advantage.[21] Surely, Charnley found herself making trade-offs at times, between the competing priorities of the short-term and long-term well-being of the company, for instance, in hiring talent. But leadership is about making those judgments, weighing costs and benefits. In assessing how economically or ethically sound a leader's decisions are, we must consider the impact of their actions over time.

The debate about the role of business in South Africa is not only about the ends but also about the means of business. One prominent businessperson told us that he believed the South African economy would prosper only if black businesspeople unabashedly pursued business for what "business was meant to be about, making profits and making money." In his mind, businesspeople concerned about "ethical soundness" over "economic soundness" were preventing the economic growth that would ultimately lead to fuller employment and lower poverty in the South African economy.

During the anti-apartheid struggle, Charnley witnessed first-hand the power of leaders using ideals to capture the hearts and minds of diverse people, leading them to achieve seemingly impossible goals. This model of action is driving the unfolding story of black business leaders in South Africa as they try to inculcate an ethic of equity into business in the face of a global economy that operates under another set of rules. The legacy of South Africa created an opportunity for reexamination of the appropriate role of business, because during apartheid business acted as an oppressor as much as government did. It was hard to imagine a new social order that would not affect how business operated. Organizations such as the BEE Commission defined a vision of what capitalism should be and identified the values to which the new generation of business leaders should aspire. Change agents such as Charnley accepted responsibility for implementing the vision and institutionalizing it in their organizations.[22]

South Africa's black business class is in the seemingly impossible situation of running profitable businesses while having to justify to society that such success makes a meaningful difference in the lives of the poor and oppressed. It is an uncomfortable new standard of legitimacy faced by few other businesspeople in the world. The risk remains that Charnley and her compatriots will turn into a new black oligarchy ruling over a democracy of haves and have-nots. Even as she brought the ethics adopted from a childhood of poverty and a life of struggle to inform corporate practice, Charnley and others like her have grown wealthy and powerful.

The story of the emerging black business leadership in South Africa encourages us to question our assumptions about business and capitalism. As corporations grow in size and influence, public pressure grows for business leaders to consider the impact of their actions on pressing societal concerns.[23] What role can and should business play in ameliorating poverty and addressing inequality? For Charnley's generation, the crucible of apartheid has prepared them to engage some of the most intractable ethical challenges of our time.

PART SIX

MEASURING SUCCESS

Perhaps the most challenging aspect of assessing business models aimed at the base of the pyramid is the question of how to measure social impact. How does a firm know that it is reducing poverty? It can certainly measure revenues and profits gained. It can also measure the number of products and services delivered to a community. But moving beyond these simple indicators to real measures of impact—to incomes increased, lives changed, and societies transformed—is no easy task. Moreover, even if a company can point to clear evidence of positive social impact, it must still grapple with questions of profitability and fairness. When does profiting from the poor become exploitation? Who makes that determination?

We start Part Six with an overview of the microfinance industry and its contributions to poverty alleviation over the past thirty-five years. In Chapter Twenty-Eight, "Microfinance: Business, Profitability, and Creation of Social Value," Michael Chu presents compelling data from Latin America showing the average return on equity (ROE) for the 2002–2004 period for a cross-section of microfinance institutions was 33.2 percent, compared to 11.2 percent for the conventional banking industry. He argues that the yardstick for measuring the industry's success should be both profitability and impact on the disposable income of the poor. In his view, competition plays a central role in reconciling these two measures, because profitability attracts competition, which in turn brings down interest rates and drives product innovation that benefits poor customers.

Chapter Twenty-Nine, "Alleviating Global Poverty Through Microfinance: Factors and Measures of Financial, Economic, and Social Performance," also looks at microfinance, but it takes a different tack. Authors Marc Epstein and Christopher Crane interviewed dozens of microcredit clients in Ghana, most reporting that they were extremely satisfied as customers. However, careful analysis of past empirical studies was unable to convincingly demonstrate that their customer satisfaction and increased business income translated into tangible improvements in nutrition, health, and housing. To better understand and assess this gap, the authors present a comprehensive assessment framework to help microfinance institutions measure and maximize their social impact.

The third paper, "Strong Double-Bottom-Line Banking" by David Porteous, documents the contributions of three development banks engaged in making loans to small and medium enterprises: Plantersbank in the Philippines, Shorebank in Chicago, and Triodos Bank in Holland. All three demonstrated superior returns to their shareholders in comparison to conventional banks in their peer group. In addition, each bank also shows ample evidence of social impact.

In Chapter Thirty-One, "H&R Block's Refund Anticipation Loans: Perilous Profits at the Bottom of the Pyramid?" David Rose, Daniel Schneider, and Peter Tufano focus on H&R Block's Refund Anticipation Loan product, which it sells to more than ten million low-income U.S. tax clients every year. The product seems popular, judging by customer demand, yet consumer advocacy groups have targeted H&R Block for its "exorbitant" interest rates. The paper argues that companies facing this "paradox of profits" must engage in the public debate about profitability and consumer protection while focusing positive attention on how their products and services bring value to poor consumers.

The fifth and final paper, "When Is Doing Business with the Poor Good—for the Poor? A Household and National Income Accounting Approach" by Herman Leonard, applies a National Income Accounting approach to measuring the impact of business operations on low-income communities. This measurement approach integrates demand- and supply-side effects into one comprehensive model centered on the value created for the poor. The paper illustrates how the model may be applied by revisiting some of the earlier case studies in this book.

CHAPTER TWENTY-EIGHT

MICROFINANCE

Business, Profitability, and Creation of Social Value

Michael Chu

At a time when the intersection of business and the poor is attracting increasing attention from both economic and social perspectives, an example often cited is commercial microfinance: provision of financial services to low-income populations on a financially sustainable basis. Microfinance is mainly associated with micro-credit and mobilization of savings, but it includes all other forms of financial services, such as housing loans, equipment leasing, insurance, and remittances. As successful microfinance institutions (MFIs) continue to enjoy rapid expansion, their products are increasingly a factor in the lives of the poor. At the same time, with virtually all the leading microfinance institutions no longer NGOs but financial entities regulated by national banking authorities, the results of their operations have become a matter of credible public record. In addition, modern microfinance has been developing for more than thirty years and so has acquired the legitimacy of longevity. Accordingly, microfinance constitutes a natural point of departure to examine meeting the needs of the base of the socioeconomic pyramid through market mechanisms—and the convergence of business and profitability with the desire for social value.

The Business of Financing the Poor

Modern microfinance began in the early 1970s at about the same time in Latin America and Asia, the endeavor of social entrepreneurs who had no idea they were laying the foundations of an industry.[1] Today, microfinance has proven capable of generating revenue streams sufficient to cover all related expenses and yield a surplus equal or superior to activities with similar risk profiles, and to do so over a sustained period of time. It is therefore part of the world of business.

This does not mean that all microfinance institutions fit this description. In fact, the vast majority of entities around the world that deploy some form of microfinance do not. As has been noted,

> A rough rule of thumb in the field places the total number of entities in the world providing some form of microfinance in the range of 7,000 to 12,000. It is probable that virtually all the significant share of any relevant measure—size of assets, number of loans, annual growth, earnings, financial returns—is concentrated in no more than fifty MFIs [microfinance institutions]. This . . . is typical of the development of an industry. While there may be many entrants, the direction of the new field is set by the handful of leaders. Accordingly, in looking at the future of microfinance, the relevant starting point is the industry as it has been defined by this core of leading MFIs.[2]

These leaders, with few exceptions, operate under general charters and statutory frameworks established by the national banking or financial authorities of their country. This is irrespective of their origin, whether NGOs, financial institutions formed specifically to enter the field, or the specialized subsidiaries or divisions of traditional commercial banks diversifying to serve a new market segment. All have grown rapidly, in terms of both the number of clients and volume of assets, and represent the dominant microfinance presence in their markets. They are the source of best practices in terms of market penetration, innovation, cost efficiency, profitability, and solvency. It is this group of MFIs that clearly meet the definition of business and in turn collectively define the entire industry.[3]

In Latin America, a comprehensive study of microfinance estimated that in December 2004, 3.3 million low-income clients were being actively served by organizations generating levels of profitability similar to or above those of conventional banking.[4] NGOs surveyed, representing the largest and most efficient in the region, had the highest return on assets (ROA) at 5.6 percent, but with less capacity to assume leverage their resulting return on equity (ROE) was the lowest at 13.2 percent. As a group, regulated finance companies dedicated to microfinance had an ROA of 3.5 percent, with an ROE of 19.5 percent. Regulated microfinance banks earned an ROA of 4.2 percent and an ROE of 31.2 percent. In comparison, conventional commercial banking in Latin America in 2004 yielded an average ROA of 1.6 percent and an ROE of 16.5 percent.[5]

The top performers in Latin American microfinance performed substantially better. Taking a three-year mean (2002–2004) to smooth out the results of 2004 as an above-average year of economic recovery for the region, Table 28.1 shows that for the top twelve performers the average ROE was 33.2 percent,[6] ranging from a high of 52.2 percent to a low of 23.4 percent.[7] By contrast, the universe of commercial banks in Latin America during this period had an average ROE of 11.2 percent.[8] In a recent comprehensive overview of microfinance in the *Economist,* the magazine made the point that, even considering a limited universe of those microfinance institutions rated by specialist MicroRate, there were seventeen entities in 2004 with ROEs that "outshone" Citigroup.[9]

Just as important, the profitability of these Latin American microfinance leaders has survived the test of time. Banco Solidario S.A. of Bolivia, or BancoSol as it is known around the world, was the first microfinance bank solely chartered under the regular banking laws of its country. BancoSol has operated in the black ever since its founding in 1992. It has had ups and downs, particularly at the onset of the intense competitive pressure that characterizes the Bolivian microfinance market, but BancoSol has consistently ranked among the most profitable and solvent institutions in the Bolivian financial system.

Although BancoSol's performance may be the most widely known, it is not an isolated case in Bolivia. Data compiled by ASOFIN, an industry association for regulated

TABLE 28.1. MOST PROFITABLE MICROFINANCE INSTITUTIONS IN LATIN AMERICA.

Microfinance Institutions	Type	Country	Average ROE 2002–2004 (Percent)
BancoSol	RU	Bolivia	26.3
Credife (Banco de Pichincha)	RD	Ecuador	50.9
Compartamos	RU	Mexico	52.2
Confía Banco Procredit	RU	Nicaragua	39.3
Banco del Trabajo	RD	Peru	33.8
Findesa	RU	Nicaragua	32.0
Fundación WWB/Cali	NGO	Colombia	31.5
Edpyme Crear Arequipa	RU	Peru	29.7
BanGente	RD	Venezuela	29.0
Banco Solidario	RD	Ecuador	25.2
FIE	RU	Bolivia	25.2
Sogesol	RD	Haiti	23.4
Simple average			33.2
Conventional banking			11.2

Note: RU = regulated "upgrading"; RD = regulated "downscaling"; NGO = nongovernmental organization.

Sources: Marulanda and Otero, 2005; Worldscope.

microfinance institutions that includes the leading industry players[10] and accounts for 84 percent of the microcredit loan portfolio of Bolivia,[11] indicate that:

- In 2004, an extremely difficult year for Bolivia in general,[12] all the ASOFIN members were profitable, with five institutions earning double-digit ROE, led by BancoSol (22.6 percent) and FFP FIE (24.7 percent). In the same period, the conventional Bolivian banking system[13] reported a loss, resulting in a negative ROE of 2.2 percent.[14]
- For the first nine months of 2005, the conventional banking system returned to profitability, with an ROE of 3.4 percent. Though one ASOFIN member was operating in the red, three continued to earn double-digit ROEs, with the leader, BancoSol, generating an ROE 6.4 times that of conventional banking.[15]
- This difference in profitability was not at the expense of asset quality. The ASOFIN members, for 2004 and the first nine months of 2005, had ratios of late payments to gross loan portfolio in the low single digits (from 2.05 percent to 6.57 percent), while the same ratio for conventional banking was above 14 percent.[16] Comparison between microfinance and regular banking is often made difficult by potentially significant differences in how similar financial terms are applied,[17] but in this case all institutions, ASOFIN members and conventional banks alike, report to the Bolivian Superintendency of Banks using uniform definitions, under a system where misreporting carries penal liabilities.
- In arriving at the profitability and asset quality indicators mentioned here, the income statements of the ASOFIN members already reflect a higher provisioning for late payments than that taken by conventional banks. Seven of the eight ASOFIN institutions have provisioned significantly above 100 percent of their late payments (with one member, FFP FIE, accounting for them three times over) compared to 85.5 percent for the traditional banks at year-end 2004, and 75.5 percent as of September 30, 2005.[18]

Consistently generating returns superior to banking at the top of the pyramid has allowed microfinance in Latin America to gradually gain acceptance as a legitimate component of the business sector. Reflecting this, microfinance institutions have begun to participate directly in the bond markets. Two recent examples are Financiera Compartamos[19] in Mexico and Mibanco in Peru.[20]

Financiera Compartamos, with 453,000 active clients and a loan portfolio of US$183.4 million as of December 31, 2005,[21] is the largest microfinance institution in Latin America. It is also among the top-earning microfinance entities in the world, with an ROE in 2004 of 48.5 percent.[22] Its client base continues to be predominantly rural, with an average outstanding loan of $404.[23] In July 2002, Compartamos made a private placement of $15 million in local-currency three-year bonds through

Banamex-Citibank, at Mexican treasury rate plus 250 basis points. Later that year, it followed with a supplemental placement of $5 million, under the same terms. In 2003, Compartamos entered the market again to place $5 million, extending the term to 3.5 years, at a slightly higher price of Mexican treasury rate plus 290 basis points. In 2004, Compartamos launched a $50 million bond program, with a first tranch of $19 million, pushing the maturity to five years.

Mibanco, a commercial bank established in Peru in 1998 from the pioneering microcredit work of its predecessor NGO, had 154,451 active clients and a loan portfolio of US$206.7 million as of December 31, 2005.[24] From 2002 to 2004, Mibanco reported an average ROE of 23 percent, a profitability "well above the average for the Peruvian banking sector during the same period."[25] In December 2002, it issued on the Peruvian capital markets $5.8 million in local-currency two-year corporate bonds via Dutch auction, at a fixed interest rate of 12 percent. In September 2003, Mibanco issued another $5.8 million of bonds, extending the maturity to two years and three months, but at a significantly lower rate of 5.75 percent. A month later, Mibanco followed it with a $2.9 million issue of eighteen-month paper at the same pricing.

The successful experience of Compartamos and Mibanco followed in the path of BancoSol, which issued $5 million in dollar-denominated two-year bonds at 13 percent, credit-enhanced by a 50 percent guarantee provided by the U.S. Agency for International Development (USAID) in March 1996.

If profitability is the minimum requirement for admission into the world of bona fide business and access to the bond markets one of its privileges, full membership into the club may be acceptance as an asset class suitable for equity investment. In 2003, Bank Rakyat of Indonesia, where microfinance is a major component (some would argue the most important source of its profits), launched an oversubscribed initial public offering that made its shares the first truly publicly traded microfinance stock.

Until then, the major equity investors in microfinance had been NGOs, multilateral development organizations and governments, and a few sophisticated socially responsible private investors. These protagonists acted alone and through specialized equity investment funds, whose numbers have been growing in recent years. The first of them was formed in 1995 through an initiative headed by ACCION International, Calmeadow of Canada, FUNDES of Switzerland, and SIDI of France. This effort "raised $23 million to create Profund, a Latin American investment pool intended to demonstrate that investing in microfinance could be commercially viable. It was designed to run for ten years, and true to its mission it sold off its last investment [in the] summer [of 2005]. By liquidating its portfolio and turning it into real cash, it became a yardstick for the investment performance of a microfinance institution."[26]

By November 2005, Profund had either fully realized or sold but not yet collected on the sale of all its assets.[27] On this basis, fund management estimated that the annualized internal rate of return over the ten years of the fund would be 6.61 percent.[28]

As the *Economist* put it, "At first sight, its returns look unexciting. . . . But on closer examination, this was a remarkable performance. All of Profund's capital was contributed in dollars and then invested in local currency. In every country it operated in, its dollar returns were reduced by local currency depreciations, reflecting the economic chaos in much of Latin America during the decade."[29]

In fact, to gauge the performance of microfinance equity investing compared to conventional asset categories, a more appropriate measure is not absolute returns but the position of Profund relative to the other equity funds deployed during the same time in the emerging markets. Applying this criterion, the IFC,[30] a Profund investor, has calculated that:

• Against a widely accepted industry benchmark of emerging-market venture capital and equity funds raised in 1995, Profund's IRR of 6.61 percent placed it squarely in the top quartile. In this universe of fourteen funds, the pooled mean return to investors was a loss of 0.37 percent and the median was a loss of 0.60 percent. The lower quartile returned a negative 8.27 percent.

• There were only two other funds that yielded a higher return to their investors, and the top performer returned 12.16 percent.

Profund's accomplishment is all the more remarkable considering the small size of the fund, $23 million. Because of this, management costs represented a larger proportion of the funds under management than normal. Profund's IRR before operating and financial expenses was 9.03 percent.[31]

Superior returns while serving the financial needs of the poor can also be found outside of Latin America. Perhaps the most successful microfinance institution in the world is also one of the least known by the general public, Bank Rakyat of Indonesia (BRI). A wholly state-owned bank until its partial privatization in 2003, it is also the oldest bank in Indonesia, tracing its origins to 1895. In the early 1970s, BRI developed an extensive national infrastructure reaching deep into rural areas to deploy agrarian credit as part of Indonesia's drive for rice self-sufficiency. This became the framework for what today is its formidable microfinance operation.[32] On June 30, 2003, BRI's assets totaled $11.1 billion, of which $5.7 billion represented government bonds, cash, and securities, and $5.3 billion was the gross loan portfolio.[33] Of that, $1.6 billion fell into what the bank calls its microloan portfolio (representing three million loans with an average balance of $532).[34] On the other side of the balance sheet, BRI funds itself with $9 billion in deposits, of which $3 billion is captured by its rural and urban microfinance operations in 29 million accounts.[35] This base of business has provided outstanding returns; for the years 2001 and 2002 and the first six months of 2003, BRI had ROAs of 1.5 percent, 1.9 percent and 2.7 percent, yielding ROEs of 24.0 percent, 28.2 percent and 38.3 percent, respectively.[36] With this level of financial return and the size of its operations, BRI has been able to advance microfinance in many ways. Mention has already been made of BRI as the first institution identified with microfinance to be publicly listed. In September 2003, it also went into the global capital markets to issue $150 million of subordinated notes due 2013.[37] As in Mexico and Peru, BRI's issues were both oversubscribed.

Financially successful microfinance institutions are also found in Africa and Eastern Europe. One of them is Uganda Microfinance Limited (UMU), a local NGO founded in August 1997 that achieved breakeven results in 2001. The following year, it reported an ROA of 4.3 percent and an ROE of 12.7 percent. By 2003, it had increased to a reported ROA of 12.36 percent and ROE of 48.4 percent. Returns for 2004 were not publicly available, but the level of profitability continued to be superior.[38] At year-end 2003, UMU had 28,099 active borrowers and 47,529 active savers.[39] In July 2005, UMU obtained a license from the Central Bank as a microfinance deposit-taking institution and became a regulated institution. Another African example is K-Rep Bank Limited, the first microfinance bank in Kenya, licensed in 1999. Its return on capital employed was 7.69 percent in 2001, 9.89 percent in 2002, 11.55 percent in 2003, and 9.93 percent in 2004.[40] In Eastern Europe and elsewhere, the experience of the Pro Credit banks, the network in fourteen countries connected to Internationale Projekt Consult GmbH (IPC), has also been profitable. A recent review of the group found that "overall, the return on equity of the banks in the network, measured in book value terms and weighted by the banks' equity, is above 10 percent."[41]

Creating Social Value

Were microfinance just a business capable of earning superior returns, its interest would be limited. Business is full of examples of high returns to first movers that manage to introduce killer concepts opening up a new market. What sets microfinance apart is its potential to contribute to economic development and respond to global poverty.

Most of the world lives under conditions where the essentials associated with basic survival and dignity are lacking or deficient: food, education, health care, shelter, clothing, safety, and respect. Countless factors affect the poor's access to these essentials, but basic lack of disposable income remains the most direct and powerful barrier to that access. No matter what hurdles the poor face, one fact stands out: if the people who survive on $365 a year were suddenly to have available the average annual U.S. disposable income of $28,000,[42] the rest of the world would mobilize rapidly to offer them all those missing essentials—regardless of race, caste, religion, or national origin. Money, as the proverbial saying goes, cannot buy happiness, but it remains the essential foundation on which lives are built.

Accordingly, whenever business intersects with the base of the pyramid, the fundamental social question is its impact on the disposable income of the poor. This can be viewed along three dimensions:

1. *Does it stretch the disposable income of the poor?* Microfinance has reduced the interest rate paid on the street from being in the thousands of percent per annum to double digits, with the lowest now in a range around 20 percent or so.

2. *Does it expand the reach of the disposable income of the poor?* In microfinance, the products offered have gone from basic credit or savings to myriad other financial instruments.

3. *Does it increase the disposable income of the poor?* Relieved of the need to meet moneylenders' high interest rates, microfinance clients can grow their enterprises and employ more people. Microfinance institutions themselves are employers at the base of the pyramid. Like construction, microfinance appears to have a broad multiplier effect.[43]

Maintaining the focus on disposable income has a further benefit: it protects the analysis of social impact from imposition of the values of the analyst over the values of the men and women at the base of the pyramid. Disposable income puts the poor and their choices squarely at the center. This is far from saying that the poor would not benefit from better information and knowledge. It is instead an affirmation that decisions, imperfect as they may be, are best made by those most cognizant of the circumstances under which the decisions are carried out.[44] It is also not a denial of the powerful qualitative benefits of microfinance such as self-respect and confidence, but a reminder that they are closely linked to increases in disposable income.

The Role of Profit in Creating Social Value

To what *precise* degree microfinance contributes to increasing the disposable income of its clients (or any other factor deemed socially relevant) is a question that by and large awaits systematic study.[45] But even if future rigorous research supports the firm conviction of practitioners and observers that the impact of microfinance on poverty is significant, the capacity of MFIs to generate outstanding returns raises the issue of the appropriate level of profitability when commerce intersects with poverty. After all, every cent of an MFI's net income is earned off the sweat of hard-working men and women at the base of the pyramid. Interest rates may not be the only factor to consider in financing the poor, but they remain a major element and it is difficult to ignore that some of the institutions earning the highest financial returns are also the ones charging the highest prices. At the top of the pyramid, relying on the market to determine pricing may make perfect sense, but is it good policy to extend that to the base? Even if market forces will eventually bring the price down, the time this takes in poor communities is measured not in pleasure deferred but in hardships suffered and life chances lost.

From a social perspective, scale is the major implication of microfinance as a bona fide business. To achieve this scale, profits in microfinance are a must, and outstanding profits critical. Because microfinance works with the poor, gaining legitimacy in the world of business does not come easily. Emerging from a sector that is so closely associated with social work and philanthropy, it has had to overcome strong prejudices regarding the poor and those that work with them. The large number of entities in microfinance and their enormous variation in performance and transparency have also made gaining legitimacy more of a challenge. Added to this is the coexistence of two contradictory conceptions of microfinance: the view that it is a "human right" and the view that it is a component of the financial system. Given all this, it is not surprising that until the late 1990s business by and large ignored microfinance. To gain awareness, microfinance had to perform "like a business," and then some. Not only did it have to generate market rates of return; it had to beat them. Without profitability, opening the bond markets and bringing in conventional commercial banking would have been impossible.

When Profit Is Good and When It Is Bad

Despite the microfinance industry's growth in both new and repeat clients, has scaling up come at too high a price for the poor? The answer lies in the realization that, from a social perspective, the real success of microfinance is not that financial institutions dedicated to the poor earn a rate of return matching or surpassing that of traditional banks. It is that these leaders have managed to create an entire industry dedicated to the base of the pyramid. Following displacement of the moneylender, competition has driven continuous improvement of the terms under which financial services reach the poor.

When BancoSol opened its doors in 1992, it charged an effective interest rate of 35 percent.[46] The rate was such a bargain compared to moneylenders' exorbitant rates that the bank enjoyed a virtual monopoly in Bolivia. Caja Los Andes was formed in 1995 as a specialized finance company.[47] At the time, market penetration was low and growth possible for both institutions. But the competitive scene changed radically in the late 1990s. Attracted by the high returns offered by microfinance, consumer credit companies piled in. With little knowledge of the target population, they introduced radical methodologies developed for totally different markets.[48] This led to one of the first shakeouts of the microfinance industry, driving the entire sector into acute crisis in 1999–2000.[49] An ensuing wave of overindebtedness exacted a social cost, but the end result brought several new benefits to the poor.

Subsequent to the crisis, the Bolivian microfinance industry remained intensely competitive, and this has had a fundamental impact on pricing. Figure 28.1 shows that effective interest rates[50] in Bolivia have dropped consistently, apparently with no end in sight. Since 1998, the price paid by the poor for credit has gone from just under 30 percent to 21.2 percent, the lowest in Latin America. Concurrently, the variety of credit products available to the poor is blossoming. When it first opened, BancoSol was characterized by a single product: solidarity loans, where people with no collateral and no ascertainable credit history could borrow by joining a self-selected group of three to five people who cross-guaranteed one another. This was a highly effective mechanism for bringing in new borrowers while preserving asset quality. But the high transaction costs of forming groups made it vulnerable to competition from individual loan products, which the competition was quick to introduce. As a result, BancoSol evolved from a monoproduct bank to one offering nine credit options by the end of the crisis in 2000. As Rhyne states, "Unquestionably, most microfinance clients benefit from the advent of competition. More people have access to financial services, they can choose their supplier, and they can demand favorable terms. . . . It is important to reiterate the effects of commercialization on service quality, methodology, and new product development and to emphasize that these emerged independent of the crisis."[51] Since then, the Bolivian competitive experience has played out in several other countries, as well, resulting in lower prices and increased product variety.

Competition is what reconciles profitability and creation of social value. In the early years of BancoSol, when the only other source of credit for the poor was the moneylender, there was little incentive to become more efficient or adapt to client needs. While price held constant, profitability improved as market penetration built on the economies of scale allowed by the existing bank infrastructure. In 1998, this model produced an ROE of just under 30 percent. Though significant in terms of solidifying BancoSol's image in the business community and strengthening its links to the capital markets, creation of social value was limited to the bank's capacity to scale up—to reach new clients and offer larger loans for existing clients. With the onset of competition (and the crisis of 1999–2000), the bank's profitability was decimated. Arguably, what BancoSol lost in profitability the poor gained through better pricing, more products, and improved services. With competitive pressures remaining intense in Bolivia, BancoSol's recent return to attractive profitability has been achieved in a declining price environment. Today, profitability improvements are the result of management skills applied to obtain efficiencies in its cost structure at a faster rate than the drop in prices. As a result, achieving an ROE of 26.3 percent in 2004 went hand-in-hand with creation of social value.

FIGURE 28.1. AVERAGE MICROFINANCE INTEREST RATE, BOLIVIA 1998–2005.

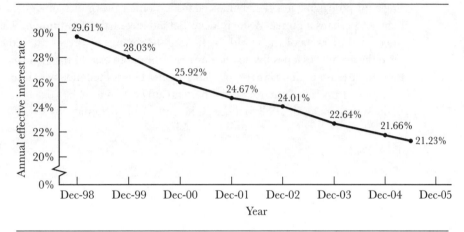

Source: ASOFIN.

Why Business at the Base of the Pyramid Matters

The case of microfinance points to a basic fact in responding to global poverty: effectiveness ultimately rests on two fundamentals, the ability to reach a large number of people and the capability to maintain that reach for however long is necessary. The need for scale is determined by the enormity of the problem: 1.3 billion people live on less than one dollar a day and 3 billion live on less than two dollars a day.[52] No matter how effective an initiative is by itself in tackling poverty, it will not be significant unless it reaches a sufficient number of the poor to make a large-scale difference. Nor will it really be consequential if it does not have staying power. Eradicating the current level of poverty will take more than one generation. Accordingly, an effective initiative must have a permanence that can survive the finite attention span and lives of individuals, whether they are at the helm of government, NGOs, philanthropy, think tanks, or academia.

The social power of microfinance lies in its ability to meet these two key requirements of *scale* and *sustainability* by turning an activity that can create social value into a business. The importance of a commercial approach is that once delivery of a good or service makes sound economic sense, the seeds are sown for eventual penetration of that market. Because the BancoSols and the BRIs of the world have proven that it is economically rational to serve the poor, it is now possible to believe that the day will come when the last woman with a stall by the side of the road who needs a loan will actually get it. What type of institution will offer it to her is less clear: a local single-purpose bank, a regional financial institution, or the branch of a global mega-bank, or perhaps all three, if she is lucky. Behind any of these institutions will stand the capital markets of the world. By linking the savings of the world to the poor, microfinance makes it possible to one day reach the entire base of the population pyramid, and to sustain that effort across generations. This is the fundamental reason the transition of microfinance from a visionary dream of NGOs to the bona fide world of business matters, most of all to those at the base of the pyramid.

CHAPTER TWENTY-NINE

ALLEVIATING GLOBAL POVERTY THROUGH MICROFINANCE

Factors and Measures of Financial, Economic, and Social Performance

Marc J. Epstein, Christopher A. Crane

The entrepreneurial women were selling food and other staples, sewing and selling clothes, and running beauty shops. They were at work in stalls in the marketplace, in front of their homes, and on the street. They were motivated, empowered, and excited to have some assistance from a local microfinance organization in building their small businesses.

In June 2005, we interviewed dozens of such entrepreneurs in Ghana—all women primarily in trading and service businesses and all borrowers of microloans from Sinapi Aba Trust. The loans gave them access to working capital and helped to smooth the economic shocks in their lives. They were satisfied with the loan and the microfinance services they received, and were full of conviction about the benefits of microfinance.

As it turns out, although the anecdotes we heard in Ghana were powerful, the results from academic and institutional research are mixed on the impact of microfinance. We wondered: Why has the value of microfinance in alleviating poverty not been demonstrated more clearly? Today, these questions are critical, with ever more funds being directed to microfinance as an important vehicle for global poverty alleviation. More and more, donors (public and private) want to better understand the payoff of their investment.

Microfinance has been used as a tool for alleviating global poverty for about forty years. In that time, billions have been loaned and many success stories have been told. Organizations such as Grameen Bank, ACCION International, and Opportunity

International have all made impressive contributions. However, the precise nature of the contributions is less clear. Furthermore, determining how microfinance can be used to make an even larger and more critical contribution to alleviating global poverty is a topic still in need of careful research and articulation.

One might expect that the large number of prior empirical studies would clearly demonstrate the positive impact of microfinance. However, the evidence we found is typically either weak or mixed. Over the years, diligent researchers from academia, nonprofit organizations, and microfinance institutions have conducted a number of studies.[1] But numerous obstacles stand in the way of a true evaluation of microfinance's impact. Studies have used multiple approaches to evaluation, employing a variety of measures and research methodologies, making comparison between studies difficult. Moreover, differences in economic and political environments, program quality, leadership, and various other contextual variables make comparison challenging. Even within studies themselves, the results are often inconclusive.

For much of its history, microfinance has been seen as logically and intuitively appealing—and primarily conducted as an act of faith. It affords access to capital and other financial services that can smooth and soften the financial impact of a crisis (such as illness) and stabilize a poor borrower's income. It also enables people to expand their businesses, increase their profits, and improve their lives.

For many observers, enabling the poor to gain access to capital and reduce their economic vulnerability is enough. But for others who want to demonstrate the payoffs to capital providers in the for-profit capital market sector or the nonprofit philanthropy sector, more conclusive evidence of impact is needed. If microfinance is to become a larger force in alleviating global poverty and expand its scale of operation, better evidence of the payoffs of microfinance investment as well as the impact on both the economic and the social welfare of borrowers is a must.

This research project was founded on two sets of questions:

1. What are the primary determinants of success for microfinance institutions? This question addresses why microfinance has been more successful in some cases than others. Is it the political or business environment? Is it the leadership of the microfinance organization? Is it the strategy, structure, or systems used to manage the organization? Is it the characteristics of the borrowers? Better articulation of these key drivers of success might lead to larger success for microfinance and greater ability to obtain additional capital for growth.

2. What are the appropriate measures of success? This question, in particular, raises numerous issues that are debated among researchers. Is the primary goal of microfinance institutions to give the poor access to capital? Or is it to create additional income for the poor? Is it necessary that borrowers not only increase their income but also improve their living conditions (better housing, nutrition, education for their children, and so forth)?

This study is an attempt to carefully specify the antecedents and consequences of investment in microfinance, examine the nature and amount of existing contributions, and consider how to enhance the contribution of microfinance to poverty alleviation. We have completed a thorough review of the literature, examined prior impact studies and data, conducted interviews with senior officers at Opportunity International, and analyzed microfinance data and field activities in Ghana.

On the basis of this research, we have developed a microfinance contribution model that articulates the antecedents and consequences of investments in microfinance to identify the key performance indicators of microfinance success. The model also specifies the performance drivers and measures that lead to this success. Finally, we suggest a set of measures for both outputs and outcomes.

Overview of Microfinance, Opportunity International, and the Ghana Field and Survey Research

The field of microfinance is less than forty years old, yet it appears to have been remarkably effective in helping the poor work their way out of poverty. Microfinance institutions (MFIs) typically make loans to individuals (mostly women) to start or expand a business. The loans can be group-based or individual, usually less than $1,000 and often less than $100. They permit access to working capital and other financial services for the poor that did not previously exist. Repayment rates for microfinance are typically between 95 percent and 100 percent, dependent, in part, on many of the input and process factors discussed here.[2]

Opportunity International

Opportunity International is one of the world's largest microfinance organizations, with more than eight hundred thousand clients in twenty-seven countries on four continents. It operates through forty-two entities, most of which Opportunity founded. Opportunity International is a 501(c)(3) nonprofit organization but operates programs in various legal forms: NGOs, finance companies, savings and loans, and chartered banks.

Opportunity International is an ideal setting in which to examine the drivers and measures of success (and failure) in microfinance. Operating throughout the world, the organization has enjoyed significant successes and suffered some failures. By analyzing operations in various countries and sectors, the size of loans, individual borrower characteristics, country economic, cultural, and political characteristics and numerous other factors, one can develop a framework that identifies the key drivers of success and develops methods to measure social, economic, and financial outcomes. This facilitates examination of the trade-offs that are often necessary in balancing social and economic benefits to various stakeholders: the microfinance organization, its funders, the individual borrowers, and the community. This process further enables us to better understand who is benefiting from microfinance institutions and how to maximize the benefits to various constituents.

Opportunity International's involvement in the conversion of NGO Sinapi Aba Trust (SAT) into a for-profit savings and loan institution (Sinapi Aba Savings and Loan) is a unique setting for evaluating alternative organizational structures in order to understand which structures yield the greatest benefit in alleviating poverty. Established in 1994, SAT currently has fifty-five thousand clients and is profitable and sustainable. It is growing rapidly and plans to continue to expand its services nationally.

Ghana Survey and Field Research

In Ghana, we conducted interviews with thirty borrowers, along with loan officers and supervisors, senior officers, the CEO, and board chairman. The loan officers and senior officers shared valuable insights into the key drivers of microfinance success and potential measures of social and economic impacts. Interviews with the borrowers offered key learnings as well. The results of all of these interviews informed development of the models and measures presented here.

Most of the borrowers were organized into group loans (or trust banks) of thirty-five to forty individuals, typically organized around affiliation through the marketplace, the community, or the church. Group social pressure and mandatory attendance at weekly meetings are important elements in SAT's high repayment rate. Weekly meetings also include compulsory business training for these new entrepreneurs.

The interview questions addressed to the borrowers were primarily focused on two sets of issues: (1) What did they do with the money borrowed? (2) What did they do with any additional profits that were facilitated by this borrowing?

Borrowers reported that the loans typically allowed them to improve their business by expanding product offerings or enabling them to buy in bulk directly from producers at reduced cost. Though much of the loan proceeds were invested in the business, we do know that some of the loans were also used for personal needs. The loans and resultant business improvements did increase personal income and permitted a higher level of personal spending on children's education, health care, and improved housing and nutrition. It also constituted a cushion for the inevitable financial shocks that affect the lives of the poor. In addition, the loans often gave borrowers an opportunity for empowerment and decision making never before considered possible, such as having a choice between public and private schooling for their children. An overall boost in borrowers' confidence and self-esteem after receiving loans was also palpable.

The field visits were convincing; microfinance had made a significant, positive impact on the economic and social conditions of the borrowers. But, just as with most other microfinance impact studies, the results of prior survey research in Ghana are mixed.

Prior Impact Assessments

Though numerous previous assessments were conducted to assess SAT's impact on its clients—and taken together, the results appear to be positive—the precise nature and amount of impact remain unclear. As a group, these Ghanaian studies (conducted in 1997, 1998, 1999, 2002, and 2004) present mixed results. Some of these studies are based on a Client Impact Monitoring System (CIMS) developed to establish a database and produce baseline numbers and appropriate measures.

Positive impact can be seen in the clients' businesses and the economic conditions of their households. There are some noticeable increases in clients' average monthly revenue, enterprise job creation, and benefits of client training in relationships with customers and suppliers. Clients' businesses are becoming more successful, and there is also some evidence that as a result they are increasing their savings and spending more on education and food. At the same time, however, this positive economic impact and increased spending in key areas does not clearly translate into tangible improvements in educational quality, nutrition, or housing. Furthermore, no assessment has been completed to measure the multiplier effects in the community and society.

Social impacts are less clear. As quality of life improved, we generally saw an increase in social activities, community involvement, and leadership, but direct connections are unclear at best and in some cases we even found evidence of negative effects. As previously noted, the impact on housing quality, home ownership, and children's education was inconclusive as well. All told, in surveys of new, intermediate, and mature clients, concrete positive impacts were difficult to discern.

The interviews themselves were more convincing. Clients strongly articulate positive economic impact on their individual status, their household, and the community by way of job creation and economic activity. It should be noted that clients do declare significant improvement in the quality of their lives in social dimensions. Education for children as well as the level of nutrition, health care, and quality of housing are often improved. From the field interviews, it appears that not only is there an improvement in their economic welfare and business success but the additional income is also used to obtain other critical, long-term benefits to the family. In addition, there is some evidence on the positive impact of microfinance in Ghana (and more generally) on the empowerment of women, including an increase in self-esteem, respect, and decision rights within the family unit.[3]

Why then aren't the results of the surveys more conclusive? In Ghana, and in impact studies in general, research methods are still in development. The industry has not yet standardized measures of success in microfinance. As a result, in some cases the wrong variables are being measured, in others the variables are not being measured well, or the research methods do not lead to clear conclusions, or too little data have been collected for adequate analysis. Thus even though field research can generate clear enough conclusions, survey data simply do not lend adequate support to back them up empirically.

Microfinance Contribution Model

Analysis of the microfinance literature demonstrates the need for further specification of the measures of microfinance success. Most microfinance impact studies include economic measures at the individual, household, and business levels, among them income, assets, and revenues.[4] Positive impact has often been shown in the areas of client business success and economic conditions in the household. Both business profits and household income increased for most borrowers after receiving a loan.[5] But here again the results are mixed, with many studies remaining unconvinced about even the economic benefits.[6]

Impact assessments have also studied the social impact that loans might have on individual borrowers, but this research is less comprehensive and less consistent. Most of these studies have not produced conclusive evidence that microfinance has a positive social impact on clients' lives.[7] Too often, studies have focused on enterprise growth, client satisfaction and retention, and default rate as the primary measures. Little research has focused on how the money (the borrowings or the profits) is used and how it has improved economic and social welfare, empowerment, and self-esteem.

In addition, we must ask what the key factors are that lead to success in microfinance. Is it the country, the political stability, relative level of corruption, senior management skills, loan officer skills, the MFI's organizational structure, type of business created by clients, characteristics of borrower (including age, gender, and experience), size of loan, sector, size of community, trust bank composition, or other internal or external factors? Why has microfinance worked well in some countries and failed in others? What are the critical internal (MFI) and external (societal) variables necessary for microfinance success?

By and large, we do not have adequate answers to these questions. It is critical that appropriate measures be developed for the social and economic impacts and the MFI's financial performance. Any discussion about the performance of microfinance in alleviating global poverty should measure both the financial success of the organization along with its success in improving the lives of the borrowers, and hopefully through a multiplier effect the lives of many others in the community.

Identifying Objectives, Drivers, and Measures

Figure 29.1 describes the critical factors that contribute to microfinance impact and success. These inputs and processes lead to the success of the client's business (intermediate output) and ultimately to the MFI's financial success and positive social and economic outcomes for clients, their households, and their communities.

The inputs in the microfinance contribution model help to establish the current context of the country and its microfinance institutions. This includes the political, social, and cultural environment of the country and its corresponding level of stability, competition, and economic opportunity. These factors, along with the financial and human resource constraints of an MFI, can help determine how the leadership will develop its strategy to affect the lives of its clients and ensure the success of the MFI. These inputs and processes lead to improvement in the clients' businesses (intermediate outputs), which in turn should lead to long-lasting impact (outcomes): improvement in the social and economic conditions of the individual borrower and their households, community, and society.

Once the objectives of microfinance have been determined, the drivers of success and their corresponding measures must be developed. The drivers specify the critical elements that influence microfinance impact and organizational success. Figure 29.2 is a visual description of the causal links that drive microfinance success.

FIGURE 29.1. MICROFINANCE CONTRIBUTION MODEL: ANTECEDENTS AND CONSEQUENCES OF MICROFINANCE INVESTMENTS.

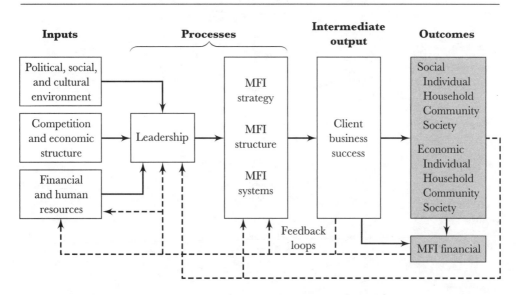

FIGURE 29.2. MICROFINANCE PERFORMANCE DRIVERS.

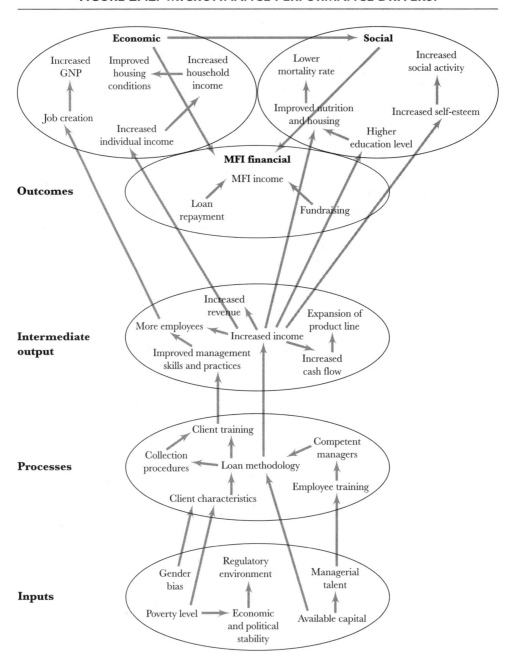

Inputs

There are three types of inputs that are important to an MFI and help guide the decisions of its leadership. The first relates to the political, social, and cultural environment in the country of operation. This includes drivers such as government corruption, business corruption, political instability, and gender bias. The second input is the country's competitive and economic structure, which comprises economic stability, regulatory environment, physical infrastructure, and the presence and success of competitors. These are variables that the MFI has little ability to change or control. Together, these two inputs determine the overall country context. These inputs can be measured by a range of indicators, among them political risk, the number of female-headed households, the prevailing interest rate, and the number of MFIs and banks currently lending to the poor.

The final input—but one not to be underestimated—is the financial and human resources of the microfinance organization itself. The MFI needs the financial resources to make loans and pay and train staff. Second, the local labor pool must supply educated individuals willing to work at a reasonable salary as a loan officer or manager. If additional spending is required to develop a capable staff, it may limit the financial viability of microfinance in a certain country setting. These two resources play a large part in determining the success of microfinance in a particular country.

Processes

Leadership within the MFI must understand the country context in order to formulate strategies, structures, and systems that will be effective. Senior executives at the MFI must be knowledgeable, support the organization, and effectively communicate the mission and vision to other members of the organization. An excellent senior leadership team and board of directors are key elements of MFI success. Effective leadership ability could be measured through client and employee ratings and years of microfinance experience, since these factors are also critical.

The organization's strategy and choice of clients and products will significantly influence the processes and outcomes achieved. Client characteristics such as business type and location, income level, and gender contribute to potential impact. Additionally, the size (average and range) of client loans is an important driver and reflects the MFI's appetite for risk. Consequently, the size of loans will have an impact on the structures and systems necessary for effective strategy implementation.

The MFI structure itself will also be affected by the inputs and strategy chosen. For example, whether an MFI chooses to issue individual loans versus using a group lending approach influences how services are delivered and the impact that those services

330 Business Solutions for the Global Poor

have on borrowers. The systems designed to implement the strategy must encourage employees to succeed and clients to participate and repay their loans. Likewise, senior loan officers must be able to implement the systems that are in place (such as employee incentives and training, credit monitoring, and IT systems) to ensure that the desired outcomes are achieved.

Intermediate Output

According to our model, client business success is an intermediate output because it is a primary contributor to overall outcomes. A well-designed and well-executed MFI strategy should lead to improved client business performance. Successful business indicators are product line expansion, better management and accounting practices, an increase in business income, and the like. If microloans do not lead to positive financial changes in the business, then positive change in the lives of the borrowers and their respective households, communities, and societies cannot be expected. After receiving a loan, the business should experience increased revenue, higher income, and creation of more jobs. It is important to remember, however, that a successful business should not be the ultimate goal of microfinance; therefore business success cannot be considered the final outcome of microfinance impact.

Outcomes

For microfinance to achieve its goals, the quality of life for individual borrowers must be improved. These improvements should also flow to the borrowers' households, immediate communities, and larger societies. Long-lasting impact should be noticeable in their economic and social lives, which could be assessed through indicators of poverty, health, education, empowerment, housing, and self-esteem. To achieve these ends, it is critical that the MFI itself remain financially stable and sustainable. To earn money, the MFI needs clients to repay their loans and continue to use the program. The MFI should also be able to create growth through additional borrowings and donations as well as expanded services.

Table 29.1 shows a selection of measures that could be used to analyze microfinance success. This is not a comprehensive list, but rather examples of the type of measure that should be considered by an organization in assessing impact. It includes many more measures than would ever be appropriate for collection or analysis. They are given as examples of the breadth of measures available, and to aid organizations in choosing just a small number that are consistent with their mission, strategy, implementation process, and outcome objectives. All impact studies must be guided by the goals and objectives of the management of the MFI and situated within a specific country context. The measures chosen should align with these organizational objectives and

TABLE 29.1. MICROFINANCE CONTRIBUTION MODEL: SELECTED METRICS FOR MICROFINANCE SUCCESS.

Inputs	Performance Measures
Political, social, and cultural environment	• Political and business corruption • Government stability • Number of female-headed households • Gender bias • Rate of reported violence against women • Education level of women • Percentage of population imprisoned • Community level of trust for group loans
Competition and economic structure	• Inflation rate • Regulatory environment • Physical infrastructure • Unemployment rate • Default rate on loans from other institutions • Poverty rate • Number of MFIs and banks lending to the poor • Government support for MFIs • Competitors' return on investment • Number or dollar amount of credit subsidies to competitors
Financial and human resources	• Dollars donated • Dollars borrowed • Dollars available for employee training • Median or average years of schooling • Median or average salary • Number of hours of training needed for loan officers

Processes	Performance Measures
Leadership	• Average years of MFI experience, loan officers and senior executives • Client ratings and turnover rate of loan officers • Board and CEO evaluation • Clearly articulated vision
MFI strategy	• Loan size and credit ratings of clients (average and range) • Demographics of market served • Percentage of women clients • Percentage of budget allocated to fundraising and marketing • Number of group and individual loans • Number of other products offered to clients (saving accounts, insurance)

continued

TABLE 29.1. *continued*

Processes	Performance Measures
MFI structure	• Number of acquisitions of other MFIs • Percentage of decisions made by loan officers • Centralized or decentralized • For-profit or nonprofit • Number of branch offices • Number of owners and governance structure
MFI systems	• Dollars invested in training (client and employee) • Percentage of employees compensated on basis of performance • Number of clients per loan officer • Percentage of clients who attend training • Hours of training (client and employee) • Percentage of clients who reapply and are granted loans • Length of repayment period • Frequency of payments (weekly, biweekly, monthly) • Quality of IT system • Success of collection procedures

Intermediate Output	Performance Measures
Client business success	• Default rate • Percentage change in profits • Number of products offered • New management skills • Improved business practices • Quality of MFI service to clients

Outcomes	Performance Measures
Social individual	• Percentage of decisions made with client's input • Number of leadership roles in community organizations or church • Reduced impact of financial shocks • Percentage who report higher level of self-esteem
Social household	• Number of household utilities • Quality of housing • Percentage of children (boys, girls) who finish school • Percentage of clients who stay married • Number of meals per day • Weekly consumption of meat, fish, milk, and eggs • Number of children who have current immunizations
Social community	• Crime rate • Average years of schooling
Social society	• Percentage change in poverty level • Percentage change in contraction of disease • Life expectancy

TABLE 29.1. *continued*

Outcomes	Performance Measures
Economic individual	• Access to more financial services • Percentage increase in personal income • Reduced impact of financial shocks • Dollars invested in personal insurance policies
Economic household	• Percentage of individual income contributed to household • Dollars and percentage spent on food and education • Number of household utilities (running water, toilets, electricity)
Economic community	• Wage rate • Number of jobs created
Economic society	• Percentage change in GNP • Income distribution
MFI financial	• Percentage of loans repaid • Dollars donated and invested • Return on investment • Number of active clients • Number of repeat clients

key performance drivers. Like the drivers, they must be tested and revised. Clear understanding and measurement of the causal relationships that drive microfinance success are critical components of this model's effectiveness.

Proving and Improving the Benefits of Microfinance

For many observers, microfinance is considered successful if borrowers report a high level of customer satisfaction. But customer satisfaction alone is not sufficient. Donors are looking for evidence of positive social and economic impact on individuals, households, communities, and society. Those impacts include (1) giving the poor increased access to working capital and other financial services and (2) protecting the poor from life's financial shocks by stabilizing their income. After all, such shocks can be significant and quickly eliminate (at least in the short run) many of the benefits created by personal financial improvement. But microfinance can do still more. It can enable borrowers to cross the poverty line—and stay across it. As such, it may be able to facilitate significant improvement in social conditions in addition to economic improvement.

We have presented a model that looks at more than dollars loaned and customers satisfied. The model includes detailed identification of the inputs and processes necessary to achieve success, incorporating the strategy, structure, systems, and leadership choices microfinance organizations make that affect success. We also proposed to more comprehensively measure the broad set of benefits that can be created through microfinance, including financial impacts on the microfinance institution, and the social and economic impacts on individual borrowers and their households, the community, and the broader society. By better understanding both the drivers and the measures of success, substantial improvement can be made that yields increased benefits for microfinance institutions and their borrowers.

CHAPTER THIRTY

STRONG DOUBLE-BOTTOM-LINE BANKING

David J. Porteous

Businesses face growing pressure to combine profit maximization with concern for their social impact. The "double bottom line approach"[1] seeks to make firms more accountable for their impact on society by measuring business performance in terms of social impact as well as financial return—people as well as profit. Since the time of Adam Smith, profit seeking has been regarded as having a positive social impact, aligning (at least in theory) the two bottom lines. In practice, however, firms wrestle with trade-offs between internal and external stakeholder groups—for example, shareholders who want profits maximized, and employees who seek higher pay, or community groups who wish to see sustainable investment in local areas.

The case studies elsewhere in this volume, building on insights contained in C. K. Prahalad's book *The Fortune at the Bottom of the Pyramid*, highlight instances where this alignment of the two bottom lines has been achieved; large profit-maximizing firms such as Hindustan Lever or Kodak have had positive social impact on low-income people. Yet what if positive social return is achieved not as a by-product of profit-making activities but as a core purpose of business? Firms pursuing blended objectives, such that neither motivation is clearly dominant, are termed here as having a "strong" double bottom line (DBL). This is to distinguish them from "weak"

My thanks are owed to the heads of the three banks: Jesus P. Tambunting of Plantersbank, Mary Houghton and Ron Grzywinski of ShoreBank Corporation, and Peter Blom of Triodos Bank, who gave their time and free access to information required for this paper. ShoreBank also extended an honorarium toward the cost of the research for this paper.

double-bottom-line cases in which one objective—profit or people—is clearly dominant, even though positive outcomes for both may still be achieved.

Strong DBL firms are usually considered dynamically unstable. On the one hand,
they are thought to be stunted in their growth because they cannot access traditional
capital sources and are vulnerable to more single-minded competitors. On the other,
they may produce a diluted social impact. In the financial sector, development banks
represent a type of strong DBL entity. However, for a development bank to stabilize
its model and sustain its social impact, the state usually has to underwrite the risk in
some form. In the absence of state support, their services are restricted to taking savings and making payments, not lending. Postal savings banks exemplify this latter
group.[2] How then can privately owned banks ever pursue a strong double bottom line
and still achieve sustainable scale?

This paper focuses on the example of three privately owned banks that together
demonstrate how strong double-bottom-line banking is indeed possible. They are
Plantersbank in the Philippines, ShoreBank in the United States, and Triodos Bank in
the Netherlands. For all their differences in context, these banks were all explicitly
founded with the intention of making a positive social impact in underserved banking
niches in their respective markets and producing reasonable positive returns for shareholders. This chapter develops and applies a measurement framework to show that
these banks have in fact achieved positive social outcomes while surpassing their mainstream peers in financial performance over the long run. It also explores the possible
trade-offs involved—after all, surely someone must pay for a strong DBL.

Unlike the microfinance institutions that are the focus of earlier chapters in Part
Six, none of these banks presently serves the global poor directly as a core business,
although their indirect interests in microfinance in poor countries are already substantial and still growing. Instead, their focus has been on financing small and medium
enterprises (SMEs) in underserved markets. However, the paradigm of private development banking that they have demonstrated and pioneered is particularly relevant
to provision of financial services to the world's poor.

The next section of this paper creates the theoretical framework for defining and
measuring the strong DBL concept. I then introduce the three banks, assess their performance (both social and financial), and explore the question of who pays for social
impact. The conclusion returns to the question of the relevance of this approach to
the business of serving the global poor.

Strong Double-Bottom-Line Measurement

To know whether a business is in fact profit-maximizing, one has to consider both its *ex ante*
intentions (what it says it aims to do) as well as its *ex post* outcomes (did it in fact do this?).

Intention

Businesses are traditionally characterized as entities seeking first to maximize return to shareholders. Representing the mainstream view, Richard Dobbs says in a recent *McKinsey Quarterly* Special Edition, "The tumultuous recent past has reinforced two fundamental beliefs. The first is that the business of business is to maximize its shareholder value by increasing its intrinsic value."[3] Businesses may nonetheless achieve positive social outcomes as a by-product while they pursue profit. This does not change their prime intention, however.

Conversely, charities seek first to maximize their positive social impact. They may, however, be constrained to earn revenue sufficient to at least break even.

Between these two polar cases where one bottom line is clearly dominant in intention, there exists a continuum of weighted intentions. Around the middle of this continuum, we distinguish a "strong DBL zone," in which both intentions are heavily and deliberately weighted, leaving two "weak DBL zones" on either side in which one intent is either heavily subordinated to the other or else is to be achieved as a by-product of the other. To illustrate, a business that combines profit maximization with (1) a "do no harm" intention with regard to social impact and (2) that produces positive social impact as a by-product only would fall into the weak DBL zone.

The weak DBL zones are at least stable, whereas a number of forces create a slippery slope leading from the strong DBL zone. They include the force of competition, which should ensure that firms not burdened by the added cost or diluted focus of two bottom lines can take away business from those that are. In fear of this effect, funders are likely to limit access to private capital for firms not maximizing profit. Consequently, these firms will be stunted in growth and probably unsustainable over time. The ongoing debate over whether companies should donate a percentage (often 1 percent) of their profit to charity illustrates this point. If this policy is questionable, how much more questionable are blended intentions in which non-profit-making motives are weighted more than 1 percent?

On the other end of the continuum, nonprofit entities with a mission to achieve positive social impact have faced increasing pressures to generate revenue.[4] Foster and Bradach account for these pressures in a recent *Harvard Business Review* article tellingly entitled "Should Nonprofits Seek Profits?" From their observation of nonprofits that also seek to produce revenue, the authors conclude: "Executives of nonprofit organizations should not be encouraged to search for a holy grail of earned income in the marketplace. Sending social service agencies down that path jeopardizes those who benefit from their programs—and it harms society itself, which depends for its well being on a vibrant and mission-driven non-profit sector."[5] In other words, charities should stay in the weak DBL zone, where their social impact intention is clearly dominant.

Outcome

Apart from having distinct intentions, business and charity should be distinguishable *ex post* by their outcomes. A firm intending to maximize shareholder value proves its intention by delivering financial results that at least match its peer group over time. Peer performance is generally the only benchmark available for measuring whether profits are in fact maximized. If a firm consistently underperforms its peers, then it loses value. In time, it either will fail or become vulnerable to takeover by a more successful firm.

Financial performance is relatively easy to measure, once the yardsticks are decided. Recent research by McKinsey and Company has proposed that the two best measures of long-run financial performance are compound revenue growth and return on invested capital since they will ultimately drive shareholder value.[6]

Similarly, social outcomes, and even social impact, can be measured, although this is generally much harder to do. Assessing social outcomes requires that social outputs (for example, the number of loans granted) be evaluated in terms of the desired change produced. Social impact assessment goes a step further in that it requires specification and measurement of an alternative comparable state, in which there was no intervention, so that the impact of the specific intervention can be isolated and attributed. Clark, Rosenzweig, Long, and Olsen have produced a catalogue of the strengths and weaknesses of the various methodologies of social impact assessment in use. Most are relatively new and have been used on a relatively limited scale. They suffer from a further weakness: only three of the nine listed allow monetization, that is, statement of impact in a quantitative form comparable to financial return. The social impact bottom line is therefore often seen as vague and fuzzy by those used to regular, rigorous disclosure of performance against quantitative benchmarks.

Table 30.1 summarizes this framework of measurement across the three DBL zones delineated. The sections that follow apply this framework to measure the intention and outcomes of the three private development banks as strong double-bottom-line institutions.

The Three Banks

The three banks that are the subject of this paper are quite different in certain ways. One (Triodos) operates internationally through branches in four European countries, another (Plantersbank) operates nationwide in the Philippines through an extensive branch network, while the third (ShoreBank) has a banking presence in only four U.S. states.

TABLE 30.1. MEASURING INTENT AND OUTCOME IN THE DOUBLE-BOTTOM-LINE ZONES.

	Zone	Intention		Measurement of Outcomes		
		Financial	Social	Output	Outcome	Impact
Traditional business	Weak DBL	Profit-maximizing	Do no harm; or acceptable as long as it is a by-product of profit maximization	Profit	Long-term revenue growth and return on invested capital, relative to peers	Economic value added, i.e., profit adjusted for opportunity cost of capital
Private development banking	Strong DBL	Blends both intents such that one is not dominant		Should draw on both		
Traditional charity	Weak DBL	May make revenue on the side	Dominant intent, defined by nature of activity	Measurement of production, depending on activity, e.g., number of people served	Desired changes produced	Outcomes less than what would have happened anyway

It is their core similarities that make them the subject of this paper, however. Chief among them is a strong and enduring commitment, as privately owned entities, to achieving social impact while making profit. Table 30.2 shows further relevant similarities. All three have been in existence for three decades or more, and they are medium-sized banks by most definitions, with asset bases ranging from $600 million to more than $2 billion. As discussed later in this paper, they are all profitable and growing their revenues fast. Their main clients are small and medium enterprises (SMEs), although they all have significant interests in microenterprise finance.

Origins and Intentions

Each bank has evolved from its own starting point, reflecting differences in local context. In each, entrepreneurs played an important role in their birth and development, and they have defined clear blended intentions for their organizations.

TABLE 30.2. BACKGROUND INFORMATION.

Name	Plantersbank	ShoreBank Corporation	Triodos Bank Group
Date of formation	1961; present stockholders acquired ownership in 1972	1973	1980 bank formed; foundation started in 1971
Countries of operation	Banking: Philippines	Banking: USA; private equity investments in developing countries	Banking: Netherlands, UK, Belgium, Spain; funds invested in 40 developing countries
Ownership	40 percent foreign institutional investors; management-controlled	75 private shareholders (individuals, corporations, and foundations) in the bank holding company, which owns 100 percent of the underlying banks	8,349 holders of depository receipts in foundation, which owns the bank; 37 percent held by 14 institutions
Mission statement	"Plantersbank is the whole-heart-and-mind partner of small and medium enterprises and professionals. We help them succeed by providing funding, financial return, and management advice. In so doing, we are a key contributor to the development of the Philippine economy and of the communities we serve."	"ShoreBank invests in people and their communities to create economic equity and a healthy environment."	"To finance companies and organizations that contribute to a better environment or that generate social or cultural added value . . . [to] offer savers and investors a way to use their money to support these initiatives."
Market focus	SME lending; treasury; cash management; savings; housing loans	Lending: community development investment; enterprise: small landlords for rehab; faith-based lending	Small businesses that are socially and environmentally friendly
Size[a] (2004, gross assets)	$620 million (23rd largest in Philippines of 42 commercial banks and 91 thrifts)	Bank $1.48 billion; group $1.66 billion	Bank $1.28 billion; group $2.25 billion

Note: [a] Here, and elsewhere, exchange rates used for conversion are 1 U.S. dollar = 54 Philippine pesos and 0.8 Euro.

In the Philippines, Jesus Tambunting, founder and chairman of Plantersbank, was an early convert to the social impact of banking. With associates, he bought a neglected development bank and discovered that there was both opportunity and need in the underserved SME sector in that country. In his own words:

> Because of the bank's small size and the provincial location of its first offices, we had no choice but to cater to the small businessmen and entrepreneurs in the region. But what started as a necessity soon turned to meaningful and gratifying work. Dealing with the small entrepreneurs opened my eyes to the wonderful realization that we were making an impact where it counted most—with the marginalized sectors and the small entrepreneurs in the countryside. . . . Our plan changed from growing the bank and becoming like other commercial banks to focusing on SMEs and proving that they are viable propositions. . . . And we vowed that no matter how big our bank became, we would always stay committed to SMEs.[7]

Triodos Bank was started by a group of four Dutch professionals with backgrounds in banking and business consultancy who had been discussing for a while how to handle money in a socially conscious way. In 1980, they formed the bank so as to put the discussion into practice. Triodos has long been involved in supporting environmentally and socially friendly small businesses and projects.

Like the founders of Triodos, the four American bankers who founded ShoreBank were dissatisfied with how conventional banking was contributing to urban blight in Chicago's poor South Side neighborhoods in the early 1970s. Together with philanthropic funders, they bought South Shore National Bank, today called ShoreBank, in 1973 and quickly refocused its operations as a neighborhood bank. Today, two of the original four founders still run ShoreBank Corporation, the group holding company.

As private financial institutions, all three recognize the importance of profit but do not pursue it single-mindedly. For example, Triodos Bank states that "profit is not everything. It is however an essential test of a company's efficiency and ability to build reserves in the future and to achieve an acceptable return for investors. Profit is, of course, also an important source of investments for new activities and developments."[8] The other two banks would agree. All three therefore have an explicit developmental mandate to make positive social impact, not externally imposed but rather internally generated and sustained.

Measuring Performance

Over similar life spans (1970s to the present), each bank has independently evolved its own double-bottom-line philosophy. Each manages its performance in terms of this philosophy.

Social Outcomes. None of the banks today measures social impact explicitly, largely because of the difficulty of defining the counterfactual to separate out their specific contribution. They do, however, measure social outputs and, to some extent, outcomes against their own developmental objectives.

For Plantersbank, positive developmental outcome arises primarily through a conscious decision to restrict its market focus to small and medium enterprises; indeed, this focus is at the core of the bank's identity. The bank currently measures social output in this area in terms of the number of SME clients served—some eight thousand at the end of 2004. The annual report regularly carries stories of the individual entrepreneurs making up this number who have grown their businesses with Plantersbank funding. These constitute anecdotal positive outcomes. On a broader level of outcome, when Plantersbank was founded the SME lending niche was originally neglected by other Philippine banks that sought to serve larger corporate customers. Today, Plantersbank faces growing competition from other private banks at the higher end of the SME market. This development cannot be entirely attributed to Plantersbank's success, but the changed market for SME funding in the Philippines is generally viewed as a positive social outcome.

ShoreBank's philosophy of change is rooted in a fundamental belief about the role of banking. As Chairman Ron Grzywinski stated in 1991[9]: "Deliberate, disciplined development banking in a disinvested community can revive a local economy, rekindle the imagination of its people and restore market forces to their normal health and interdependency." ShoreBank has played this role demonstrably in the South Shore community of Chicago. At a time when other banks were disinvesting by redlining the area, thereby restricting access to mortgage loans, ShoreBank provided credit. In the process, it created a new local market niche: financing acquisition of multifamily rental buildings by small local landlords who rehabilitated and rented out the buildings to low-income tenants without any public subsidy. This product line is the most profitable in ShoreBank's loan portfolio today and has produced to date forty-seven thousand units of improved rental housing. The portfolio also includes loans to small businesses and to faith-based and nonprofit organizations, which stabilize the social fabric of a community.

ShoreBank monitors and reports regularly on its output of what it calls "community development lending": loans to designated priority communities, to minority-owned companies and faith-based and other nonprofit organizations. Its benchmark is delivery of new loans annually in excess of twice average capital, with recent performance in excess of three times. In 2004, ShoreBank reported that its cumulative community development lending exceeded $2 billion. The South Shore community has experienced substantial revitalization over the more than three decades since ShoreBank started its refocused activities.

As with Plantersbank, not all of this positive social outcome can be attributed to ShoreBank alone; other forces of change within the Chicago metropolitan area and housing sector in the country as a whole over the 1990s have made a big difference. However, ShoreBank's demonstration that community development lending in depressed neighborhoods is possible has had a materially positive outcome, both directly and indirectly, in the communities it serves.

Triodos Bank carries on banking business across a range of geographies, making it harder to measure the overall outcome in any particular local community. However, more like Plantersbank, Triodos restricts the type of business it will fund. As its Website declares: "Triodos Bank only finances enterprises which add social, environmental and cultural value—in fields such as renewable energy, social housing, complementary health care, fair trade, organic food and farming and social business. . . . We do this with the support of depositors and investors who wish to contribute to social justice within the context of a more sustainable economy." Of outstanding loans at the end of 2004, loans associated with culture and society made up 41 percent (US$286 million), nature and environment 34 percent (US$231 million), and social business 21 percent (US$134 million). In common with the other banks, the Triodos annual reports also highlight pictures of clients supported by loans as anecdotal confirmation of positive outcomes.

Beyond its SME lending in sectors that at the outset at least were underserved, Triodos sees its social impact in more general terms: it "is actively engaged in finding positive solutions to social problems where money in general and banks in particular can play a significant role."[10] To Triodos, sustainable banking means not only supporting sustainable development but also offering competitive products to its clients, innovating those products, and engaging in public debate about the benefits and challenges of socially responsible banking. Triodos has been innovative in creating and managing off-balance-sheet funds, including the first green energy fund in the Netherlands and some of the earlier funds investing in global microfinance.

The banks therefore assess the direct social outcome of their business based on the business filters they use. Because they restrict activities to types of business with generally accepted positive spillovers for their societies, they count all outputs as socially beneficial. Outcome reporting tends to be anecdotal, as exemplified by the pictures or stories in annual reports, and all three banks accept that they can do more in this respect. The impetus for development and use of more sophisticated outcome measurement frameworks is growing. ShoreBank Corporation, for example, has recently developed a "theory of change" framework in which the indicators of targeted positive social change are set for each business unit according to local business conditions. These indicators will be monitored over time so that outcome can be measured in the future. Within the ShoreBank group, a small community development financial institution called Shorebank Enterprise Pacific (SEP) in Ilwaco, Washington, has made the most progress to date in applying a holistic performance management framework, called 3E Metrics, which tracks social and environmental outcomes with hard data points.[11]

These moves at least bring social outcome to the same level as other "hard" or quantitative outcomes such as return on equity. As the supply of socially responsible investment grows,[12] so will the need for an independent evaluation of social impact.

Financial Outcomes. The two measures of long-run financial performance suggested by McKinsey and Company—return on equity and compound growth in revenue—are used in Table 30.3 to compare each bank against its defined peer group. Comparison among the three banks is not meaningful because their contexts are vastly different in return and growth profiles.

In the past five years, all three banks have consistently grown two to three times faster than their peers in terms of revenues. Two of the three have also grown assets faster, which for lending banks generates most revenue. The third, ShoreBank, has almost matched its national peers in asset growth and exceeded the growth of peer banks in its home state.

At the level of return on equity, both Plantersbank and ShoreBank have exceeded the recent five-year average of their peers.[13] This has been achieved consistently rather than through a few years of exceptional performance. Plantersbank's profitability has exceeded the volatile Philippine bank average in all but two of the past ten years, and in those two years it equaled them. ShoreBank has shown a steadily increasing level of profitability since establishment, exceeding its U.S. peer group in each of the past three financial years and having come very close in the preceding three years.

In the case of Triodos, average return on equity is under half that of its peer group but is at the target level of 4 percent used as guidance by the board over this period. Triodos openly states that it prioritizes "above all, stable returns," rather than the level of return per se. Using the standard deviation of return on equity 1999–2003 as a measure of earnings stability, Triodos has outperformed three of its peer competitors, but not the giant Rabobank.

Who Pays for Social Impact?

All three banks have achieved positive social outcomes, while in general outperforming their peers according to most long-run financial measures. Some might question at whose cost this impact has been achieved; in other words, who subsidized the financial return?

TABLE 30.3. DIVIDING THE COSTS AND BENEFITS.

Stakeholder Group	Plantersbank	ShoreBank	Triodos
Shareholders:			
• Average ROE 1999–2004[a]	8.4% (5.0%)	15.1% (14.2%)	4.0% (9.2%)
• Total real return to shareholders from establishment, per annum and cumulative	7.5% (1,087%)	1.32% (group) (51%)	1.04% (29.6%)
• Annual growth in revenue[b] 1999–2003	15.2% (5.7%)	12.3% (12.8%)	20.2% (10%)
Employees:			
Compensation	Competitive but not top of market	Salaries benchmarked at 75th percentile for senior managers and at 50th for all other employees	Benchmarked to market at lower and middle levels; deliberately lower than market for top levels
Borrowers:			
Interest rates on lending	Higher than market by 100-200 points; SME niche	Higher than general market in rehab niche and at market for all other products	Market-competitive
Depositors:			
Interest rates on deposits	Market-competitive	Market-competitive	Market-competitive
Peer group	Philippine commercial banking sector	U.S. bank peer group by asset size ($1–10 billion), regionally and nationally	Three Dutch cooperative banks: Rabobank, SNS Bank, Friesland Bank[c]

Notes: [a] Peer groups in parentheses.

[b] Revenue for a bank is defined as adjusted operating income, that is, total revenue (interest and fee income) less interest paid.

[c] The Dutch co-op banks differ from Triodos in geographic market focus, age, size, and especially mission but represent the closest peer group against which Triodos can be compared.

Already, it is clear that shareholders are hardly paying a price for the positive social outcomes observed, at least in the past five years. On the contrary, they appear to be enjoying premium returns in two of the three banks. In the third, shareholders are comfortable in that their target level of return has been achieved.

Other stakeholders may be picking up the burden, however:

- Employees, who may be paid less than in equivalent jobs elsewhere
- Borrowers, who may pay higher rates than they would elsewhere
- Depositors, through accepting lower interest rates on deposits

Table 30.3 reflects the policies and outcomes of these banks, which determine the distribution of the "cost" of social impact.

The table shows that in all cases depositors do not receive lower rates for the social benefit their deposits may bring when lent out. The banks vie for retail funding in competitive markets where there is little evidence that depositors accept a "discount" on interest rates received in return for social impact.

Furthermore, in general employees do not pay either, because most salaries are marked to market. However, Triodos intentionally pays lower-than-market salaries at the senior management level. This follows from the belief that the extrinsic rewards of the job are highest at this level, and that paying lower salaries to executives is both an important signal to the rest of the organization as well as a good screen for the real motivation of top managers.

Borrowing clients appear to pay in part through slightly higher interest rates on their loans, but this is probably more apparent than real. For one thing, market comparison rates are generic, whereas each institution tends to have specialized niches (such as housing rehabilitation for ShoreBank or smaller SME clients for Plantersbank) in which the comparable rates may well be higher than the average. Certainly, in each case there are competitors who could lure borrowers away if interest rates were uncompetitive. The growing balance sheets of all three entities suggest that borrowers are not defecting; these institutions are attracting new loan clients faster than their peers are.

In summary, therefore, although initial shareholders have had to be patient in most cases for their returns, the experience of these banks indicates that there may not be a trade-off between financial and social performance in the long run.

Role as Market Development Agents

Is the highly positive experience of these three banks generalizable, or is it merely coincidence? The sheer diversity of the banks' contexts and the length of their track records rule out luck alone as a sufficient explanation. Closer analysis indicates that some quite conventional forces have been at work, helping to generate the observed performance: all three banks have specialized in market niches which they pioneered, even if today they are not market leaders by size. Specialization has enabled them to reap the economies of scale observed in financial intermediation.[14] However, getting to sufficient scale has required deliberate and careful management of growth, especially in a banking environment where banks are required by law to maintain capital proportional to assets. This formula for success—managing growth while specializing—is not unique to strong DBL businesses.

What is unique is the choice of market sector; each bank chose deliberately to focus on underserved sectors of the local banking market. In these sectors, the banks have been deliberate market catalysts, demonstrating success in a way that has attracted the attention of competitors. Broad-based market development that extends access to financial services, while over time reducing their relative price, is indeed a socially desirable outcome. Nongovernmental organizations and charities sometimes serve as market pioneers, but these banks have from the outset been businesses, and as businesses they have been able to translate their blended intentions into returns on both bottom lines that exceed their peer groups.

Conclusion

The experience of these banks demonstrates that strong double-bottom-line banking is indeed possible. More so, their experience suggests that in certain circumstances there may be little or no trade-off in long-run outcomes between the bottom lines. Businesses that blend social mission with profit seeking in a strong DBL manner can achieve outcomes matching or exceeding single-minded peers.

Consequently, the standard dichotomy between businesses that intend to maximize profit and those that do not is not adequate or even helpful in understanding or predicting the outcomes. This is not to argue, however, that it is easy to survive the tensions in the strong DBL zone.

On the contrary, building the resilience to manage the tensions is at the heart of private development banking. The regulatory framework for banking, which requires that banks remain solvent, is in many ways an ally in this respect; it maintains one side of the tension by mandating that banks must be profitable over time. To survive, private development banks must remain flexible and entrepreneurial. Unlike their publicly owned counterparts, which may crowd out the private sector with their entrenched advantages (such as government backing), private development banks must innovate continuously to stay ahead of the competition that inevitably follows their success. This self-sustaining push to innovate for impact, disciplined by market forces and regulation, is a core aspect of the emerging paradigm of private development banking.

Private development banking is a highly relevant approach for reaching the billions of people who today lack adequate access to financial services. The global poor by and large do not live in ready-made formal financial service markets. Consequently, they are less amenable to banking approaches predicated on quick return from "impatient" capital. Indeed, a get-rich-quick approach by certain consumer lenders has already generated a political and social backlash in developing countries such as Bolivia and South Africa.[15] In many cases, creating sustainable retail financial markets requires active participation of banks with a developmental focus and a long-term horizon.

ShoreBank Corporation and Triodos Group already manage private equity funds with extensive and growing portfolios of investments in microfinance institutions throughout the world, serving close to three million lower-income people. Some of these investments will help form the next generation of private development banks with even wider reach.

These microfinance interests alone will ensure that these three banks have a place in serving the global poor in the twenty-first century. However, their more enduring contribution may well be that together they pioneered and demonstrated the paradigm of private development banking to often skeptical investors and regulators.

CHAPTER THIRTY-ONE

H&R BLOCK'S REFUND ANTICIPATION LOANS

Perilous Profits at the Bottom of the Pyramid?

David T. Rose, Daniel Schneider, Peter Tufano

At a recent meeting, a big-city mayor angrily confronted an H&R Block executive: "Why do you charge poor people $130 to do tax returns? At our volunteer sites, we do them for free!" At a Chicago meeting, the leader of a large volunteer tax site refused to shake hands with a Block executive. In a meeting in Washington, a senior banking regulator railed about Block "ripping off consumers."

Again and again, this story plays out. H&R Block, the nation's largest tax preparation firm, serves more than nineteen million filers each year, of which 57 percent have an annual household income below $30,000. It delivers roughly 22 percent of the federal earned income credit payments. Many financial service providers have "fired" poorer consumers, but Block embraces its low-income clientele, helping them secure tax refunds of $35 billion annually. Block customers are reasonably satisfied, with Block's satisfaction scores in the high 80s (out of 100) and 70 percent customer retention. Yet Block is open to substantial criticism for a product that consumers demand but activists and some lawmakers abhor: the refund anticipation loan (RAL,

This paper draws from a substantially longer piece entitled "H&R Block's Refund Anticipation Loan: A Paradox of Profits?" We would like to thank H&R Block for supplying data for this project, and Joe Badaracco, Joshua Margolis, Felix Oberholzer-Gee, Lynn Paine, Sandra Sucher, and participants at the IIBS Conference on Global Poverty for their thoughtful comments. Financial support for this research project was provided by the division of research of the Harvard Business School.

David Rose is assistant vice president of competitive strategy at H&R Block. This paper is not endorsed by H&R Block and does not reflect the views of the organization.

pronounced to rhyme with "pal"). This product gives consumers nearly immediate access to funds, albeit in a costly manner.

Consumer demand for RALs is strong, with more than four million of Block's sixteen million retail office customers choosing the product. RALs are profitable for Block as well, contributing better than $100 million to earnings annually. Yet a product that its users and Block shareholders both seem to like creates so much trouble that Block executives debate whether or not they should continue to offer it. At the heart, offering RALs opens them up to difficult questions: How can you justify charging poor people so much for this product and earning such profits by selling to the poor? Many would urge business to serve poor customers, holding out the promise of the "fortune at the bottom of the pyramid," to use C. K. Prahalad's description. However, Block's experience reminds us that our commercial treasure seeker must also answer—in public— some hard questions: Is your price "fair"? Are your profits "too high"? Asked by consumer advocates, regulators, and the media—but not necessarily by consumers— these questions form what we call "the paradox of profits." Put simply, a business cannot serve the poor unless it is profitable. Yet firms that profit by selling to the poor are subject to criticism that can result in costs that make firms reconsider whether serving the poor is a good use of their resources, time, and reputation.

The questions that Block executives faced ("Are your prices and profits too high?" and "Are you selling the wrong products?") have a long history. Although economists see prices and profits as merely determined by supply-and-demand curves, the question of "fairness" is one that businesses have faced throughout history with few definite answers. The question has appeared regularly in a governmental context, around issues such as wartime profiteering and price gouging. In addition, Abrahamic religious traditions historically mandated against usury, and the Islamic prohibition on *riba* continues to shape business policy. Professionals such as doctors and lawyers, as well as investment managers, must demonstrate fiduciary duties of care and loyalty toward their clients. Norms about an appropriate level of profit have recently been discussed in the context of consumer protection as advocates and scholars study whether the poor pay higher prices than do well-off consumers. These inquires raise a fundamental ethical question: Should private firms be permitted to derive substantial profits from poor and vulnerable consumers with insubstantial resources? This question has remained unsettled for centuries.

H&R Block and Its Refund Anticipation Loans

In this section of the paper, we show how this ethical debate has played out for H&R Block. We then draw on the case to discuss how firms can address the paradox of profits head-on, using the example of Block's recent strategic initiatives to engage its potential critics.

Background on H&R Block

Founded in 1955 by Henry and Richard Bloch, by 2005 H&R Block was a $4.2 billion (in revenue) financial services company. The $2 billion tax preparation unit accounts for most of revenues, with the rest coming from its accounting services, subprime mortgage, and personal financial advisory divisions. The firm's explicit strategy is to be "America's financial partner"—especially a partner of the less affluent.

Block's primary strategy is to leverage existing relationships with tax clients to inexpensively acquire clients in its other business units. Block's distribution system consists of some twelve thousand offices and a field force of about a hundred thousand seasonal employees. Block prepares tax returns for sixteen million filers through its retail offices each year, or approximately 16 percent of U.S. households. Block's tax preparation clients tend to be low-income. More than 57 percent of its retail customers are in households with adjusted gross income under $30,000 (representing 33 percent of all U.S. households with incomes below that figure), and approximately 40 percent of clients are unbanked. The company's existing distribution capabilities—tax professionals, locations, and ready information access—enable it to offer other financial and advisory services that might appeal to the many low-income customers who are undeserved by "mainstream" financial services providers. For example, Block clients can deposit their refunds directly onto a debit card and avoid costly check-cashing fees. Block offers IRAs and savings accounts as well, which can be opened with a client's tax refund. Although these products are generally more palatable to consumer advocates, demand and profits are much less compared to RALs.

Refund Anticipation Loans: Product Structure

The millions of H&R Block clients who purchase RALs each take out a very short-term loan, averaging $2,800, secured by the refund. The loan allows the client to speed up the receipt of funds to one to two days.[1]

From a client's perspective, the RAL transaction begins when the H&R Block tax professional presents various options for receiving funds. (If the client is a repeat customer, she will often ask for the RAL directly.) At this point, a client is advised of both delivery times and costs for a RAL versus a refund.[2] Prepared scripts encourage the client to first consider less costly methods, such as receiving her refund via direct deposit if a bank account exists. If the client chooses a RAL, she and the tax professional review the annual percentage rate (APR) and other fees. Finally, an application is submitted to the lending bank (HSBC) and the return is submitted to the IRS. The IRS then supplies a Debt Indicator (a measure identifying offsets such as for taxes, child support, or other debt), which is used by the lender to minimize losses. If the transaction is approved, the client returns within two days to pick up a check.

Operationally, fulfillment of the RAL is complex. Under the client's instruction, the refund travels from the Treasury to HSBC, which uses the proceeds to settle the client's loan. Because the IRS requires that all refunds received by direct deposit be routed to a bank account owned by the filer, HSBC complies by opening up a temporary bank account in the name of the RAL purchaser. The IRS direct-deposits the refund to this account in eight to fifteen days, which is "swept" to debit the loan amount and fees. The account is then closed.

An average Block RAL client pays about $90 for the loan. Block's partner, HSBC, discloses that it charges $27.95 to open the temporary bank account and then adds a financing charge of between $7 and $77 (for a RAL of between $200 and $5,000). Total fees were somewhat less for Block RAL clients, ranging from $29.95 to $109.95 (for a RAL of between $200 and $9,999).[3] Given an average loan of $2,800 and an average loan period of 11 days, these fees represent an APR of approximately 110 percent.[4]

The RAL Market

Block CEO Mark Ernst observed that "refund anticipation loans are a product that . . . consumers love."[5] This preference is manifested in strong demand. In 2000, Block sold nearly 4.5 million RALs (representing well over 50 percent of the market) and sold nearly 4.3 million RALs in 2004. More than a quarter of its sixteen million annual retail clients sought RALs, a level that was essentially unchanged between 2002 and 2004 (ranging from 26.3 percent to 27.3 percent).[6] The share of Block clients purchasing a RAL is lower than that of its main retail competitor, Jackson Hewitt Tax Service, which reports that 40 percent of its clients purchased a RAL.[7]

The typical consumer who purchases a RAL from Block has a household income below $30,000. Most use some form of "alternative financial services" such as check cashing, payday loans, or money transfers. In many respects, RAL purchasers are like the majority of Block's low-to-moderate-income (LMI) clients, and data from a recent survey of RAL users (not limited to Block) confirm this view.[8] Overall, 18 percent of respondents had purchased a RAL. Purchasers tended to be:

- Less well educated: 30 percent of respondents without a high school degree and 23 percent of those with only a high school diploma had purchased a RAL; just 12 percent of those who graduated from college had done so.
- Less well off: 25 percent of those with household income of under $50,000 reported purchasing a RAL.
- Ethnic minorities: 28 percent of African Americans and 21 percent of Latinos had purchased a RAL versus just 17 percent of whites.

A second survey[9] finds a lower rate of RAL purchase, but purchasers still disproportionately low-income and less educated. This demographic profile reflects the RAL's consumer-value proposition. RALs enable cash-strapped consumers to receive money quickly to pay existing debts, have tax preparation fees deducted from the loan (no out-of-pocket expenses), and have money on hand if needed. Figure 31.1 shows the data on why Block clients opted to purchase RALs.

RAL Economics

A product that meets with ample demand in the marketplace, RALs represent a significant source of revenue and profits for Block.

RAL Revenue. RALs are an important source of revenue for Block. In 2004, they generated $175 million in revenue, approximately 8.4 percent of total revenues from U.S. tax operations. Over the last six years, RAL revenues have increased fairly steadily, from $90.1 million in 1999 to $133.8 million in 2001 to $139.1 million in 2003.[10] As a share of total revenue from all U.S. tax sources, RAL revenues ranged between 6.43 percent and 8.74 percent. See Figure 31.2.

Although Block is the visible merchant of RALs, operationally it retails a loan product developed by HSBC, which holds patents on the RAL process. Block renegotiated its ten-year contract with HSBC to move from receiving a flat fee per loan to participating in the upside of the loans in exchange for taking on a share of risk.

FIGURE 31.1. REASONS FOR GETTING A RAL FROM H&R BLOCK.

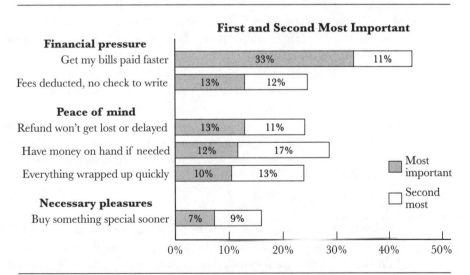

Source: H&R Block survey of seventeen hundred refund clients conducted in July 2003.

FIGURE 31.2. RAL REVENUES AS A PERCENTAGE OF TOTAL U.S. TAX REVENUE 1999–2004.

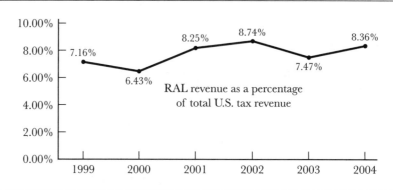

Source: H&R Block 10-K, 1999–2004.

When Block first introduced RALs, it was hoped that the product would deliver both revenues and a means to differentiate the firm. Over time, the latter benefit has eroded as other tax preparation firms offered RALs. This trend is due mainly to the increased number of electronic return originators or EROs (tax preparers who can file returns electronically). The number of EROs has been growing at more than 15 percent annually to one hundred thousand in 2003. An ERO cannot offer RALs without a bank partner, but banks such as HSBC, Santa Barbara Bank & Trust, Bank One/JP Morgan Chase, River City, and Republic have all developed proprietary RAL products. In 2004, HSBC offered RALs through eighty-one hundred non-Block offices[11] in addition to Block offices.

Though RALs may not differentiate Block, they do offer a valuable (but unanticipated) side benefit. Block clients who purchase multiple services are slightly more likely to return to Block for tax preparation the following year. Retention differentials are economically significant given the high cost of recruiting new clients. Block estimates that it spends $115 million annually on marketing to replace the five million clients it loses each year, a cost that is steadily rising as Block increases the share of the U.S. population that has been to Block at one time (50 percent) and is unlikely to return (6 percent–7.5 percent).[12]

RAL Costs. The primary costs of offering RALs are operational expenditures and losses from delinquency. Block and HSBC maintain systems that link individual offices to the IRS. Block must train its staff, slow down its tax prep process to explain and consummate the RAL purchase, and operate a customer service infrastructure to support RALs. The company must maintain the technology used to print the RAL checks, and

HSBC must open, sweep, and close the accounts. The lender also incurs the cost of borrowing the funds for the loans.

The largest single cost is that of bad debts. Even though a check from the U.S. government has no credit risk, the size of a refund check can be smaller than originally estimated on a filer's tax form. These differences can be due to errors, or to various hold-backs on the refund on account of legal claims such as unpaid child support, back taxes, and student loan debt. HSBC takes steps to try to minimize these losses through examination of a filer's Debt Indicator, furnished by the IRS and offering an assessment of any offsets that the government may make against the filer's refund. Though use of the Debt Indicator cuts losses, it is an imprecise measure. Nevertheless, Block and its partner report a relatively low loss rate (under 100–150 basis points) compared to other short-term credit products. For instance, a recent study of two large monoline payday lenders found an annual loss rate of 15.1 percent (as a ratio of losses to total revenue).[13]

RAL Profitability. RAL fees represented less than 4 percent of Block's $4.2 billion in 2004 sales, but it is estimated that they accounted for 7–10 percent of Block's pretax net income. RALs also made a disproportionate contribution to Block's growth rate. The companywide compound annual growth rate of Block's operating income from 1998 to 2002 was 19 percent, with RALs accounting for more than three percentage points of the growth.[14]

Analysts estimated that Block had pretax income margins of roughly 26–30 percent companywide, 28–31 percent on its core tax preparation business, and 46–58 percent on its mortgage business, and that it sustained losses in the investment and business services divisions. RAL margins are generally between those of Block's tax business and the mortgage business. Although some analysts estimate RAL margins near 50 percent (extrapolating from Block's agreement with HSBC), after considering the full costs of technology, training, and other infrastructure, the profit margin is probably lower, yet still attractive.

RALs are a profitable part of the Block business, and a product demanded by consumers. It would seem that this is a proverbial win-win, but this naïve supposition is far from correct.

RAL Criticism

Whereas the company interprets the high level of demand and consumers' willingness to accept RAL pricing as indicative of the high value they place on RALs, consumer advocates have interpreted this demand quite differently. The "high" price of RALs, combined with suspicions about "high" profit margins, has led to substantial criticism of Block. This criticism has taken two forms: complaints (and calls for boycotts) from consumer advocates, and costly litigation.

Groups such as the Consumer Federation of America (CFA) and the National Consumer Law Center (NCLC) contend that few RAL purchasers realize they are entering into a loan and allege that there are not adequate disclosures made at the point of sale. These groups point to survey data suggesting that many RAL purchasers did not realize they were in fact entering into a short-term loan agreement.[15]

Grassroots efforts, led by groups such as the Association of Community Organizations for Reform Now (ACORN), target Block and RALs. In 2004, ACORN organized a campaign against Block offices in sixteen states. The protests in front of Block offices were covered by twenty-nine newspapers, thirty-four TV broadcasts, and two radio broadcasts. Although other national tax preparation firms sell RALs, Block felt it was singled out for its size and name recognition. Smaller campaigns have been launched against Block's competitors as well. In 2003, ACORN held protests outside thirty Jackson Hewitt offices across the United States, and in 2005 protesters converged at the headquarters of Liberty Tax.[16] However, these activities have generated far less media coverage.

RALs have led to twelve lawsuits (mostly class action) against Block alleging that the company made inadequate disclosures to clients and engaged in deceptive advertising and sales practices (generally based on conduct prior to 1996). More fundamental objections are raised about the rates charged on these short-term loans. Annualized APRs can reach as high as 156 percent, a rate that some consumer advocates deem usurious. RALs are sold by nationally chartered banks, a designation that allows these institutions to avoid state lending rate caps though not criticism about equity and fairness.

Block successfully defended against most claims but paid out a substantial settlement in a Texas case, *Haese* v. *H&R Block*, which resulted in a pretax expense of $43.51 million. The uncertainty regarding RAL-related litigation has depressed Block's market value, with most analysts citing the risk of litigation as a key concern.[17] For example, when the Texas litigation was announced in November 2002, Block's stock declined 30 percent in a six-day period, accounting for more than $2 billion in lost market value. The stock regained some of that value, but even after the positive rebound the stock suffered nearly a $1.5 billion market-adjusted loss. Similarly, stock price drops on November 7 and 8 came on the heels of an announcement by the judge in the case of a ruling unfavorable to Block.[18] Although the stock rebounded as the legal uncertainty subsided, litigation risks remain a black cloud over the stock (see Figure 31.3).

In addition, policy makers have introduced legislation to curtail, if not ban, RAL sales. Laws in nine states and several cities impose additional disclosure requirements on RALs. Federal legislation introduced in the House and Senate would ban RALs that are made on the basis of expected earned income tax credit (EITC) refunds.[19] Although Block has made considerable investments in improving disclosures and enforcing compliance to best practices across its network, much uncertainty remains with respect to the role of RALs in the company's strategy.

FIGURE 31.3. H&R BLOCK DAILY STOCK RETURNS, NET OF S&P 500, 10/31/02 TO 11/29/02.

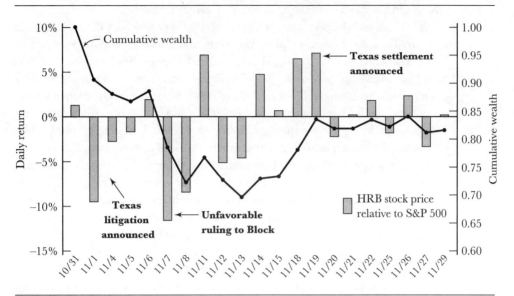

Note: The bars and left scale show the net daily return, which is calculated as daily return on HRB stock less return on the S&P 500. The line and right scale show the cumulative excess wealth over this period, which is the product of 1 plus the net daily returns from the day before the litigation was announced through the day shown on the horizontal scale.

Source: www.finance.yahoo.com.

Addressing the Paradox

Block's experience with RALs reflects the essence of a more general conundrum. A firm sells a product that meets customer needs and enjoys a high level of customer satisfaction and profit. Its success encourages entry by competing firms. Yet the firm faces criticism and legal pressure for offering the product to low-income users and "profiting from the poor." The fortune at the bottom of the pyramid is like the treasure sought in an adventure film—fraught with traps and dangers.

In Block's case, criticism of RALs revolves around a trio of issues: appropriateness, disclosure, and pricing. However, we suspect that most of the critics would be silenced if RALs were offered at no charge. Put simply, critics believe that Block and its partners charge the poor too much for RALs and earn profits that are simply too high. In a companion piece, we briefly chronicle the long history of the debate over "too much" and "too high." In fundamental terms, this debate has been active for centuries.

Economists, moral philosophers, religious thinkers, political scientists, consumer advocates, politicians, legal scholars, judges, and others have offered contradictory advice. On questions of fairness, there are no simple answers.

This is of little help to Block. Organized consumer advocacy directed at RALs surely results in legal expenses, marketing costs, and diversion of management time. More important, however, is possible reputational damage. Block enjoys 98 percent brand awareness but, perversely, faces high costs in acquiring new customers. Also, given its name recognition, Block may suffer from adverse media attention that sours not only current RAL purchasers but other existing and prospective customers as well. This potential loss is not just theoretical; empirical research has suggested a positive relationship between a firm's reputation and its financial performance.[20]

Block is subject to what some have called "brand-jacking."[21] Consumer advocates, as well as members of the media, have limited resources and must budget them carefully. Targets of greater and more forceful advocacy and media attention may be firms that (1) are more visible, (2) earn greater profits (or at least appear to by dint of high prices), or (3) are larger. To maximize impact, large well-known firms or brands are targeted. In this instance, Block feels singled out for legal and media attention, while believing that other RAL providers "fly under the radar screen."

In our companion piece, we discuss the implications of this hypothesis for industrial organization. In brief, we hypothesize that these phenomena can lead to circumstances where certain types of firms serving the poor may enjoy a comparative advantage. These firms are ones that are less visible, appear less profitable, and are smaller. Costs and prices will rise as larger and more profitable firms exit, leaving smaller and less efficient firms to serve the market. As an unintended consequence, rather than leading to lower costs and greater transparency, media criticism and advocacy could lead to higher costs and prices.

We are not seeking pity for profitable firms. Criticism about profits is a legitimate and expected cost of doing business in a capitalist system with free speech. In this chapter, we focus instead on various strategies that firms, their critics, and other responsible members of a civil society can use to leverage this debate for the good of all.

- *Publicly identify opportunities for business to serve poorer customers—and how this benefits these consumers.* C. K. Prahalad's book *The Fortune at the Bottom of the Pyramid* challenges businesses to discover profit opportunities that exist among poorer customers. Prahalad suggests that public discussion could lower the cost of entry by providing free "market research" to potential entrants; his book serves this function. Academics, nonprofits, and government agencies could serve a similar function. For example, the D2D Fund identifies opportunities to serve the poor in the financial services sector, conducts R&D in the form of pilots, and makes this information broadly available to potential entrants and policy makers. In a similar way, Block has begun to focus attention on the opportunities to serve the poor by highlighting the costs that its customers face in transforming their tax refund into cash (by way of check cashers) and the opportunities for refund-time savings.

• *Focus positive attention on products and services that aid poorer customers.* The media and consumer advocates generally target firms for criticism, not praise. This provides little positive feedback for those that do serve the poor in a manner that is beneficial for both customer and firm. Again, *The Fortune at the Bottom of the Pyramid*—and this volume—achieve the latter goal by highlighting Proctor & Gamble, Unilever, CEMEX, and ICICI, whose business with the poor is a proverbial win-win. Best-practice role models should be profiled in business schools, trade associations, and policy discussions and in the media. In so doing, advocates can lower the marketing costs of responsible firms and perhaps lower the prices consumers face. Block has adopted a strategy of informing others how it serves low-income consumers. These initiatives include disclosure of its activities, through cooperating with academics and policy makers; attending meetings of policy makers, academics, and community activists; and joining boards of industry groups aimed at addressing the problems of the poor. For example, Chairman and CEO Ernst joined the advisory board of the Aspen Institute's Initiative on Financial Security.

• *Enter into the debate about profitability and consumer protection.* It is important that the question "How much profit is too much?" be debated outside of courtrooms and media headlines. Like most difficult issues, reasonable people may disagree—but this makes it even more critical to have reasoned debate. In the RAL context, consumer advocates question the value consumers derive from receiving their refund "a few days" earlier than otherwise. Useful debate might include discussion of what the competing sources of unsecured borrowing are, how the prices of those products compare to RALs, and the cost structure of delivering RALs. How does one incorporate the risks borne by firms—including litigation risk, or capital investments made by them—in our definition of fair profit? Should the concept of fair profits be determined *ex ante* rather than by simply arguing *ex post* that the most successful businesses enjoy excess profits? A more fundamental question is, Who has the right to say whether prices or profits are too high? As part of this debate, we need to establish a sense of context. The prevailing term for promoters of hedge funds is "2 and 20." They receive 2 percent of the money under management each year plus an additional 20 percent of the capital appreciation earned by the fund.[22] For a large hedge fund, we suspect that these revenue levels would correspond to gross margins well above 100 percent. In the mutual fund industry, courts have held that pretax margins of up to 70 percent are not inconsistent with the fiduciary duty that boards owe to fund shareholders.[23] The RAL business generates pretax profits far below either of them, and the tax preparation business even lower. Yet there is a sense of outrage around profits for tax preparation and RALs that does not extend to purveyors of mutual or hedge funds. What determines a fair level of profitability, beyond what consumers and competition will support? Whose sense of fairness matters? Though it would be naïve to think we can resolve these issues, we need to create forums where they can be debated rationally.

• *Use partnerships with nonprofits and governments.* Partnering with nonprofits and governments can have three salutary effects. First, by leveraging "soft" marketing by their partners or their intimate knowledge of the LMI customer, it may be less costly to deliver products. Second, within these partnerships the debate over pricing and profits can be informed and carried out by means of case studies. For-profit businesses can better understand the perspective of their customers; advocates can better understand that for-profit partners cannot meet budget shortfalls by soliciting donations, and their partnerships become the venue for the debate. Third, when successful, these partnerships become a powerful example of the capacity of business (and collaborative partnerships) to serve the poor, and thus encourage broader activity. Block has realized the power of these partnerships and in 2004 implemented six new programs with various partners:

1. Partnering with Operation Hope in Los Angeles to help improve financial literacy in low-income inner-city neighborhoods as well as increase access to financial services
2. Partnering with the Texas Children's Health Insurance Program (CHIP) to increase access to benefits in the rural areas of the state
3. Partnering with a nonprofit organization in Tulsa, Oklahoma, offering free tax preparation services for low-income residents of the city
4. Working with the city of San Francisco (including donation of funds) to increase awareness and uptake of the earned income tax credit (EITC)
5. Partnering with the Miami mayor's office to increase EITC awareness in the city
6. Conducting a pilot in St. Louis, Missouri (working with scholars at Harvard, UC Berkeley, MIT, and the Brookings Institution) to test alternative policies for increasing saving in low-income households

These programs have generated positive business results as well as better understanding of Block's strategy in several high-profile publications such as the *San Francisco Chronicle*, the *Wall Street Journal*, and the *New York Times*.[24] From the firm's perspective, they highlight the fact that it is actually serving the needs of their low-income clients. This serves to advance the firm's interests in city, state, and federal governments.

• *Research the implications of the consumer debate on public welfare.* In our companion piece, we raise—but do not answer—questions about the role of consumer advocacy. When does consumer advocacy lead to entry, lower prices, and enhanced welfare? When does it backfire and lead to exit, higher prices, and reduced welfare? What is the incremental cost of serving certain classes of customers? How do we reconcile the demands of consumers and those of consumer advocates (which may not be the same)? There are strong opinions, but precious little data, to answer some of these hard questions. For example, in assembling data on various contentious financial products, we found a large amount of advocacy literature—from consumer advocates as well as business defenders—but less neutral research without an obvious point of view. Academia can serve an important purpose in working to promote objective data that can inform this set of discussions. Businesses and advocacy groups can help by jointly cooperating with third-party researchers.

Block has recently seen how independent research can inform public policy and business practice. In early 2005, Block's St. Louis pilot program yielded new insights for policy makers about the impact of matching programs on stimulating savings among the poor. It also gave Block insights about how to motivate its salesforce. In 2006, Block is conducting additional experiments that hopefully will produce still more insight into the intersection of public policy with other aspects of its business.

Block is a firm embroiled in a long-standing debate: What level of profit is fair? The paradox of profits—if it exists—is that profits are necessary to encourage private firms to serve the poor, but profits themselves can create additional costs for these firms in the form of damaged reputation, public attacks, and associated litigation. Without attacking or defending Block, we seek to use its example to bring the question of fairness of profits into the open. A debate in a well-lit room, informed by substantial evidence, seems far preferable to optimistically hoping that those who serve the poor will be lauded, or cynically assuming that reputable people can never profit from serving the poor.

CHAPTER THIRTY-TWO

WHEN IS DOING BUSINESS WITH THE POOR GOOD—FOR THE POOR?

A Household and National Income Accounting Approach

Herman B. Leonard

Much has been made in recent years of the potentially large benefits to businesses of selling goods to people at the "bottom of the pyramid." By inventing new products or reconfiguring existing products in ways that make them both valuable and accessible to the poor, it is alleged, substantial profits can be made—and many examples have now been offered, in this volume and elsewhere.

Throughout much of the discussion and literature on this BOP approach, there is a working presumption that this phenomenon is of benefit to the consumers thereby served. An array of benefits are described: the products are themselves assumed to be valuable; poor people are brought into a market economy that will confer other advantages upon them; and they may be exposed to other products, opportunities, and exchange vehicles (for example, the banking system, credit devices, and so on) that will expand the range of possibilities available to them. Indeed, some have described actions by firms seeking to target low-income consumers as part of the firms' corporate social responsibility agenda, presumably implying that social benefits are being generated.

To the extent that new profits are being made through sales to BOP consumers, then by definition goods are being sold to the poor in excess of the cost of producing them. Private net financial benefits are being realized—most of them, most of the time, *outside* the low-income communities purchasing the goods. These activities may (and indeed are often alleged to) have substantial profit margins. By voluntarily purchasing these products, the low-income community is signaling that it is on balance better off with them. However, it would obviously be better off still if it could obtain such products at closer to their cost. In some cases, where profit margins are particularly high, some might regard the situation as exploiting low-income consumers (rather than "serving" them). The situation is particularly likely to be seen as exploitive where high profit margins are created or sustained through monopoly, regulation, or other anticompetitive forces (such as restrictions on use of intellectual property). For example, state-owned monopolies on production and distribution of salt were used for centuries as a way to extract income from poor communities, because people literally could not live without salt in their diet. Few would regard this long-standing historical form of "doing business with the poor" as much of a benefit to the poor.[1] Under what circumstances, then, can we say that substantial benefits to a low-income community are being produced, and under what circumstances can we say instead that the poor are being exploited? Under what circumstances are sales to the BOP good *for the poor*—both as individual consumers and as a community? In cases where a venture explicitly seeks to create social benefits, how can we best design BOP strategies to produce greater benefits to the consumers from whom these new profits are being earned?

This paper develops a conceptual framework for examining the wider range of impacts that doing business with the poor has on the poor. It then presents a list of design features for business ventures directed at low-income markets that help increase the benefits received by the poor. This framework is applied to three examples of BOP activity described elsewhere in this volume.

The Impacts of Consumer Sales to the Poor on Low-Income Communities

Providing products that low-income consumers desire and can afford offers them some obvious benefits. To be sure, the greatest benefit of a free economy is that it generates products that consumers value, and their voluntary purchase and use of these products is the best indication that the products are generating perceived consumer value. But products can have many primary effects (those of direct consumption), secondary effects (results flowing indirectly from their use), and tertiary effects (consequences that flow from other changes made by the consumers who use them). For example, consider a new communications device that can be manufactured cheaply enough to be affordable to residents of a low-income community and that can be sold in a way that meets their cash (or credit) constraints. This device has immediate primary effects within the community, as customers use it to stay in touch with one another, make plans, and "visit" with friends. Secondary effects may include the ability of local entrepreneurs to develop new income-generating opportunities in the community (applying the device as a business tool rather than just as a consumption item). Finally, the desire to purchase such devices may induce people operating in an informal non-market exchange economy to make products for sale or take wage-paying jobs in order to purchase this product. A widening circle of impacts thus spreads as consumers develop new ways to use the product to their benefit—and adapt their lives so that they can afford it.

Consider, by contrast, the development of a new package delivery product. An entrepreneur develops a nationwide transport network to track and move packages at low cost from a set of "collection points" in low-income communities. Using simple technology, household-based local entrepreneurs can become drop-off and pick-up points for packages to be sent to any other collection point in the network. Like the communications device, this product has immediate consumption benefits, and indirect benefits such as the ability of other local entrepreneurs to obtain supplies or to ship locally produced goods outside their immediate community at reasonable cost. But this product has another important impact in the low-income communities where it is sold: it directly generates income in the community, because it is in part "manufactured" or produced within the community. Products that confer substantial benefits on their consumers are generally a good thing for a low-income community, but products that yield local income are likely to be an even better thing.

Tracking the Impacts of BOP Ventures: An Income-Accounting Approach

Both consumption and income generation are clearly important benefits to low-income communities associated with BOP sales. One way to examine these impacts is by constructing a formal accounting of the flows associated with BOP activities, examining both household and total community income. Macroeconomists use a "national income accounting" framework to track generation and use of income. We can begin by identifying a low-income community as a separate entity, and consider the flows of its income generation and consumption in a "trade" model that includes flows between the community and the rest of the world.

Household Income Flows

Let us first look at the flow of income and spending in a given household. Households in the low-income community divide their total time L among leisure, work in the market economy (L_m), work in producing products directly for the market exchange economy (L_e, for example, when a family sells vegetables grown in the garden), and work producing commodities it will consume itself (L_h, for example, when it uses home-produced clothing). Income earned by the household is thus:

$$Y = wL_m + p_eE(L_e) + rK,$$

where $E(L_e)$ is the amount of exchange product generated by the amount of work L_e, p_e is the market price of products produced at home for exchange, and rK is capital income (the amount of earnings received as a result of accumulated savings).

In addition, the household may receive government cash income payments (G_b) or remittances from family members working outside the community, R. Its overall cash income is thus:

$$Y = wL_m + p_eE(L_e) + rK + G_b + R$$

and the household's disposable income, after taxes T, is:

$$Y_d = wL_m + p_eE(L_e) + rK + G_b + R - T$$

If the household saves an amount S, then its consumption spending will be:

$$Y_c = Y_d - S = wL_m + p_eE(L_e) + rK + G_b + R - T - S$$

Households presumably act to maximize their self-perceived welfare by choosing how much labor to devote to market activities, exchange activities, and own-production (with the remaining time going to leisure), how much to save, and what commodities to purchase with their income spendable on consumption, Y_c. In addition to the vector of commodities they buy in the market economy, C_m, households manufacture a vector of commodities for their own use, $C_h = H(L_h)$, where $H(L_h)$ is the amount of own-use products produced by the level of effort L_h.[2] Thus, if household utility can be thought of as a function of commodity consumption, government services, leisure, and accumulated capital,[3]

$$U = U(\text{consumption, government services, leisure, capital}),$$

then households consume a vector of commodities,

$$C = C_m + C_h = C_m + H(L_h)$$

and can be thought of as maximizing their welfare,

$$\max U = U(C_m + H(L_h), G_s, L - (L_w + L_e + L_h), K(1 - \delta) + S) \text{ (equation 1)}$$

(where G_s is the amount of government services provided and δ is the rate of depreciation of accumulated capital) by choosing (1) how much to work in the wage economy, L_w; (2) how much to work directly to produce commodities for market exchange, L_e; (3) how much to work to produce home-manufactured commodities, L_h; (4) how much to save, S; and (5) the bundle of purchased market commodities C_m, subject to the constraint that

$$pC_m = Y_c = Y_d - S = wL_m + p_eE(L_e) + rK + G_b + R - T - S, \text{ (equation 2)}$$

that is, the cost of the commodities purchased in the market economy must not exceed the household's available disposable income.

Equations (1) and (2) define the individual household's challenge of dividing its time and purchases to produce the best results (as perceived from its vantage point, and given the information and choices available to the household).

Community Income Flows

The flows of income in individual households aggregate to the flow of income in the community as a whole, with the important difference that each transaction has two "sides." When a household spends its funds on a consumption item, it "produces" consumption; but if the commodity is purchased from someone else in the community, the transaction also produces income. Indeed, no matter where the purchase is made, income is generated, so from the perspective of a low-income community it becomes important whether the commodity was purchased from within the community or outside. If purchased from within, it drives income in the community; if "imported," then it drives income elsewhere. This implies a key distinction for BOP ventures. "Doing business with the poor" is generally understood to begin with a sale of a product to a member of a low-income community, thus referencing in the first instance the *consumption* side of the transaction. But for every sale, there is both a consumption and an *income* side to the transaction. Income from the sale is necessarily generated *somewhere*, and thus a key question from the perspective of the low-income community is, *Where?* Is the income side of the transaction also within the community—is the product, or some part of it, produced in the community? Or is it an import? A consumer product represents and produces value in consumption, but to the extent to which the value embodied in the product was added to the product locally, the community is better off by virtue of value on both sides of the transaction.

A simple way to view this is within the framework of what economists call national income accounting. In a closed economy, the income generated by any sale or activity produced is within that economy, so that

$$Y = C + I + G,$$

where Y is the total income produced in the community, C is total community consumption, I is the amount of investment, and G is the amount of government services provided. This equation, known as the national income accounting identity, expresses the fact that when a consumer spends a dollar on a commodity, that dollar is received as income by someone or by some group of people within the community. The storekeeper may get a part of it, the owner of the business that made the product gets some of it, his or her workers get some of it, the truck driver who delivered it gets some of it, and so on. But all of it goes somewhere, so that each dollar of spending necessarily creates a dollar of income. Similarly, spending by firms on investment items (new equipment, for example) and spending by government (paying teachers to produce public education) generates a dollar of income for each dollar of spending.

If the economy is "open"—that is, if the community we are examining trades with others—then when a second community purchases commodities produced by the first, income is also generated within the first community. By contrast, any purchase of commodities from the second community produces *consumption* in the first community, but it does not produce *income* in the first community. Letting X designate exports to the outside world and M designate imports from the outside, we thus have:

$$Y = C + I + G + (X - M),$$

that is, income produced in the community is the sum of consumption, investment, and government spending *plus* net exports purchased from the community by those outside it. Of course, imported goods and services can be consumption goods C_m, investment goods I_m, or government activities G_m, which is to say,

$$M = C_m + I_m + G_m$$

so it may be more insightful to write this equation as:

$$Y = (C - C_m) + (I - I_m) + (G - G_m) + X. \text{ (equation 3)}$$

Therefore the amount of income generated in the community is the amount of consumption that is not met through imported commodities, together with the amount of investment that is not carried out through purchases of investment goods outside the community, together with the amount of government activity that is produced from within the community, plus the amount of exports to the outside world.

Equation (3) defines the fundamental identity of aggregate community income: income in the community is generated to the extent (and only to the extent) to which it is able to (1) engage in consumption of commodities produced locally, (2) make investments from locally produced materials, and (3) produce locally generated government services, *or* (4) generate export products purchased by those outside the community. Increasing income generated in the low-income community requires interventions or changes that alter one or more of these balances—that increase locally produced consumption, increase investment activities using local materials, provide government services using inputs from the local community, or expand exports. There are other ways to raise the spending power of the low-income community, such as government income supplements or remittances, but if one of the central purposes of socially oriented programs focused on the BOP is to increase current income actually produced in the community, then these are the only options.

The Income and Welfare Dynamics of a New Product Introduction

Our formulation of household and aggregate income flows generated within a community offers a lens through which to view the low-income community effects of a BOP venture. Equations (1) and (2) lay out the individual household framework; households maximize

$$\max U = U(C_m + H(L_h), G_s, L - (L_w + L_e + L_h), K(1 - \delta) + S) \text{ (equation 1)}$$

subject to

$$pC_m = Y_c = Y_d - S = wL_m + p_e E(L_e) + rK + G_b + R - T - S, \text{ (equation 2)}$$

while in the aggregate low-income community as a whole,

$$Y = (C - C_m) + (I - I_m) + (G - G_m) + X \text{ (equation 3)}$$

Consider first what happens when a new BOP product, manufactured outside the low-income community, is offered for sale within it. In the first instance, household income is unaffected. To the extent that households choose to purchase the new product, they must do so either by displacing existing consumption or by increasing time spent on income-earning activities (through wage-earning or through home production of goods for sale), or by "dis-saving" (selling assets, or borrowing). Opportunities for additional income generation may not be available or may not be desirable; households may already be constrained by a lack of employment opportunities. If opportunities for additional income generation are available and households choose to earn additional income to purchase the product, their choices indicate that on balance they value the product in excess of the loss of leisure required to finance it. In addition to the value of the consumption of the product, total income in the low-income community is raised (at the expense of leisure time).

If, by contrast, the purchase of the new product is at the expense of consumption of other products, then it matters whether the consumption forgone was locally produced or not. If so, then the reduction in consumption of these other commodities also produces a loss of income to others within the low-income community. In the context of equation (3), C remains fixed (because the consumer trades consumption of one commodity for another), while C_m rises—which implies that Y, income within the community, is actually falling. In this circumstance, the product itself may have important benefits to the individual(s) or groups using it, but one consequence of introduction is diminished income produced within the community.

Products that are partly or completely manufactured within the community confer additional benefits through generating some of the income necessary to consume them.[4] In addition, some products may prove useful in developing business opportunities, or they may help people in the low-income community develop relationships, experience, and greater comfort with banking, credit, and other forms of transactions possibly enabling them to expand their potential earnings.

A Checklist for Designing BOP Ventures Likely to Be Good for the Poor

New products designed to serve the needs and aspirations of low-income consumers can foster both profitable business opportunities and benefits to consumers as well as low-income communities more generally. Some kinds of products are, however, more likely to confer wider social benefits than others. Products that supply core needs of the community through noncompetitive and high-margin transactions are likely to be viewed as exploitive. By contrast, new products that confer significant benefits previously unavailable at a fair price and that expand the income-earning opportunities for members of the community are likely to be viewed as of great benefit to the poor and the community they live in. Examining these potential benefits through the framework of household and community income and expenditure generation allows us to identify a series of characteristics likely to predispose a given project to generating greater net benefit to the poor. The checklist that follows can help assess how existing products and projects might be seen; it implicitly guides which design features of future projects can provide the most benefit to low-income communities.[5]

Checklist for Prospective BOP Projects

☐ *Consumption benefits.* Does the product provide substantial net benefits to the direct consumer?

☐ *Expansion of business opportunities.* Does the product create opportunities for building entrepreneurial activities, or expand opportunities to develop, create, or market locally produced goods and services?

☐ *Local income production in the manufacturing process.* Is the product, or any component of it, locally manufactured, or produced by members of the low-income community?

☐ *Wage impacts.* Does the local manufacture of the product generate higher wages than what prevailed in the community before?

☐ *Expansion of formal labor market opportunities.* Does the local manufacture of the product enhance opportunities for additional wage-earning activity that was previously unavailable?

☐ *Expansion of desirable wage-earning opportunities.* Does the local manufacture of the product foster opportunities for additional wage-earning activity that members of the low-income community find desirable?

☐ *Encouragement of savings.* Does the product encourage or create opportunities to enhance saving by the consumer or others in the community?

☐ *Encouragement of formal banking, credit, and other business-related opportunities.* Does the product create opportunities for development of lower-cost and more comprehensive banking or other financial arrangements for consumers or other people in the low-income community?

Applying the Framework

The papers in this volume have presented a range of examples of projects and business activities that involve transactions with low-income people. Let us examine three examples to illustrate how the community-income accounting approach might help us understand more fully a broader range of their likely social impacts.

Monsanto and Small Farmers in Mexico

In Chapter Eighteen, "Building New Business Value Chains with Low-Income Sectors in Latin America," Austin and colleagues describe the challenges Monsanto faced in trying to bring its products to small farmers. It recognized that there might well be an enormous, untapped market among small farmers, but Monsanto knew nonetheless that it did not have a good understanding of these "consumers"; nor did it have appropriate distribution mechanisms to reach this market efficiently. Partnering with the Mexico Foundation for Rural Development brought it expertise in what farmers needed as well as in preexisting relationships that could be used to design a new distribution system to effectively reach this new market segment.[6]

From a community-income accounting perspective, Monsanto is selling what is presumably a collection of productivity- and income-enhancing materials and intermediate products to small farmers. In the short run, farmers will have to reduce their consumption of other purchased commodities, borrow, sell assets, or earn more in other activities to afford purchase of these new inputs to their farming production process. To the extent to which these commodities are produced elsewhere (and not in the low-income community itself), these products are imports (and therefore produce little or no direct additional income in the community), and to the extent that farmers reduce their consumption of locally produced commodities to buy them, the local income effect in the short run is negative. The long-term income effect, however, may be positive, and potentially substantial; by increasing the productivity of small farmers, these products may allow them to produce a larger volume of more competitive products that are (from the perspective of the low-income community) mostly exports. Thus this intervention amounts to an investment by farmers (and, perhaps, by the community as well), as purchases are displaced (and possibly local income falls) in the short run but larger incomes result from a more prosperous "export sector" from the low-income community in the long run.

Hindustan Lever Limited's Project Shakti

As described by V. Kasturi Rangan, Dalip Sehgal, and Rohithari Rajan in Chapter Thirteen, "The Complex Business of Serving the Poor," Hindustan Lever Limited (HLL) sought, over the course of decades, to increase the fraction of Indian society that its products could reach. Constantly seeking inroads into doing business with less-well-off members of the society, it developed products at lower price points, designed new products that could be produced for substantially lower cost, and reengineered distribution systems. Fifty years after India's independence, however, HLL still found itself unable to draw into the customer base five hundred million of the country's poorest citizens. Project Shakti involved reorganization of HLL's distribution chain for products marketed to this BOP group by developing local entrepreneurs as company agents to sell HLL products directly in their villages. The entrepreneurial network, backed by training and microcredit, has grown rapidly, producing correspondingly rapid growth in sales.

From a community-income perspective, this strategy has two counterbalancing effects. Sales to low-income members of society in rural India are likely to be almost exclusively of import products, and HLL's products are consumption goods, so they will probably not foster opportunities for business or income development or growth. Thus the net effect of these sales on *income* in the low-income community depends critically on whether they displace other items that would have been consumed, or encourage people to increase their incomes so that they can afford to buy these newly available products. In particular, the net effects depend importantly on whether the displaced consumption was of commodities or services produced within the low-income community. Given the relatively low income of the communities in question, and the prevalence of barter and exchange within the low-income community, this displacement seems at least in part to be a substitution of local products by imported products, lowering local incomes. In the HLL model, however, this effect is likely to be offset to a considerable extent—and possibly more than completely offset—by the fact that the new distribution mechanism is designed around a local entrepreneur who is a member of the local community and whose income is being earned in the community. To put it another way, to the extent that a part of the finished goods cost is local cost of distribution, the Project Shakti model is built around a production process that includes at least some local "manufacturing." HLL profits from the fact that this is a much-lower-cost form of distribution than it was otherwise able to arrange, thus lowering total delivered cost to these villages and making it economically viable to deliver and sell products there. The community benefits not only from the consumption value of the new products but also from the fact that the involvement of the local distributor reduces the extent to which those products are imports to the community.

HLL's Project Shakti model is powerful because it is driven by a profit engine; since it works, HLL actively wants to expand it. But it is also powerful because HLL is in effect "sourcing" some of its inputs—the distribution services, in this case—from the low-income community it is serving.

When "Doing Business with the Poor" Means Buying Instead of Selling

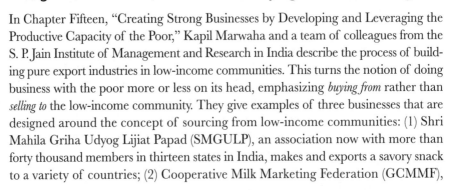

In Chapter Fifteen, "Creating Strong Businesses by Developing and Leveraging the Productive Capacity of the Poor," Kapil Marwaha and a team of colleagues from the S. P. Jain Institute of Management and Research in India describe the process of building pure export industries in low-income communities. This turns the notion of doing business with the poor more or less on its head, emphasizing *buying from* rather than *selling to* the low-income community. They give examples of three businesses that are designed around the concept of sourcing from low-income communities: (1) Shri Mahila Griha Udyog Lijiat Papad (SMGULP), an association now with more than forty thousand members in thirteen states in India, makes and exports a savory snack to a variety of countries; (2) Cooperative Milk Marketing Federation (GCMMF),

India's largest marketing organization for food products, deliberately sources from low-income communities; and (3) SEWA Trade Facilitation Centre (STFC) extends support, product design, and marketing assistance to artisans, helping them build exports from their communities. The income-producing impact of export industries is straightforward, and to the extent that businesses can perceive opportunities to source materials and labor from low-income communities, doing business with the poor can have an unambiguously positive impact on the income of the poor.

Conclusion

Inventing new products and redesigning existing ones to make them valuable and accessible to people in low-income communities can confer great benefits on the innovating companies and on the poor themselves. Not all such relationships, however, are likely to be equally good for the poor. In some cases, high profit from such activities will signal that great social benefits have been created; in other cases, such profit indicates that great value has been created but captured by private interests remote from the low-income community (firm owners, managers, workers in another location, intermediaries, and others).

How do we know when doing business with the poor is good not only for business but also for the poor? We have identified several characteristics of products and projects that make this probable. The principal benefit of good products remains that they bestow consumption benefits. But the best products for socially productive BOP ventures also:

- Generate income directly in the low-income community
- Expand wage-earning opportunities among low-income people
- Raise prevailing wages
- Create opportunities to develop new businesses or expand existing business in low-income areas
- Foster rapid growth in local incomes
- Help low-income residents expand saving and investment
- Make available opportunities to develop banking, credit, and other relationships

Part of the challenge of socially valuable entrepreneurship focused on the BOP is to design products and ventures in a way that serves the larger social interests of the people fueling the transaction, rather than simply finding ways to create, capture, and then drain value from low-income communities.

CONFERENCE PARTICIPANTS

Name	Title	Affiliation
Gerardo C. Ablaza Jr.	President and CEO	Globe Telecom, Inc.
Ibrahim Abouleish	Founder	Sekem
Fauzia Erfan Ahmed	Director	Women's Studies Program, Indiana University
Frederick Ahwireng-Obeng	Professor of economics	Wits Business School
Ravi Anupindi	Associate professor	Ross School of Business, University of Michigan
Antonino T. Aquino	President	Manila Water Company
Luis Fernando Arboleda	Management consultant	
Nava Ashraf	Assistant professor	Harvard Business School
Jaime Augusto Zobel de Ayala II	Chairman and CEO	Ayala Corporation
James E. Austin	Eliot I. Snider and Family Professor of Business Administration	Harvard Business School

Name	*Title*	*Affiliation*
Urs Baerlocher	General counsel, head legal and general affairs	Novartis International AG
Chris Beshouri	Managing partner	McKinsey and Company
Peter Blom	CEO	Triodos
David E. Bloom	Professor	Harvard School of Public Health
Joseph Bower	Donald K. David Professor of Business Administration	Harvard Business School
David Brown	Associate director for international programs	Hauser Center for Nonprofit Organizations, Harvard University
Valeria Budinich	Vice president, Full Economic Citizenship Initiative	Ashoka
Zoë Chance	Doctoral candidate in marketing	Harvard Business School
Ricardo Charvel	Vice president, institutional relations and communication	CEMEX—Mexico
Michael Chu	Senior lecturer	Harvard Business School
Christopher A. Crane	President and CEO	Opportunity International
Guillermo D'Andrea	Chairman, Marketing Department	IAE, Universidad Austral
Srikant Datar	Professor and senior associate dean	Harvard Business School
Rohit Deshpandé	Sebastian S. Kresge Professor of Marketing	Harvard Business School
Melchior Dikkers	MBA student and researcher	IAG/PUC-Rio (Pontifical Catholic University of Rio de Janeiro)
Andreas Eggenberg	Executive director	Amanco Agricultural Solutions

Name	*Title*	*Affiliation*
David Ellwood	Dean	Kennedy School of Government, Harvard University
Marc J. Epstein	Distinguished research professor	Rice University
Gerardo Lozano Fernández	Professor	EGADE
Sanjay Gandhi	Global project manager, Growing Sustainable Business Initiative	United Nations Development Programme (UNDP)
Victoria Garchitorena	President	Ayala Foundation
Aurelia Garrido	Strategic initiatives coordinator	AVINA Foundation
Neil Gershenfeld	Director	Center for Bits and Atoms, MIT
Ray A. Goldberg	Moffett Professor of Agriculture and Business Emeritus	Harvard Business School
Michael Gordon	Professor	Ross School of Business, University of Michigan
Allen Grossman	MBA Class of 1957 Professor of Management Practice	Harvard Business School
Ron Grzywinski	Chair	ShoreBank Corporation
Doug Guthrie	Professor of sociology and management	Stern School of Business, New York University
Allen Hammond	Vice president for innovation and special projects	World Resources Institute
Robert Hart	President and CEO	Globeleq
Stuart Hart	S. C. Johnson Professor of Sustainable Global Enterprise	Cornell University, Johnson School of Management
Ricardo Hausmann	Director and professor of the practice of economic development	Center for International Development, Kennedy School of Government

Name	Title	Affiliation
Harriet Hentges	Partner	Clifton Partnership
Kerry Herman	Senior researcher, Global Research Group	Harvard Business School
Pablo Sánchez Hernando	Research assistant	IESE Business School
Gustavo Herrero	Executive director, Latin America Research Center	Harvard Business School
Linda A. Hill	Wallace Brett Donham Professor of Business Administration	Harvard Business School
Kurt Hoffman	Director	Shell Foundation
John Hoffmire	Director, Center on Business and Poverty	University of Wisconsin–Madison
Mary Houghton	President	ShoreBank Corporation
Matthew Humbaugh	Business outreach coordinator, Growing Sustainable Business Initiative	United Nations Development Programme (UNDP)
Wilson A. Jácome	Director, Advanced Management Program	IDE Business School
David J. Jhirad	Vice president for science and research	World Resources Institute
Michele Kahane	Director, special projects	Center for Corporate Citizenship, Boston College
Rosabeth Moss Kanter	Ernest L. Arbuckle Professor of Business Administration	Harvard Business School
Robert S. Kaplan	Baker Foundation Professor	Harvard Business School
Tarun Khanna	Jorge Paulo Lemann Professor	Harvard Business School
Sirkka Korpela	Senior advisor	World Monitors

Name	*Title*	*Affiliation*
Anil B. Kulkarni	Professor	S. P. Jain Institute of Management and Research
Raúl Zavalía Lagos	Executive director	Fundación Pro Vivienda Social
Francisco A. Leguizamón	Professor	INCAE
Herman B. Leonard	Professor of business administration (HBS) and George F. Baker Jr. Professor of Public Management (HU)	Harvard Business School and Kennedy School of Government, Harvard University
George Lodge	Jaime and Josefina Chua Tiampo Professor of Business Administration, emeritus	Harvard Business School
Ted London	Senior Research Fellow	Ross School of Business, University of Michigan
Luis E. Loría	Director	Economic Environment & Enterprise (e3)
Monique Maddy	Global poverty expert	Google
Fikile Magubane	Consul general	South African Consulate General
Johanna Mair	Professor	IESE Business School
Sonia Marciano	Senior lecturer	Harvard Business School
Patricia Márquez	Professor	IESA
Kapil Marwaha	Adjunct faculty, Center for Development of Corporate Citizenship	S. P. Jain Institute of Management and Research
John McArthur	Dean emeritus	Harvard Business School
Mark Milstein	Scholar in residence (Cornell) and business research director (WRI)	Cornell University and World Resources Institute
Thomas S. Mondschean	Professor	DePaul University

Name	*Title*	*Affiliation*
Ajay S. Mookerjee	Executive director, India Research Center	Harvard Business School
Anabel Pérez Moreno	Senior vice president, retail banking	Venezolano de Crédito Banco Universal
Paulo Cesar Motta	Professor of marketing	IAG/PUC-Rio (Pontifical Catholic University of Rio de Janeiro)
Andrew Natsios	Administrator	USAID
Mthuli Ncube	Professor of finance	Wits Business School
Jane Nelson	Director, CSR Initiative	Kennedy School of Government, Harvard University
Raymond Offenheiser	President	Oxfam America
Andrin Oswald	Assistant to the chairman and CEO	Novartis AG
Marcelo Paladino	Head of Business, Society, and Economics	IAE Business School, Universidad Austral
Krishna Palepu	Professor, senior associate dean for international development	Harvard Business School
Roslyn Payne	President	Jackson Street Partners, Ltd.
Djordjija Petkoski	Lead specialist and program leader	World Bank
Tom Piper	Baker Foundation Professor	Harvard Business School
David J. Porteous	Director	Bankable Frontier Associates
Luis Reyes Portocarrero	General director	TIA, S.A.
Andrea M. Prado	Ph.D. student	INCAE, New York University
C. K. Prahalad	Paul and Ruth McCracken Distinguished University Professor	Ross School of Business, University of Michigan

Name	*Title*	*Affiliation*
John A. Quelch	Senior associate dean, Lincoln Filene Professor of Business Administration	Harvard Business School
Rohithari Rajan	Market development manager, Rural	Hindustan Lever Ltd.
Ravi Ramamurti	Professor of international business	Northeastern University
V. Kasturi Rangan	Malcolm P. McNair Professor of Marketing	Harvard Business School
Ezequiel Reficco	Senior researcher	Harvard Business School
Margaret Reid	Senior vice president, consumer products	VISA International
Nicolas Retsinas	Director, Joint Center for Housing Studies	Kennedy School of Government, Harvard University
David Rose	Assistant vice president, competitive strategy (H&R Block), Ph.D. candidate (WPI)	H&R Block and Worcester Polytechnic Institute
Carlos Rufin	Assistant professor of management	F. W. Olin Graduate School of Business, Babson College
Tony Salvador	Director, ethnography and design research, Channel Products	Intel
Stéphanie Schmidt	Director	Ashoka
Daniel Schneider	Research associate	Harvard Business School
Ann Scoffier	Senior vice president for marketing and deposit development and corporate secretary	City *First* Bank of D.C.
Bruce R. Scott	Paul W. Cherington Professor of Business Administration	Harvard Business School

Name	*Title*	*Affiliation*
Christian Seelos	Visiting lecturer	IESE Business School
Arthur I. Segel	Professor of management practice	Harvard Business School
Erik Simanis	Ph.D. student and director, BoP Protocol Project	Johnson School of Management, Cornell University
Raj Singh	Executive vice president	Nestlé India
Kunal Sinha	Executive director, Discovery	Ogilvy & Mather India
S. Sivakumar	Chief executive, Agri Businesses	ITC Limited
Howard Stevenson	Senior associate provost for planning and resources	Harvard University
Amb. Jesus Tambunting	Chair and CEO	Plantersbank
R. S. Tucker	Director	Standard Bank
Peter Tufano	Sylvan C. Coleman Professor of Financial Management	Harvard Business School
David Upton	Albert J. Weatherhead III Professor of Business Administration	Harvard Business School
Sushil Vachani	Associate professor	Boston University
Carolyn Welch	Community affairs team leader	Board of Governors of the Federal Reserve System
Annie Woollam	Business research analyst	World Resources Institute

NOTES

Introduction

1. In 2000, under the auspices of the UN, 180 world leaders made a declaration adopting eight Millennium Development Goals to be reached by 2015. They included halving extreme poverty, as well as halting the spread of HIV/AIDS, providing universal primary education, and reducing child mortality.
2. United Nations (2005). According to the UN, many countries in sub-Saharan Africa have seen the poverty rate increase in the past ten years. The rate in other parts of the developing world outside of Asia has shown little movement.
3. Ibid.
4. See Prahalad and Hammond (2002) and Hart (2005).
5. Prahalad (2004).
6. Hammond and Prahalad (2004).
7. Rangan and McCaffrey (2004).
8. The term *submerged market* is drawn from Rangan (2002) to characterize markets that are fragmented, informal, and sometimes temporary.
9. For more on South African government initiatives to economically empower the black community, see Hill and Farkas (Chapter Twenty-Seven); Tucker, Mondschean, and Scott (Chapter Twenty-Three); and Ahwireng-Obeng and Ncube (Chapter Twenty-Six).
10. See Kanter (Chapter Twenty) and Welch and Scoffier (Chapter Twenty-One).

Chapter One

1. Daley-Harris (2004).
2. Rangan and Walker (1999).

3. Palmer and Millier (2004).
4. During my time at Grameen Bank, I was impressed by both the local branch manager in the field and the senior leadership in Dhaka. An excellent organization, the Grameen Bank consists of staff who are deeply committed to poverty alleviation and to the people whom they serve.
5. Agarwal (1994).
6. Based on sex segregation within the household and outside, *purdah* is a complex social institution prevalent in many communities in South Asia. Imbued with notions of respectability and male honor, in essence it defines the male world as separate from the female world. It can lead to seclusion of women, seriously interfering with their efforts to enter the labor market and thereby increasing their psychological and economic dependence on men.
7. Pitt and Khandakar (1995).
8. Bhuiya, Sharmin, and Hanifi (2003); Rahman (1999).
9. Khan and others (1998).
10. Stark and Flitcraft (1991).
11. Stark and Flitcraft (1991), p. 133.
12. Wood and Sharif (1997).
13. Agarwal (1994).
14. Center for Reproductive Rights (2004).

Chapter Two

1. World Bank figures (http://www.economist.com/World/la/PrinterFriendly.cfm?Story_ID=2193852).
2. Following the convention adopted by the World Bank, those that live on less than US$2 per day are considered poor, and those that live on less than US$1 per day are considered extremely poor, also referred to as indigent or destitute. (Economic Commission for Latin America and the Caribbean, 2005.)
3. Unless stated otherwise, the sign $ stands for U.S. dollars.
4. Two separate studies by AC Nielsen and ANTAD suggest that average tickets for emerging segments may reach up to 50 percent of what middle-class and higher-income consumers spend in the supermarket. It should be noted that the reported average ticket sizes by socioeconomic status do not take into account frequency of shopping and that emerging consumers shop much less frequently in large supermarkets.
5. According to Napoleon Franco & Cia., Colombia is one exception for televisions, stoves, and radios, with penetration lower at 65–85 percent.
6. Overall, few of the focus group participants stated they shopped at hard discount supermarkets (especially in Mexico and Colombia, where almost all participants claimed they "never shopped" at discount supermarkets). In Argentina, shopping incidence was the highest observed for this format. It should be noted that the sample size is not statistically sufficient to make a quantitative assessment and that many consumers interviewed may not happen to live or work near these stores.
7. Undoubtedly, relatively low penetration of freezers and microwave ovens in emerging segments drives low penetration of ready-to-eat meals and frozen foods—in part. However, many of the group participants enjoy preparing meals from scratch as an extension of caring for the family, and it is not clear that they would "pantry load" frozen meal components such as chicken, meat, and vegetables, even if they owned a freezer.

8. Sheth, Newman, and Gross (1991).

9. Most discussion group participants did not consider public buses and subways to be a viable means of transport for bringing purchases back home when heavy or numerous packages were involved; instead, consumers tended to reference the price of a pirate taxi ride, or "collective," or shared van/taxi service when referring to the transport expenses that were factored into the total purchase cost.

10. Ring, Tigert, and Serpkenci (2002).

11. One potential explanation for higher shelf prices in Argentine chain supermarkets and hypermarkets is that large retailers are raising markups while small retailers are selling at or just above final delivered cost of product to weather the economic crisis. Additionally, large self-service wholesalers are growing in importance in the area where retail surveys were conducted, which may lead to sharing of purchasing scale benefits with small retailers.

12. Figures in local currency converted to U.S. dollars with February 2003 exchange rates.

13. Gross margins for large supermarkets vary considerably by individual retailer, geographic location, and format (hard discount, supercenter/hypermarket, or high-end specialty grocery). For a small sample of chain retailers, we observed gross margins for large chain retailers of 20–32 percent of net sales (per financial statements available during first quarter 2003).

14. Recognizing again the small size of our sample for large chain retailers and the variety of formats. Monthly sales per full-time employee for the large players ranged from approximately $4,000 to $9,000.

15. Note that surveys were conducted in major metropolitan markets, where there is relatively high concentration of retail outlets per square kilometer and multiple distributors. Both of these factors facilitate small retailers' frequent replenishment.

16. All of the countries in this study levy VAT taxes, and large-scale retailers' reported figures naturally exclude this tax as an income statement expense since it is ultimately passed on to consumers. VAT debits and credits do appear in balance sheet accounts such as tax-related receivables and payables. Care must therefore be taken in comparing tax expenses in the published income statements of chain retailers (excluding VAT) with small-scale retailers' tax expenses (a flat tax that in many cases "includes" VAT). Adjusting for this, the total tax pie (with VAT) is higher under the standard tax regime that large retailers face compared to small-business tax regimes.

17. Most Latin American governments require employers to pay their workers a complementary annual compensation, usually equivalent to a one-month salary.

18. Assumes 18 percent VAT tax and 3 percent sales tax; actual numbers vary by country.

Chapter Three

1. Natarajan (2004).

2. Natarajan (2004), cited in Prahalad (2005).

3. Natarajan (2004).

4. Kashyap (2004b).

5. Ogilvy & Mather internal data.

6. Natarajan (2004).

7. Indian Ministry of Statistics and Programme Implementation (1994–2002).

8. Registrar General and Census Commissioner (2005).

9. Ogilvy & Mather internal analysis using National Readership Survey data.

Chapter Five

1. United Nations Development Programme (2005b).
2. Bloom, Zaidi, and Yeh (2005).
3. Bloom and Sachs (1998).
4. Authors' calculations based on United Nations Development Programme (2005b).
5. United Nations Development Programme (2005b).
6. United Nations Development Programme (2005b).
7. United Nations Development Programme (2005b).
8. Baker and van der Gaag (1993); Berman, Nwuke, Rannan-Eliya, and Mwanza (1995); World Bank (1995).
9. Hanson and Berman (1998).
10. For more on the effects of low pay and lack of resources in the public sector, see Jan and others (2005).
11. Nieves, La Forgia, and Ribera (2000).
12. Marek, Yamamoto, and Ruster (2003).
13. Philip Musgrove (1999) reviews nine considerations affecting the choice between public and private financing of health care, centering on cost-effectiveness. Musgrove's conclusion: "Public funds should finance public and semi-public goods that are cost-effective and for which demand is inadequate; cost-effective interventions that preferentially benefit the poor; and catastrophically costly care, when contributory insurance will not work or there are good reasons to finance insurance publicly." A much longer discussion, which includes more on insurance considerations, is Musgrove (1996).
14. World Bank (2005); data for 2002.
15. World Bank (2005).
16. Khanna, Rangan, and Manocaran (2005).
17. These ideas are developed quite generally in several papers, the earliest of which are Khanna and Palepu (1997, 2000) and Khanna (2000). Econometric evidence on the benefits of compensating for institutional voids in rural areas of India is provided by Fisman and Khanna (2004).
18. Acharya and Ranson (2005).
19. Acharya and Ranson (2005).
20. Schofield (2005).

Chapter Six

1. Berwick (2002).
2. Berwick (2002).
3. Bonnel (2000).
4. Gara (2005).
5. Sidley (2002).
6. Deshpande and Winig (2003).
7. McNeil (2000).
8. Leggett (2004).
9. "Aspen's Upward Slope" (2005).

10. Vachani and Smith (2004).
11. Product patents were eliminated in favor of process patents. After 1970, no molecule or drug combination could be patented; only its processing method was protected.
12. Huang and Hogan (2002).
13. Hamied (2005).
14. Deshpandé and Winig (2003).
15. Deshpandé and Winig (2003).
16. Vachani and Smith (2004).
17. Deshpandé and Winig (2003).
18. Hamied (2005).
19. Biswas (2003).
20. Deshpandé and Winig (2003).
21. Oliveira-Cruz, Kowalski, and McPake (2004).
22. Biehl (2004).
23. Phillips and Moffett (2005).
24. Biehl (2004).
25. Far-Manguinhos (n.d.).
26. Serra (2003).

Chapter Seven

1. London and Hart (2004).
2. Prahalad and Hart (2002).
3. Sánchez and Rodríguez (2005).
4. Ellison and Rodríguez (2003).
5. Miroslava and Arenas (2003).
6. Sánchez and Rodríguez (2005).
7. Sánchez, Ricart, and Rodríguez (2005).
8. London and Hart (2004).
9. Hart (2005), p. 208.
10. Khanna and Palepu (1997).
11. Peng and Heath (1996).
12. Prahalad and Ramaswamy (2004).

Chapter Eight

1. International Energy Agency (2004); United Nations, UN-Energy (2005); United Nations Development Programme (2005a).
2. Department for International Development (2002); United Nations Development Programme (2005a).
3. International Energy Agency (2004).
4. International Energy Agency (2004).
5. International Energy Agency (2004).
6. International Energy Agency (2004).
7. Jhirad and Mintzer (1992).

8. International Energy Agency (2003).
9. Department for International Development (2002).
10. United Nations Development Programme (2004).
11. "Sarvodaya [SEEDS] sees these projects as primarily social projects, and thus does not approach the market with the aggressiveness of a private company. Without other MFIs in the market, credit delivery through Sarvodaya may simply be too slow for the market expansion desired by suppliers." (Martinot, Ramankutty, and Rittner, 2000, p. 25).
12. 1 U.S. dollar = average Rs. 46.00 between 1999 and 2002.
13. Sharan (2004).
14. Mugica and London (2004). On the basis of current expenditures on nonrenewable energy sources such as kerosene and batteries, studies place the average ability to pay for electricity services at under five dollars per month. (Goldemberg, Lèbre La Rovere, and Teixeira Coelho, 2004).
15. One reason the service may be canceled is that the grid reaches the customer; it is able to supply cheaper, higher-voltage electricity constantly. In this case, it has been negotiated with the customers that even though the battery and solar panels must be deinstalled and returned to IDEAAS, the customer can retain the wiring.
16. E+Co (2005).
17. E+Co (2003).
18. The target of eight hundred million people is based on Renewable Energy Task Force (2001).
19. Drewienkiewicz (2005).

Chapter Nine

1. Urban poverty is rapidly growing as a result of migration from countryside to cities. UN-HABITAT "estimates that in 2001 there were 924 million slum dwellers in the world and that without significant intervention to improve access to water, sanitation, secure tenure, and adequate housing this number could grow to 1.5 billion by 2020" (http://ddp-ext.worldbank.org/ext/GMIS/gdmis.do?siteId=2&goalId=11&targetId=25&menuId=LNAV01GOAL7SUB3, accessed on July 28, 2006); the eleventh Millennium Development Goal is to "have achieved by 2020 a significant improvement in the lives of at least 100 million slum dwellers."
2. Gómez-Ibáñez (2003).
3. In Latin America, privatization of water utilities has taken place in Argentina, Bolivia, Brazil, Chile, Colombia, Ecuador, Honduras, Mexico, Peru, and Uruguay. Other countries in the region did not privatize but established management contracts with foreign utilities to operate local companies (Hall and Lobina, 2002).
4. "Argentina's Changing Economy" (2005); Hall and Lobina (2002).
5. Prahalad (2004); Prahalad and Hammond (2002).
6. In fact, a powerful incentive for slum residents to pay for utility services is the fact that utility bills constitute legal proof of residence, giving residents the right to ask for municipal services such as education, and in some cases even squatters' rights to the land.
7. According to a National Bureau of Standards poll, respondents consistently rated AAA over 4.0 on a scale of 0 to 5 (with 5 being the highest mark) with regard to being (1) a modern company, (2) one that improves continuously, (3) responsible, (4) concerned with the community, (5) satisfactory in providing ample coverage, and (6) a leader in the business community.

8. Hall and Lobina (2002).

9. Hart and London (2005).

10. In the case of telecommunications, cellular technology has eliminated dependence on physical networks and greatly reduced the economic obstacles to reaching the poor.

Chapter Ten

1. An exception seems to be Aguas Argentinas, a water utility that has developed an innovative service provision plan involving authorities and community and local actors. See Paladino (2001); and Mele and Paladino (2005).

2. This program was called "Gas para todos" (gas for all) and was created to connect five hundred thousand new customers. Nevertheless, it had limited success because many customers consumed more gas than they could pay for, and stopped paying their service bills.

3. INDEC (Argentine National Index and Census Institute), 2001, www.indec.mecon.ar.

4. INDEC (2001) and Permanent Household Survey (Encuesta Permanente de Hogares, 2001).

5. Based on Paladino and Blas (2005).

6. Over a ten-year period, FPVS lent ARS$12 million to eight thousand families, 95 percent of which was repaid.

7. www.fpvs.org.

8. Gas Natural BAN.

Chapter Eleven

1. Chandler, 1990; Cole, 1946; McCraw, 1997; Schumpeter, 1947a, 1947b.

2. Axelrod (1984).

3. On community welfare, Arrow (1972) and Mauss (1990); on value of the company, Jensen and Meckling (1976); on employee growth, Baron and Kreps (1999).

4. Prahalad and Hammond (2002).

5. Indicadores Básicos en Ecuador (2003).

6. Prahalad and Hammond (2002).

7. Arrow (1972); Axelrod (1984); Smith and Smith (1976).

8. Kotler and Lee (2005).

9. von Hippel (1988).

Chapter Thirteen

1. By 2004, Unilever had a 51 percent equity position in the Indian company with the rest of the shares being owned by local institutional and individual shareholders. HLL's predecessor company started operating in India as early as 1933 to manufacture and market soap. In 1956, the entity known as HLL was formed.

2. P&G had operated in India through its Vicks and Clearasil franchise since the 1960s, but only in the late 1980s did it seriously approach the consumer market for soaps and detergents.

3. *Vani* is a Hindi word that means "voice" or "speech." It is also a commonly used female name.

Chapter Fourteen

1. Harvard Joint Center for Housing Studies (2005).

2. Prahalad (2005).

3. XII Population and Housing Census, INEGI (Instituto Nacional de Estadística, Geografia e Informática), México, 2000.

4. Flores, Flores Letelier, and Spinosa (2003).

5. Softec (2003).

6. Data from CEMEX.

7. All customer, distributor, and promoter interviews were conducted over a two-day period, April 7–8, 2005.

8. De Soto (2000).

9. In a *tanda*, ten families contribute MXN$100 per week to a communal pool for ten weeks. Every week, a lottery is held, and a different family withdraws MXN$1,000.

10. Data from CEMEX.

11. Putnam (2000).

12. Flores, Flores Letelier, and Spinosa (2003).

13. Data from CEMEX.

14. PH counts accumulated clients as all the clients that have passed through the program throughout its history, regardless of whether they are active or not during a given year. On average, 65.4 percent of accumulated clients are active during a year. Of total active clients, only 58.8 percent pay their membership fee during the fifty-two weeks of the year on average. For the cost and revenue projections, we have assumed that these fractions remain unchanged as the program expands.

15. This assumes a 400 percent increase in cement consumption per family per year and does not take into account decreased sales attributable to those families who complete their homes and no longer need to purchase cement.

16. Data from CEMEX.

17. Prahalad (2004).

18. Willard (2002).

19. Survey data from CEMEX.

20. Softec (2003) and Federal Reserve (http://www.federalreserve.gov).

21. Banco de México (www.banxico.gob.mx).

Chapter Fifteen

1. After all, how many low-cost units can one consume on a survival budget of one or two dollars a day?

2. As referenced in Singh (2005), p. 46.

3. Though beyond the scope of discussion of this paper, it may be worthwhile to draw attention to the Eastern philosophy that advocates limitation of wants in order to take care of one's needs and not succumb to greed. This is a counterpoint to the entire edifice of mainstream economic thinking that is based on continuous expansion of goods to satisfy unlimited wants (Nayak, 2005). We were told that one cause of disgruntlement among the farmers is their desire to increase their consumption of items not linked to productivity, in the face of limited resources.

4. Gandhian business principles include *Sarvodaya* (nonviolent socialism) and collective trusteeship.

5. "Private Dairies Unfair to Farmers" (2005).

6. Candler and Kumar (1998), chapter 8.

7. Candler and Kumar (1998), chapter 7.

8. Candler and Kumar (1998), chapter 8, p. 56.

9. Candler and Kumar (1998), chapter 7, p. 52.

Chapter Sixteen

1. Purchasing power parity.

2. Agrawal and Agrawal (2004).

3. The e-Choupal experiment for soybeans procurement has been well documented in Prahalad (2005) and Upton (2003).

4. A CA can be either a seller's (farmer's) agent or a buyer's (for instance, ITC).

5. Quantifying this benefit requires a detailed econometric study, which ITC plans to commission shortly.

6. Several agencies, government and private, have in the past tried to sell to the farmer, an act that asks a farmer to part with his money. If not done right, its potential to build a trusting relationship is questionable.

7. "Agricultural Statistics at a Glance" (2004).

8. Increased production and yield were made possible by expansion of farm areas, double cropping, and use of high-yielding seed varieties.

9. The foods division is part of ITC's fast moving consumer goods segment of the business, which includes cigarettes, foods, lifestyle retailing, and others.

10. See Anupindi and Sivakumar (2006) for a detailed discussion of the agribusiness value chain reengineering using e-Choupal.

11. See Anupindi and Sivakumar (2005) for more details.

Chapter Seventeen

1. The essential amino acids are present in nearly ideal proportions, as defined by the World Health Organization.

2. The number reached US$3.2 billion if including purchases of milk ingredients.

Chapter Eighteen

1. SEKN (www.sekn.org) is a collaboration formed to address the need for generating social enterprise intellectual capital developed in Latin America. It was created in 2001 through the participation of a group of leading Latin American business schools and the Harvard Business School in partnership with the AVINA Foundation.
2. de Ferranti, Perry, Ferreira, and Walton (2004).
3. Austin (2000); Austin and others (2004).
4. Prahalad (2005).
5. Austin and Reavis (2002).
6. Interviewed on Feb. 24, 2004.
7. Prahalad (2004).

Chapter Nineteen

1. This includes Mexico, Brazil, Turkey, Russia, India, China, Indonesia, Thailand, Malaysia, and the Philippines. GDP is on a PPP basis.
2. After Abraham Maslow's hierarchy-of-needs theory, which contends that humans are motivated by certain basic needs that must be fulfilled before "higher needs" can be realized. See Maslow (1943).
3. In our work, we also developed a detailed case on Globe Telecommunications that illustrates many of the same general principles outlined in this paper. The case is available from Globe Telecommunications.
4. As of 2005, the ownership is Ayala Corporation, International Finance Corporation, United Utilities, and Mitsubishi.
5. See Davis (2005).

Chapter Twenty

1. This section about FBC is taken from Kanter (2005).
2. This section about ABN AMRO Real is taken from Kanter and de Pinho (2005).

Chapter Twenty-One

1. Immergluck (2004).
2. Code of Federal Regulations, Title 12: *Banks and Banking, Part 225—Bank Holding Companies and Change in Bank Control* (Regulation Y), Subpart I—Financial Holding Companies, Interpretations. http://ecfr.gpoaccess.gov/cgi/t/text/text-idx?c=ecfr&sid=5a24472a6650360617ef8b9ebdbac02f&rgn=div8&view=text&node=12:3.0.1.1.6.9.6.32&idno=12.

3. Federal Reserve Board of Governors, *Community Development Investments*. http://www. federalreserve.gov/CommunityAffairs/cdi/default.htm.

4. Federal Reserve Board of Governors, and Office of the Comptroller of the Currency, Part 24, *Community Development Investments*. www.occ.treas.gov/cdd/pt24toppage.htm.

5. 12 USC Title 12: *Banks and Banking, Chapter 30, Community Reinvestment*, U.S. Code Online, 12 U.S.C. 2901. http://www.gpoaccess.gov/uscode/index.html.

6. Sampson (1999).

7. U.S. Census Bureau, American Survey Reports, Income, Earnings, and Poverty. *2004 American Community Survey*, Aug. 2005. www.census.gov/prod/2005pubs/acs-01.pdf.

8. U.S. Department of Housing and Urban Development, *HUD's Mission*. www.hud.gov/ library/bookshelf18/hudmission.cfm.

9. Georgetown University, Office of Communications, *Fact Sheets*. http://explore.georgetown. edu/documents/?DocumentID=738&PageTemplateID=52.

10. Interview with Clifton Kellogg, president and CEO, and Ann Scoffier, vice president of resource development, City *First* Bank of D.C., N.A., Sept. 28, 2005.

11. National Community Investment Fund, www.ncif.org.

12. U.S. Code, Title 12: *Banks and Banking, Chapter 46: Government Sponsored Enterprises*, Subchapter I—Supervision and Regulation of Enterprises, Section 4565. http:// frwebgate2.access.gpo.gov/cgi-bin/waisgate.cgi?WAISdocID=178163366225+0+0+0& WAISaction=retrieve.

13. 12 USC Title 12, *Banks and Banking, Chapter 30, Community Reinvestment*, U.S. Code Online, 12 U.S.C. 2901. http://www.gpoaccess.gov/uscode/index.html.

14. Certificate of Deposit Account Registry Service. http://www.cdars.com/.

15. "Report on the Condition of the U.S. Banking Industry: Fourth Quarter, 2004." *Federal Reserve Bulletin*, Spring 2005. www.federalreserve.gov/pubs/bulletin/2005/spring05_bsr.pdf.

16. "Report on the Condition . . ." (2005).

Chapter Twenty-Two

1. Swanstrom (1985).

2. The original pledge was $350 billion over a ten-year period, beginning in 1999. In 2004, however, this figure was expanded to $750 billion. See Bank of America (2004).

3. Interview with Doug Woodruff, president of community banking, Bank of America.

4. See, for example, Marsico (2005). Some scholars do go very deep into a sophisticated analysis of the CRA. For example, Macey and Miller (1993) argue that the 1977 version of the CRA had little impact. However, they chart the law's efficacy at bringing about true change in the area of urban development to the revamping of the law by Congress in 1989. We do not dispute this argument, but we maintain that introduction of the LIHTC and the synergistic relationship between the two was as important as the change in the law in 1989.

5. Guthrie (2004); Guthrie and McQuarrie (2005).

6. The data for this chapter come from two sources. First, as part of the Corporate-Community Relations Study, we conducted 150 in-depth interviews with individuals working in the local development sector in three U.S. cities. Qualitative data and background information on the economic systems and the political processes we describe here come from these interviews. Interviews were semistructured, organized around the issue of building low-income housing and public-private partnerships more generally. These interviews

give us insight into the pressures, practices, and views of the advocacy community outside the government working with the LIHTC. All interviews were recorded and transcribed. Second, we analyzed the Congressional Record for the 99th to 107th Congresses, covering the years 1985–2002, to track the politics of the debate over LIHTC legislation. To gather these data, we conducted general searches on the Lexis Nexis Government Documents/Congressional Records section. Lexis Nexis allows general and Boolean searches for document text. To be sure that we captured all records that refer to the LIHTC, we conducted general searches on "low-income housing tax credit." In addition, we conducted searches on relevant issues that have emerged as related to the LIHTC: "passive loss," "capital gains," "real estate development." This yielded more than five hundred pages of subcommittee and floor records, which we then pared down to the relevant information for the legislation under scrutiny. In conjunction with the relevant documents that constitute the actual legislation and its amendments, we treat this body of documents as the history of the legislation in Congress.

7. The literature on the postwar crisis in American cities is huge. Although the roots of the crisis remain a debate among scholars and policy makers alike, the fact of the crisis is basically undisputed. See, for example, Wilson (1987); Venkatesh (2000); and Massey and Denton (1992).

8. Redlining is the practice whereby lenders assess specific communities as high-risk areas—historically denoted (literally and figuratively) by drawing red lines around them—on the basis of race and ethnicity. The practice became institutionalized in private and governmental housing policies in 1933 when University of Chicago economist Homer Hoyt was hired by the federal government to develop the underwriting criteria for the Federal Housing Authority. Hoyt had gained attention through his writing about the relationship between racial groups and property values, arguing specifically that Italians, African Americans, and Mexicans were high-risk groups for their impact on property values. In the FHA underwriting criteria, specific groups were not named, but warnings about the negative impact of racial groups on property values were. This language was also adopted by the American Institute of Real Estate Appraisers in 1933. See, for example, Dedman (1988); and Massey and Denton (1992).

9. The Fair Housing Act (1968 [42 U.S. Congress §§ 3601–3619]), the Equal Credit Opportunity Act (1974 [15 U.S. Congress §§ 1691–1691f]), the Home Mortgage Disclosure Act (1975 [12 U.S. Congress §§ 2801–2809]), and the Community Reinvestment Act (1977 [12 U.S. Congress §§ 2901–2908]).

10. For discussion, see, for example, Hossain (2004).

11. It is important to note that banks are assessed on a given establishment's relationship to its locale. In other words, large multiestablishment banks such as Bank of America or Citigroup, which have been involved in many mergers and serve many local markets, are not assessed an overall CRA rating. Instead, each establishment-level bank is rated with regard to its CRA practices. The corporate bank is also given an overall CRA rating that is a composite of the whole. The vast majority of banks fall into the categories of "needs to improve" (78 percent) or "substantial noncompliance" (19 percent).

12. See Guthrie and McQuarrie (2005).

13. See, for example, the comments by Senator Packwood (R-Ore.), chair of the Senate Finance Committee, which oversaw the production of the act: legislative day of Wednesday, Sept. 24, 1986, 99th Cong. 2nd Sess., 132 Cong Rec S 13782, vol. 132 no. 129, though submitted to the Senate Congressional Record on Sept. 26, 1986.

14. Recall that the passive-loss write-off as exercised by individuals created incentives for new owners to let properties depreciate in value. Under this system, there were two key features

of the LIHTC that changed this dynamic. First, all of the depreciation values are paper values that were structured (as expected values) at the beginning of the deals. As such, developers could work hard to increase property values over the ten-year life of the LIHTCs without upsetting the agreed-on depreciation values that mattered for the corporations. Second, developers were partial owners of the properties (with corporations), so there were equal incentives for them to figure out how to help the properties appreciate by the time they would aspire to sell the property, thus having the positive effect on inner-city development that private investment in housing development should have.

15. According to Ohio's State Development Office, for the Cleveland metropolitan area (which includes Cleveland, Elyria, Loraine, and East Cleveland), 5,218 tax credit units have been built since 1987; 4,677 of them are in the city of Cleveland.

16. Banks are more closely regulated by the federal government than other C-corporations, mainly because they are federally insured. However, corporations and banks in general have both become delinked from the welfare state in terms of tax commitments. By the middle of the twentieth century, corporate and individual income taxes each represented about 9 percent of gross domestic product. Individual income taxes still represent about 9 percent of GDP today, but corporate income taxes have fallen steadily to about 1 percent.

Chapter Twenty-Three

1. Unless otherwise stated, the term *black South Africans* is intended to refer to nonwhite South Africans.

2. For a detailed description of the negotiation process that led to the agreement of a Financial Sector Charter for South Africa, see Tucker (2005).

3. South African Financial Sector Charter (2003).

4. "Black influenced" companies are defined as between 5 percent and 25 percent ownership by black people and with participation in control by black people; "black empowered" companies are more than 25 percent owned by black people and see substantial participation in control vested in black people; "black companies" are more than 50 percent owned and controlled by black people.

5. Banking Association of South Africa (May 18, 2005).

6. "Carrot Trumps Stick" (2005).

7. South African Financial Sector Charter (2003).

Chapter Twenty-Four

1. Baumol (2004).

2. World Bank (2003).

3. Abramovitz (1995); Chanda and Putterman (2004).

4. Seelos and Mair (2005b).

5. This section is drawn from Seelos and Mair (2005a).

6. Seelos and Mair (2005a).

7. Seelos and Mair (2005a).

8. "Sekem/Dr. Ibrahim Abouleish (2003)." Right Livelihood Award. http://www.rightlivelihood.org/recip/2003/sekem.htm.

9. Seelos and Mair (2005c).

10. Easterly (2001).

Chapter Twenty-Five

1. For more background on social entrepreneurship, see Bornstein (2004).

2. Ashoka is the largest global community of social entrepreneurs. Since its establishment twenty-five years ago, it has invested in more than seventeen hundred social entrepreneurs in sixty countries. Ashoka pioneered the "social venture capital" approach as a way to address major social challenges with systemic responses. Ashoka Fellows are selected for their innovative and practical ideas to address social needs. The work described here is part of Ashoka's Full Economic Citizenship initiative, a global program designed to enable and mobilize commercial partnerships between social entrepreneurs and businesses to develop sustainable and profitable markets while delivering social impact (www.ashoka.org).

3. With an estimated volume of resources of more than US$1 trillion and nineteen million jobs at the global level (excluding religious congregations), the nonprofit sector is already equivalent to the eighth-largest economy in the world (Sustainability, 2003).

4. These social networks range from the most basic form of human interaction at the grassroots community level (schools, churches, health centers, parks) to a more sophisticated array of actions undertaken by citizen groups to mobilize communities toward a common goal. Examples are small farmer cooperatives, reproductive health programs, youth learning initiatives, environmental groups, and many other forms of community organization addressing some social issue.

5. For a detailed description of the framework behind these principles, see Budinich (2005).

6. "Of the 4.9 million gallons of water used for irrigation annually—32 percent of the total water usage in Mexico—more than 60 percent will be lost due to the inefficiency of agricultural irrigation systems" ("Agricultural Irrigation Equipment," 2003).

7. Under the present system, most of the Mexican government subsidies for irrigation go to medium- and large-scale farmers. This situation changes for small farmers when a well-established company such as Amanco furnishes the pro-forma quotes required and a system to secure the remainder of the financing is in place.

8. See www.ashoka.org for a description of the search and selection process of Ashoka Fellows.

Chapter Twenty-Six

1. Kilby (1971).

2. Lichtenstein and Lyons (2001).

3. Wennekers and Thurik (1999).

4. Lichtenstein and Lyons (2001).

Chapter Twenty-Seven

1. Margolis and Walsh (2003).
2. Milton Friedman's argument that the sole concern of business should be shareholder maximization is alive and well. See, for example, Crook (2005) and Friedman (1962). For readings that make the counterargument, see, for example, Damon (2004); Greider (2003); Handy (2002); and Sen (1993).
3. Drawing on the traditions of oral history and ethnography, this chapter is adapted from a larger research effort to profile and examine South African black business leaders' formative experiences and leadership. In conducting this research, we initially interviewed more than two hundred black and white South African leaders in the business, government, and not-for-profit sectors over five years. On the basis of these interviews, we chose four black business leaders whose paths to business were representative of those followed by the majority of their peers (and representative of the race and ethnicity of Africans, coloreds, and Indians in South Africa). We conducted an additional series of in-depth interviews and field-based observations with our four protagonists, their colleagues, mentors, friends, and in some cases families.
4. For a discussion of the experiences of black businesspeople, see Luhabe (2002).
5. This ranking uses Gini coefficients to order inequality. South Africa ranks fifth lowest among the eighty-eight countries with recorded Gini coefficients (World Bank, 2001b).
6. Jenkins and Thomas (2000).
7. In South Africa, there were four general race group categorizations: white, African, Indian, and colored. The latter three were collectively referred to as black. Charnley was classified as colored because her ancestors came from more than one race group. We have included a racial identifier of individuals in this chapter as they are introduced. We find it difficult to think through the complexities facing the workforce in South Africa without having that information.
8. Iqbal Survé, one of the individuals we are profiling in our research, coined the phrase "gentler capitalism" in our first interview with him.
9. President Mandela and the ANC were elected as part of a fragile coalition government in a post–Cold War environment. Although a violent revolution was averted, the new ANC government recognized that the liberation movement, which succeeded with aid from the trade unions and the communist party, would not remain patient in the face of one of the most inequitable distributions of income in the world. The ANC promised free education for all, a million new homes over five years to help combat the country's acute homeless problem, and extension of electric and water service to millions of homes. Once in power, however, the ANC found itself in a quandary. Many hoped the ANC, with its socialist roots, would favor nationalization and radical redistribution of wealth. After consulting with their traditional constituencies and international financiers, however, Mandela's government adopted a tight fiscal policy intended to stimulate long-term growth through debt reduction and decreased inflation. Its macroeconomic strategy was characterized by privatization, deregulation, fiscal austerity, and trade liberalization to encourage domestic and foreign investment. This decision was not without controversy; some accused the government of abandoning its social agenda.
10. Data summarizing the gains and losses over time of the number and market capitalization of the so-called black chip companies listed on the Johannesburg Stock Exchange are

difficult to summarize succinctly in part because the definition of *black-chip company* has changed over time.

11. Calculation of unemployment in South Africa is, as in many countries, imprecise. In their article, Kingdon and Knight (2004) employ "broad" and "narrow" definitions of unemployment, which for Africans in 2000 ranged from 41.2 percent to 26.2 percent.

12. Black Economic Empowerment Commission Conference, October 2000.

13. This narrative is based on data collected principally between 1997 and 2003. Much of it is also included in a series of Harvard Business School cases on Irene Charnley at Johnnic Group (A), 9–405–059, (B) 9–403–171, and (C) 9–403–171.

14. In 1950, the South African government mandated that individuals live only with people who were of the same race. Charnley's mother and father's parents were Xhosa, white, Malay, and Italian; they were classified as colored.

15. In the mid-1990s, Anglo American disposed of "noncore" assets, including those represented by Johnnic. Its core activities were in mining gold, diamonds, platinum, ferrous metals, industrial minerals, and base metals.

16. MTN and Johnnic have won multiple awards for BEE, including Businessmap's Anglo American Award for Top BEE Market Performer 2004. In 2000, Johnnic was third place in Empowerdex's annual listing of most empowered boards.

17. For a detailed analysis of inequality and the difficulty of addressing it in South Africa, see May (2000); Seekings and Nattrass (2005); and Wilson and Ramphele (1989).

18. MTN also publishes an annual economic and sustainability report to assess financial and social achievements.

19. MTN Group Employment Equity Plan, 1998.

20. Paine (2003), p. 243.

21. For discussion of the potential costs and benefits of targeting the poor as a market, see Prahalad (2005). Clearly, there are profits to be made. But as Paine's model suggests, the overlap can be less than perfect between making profits and engaging in socially responsible behavior.

22. For discussion of how to develop leaders of moral courage and capability, see Hill (2006).

23. See, for example, Elkington (1998) and Tichy, McGill, and St. Clair (1997).

Chapter Twenty-Eight

1. In 1971, Opportunity International, a nongovernmental organization (NGO) from the United States, started lending in Colombia; ACCION International, another U.S. NGO, issued its first microcredit loan in Recife, a poor area of Brazil in 1973; in 1970, an entrepreneur established Bank Dagang Bali in Indonesia to lend to and capture savings from people who had no access to the financial system; and Grameen, a Bangladeshi NGO, was founded in 1976 to empower women and improve their economic lot. None of these early pioneers knew each other at the time.

2. Chu (2005), p. 100.

3. In a normal market environment, those microfinancing entities not able to meet the requirements of financial viability would in time disappear. However, because microfinance takes place among the poor, donors (from the developmental agencies and from private philanthropy) continue to play an important role. Donor funds have been critical to the

creation of the field, and donors can still play a vanguard role in its development, but grant monies have also served to prevent the shakeout that typically rationalizes emerging industries as they mature.

4. Marulanda and Otero (2005).

5. Worldscope database, RIMES Technologies, accessed Nov. 15, 2005.

6. Simple average, not weighted for asset volume.

7. Marulanda and Otero (2005), p. 12.

8. Worldscope database, simple average of the years.

9. "The Hidden Wealth of the Poor" (2005).

10. Asociación de Entidades Financieras Especializadas en Micro Finanzas (ASOFIN), La Paz, Bolivia, whose members are BancoSol and Banco Los Andes ProCredit (banks); EcoFuturo, Fie S.A., Prodem, Fortaleza, and Fácil (fondos financieros privados or FFPs, regulated institutions chartered as single-purpose microfinance entities); and AgroCapital (FFP license pending); www.asofinbolivia.com.

11. As of June 30, 2005. ASOFIN, *Resumen Institucional, Junio 2005,* p. 7.

12. The year was marked by severe political upheaval, with major highways cut, isolating key cities and leading to the economic standstill of the country and the ousting of the constitutionally elected president.

13. Excluding the two microfinance banks, BancoSol and Banco Los Andes Procredit.

14. ASOFIN, Boletín Informativo, Sept. 30, 2005 (www.asofinbolivia.com).

15. ASOFIN (2005).

16. ASOFIN (2005).

17. For example, the Grameen Bank arrears rate includes only amounts overdue at least a year (see Robinson, 2001, p. 93, table 2.8).

18. Robinson (2001).

19. Financiera Compartamos is a SOFOL (Sociedad Financiera con Objetivo Limitado), a single-purpose finance company licensed and regulated by the Mexican Superintendency of Banks. It is not permitted to take deposits from the public.

20. The discussion that follows is based on Lopez (2005).

21. Financiera Compartamos.

22. MIX Market (www.mixmarket.org).

23. As of Dec. 31, 2005 (Financiera Compartamos).

24. Mibanco.

25. Lopez (2005), p. 53.

26. "Hidden Wealth" (2005), pp. 8–9.

27. As of Nov. 3, 2005, Profund was in the process of collecting the cash proceeds related to its last sales of assets.

28. Profund International, S.A., Presentation to the General Assembly of Shareholders, Nov. 3, 2005.

29. "Hidden Wealth" (2005), p. 9.

30. International Finance Corporation of the World Bank, information shared at Profund meeting, Nov. 3, 2005.

31. Profund, presentation to shareholders, Nov. 3, 2005.

32. For an analytical history of BRI and the extensive microfinance experience of Indonesia, see Robinson (2002).

33. PT Bank Rakyat Indonesia Persero, offering circular, Oct. 31, 2003, p. 39.

34. PT Bank Rakyat Indonesia Persero (2003), pp. 75, 81.

35. PT Bank Rakyat Indonesia Persero (2003), p. 81. The number of savings accounts is not equivalent to number of clients, because customers may have more than one account.

36. PT Bank Rakyat Indonesia Persero (2003), p. 39.

37. PT Bank Rakyat Indonesia Persero (2003), p. 37.

38. For 2001–2003, UMU Website (www.umu.co.ug); for 2004, author information, public disclosure permission pending.

39. UMU Website (www.umu.co.ug).

40. K-Rep Bank Limited, Deloitte Management Letter, Dec. 31, 2004.

41. Schmidt and von Pischke (2005).

42. The disposable personal income per person in the United States in 2003 was $28,227 (U.S. Census Bureau, www.census.gov).

43. This is beginning to find support in macroeconomic studies. As reported in the *Economist:* "Hidden Wealth," p. 2.

> A World Bank report by Thorsten Beck, Asli Demirguc-Kunt and Soledad Martinez published [in October 2005] shows strong correlation between lack of financial access and low incomes. . . . Earlier research by the first two authors and Ross Levine concluded that a sound financial system boosts economic growth and particularly benefits people at the bottom end of the income ladder. A long-term study in Thailand by Robert Townsend of the University of Chicago and Joe Kaboski of Ohio State University showed that families with access to credit invested more, consumed more and saved less than those without such access.

44. This approach differs from those of other observers who are interested in measuring qualitative factors defined by the analyst rather than the microfinance client.

45. Limited studies undertaken by developmental agencies such as USAID and some microfinance entities are well regarded, but as Marguerite Robinson (2001, p. 123) has said, "Overall, however, the microfinance industry has little systematic, reliable information on the impact of its services on its clients and their households."

46. For dollar loans. Given the dollarization of the Bolivian economy, the bulk of BancoSol's loans are dollar-denominated (source: BancoSol).

47. Originally a Fondo Financiero Privado (FFP), it is now licensed as a bank, operating as Banco Los Andes ProCredit.

48. Basically, salaried consumers employed in the formal sector.

49. For a review of the crisis, see Rhyne (2002).

50. Calculated as the ratio of financial income to loan portfolio (source: ASOFIN).

51. Rhyne (2002), pp. 131, 136.

52. Wolfenson (1998).

Chapter Twenty-Nine

1. See, for example, Snodgrass and Sebstad (2002); Morduch (2000); Coleman (2005); Hoque (2004); Sebstad and Chen (1996); Simanowitz and Walter (2002); Cheston and Reed (1999); Brau and Woller (2004); and Armendariz de Aghion and Morduch (2005).

2. For further details about microfinance, see Drake and Rhyne (2002); Daley-Harris (2002); Jurik (2005); Brau and Woller (2004); and Polakow-Suransky (2003).

3. Cheston and Kuhn Fraioli (2002); Kuhn Fraioli (2003). For more detail on Opportunity International and field and survey data in Ghana along with prior studies, see Epstein and Crane (2006); Afrane (2002); Hishigsuren (2004); and Hishigsuren, Beard, and Opoku (2004).

4. Sebstad and Chen (1996).

5. Copestake and others (2001); Dunn and Arbuckle (2001).

6. For example, Hoque (2004). See also Coleman (2005).

7. For example, Kabeer and Noponen (2005); Dunn and Arbuckle (2001).

Chapter Thirty

1. In fact, all three banks in this paper have a "triple bottom line" whereby the effect on the *environment* is also measured and assessed; but this paper focuses primarily on social impact, hence the narrower reference to double bottom line.

2. CGAP has recently reported 750 million small savings and loan accounts at double-bottom-line banking institutions (Christen, Rosenberg, and Jayadeva, 2004). Many of these banks are members of the World Savings Bank Institute, an association for banks committed at some level to a double-bottom-line approach. WSBI has 101 members, almost all of which are state-owned; many focus only on taking retail savings without extending any credit. Cooperative banks in some countries are notable exceptions, although they are restricted to members only. Other notable exceptions that deserve further research are the giant Bangladeshi microfinance NGOs such as BRAC and ASA, which are consistently profitable and yet have great impact on the well-being of their clients.

3. Dobbs (2005).

4. Despite the pressures on nonprofits to generate revenues, Foster and Bradach (2005) show that the percentage of earned income in total income reported by U.S. nonprofits did not change much between 1977 and 1997.

5. Foster and Bradach (2005), p. 100.

6. Dobbs and Koller (2005).

7. Speech to MAP Inaugural Meeting, Jan. 26, 2004.

8. Triodos Annual Report, 2003, p. 21.

9. Grzywinski (1991), p. 95.

10. Annual Report 2004, p. 7.

11. http://www.sbpac.com/bins/site/templates/subtemplate.asp?area_2=Our+Story%2FMetrics&objectid=C8221190%2D3&NC=4663X.

12. The Social Investment Forum reports that in 2003 more than US$2 trillion was counted as socially responsible investment in the United States, double the 1997 figure.

13. At the level of ShoreBank Corporation, returns from the core bank shown in Table 30.2 are explicitly diluted as the result of other market development activities to a group return of 7.9 percent. Note that for Triodos geographic expansion takes place through establishment of new branches, the cost of which is borne by the bank, whereas for ShoreBank it has been largely carried by the holding company.

14. For a survey of recent empirical evidence to this effect, see Bossone and Lee (2002).
15. See Rhyne (2002) on Bolivia, and Porteous and Hazelhurst (2004) on South Africa.

Chapter Thirty-One

1. From a client's perspective, the loan "term" may seem like the time from when the money is received to when the consumer might otherwise have expected it (one to eight weeks depending on whether a filer chose direct-deposit or mail). However, the actual loan is paid off in an average of eleven days.
2. Clients also have the option of purchasing a Refund Anticipation Check, which delivers funds more slowly at lower cost, or an Instant RAL, which delivers the funds faster but is more costly than a RAL. Clients may also opt not to purchase any such "settlement product" and decide to receive their refund by direct deposit or by paper check.
3. Wu and Fox (2005).
4. The Truth in Lending Act requires that the interest rates be stated in annualized terms. Calculated this way:

($90 finance charge/($2,800 loan amount − $90 finance charge)) × (365 days/11 days)

the APR is 110 percent. Alternatively, one can express the cost of a RAL as 3–4 percent of a tax refund.
5. Ernst (2003).
6. H&R Block (2005).
7. Jackson Hewitt (2005).
8. Wu and Fox (2005).
9. Elliehausen (2005).
10. Tufano and Schneider (2005).
11. Wu and Fox (2005).
12. Tufano and Schneider (2005).
13. Flannery and Samolyk (2005).
14. Gutek and Shroff (2002).
15. Wu and Fox (2005).
16. ACORN (2004, 2005).
17. For example, Morgan Stanley analysts note that "RAL is a high-margin product that has also hurt Block's reputation" (Gutek and Shroff, 2002), p. 7.
18. Freed (2002).
19. Wu and Fox (2004, 2005).
20. Roberts and Dowling (2002).
21. Thanks to C. K. Prahalad for calling attention to this term. When used in this context, brand-jacking refers to the practice by activists of targeting the leading brand in an industry in order to maximize the efficacy of their actions, with the hope that any changes implemented by the brand leader will diffuse through the remainder of the industry. See "Runner-up, up and away" (2005) for a recent discussion of this phenomenon.
22. "Hedge Funds: The New Money Men" (2005).
23. Freeman and Brown (2001).
24. Gordon (2005); Mullins (2005); "H&R Blockbuster" (2005).

Chapter Thirty-Two

1. Indeed, through the Salt March of 1930, in one of his first major acts of organized civil disobedience, Gandhi famously sought to liberate the poor in India from the yoke of the British salt monopoly that operated as a tax, in his words, on "the poorest of the poor."

2. Households distribute their own production time L_h across a series of household production activities, producing a vector of consumable items C_h.

3. It is somewhat unusual to include accumulated capital in a utility function, but it is a simple way to compress what would be a multiperiod optimization problem into a single time period. This works because the only durable impact current decisions have on the future is through the accumulated capital stock. The only decision of the current period with a footprint on the future is how much net saving to carry out.

4. In Chapter Fifteen of this book, Kapil Marwaha and colleagues from the S. P. Jain Institute of Management and Research in India describe a related concept as "serving and being served by the poor," through which they suggest that products designed to meet needs of low-income consumers also be designed so that low-income communities offer inputs into the manufacture, distribution, or sale of the products.

5. Similar issues are raised in another form by Stuart Hart and a group of colleagues working on the development of a "protocol" to guide business initiatives focused on the base of the pyramid. See Simanis and others (2005).

6. In a related example, Budinich, Manno Reott, and Schmidt in Chapter Twenty-Five describe "hybrid value chains" in which commercial businesses and community organizations partner to complete value chains that neither can independently construct. A relationship between a commercial manufacturer of irrigation systems and "citizen sector organizations" that have much more experience in reaching low-income communities and a much better understanding of the needs of and constraints faced by members of those communities allows the manufacturer to sell systems to groups that would otherwise almost surely be beyond its marketing reach.

REFERENCES

Abramowitz, M. "The Elements of Social Capability." In B. H. Koo and D. H. Perkins (eds.), *Social Capability and Long-Term Growth*. New York: St. Martin's Press, 1995.

Acharya, A., and Ranson, M. K. "Health Care Financing for the Poor: Community-Based Health Insurance Schemes in Gujarat." *Economic and Political Weekly*, Sept. 17, 2005, pp. 4141–4150.

ACORN. "ACORN Brings Message to Liberty Tax Headquarters and Owner's Home: 'Stop Refund Loan Rip-Offs.'" 2005. http://www.acorn.org/index.php?id=4174&tx_ttnews%5Btt_news%5D=17038&tx_ttnews%5BbackPid%5D=8306&cHash=9b6a099c7e (accessed Feb. 27, 2006).

ACORN. "ACORN Presents Jackson-Hewitt with 'Turkey of the Year' Award." 2004. http://www.acorn.org/index.php?id=8313&tx_ttnews[tt_news]=12997&tx_ttnews[backPid]=8879&cHash=bde5f5831a (accessed Feb. 27, 2006).

Afrane, S. "Impact Assessment of Microfinance Interventions in Ghana and South Africa: A Synthesis of Major Impacts and Lessons." *Journal of Microfinance*, Spring 2002, pp. 37–58.

Agarwal, B. *A Field of One's Own: Gender and Land Rights in South Asia*. Cambridge, UK: Cambridge University Press, 1994.

Agrawal, P., and Agrawal, A. "Implementing a Rural Roads Project in Madhya Pradesh." In S. Morris (ed.), *India Infrastructure Report 2004*. New York: Oxford University Press, 2004.

"Agricultural Irrigation Equipment." (Report.) U.S. and Foreign Commercial Service and U.S. Department of State, Jan. 30, 2003.

"Agricultural Statistics at a Glance." New Delhi: IFFCO, Aug. 2004.

Anupindi, R., and Sivakumar, S. *ITC's e-Choupal: A Platform Strategy for Rural Transformation (Unabridged)*. Ann Arbor: Ross School of Business, University of Michigan, 2005.

Anupindi, R., and Sivakumar, S. "Supply Chain Reengineering in Agri-Business: A Case Study of ITC's e-Choupal." In H. L. Lee and C.-Y. Lee (eds.), *Supply Chain Issues in Emerging Economies*. New York: Elsevier-Springer, 2006.

"Argentina's Changing Economy." *Economist*, Sept. 29, 2005.

Argentine National Index and Census Institute (INDEC). 2001. www.indec.mecon.ar.

Armendariz de Aghion, B., Morduch, B., and Morduch, J. *The Economics of Microfinance*. Cambridge, Mass.: MIT Press, 2005.

Arrow, K. J. "Gifts and Exchanges." *Philosophy and Public Affairs*, 1972, *1*(4), 343–362.

"Aspen's Upward Slope: Can South Africa's Top Generics Manufacturer Become a Global Giant?" *Economist*, Oct. 6, 2005. http://www.economist.com/displayStory.cfm?story_id=4492884.

Austin, J. *The Collaboration Challenge: How Nonprofits and Businesses Succeed Through Strategic Alliances* (1st ed.). San Francisco: Jossey-Bass, 2000.

Austin, J., and others. *Social Partnering in Latin America: Lessons Drawn from Collaborations of Businesses and Civil Society Organizations*. Cambridge, Mass.: Harvard University Press, 2004.

Austin, J., and Reavis, C. "Starbucks and Conservation International." HBS case no. 9-303-055. Boston: Harvard Business School Publishing, 2002.

Axelrod, R. M. *The Evolution of Cooperation*. New York: Basic Books, 1984.

Baker, J. L., and van der Gaag, J. "Equity in Health Care and Health Care Financing: Evidence from Five Developing Countries." In E. van Doorslaer, A. Wagstaff, and F. Rutten (eds.), *Equity in the Finance and Delivery of Health Care: An International Perspective*. Oxford: Oxford University Press, 1993.

Bank of America. "Investing in Our Communities." Document no. 00-25-3925B, 2004.

Bank of America. *2004 4Q Investor Fact Book*. Charlotte, N.C.: Bank of America, 2005a. http://www.bankofamerica.com (accessed Nov. 7, 2005).

Bank of America. *2004 Annual Report*. Charlotte, N.C.: Bank of America, 2005b. http://www.bankofamerica.com/annualreport/2004/ (accessed Nov. 7, 2005).

Banking Association of South Africa. "One Million Mzanzi Account Holders." Press release, May 18, 2005.

Baron, J. N., and Kreps, D. M. *Strategic Human Resources: Frameworks for General Managers*. New York: Wiley, 1999.

Baumol, W. "Entrepreneurial Cultures and Countercultures." *Academy of Management Learning and Education*, 2004, *3*, 316–326.

Berman, P., Nwuke, K., Rannan-Eliya, R., and Mwanza, A. *Zambia: Nongovernmental Health Care Provision*. Boston: Data for Decision Making Project, Harvard School of Public Health, 1995.

Berwick, D. "We All Have AIDS: Case for Reducing the Cost of HIV Drugs to Zero." *British Medical Journal*, 2002, *324*, 214–218.

Bhuiya, A., Sharmin, T., and Hanifi, S.M.A. "Nature of Domestic Violence Against Women in a Rural Area of Bangladesh: Implication for Preventive Interventions." *Journal of Health Population and Nutrition*, 2003, *21*(1), 48–54.

Biehl, J. "The Activist State: Global Pharmaceuticals, AIDS and Citizenship in Brazil." *Social Text 80*, 2004, *22*(3), 105–132.

Biswas, S. "Indian Drugs Boss Hails AIDS Deal." *BBC News*, Oct. 29, 2003. http://news.bbc.co.uk/2/hi/south_asia/3220619.stm.

Bloom, D. E., Zaidi, A., and Yeh, E. "The Demographic Impact of Biomass Use." *Energy for Sustainable Development*, Sept. 2005, *9*(3), 40–48.

Bloom, D., and Sachs, J. "Geography, Demography, and Economic Growth in Africa." *Brookings Papers on Economic Activity*, 1998, *2*, 207–295.

Bonnel, R. "Economic Analysis of HIV/AIDS." World Bank AIDS Campaign Team for Africa, Sept. 2000.

Bornstein, D. *How to Change the World: Social Entrepreneurs and the Power of New Ideas.* New York: Oxford University Press, 2004.

Bossone, B., and Lee, J. K. "In Finance, Size Matters." IMF Working Paper no. 02/113, 2002. http://www.imf.org/external/pubs/cat/longres.cfm?sk=15884.0.

Brau, J., and Woller, G. "Microfinance: A Comprehensive Review of the Existing Literature and an Outline for Future Financial Research." *Journal of Entrepreneurial Finance and Business Ventures,* 2004, *9*(1), 1–26.

Budinich, V. "A Framework for Developing Market-Based Strategies That Benefit Low-Income Communities," 2005. www.changemakers.net/.

Candler, W., and Kumar, N. "India: The Dairy Revolution." World Bank Evaluation Department, Report no. 20844. Washington, D.C.: World Bank, 1998.

"Carrot Trumps Stick." *Business Day,* Apr. 1, 2005.

Center for Reproductive Rights. "Women of the World: Laws and Policies Affecting Their Reproductive Lives, South Asia." New York: Center for Reproductive Rights, 2004.

Chanda, A., and Putterman, L. "The Quest for Development: What Role Does History Play?" *World Economics,* 2004, *5,* 1–31.

Chandler, A. D. *Strategy and Structure: Chapters in the History of the Industrial Enterprise.* Cambridge, Mass.: MIT Press, 1990.

Changemakers, Aug. 2005. www.changemakers.net.

Cheston, S., and Kuhn Fraioli, L. "Empowering Women Through Microfinance." In S. Daley-Harris (ed.), *Pathways out of Poverty.* Bloomfield, Conn.: Kumarian Press, 2002.

Cheston, S., and Reed, L. "Measuring Transformation: Assessing and Improving the Impact of Microcredit." Microcredit Summit Meeting of Councils in Abidjan, Côte d'Ivoire, June 24–26, 1999.

Christen, R., Rosenberg, R., and Jayadeva, V. "Financial Institutions with a Double Bottom Line: Implications for the Future of Microfinance." CGAP Occasional Paper no. 8, www.cgap.org, 2004.

Chu, M. "Microfinance: The Next Ten Years." In A. Pakpahan, E. M. Lokollo, and K. Wijaya (eds.), *Microbanking: Creating Opportunities for the Poor Through Innovation.* Jakarta, Indonesia: PT Bank Rakyat Indonesia (Persero), 2005.

Clark, C., Rosenzweig, W., Long, D., and Olsen, S. "Double Bottom Line Project Report: Assessing Social Impact in Double Bottom Line Ventures." 2003. http://www.riseproject.org/DBL_Methods_Catalog.pdf.

Cohen, J. "South Africa's New Enemy." *Science Magazine,* 2000, *288*(5474), 2168–2170.

Cole, A. H. "An Approach to the Study of Entrepreneurship: A Tribute to Edwin F. Gay." *Journal of Economic History,* 1946, *6* (Issue Supplement: The Tasks of Economic History), 1–15.

Coleman, I. "Defending Microfinance." *Fletcher Forum of World Affairs,* Winter 2005, 181–190.

Copestake, J., and others. "Impact Monitoring and Assessment of Microfinance Services Provided by CETZAM on the Zambian Copperbelt 1999–2001." Bath, UK: University of Bath, 2001.

Crook, C. "The Good Company." *Economist* (Special Edition: "The Good Company: A Skeptical Look at Corporate Social Responsibility"), Jan. 25, 2005, *374*(8410).

Daley-Harris, S. "State of the Microcredit Summit Campaign Report." Microcredit Summit Campaign, Washington, D.C., 2004. http://www.microcreditsummit.org/pubs/reports/socr/2003/SOCR03-E[txt].pdf (accessed Dec. 29, 2004).

Daley-Harris, S. *Pathways out of Poverty: Innovations in Microfinance for the Poorest Families.* Bloomfield, Conn.: Kumarian Press, 2002.

Damon, W. *The Moral Advantage: How to Succeed in Business by Doing the Right Thing.* San Francisco: Berrett-Koehler, 2004.

Davis, I. "The Biggest Contract." *Economist,* May 28, 2005, pp. 87–89.

De Ferranti, D., Perry, G., Ferreira, F., and Walton, F. "Inequality in Latin America: Breaking with History? World Bank Latin American and Caribbean Studies." Washington, D.C.: World Bank, 2004.

De Soto, H. *The Mystery of Capital.* London: Black Swan, 2000.

Dedman, W. "Southside Treated like Bank's Stepchild." (In series "The Color of Money.") *Atlanta Journal Constitution,* May 2, 1988, p. A1.

Department for International Development (DFID). *Energy for the Poor: Underpinning the Millennium Development Goals.* London: DFID, 2002.

Deshpandé, R., and Winig, L. "Cipla." HBS case no. 9-503-085. Boston: Harvard Business School Publishing, June 23, 2003.

Development Finance Forum. "Capital Plus: The Challenge of Development in Development Finance Institutions." 2004. www.dfforum.com.

DeYoung, R., and Hunter, W. C. "Deregulation, the Internet and the Competitive Viability of Large Banks and Community Banks." In B. E. Gup (ed.), *The Future of Banking.* Westport, Conn.: Forum Books, 2003.

Dobbs, R. "Managing Value and Performance." *McKinsey Quarterly 2005* (special ed.). www.mckinseyquarterly.com.

Dobbs, R., and Koller, T. "Measuring Long-term Performance." *McKinsey Quarterly 2005* (special ed.). www.mckinseyquarterly.com.

Drake, D., and Rhyne, E. *The Commercialization of Microfinance: Balancing Business and Development.* Bloomfield, Conn.: Kumarian Press, 2002.

Drewienkiewicz, R. *Documentation and Analysis of Business Models Within the E+Co Portfolio.* Global Village Energy Project, United Nations Development Programme. New York: UNDP, 2005.

Dunn, E., and Arbuckle, J. C., Jr. "The Impacts of Microcredit: A Case Study from Peru." Washington, D.C.: Assessing the Impact of Microfinance Services (AIMS), USAID, 2001.

E+Co. "Business Plan." 2003. http://www.energyhouse.com/investments_portfolio.htm.

E+Co. "E+Co Portfolio Performance Summary." 2005. http://www.energyhouse.com/investments_portfolio.htm.

Easterly, W. R. *The Elusive Quest for Growth: Economists' Adventures and Misadventures in the Tropics.* Cambridge, Mass.: MIT Press, 2001.

Economic Commission for Latin America and the Caribbean (CEPAL). *Panorama Social de América Latina 2004.* Santiago, Chile: United Nations Press, 2005.

Elkington, J. *Cannibals with Forks: The Triple Bottom Line of 21st Century Business.* Gabriola Island, B.C., Canada: New Society, 1998.

Elliehausen, G. "Consumer Use of Tax Refund Anticipation Loans." Washington, D.C.: Credit Research Center, McDonough School of Business, Georgetown University, http://msb.georgetown.edu/faculty/research/credit_research/pdf/M37.pdf, 2005, (accessed Mar. 3, 2006).

Ellison, B., and Rodríguez, M. Á. "Hindustan Lever Reinvents the Wheel." IESE case no. DG-1424. Barcelona, Spain: IESE Publishing, 2003.

Epstein, M. J., and Crane, C. A. "Alleviating Global Poverty Through Microfinance: Factors and Measures of Financial, Economic, and Social Performance (A)." Working paper, Rice University, 2006.

Ernst, M. "The Money Gang." (Interview by C. Ramos and P. Kiernan.) *Cable News Network,* Feb. 25, 2003. http://lexis-nexis.com (accessed June 30, 2004).

Far-Manguinhos. http://www.far.fiocruz.br/not_arvs_vis.htm (accessed July 14, 2006).

"Financial Sector Charter and Scorecard." South African Ministry of Finance, Oct. 2003.

Fisman, R., and Khanna, T. "Facilitating Development: The Role of Business Groups." *World Development,* 2004, *32*(4), 609–628.

Flannery, M., and Samolyk, K. "Payday Lending: Do the Costs Justify the Price?" Working paper, 2005. http://www.chicagofed.org/cedric/files/2005_conf_paper_session1_flannery.pdf (accessed Apr. 21, 2005).

Flores, F., Flores Letelier, M., and Spinosa, C. "Developing Productive Customers in Emerging Markets." *California Management Review,* Summer 2003, *45*(4), 77–103.

Foster, W., and Bradach, J. "Should Nonprofits Seek Profit?" *Harvard Business Review,* Feb. 2005, pp. 92–100.

Freed, J. "Judge Says He Will Rule Against Block in Refund Loan Case." *Associated Press,* Nov. 7, 2002.

Freeman, J. P., and Brown, S. L. "Mutual Fund Advisory Fees: The Cost of Conflicts of Interest." *Journal of Corporation Law,* 2001, *26*(3), 609–673.

Friedman, M. *Capitalism and Freedom.* Chicago: University of Chicago Press, 1962.

Gara, R. "AIDS Target Won't Be Met, Says Report." *Health News,* June 29, 2005.

Goetz, A. M., and Sen Gupta, R. "Who Takes Credit? Gender, Power, and Control over Loan Use in Rural Credit Programmes in Bangladesh." *World Development,* 1996, *24*(1), 45–63.

Goldemberg, J., Lèbre La Rovere, E., and Teixeira Coelho, S. "Expanding Access to Electricity in Brazil." *Energy for Sustainable Development,* 2004, *8*(4), 86–94.

Gómez-Ibáñez, J. A. *Regulating Infrastructure: Monopoly, Contracts, and Discretion.* Cambridge, Mass.: Harvard University Press, 2003.

Gordon, R. "San Francisco Bonus for Families Earning IRS Tax Credit." *San Francisco Chronicle,* Feb. 3, 2005, p. A1.

Greider, W. *The Soul of Capitalism: Opening Paths to a Moral Economy.* New York: Simon & Schuster, 2003.

Grzywinski, R. "The New Old Fashioned Banking." *Harvard Business Review,* May/June 1991, pp. 87-98.

Gutek, C., and Shroff, S. "Closer Look at RALs: We've Been Too Conservative." New York: Morgan Stanley Equity Research, Sept. 30, 2002.

Guthrie, D. "An Accidental Good: How Savvy Social Entrepreneurs Seized on a Tax Loophole to Raise Billions of Corporate Dollars for Affordable Housing." *Stanford Social Innovation Review,* Fall 2004, pp. 34–44.

Guthrie, D., and McQuarrie, M. "Privatization and the Social Contract: Corporate Welfare and Low-Income Housing in the United States Since 1986." *Research in Political Sociology,* 2005, *14,* 15–50.

"H&R." *New York Times,* May 17, 2005, Section A, p. 20.

H&R Block. *2004 Annual Report.* Kansas City: H&R Block, http://www.corporate-ir.net/ireye/ir_site.zhtml ?ticker=HRB&script=700, n.d. (accessed Nov. 7, 2005).

Hall, D., and Lobina, E. "Water Privatisation in Latin America, 2002." London: Public Services International Research Unit, 2002.

Hamied, Y. K. "Trading in Death." *IDMA Bulletin,* 2005, *36*(7), 20–25.

Hammond, A. L., and Prahalad, C. K. "Selling to the Poor." *Foreign Affairs,* May/June 2004, *142,* 30–37.

Handy, C. "What's a Business for?" *Harvard Business Review,* 2002, *80*(12), 49–55.

Hanson, K., and Berman, P. "Private Health Care Provision in Developing Countries: A Preliminary Analysis of Levels and Composition." (Review article.) *Health Policy Plan,* 1998, *13,* 195–211.

Hart, S. L. *Capitalism at the Crossroads: The Unlimited Business Opportunities in Solving the World's Most Difficult Problems.* Upper Saddle River, N.J.: Wharton, 2005.

Hart, S. L., and London, T. "Developing Native Capability: What Multinational Corporations Can Learn from the Base of the Pyramid." *Stanford Social Innovation Review,* Summer 2005, 28–33.

Harvard Joint Center for Housing Studies. "More Than Shelter: Housing as an Instrument of Economic and Social Development." Bellagio Conference, May 2005.

"Hedge Funds: The New Money Men." *Economist,* Feb. 17, 2005, www.economist.com (accessed May 17, 2005).

"The Hidden Wealth of the Poor: A Survey of Microfinance." *Economist,* Nov. 5, 2005, survey.

Hill, L. "Exercising Moral Courage: A Developmental Agenda." In D. Rhode (ed.), *Leadership: The Theory and Practice of Power, Judgment, and Policy.* San Francisco: Jossey-Bass, 2006.

Hill, L. "Irene Charnley at Johnnic Group (A)." Harvard Business School case no. 9-405-059. Boston: Harvard Business School, Jan. 2005.

Hill, L. "Irene Charnley at Johnnic Group (B)." Harvard Business School case no. 9-403-171. Boston: Harvard Business School, Jan. 2005.

Hill, L. "Irene Charnley at Johnnic Group (C)." Harvard Business School case no. 9-405-061. Boston: Harvard Business School, Jan. 2005.

Hishigsuren, G. "Impact Assessment Findings Using the SEEP-AIMS Tools at Sinapi Aba Trust, Ghana." Sussex, Brighton: Imp-Act Programme, Institute of Development Studies, University of Sussex, Brighton, 2004.

Hishigsuren, G., Beard, B., and Opoku, L. "Client Impact Monitoring Findings from Sinapi Aba Trust, Ghana." Sussex, Brighton: Imp-Act Programme, Institute of Development Studies, University of Sussex, Brighton, 2004.

Hoque, S. "Micro-Credit and the Reduction of Poverty in Bangladesh." *Journal of Contemporary Asia,* 2004, *34*(1), 21–32.

Hossain, R. "The Past, Present and Future of the Community Reinvestment Act (CRA): A Historical Perspective." Working Paper Series 2004-30. Storrs: Department of Economics, University of Connecticut, 2004.

Huang, Y., and Hogan, H. F. "India's Intellectual Property Rights Regime and the Pharmaceutical Industry." HBS case no. 9-702-039. Boston: Harvard Business School Publishing, Mar. 22, 2002.

Hulme, D., and Shepherd, A. "Conceptualizing Chronic Poverty." *World Development,* 2003, *31*(3), 403–423.

Immergluck, D. *Credit to the Community: Community Reinvestment and Fair Lending Policy in the United States.* Armonk, N.Y.: M. E. Sharpe, 2004.

Indian Ministry of Statistics and Programme Implementation. *National Sample Survey,* Round 50 (July 1993–June 1994), Round 55 (July 1999–June 2000), and Round 57 (July 2001–June 2002).

Indicadores Básicos en Ecuador. Prepared by Ecuadorian Ministry of Health, National Institute of Statistics and Census, and Pan-American Health Organization (Organización Panamericana de la Salud), 2003.

International Energy Agency. *2003 Insights, World Energy Investment Outlook.* Paris: IEA, 2003.

International Energy Agency. *World Energy Outlook 2004.* Paris: IEA, 2004.

Jackson Hewitt. *2005 Annual Report.* Parsippany, N.J.: Jackson Hewitt, http://library.corporate-ir.net/library/17/177/177359/items/163879/AR2005.pdf (accessed Nov. 7, 2005).

Jan, S., and others. "Dual Job Holding by Public Sector Health Professionals in Highly Resource-Constrained Settings: Problem or Solution?" *WHO Bulletin,* 2005, *83*(10), 771–776.

Jenkins, C., and Thomas, L. "The Changing Nature of Inequality in South Africa." Working paper no. 203, Helsinki, Finland: United Nations University's World Institute for Development Economics Research, 2000.

Jensen, M. C., and Meckling, W. H. "Theory of the Firm: Managerial Behavior, Agency Costs and Ownership Structure." *Journal of Financial Economics,* 1976, *3,* 305–360.

Jhirad, D., and Mintzer, I. "Electricity: Technology Opportunities and Management Challenges to Achieving a Low-Emissions Future." In I. Mintzer (ed.), *Confronting Climate Change: Risks, Implications and Responses.* Cambridge: Cambridge University Press, 1992.

Jurik, N. C. *Bootstrap Dreams: U.S. Microenterprise Development in an Era of Welfare Reform.* New York: Cornell University Press, 2005.

Kabeer, N., and Noponen, H. "Social and Economic Impacts of PRADAN's Self Help Group Microfinance and Livelihoods Promotion Program: Analysis from Jharkhand, India." Imp-Act Working Paper no. 11. Sussex, Brighton: Institute of Development Studies, University of Sussex, Brighton, 2005.

Kanter, R. M. "First Community Bank (A)." HBS case no. 9-396-202. Boston: Harvard Business School Publishing, rev. Dec. 5, 2005.

Kanter, R. M., and de Pinho, R. R. "ABN AMRO Real: Banking on Sustainability." HBS case no. 9-305-100. Boston: Harvard Business School Publishing, rev. Oct. 25, 2005.

Kashyap, P. "Rural Marketing: Issues, Opportunities and Challenges." Presentation at Rural Marketing Summit, Oct. 2004a, organized by Federation of Chambers of Commerce in India.

Kashyap, P. "Selling to the Hinterland." In *Businessworld Marketing Whitebook, 2003–04.* Calcutta: Businessworld, 2004b.

Khan, M. R., and others. "Domestic Violence Against Women: Does Development Intervention Matter?" Joint Project working paper no. 28. Dhaka: BRAC, ICDDR, 1998. Quoted in D. Leon and G. Walt (eds.), *Poverty, Inequality and Health: An International Perspective.* Oxford: Oxford University Press, 2001.

Khanna, T. "Business Groups and Social Welfare in Emerging Markets: Existing Evidence and Unanswered Questions." *European Economic Review,* 2000, *44*(4–6), 748–761.

Khanna, T., and Palepu, K. "Is Group Affiliation Beneficial in Emerging Markets? An Empirical Analysis of Diversified Indian Business Groups." *Journal of Finance,* 2000, *55*(2), 867–891.

Khanna, T., and Palepu, K. "Why Focused Strategies May Be Wrong for Emerging Markets." *Harvard Business Review,* 1997, *75*(4), 41–50.

Khanna, T., Rangan, K., and Manocaran, M. "Narayana Hrudayalaya Heart Hospital: Cardiac Care for the Poor." HBS case no. 9-505-078. Boston: Harvard Business School Publishing, 2005.

Kilby, P. *Entrepreneurship and Economic Development.* New York: Free Press, 1971.

Kingdon, G., and Knight, J. "Race and the Incidence of Unemployment in South Africa." *Review of Development Economics,* May 2004, *8*(3), 198–222.

Kotler, P., and Lee, N. *Corporate Social Responsibility: Doing the Most Good for Your Company and Your Cause.* Hoboken, N.J.: Wiley, 2005.

"K-Rep Bank Limited." *Deloitte Management Letter,* Dec. 31, 2004.

Kuhn Fraioli, L. K. "In Search of a 'Recipe' for Empowerment and Transformation: An In-Depth Look at Microcredit and Training at Work in the Lives of Ghanaian Women." Working Paper. Oakbrook, Ill.: Opportunity International, 2003.

Leggett, T. "Drugs, Sex Work, and HIV in Three South African Cities." *South Africa Health Info,* Feb. 20, 2004, http://www.sahealthinfo.org/admodule/drugs.htm.

Lichtenstein, G. A., and Lyons, T. S. "The Entrepreneurial Development System: Transforming Business Talent and Community Economies." *Economic Development Quarterly,* 2001, *15*(1), 3–20.

London, T., and Hart, S. L. "Reinventing Strategies for Emerging Markets: Beyond the Transnational Model." *Journal of International Business Studies,* 2004, *35*(5), 350–370.

Lopez, C. "Microfinance Approaches the Bond Market: The Cases of Mibanco and Compartamos." *Small Enterprise Development,* Mar. 2005, *16*(1), 50–56.

Luhabe, W. *Defining Moments: Experiences of Black Executives in South Africa's Workplace.* Pietermaritzburg: University of Natal Press, 2002.

Macey, J., and Miller, G. "The Community Reinvestment Act: An Economic Analysis." *Virginia Law Review,* 1993, *79*, pp. 291–348.

Manzetti, L., and Rufin, C. "Private Utility Supply in a Hostile Environment: The Experience of Water/Sanitation and Electricity Distribution Utilities in Northern Colombia, the Dominican Republic, and Ecuador." (Report to Inter-American Development Bank.) Washington, D.C.: Inter-American Development Bank, 2004.

Marek, T., Yamamoto, C., and Ruster, J. "Policy and Regulatory Options for Private Participation." Public Policy for the Private Sector, note no. 264. Washington, D.C.: World Bank Group Private Sector and Infrastructure Network, June 2003.

Margolis, J. D., and Walsh, J. P. "Misery Loves Companies: Rethinking Social Initiatives by Business." *Administrative Science Quarterly,* 2003, *48*, 265–305.

Marsico, R. *Democratizing Capital: The History, Law, and Reform of the Community Reinvestment Act.* Durham, N.C.: Carolina Academic Press, 2005.

Martinot, E., Ramankutty, R., and Rittner, F. "The GEF Solar PV Portfolio: Emerging Experience and Lessons." Monitoring and Evaluation Working Paper no. 2. Washington, D.C.: Global Environment Facility, 2000.

Marulanda, B., and Otero, M. *The Profile of Microfinance in Latin America in 10 Years: Vision and Characteristics.* Boston: ACCION International, 2005.

Maslow, A. H. "A Theory of Human Motivation." *Psychological Review,* 1943, 370–396.

Massey, D., and Denton, N. *American Apartheid: Segregation and the Making of the Underclass.* Cambridge, Mass.: Harvard University Press, 1992.

Mauss, M. *The Gift: The Form and Reason for Exchange in Archaic Societies.* New York: Norton, 1990.

May, J. *Poverty and Inequality in South Africa: Meeting the Challenge.* Cape Town: David Philip, 2000.

McCraw, T. K. *Creating Modern Capitalism: How Entrepreneurs, Companies, and Countries Triumphed in Three Industrial Revolutions.* Cambridge, Mass.: Harvard University Press, 1997.

McNeil, D., Jr. "Medicine Merchants. Drug Companies and the Third World: A Case in Neglect." *New York Times,* May 21, 2000, p. A1.

Mele, D., and Paladino, M. "Corporate Community Involvement Promoting a Multi–Stakeholder Commitment." Paper presented at Academy of Management Conference, Honolulu, Aug. 2005.

Miroslava, R., and Arenas, F. *CEMEX: Patrimonio Hoy.* IPADE, México, 2003.

Morduch, J. "The Microfinance Schism." *World Development,* 2000, *28*(4), 617–629.

Mugica, Y., and London, T. "Distributed Solar Energy in Brazil: Fabio Rosa's Approach to Social Entrepreneurship." (Teaching case study.) Chapel Hill: Kenan-Flagler Business School, University of North Carolina, 2004.

Mullins, B. "H&R Block Proposal Could Help Unite Congress on Social Security." *Wall Street Journal*, May 10, 2005, Sect. A, p. 4.

Musgrove, P. "Public Spending on Health Care: How Are Different Criteria Related?" Health Policy, 1999, *47*, 207–223.

Musgrove, P. "Public and Private Roles in Health: Theory and Financing Patterns." Health, Nutrition, and Population (HNP) Discussion Paper. Washington, D.C.: World Bank, July 1996.

Natarajan, I. *Indian Market Demographics.* New Delhi: National Council for Applied Economic Research, 2004.

Nayak, P. "Gandhian Economics Is Relevant." *Times of India*, Oct. 3, 2005.

Nieves, I., La Forgia, G., and Ribera, J. "Large-Scale Government Contracting of NGOs to Extend Basic Health Services to Poor Populations in Guatemala." In M. Rosenmöller (ed.), *Challenges of Health Reform: Reaching the Poor.* Barcelona: Estudios y Ediciones IESE, 2000, 117–132.

Nowak, J. "Back to the Future—A Case Study of ShoreBank." Development Finance Forum, www.dfforum.com, 2004.

Oliveira-Cruz, V., Kowalski, J., and McPake, B. "The Brazilian HIV/AIDS 'Success Story'—Can Others Do It?" *Tropical Medicine and International Health*, 2004, *9*(2), 192–197.

Paine, L. *Value Shift: Why Companies Must Merge Social and Financial Imperatives to Achieve Superior Performance.* New York: McGraw Hill, 2003.

Paladino, M. "Aguas Argentinas: Public-Private Cooperation for the Common." IAE–Universidad Austral, 2001.

Paladino, M., and Blas, L. "El Tendido de la red de gas en Cuartel V, Moreno. Cooperación para el Desarrollo." In J. Llach (ed.), *El renacer de lo local—Buenas prácticas de gobiernos subnacionales.* Buenos Aires: IAE, Escuela de Dirección y Negocios de la Universidad Austral, 2005.

Palmer, R. A., and Millier, P. "Segmentation: Identification, Intuition and Implementation." *Industrial Marketing Management*, 2004, *33*, 779–785.

Peng, M. W., and Heath, P. S. "The Growth of the Firm in Planned Economies in Transition: Institutions, Organizations, and Strategic Choice." *Academy of Management Review*, 1996, *21*(2), 492–528.

Permanent Household Survey (Encuesta Permanente de Hogares), 2001.

Phillips, M., and Moffett, M. "Brazil Refuses US AIDS Funds, Rejects Conditions." *Wall Street Journal*, May 2, 2005.

Pitt, M., and Khandakar, S. "The Impact of Group-Based Credit Programs on Poor Households in Bangladesh: Does the Gender of Participants Matter?" World Bank paper, 1995.

Plantersbank. *Annual Report.* Various years. www.plantersbank.ph.

Polakow-Suransky, S. "Giving the Poor Some Credit: Microloans Are in Vogue. Are They a Sound Idea?" *American Prospect*, Summer 2003, pp. A19–A21.

Porteous, D., and Hazelhurst, E.. *Banking on Change.* Cape Town: Doublestorey, 2004.

Prahalad, C. K. *The Fortune at the Bottom of the Pyramid: Eradicating Poverty Through Profits.* Philadelphia: Wharton School Publishing, 2004. (2005 edition also cited)

Prahalad, C. K., "Strategies for the Bottom of the Economic Pyramid: India as a Source of Innovation." *Reflections: The SOL Journal on Knowledge, Learning and Change*, 2002, *3*(4), 6–14.

Prahalad, C. K., and Hammond, A. L. "Serving the World's Poor, Profitably." *Harvard Business Review*, Sept. 2002, *80*(9), 48–57.

Prahalad, C. K., and Hart, S. L. "The Fortune at the Bottom of the Pyramid." *Strategy + Business,* Jan. 26, 2002, pp. 1–14.

Prahalad, C. K., and Ramaswamy, V. *The Future of Competition: Co-Creating Unique Value with Customers.* Boston: Harvard Business School Press, 2004.

"Private Dairies Unfair to Farmers." *Business Standard,* Oct. 7, 2005.

PT Bank Rakyat Indonesia (Persero). *Offering Circular.* Oct. 31, 2003.

Putnam, R. *Bowling Alone: The Collapse and Revival of American Community.* New York: Simon & Schuster, 2000.

Rahman, A. *Women and Microcredit in Rural Bangladesh: An Anthropological Study of the Rhetoric and Realities of Grameen Bank Lending.* Boulder, Colo.: Westview Press, 1999.

Rangan, V. K., and Walker, P. "Marketing's Role in Addressing the Poor as Customers." Working paper, Harvard Business School, 1999.

Rangan, V. K. "Comments on Prahalad." *Reflections: The SOL Journal on Knowledge, Learning, and Change,* 2002, *3*(4), 15–16.

Rangan, V. K., and McCaffrey, A. "Globalization and the Poor." In J. Quelch and R. Deshpandé (eds.), *The Global Market: Developing a Strategy to Manage Across Borders.* Jossey-Bass: San Francisco, 2004.

Rangan, V. K., and Rajan, R. "Unilever in India: Hindustan Lever's Project Shakti— Marketing FMCG to the Rural Consumer." HBS case no. 9-505-056. Boston: Harvard Business School Publishing, 2005.

Registrar General and Census Commissioner. *Census of India 2001,* Social and Cultural Tables, Series C. New Delhi, 2005.

Renewable Energy Task Force (G8). "Chairman's Report." 2001. http://www.g8.utoronto.ca/meetings-official/ g8renewables_report.pdf.

Rhyne, E. "Commercialization and Crisis in Bolivian Microfinance." In D. Drake and E. Rhyne (eds.), *The Commercialization of Microfinance: Balancing Business and Development.* Bloomfield, Conn.: Kumarian Press, 2002.

Rhyne, E. *Mainstreaming Microfinance.* Bloomfield, Conn.: Kumarian Press, 2001.

Ring, L. J., Tigert, D. J., and Serpkenci, R. R. "The Strategic Resource Management (SRM) Model Revisited." *International Journal of Retail and Distribution Management,* 2002, *30*(11), 544–561.

Roberts, P., and Dowling, G. "Corporate Reputation and Sustained Superior Financial Performance." *Strategic Management Journal,* 2002, 1077–1093.

Robinson, M. S. *The Microfinance Revolution: Sustainable Finance for the Poor.* Washington, D.C.: World Bank, 2001.

Robinson, M. *The Microfinance Revolution.* Vol. 2: *Lessons from Indonesia.* Washington, D.C.: World Bank, 2002.

Rockefeller Foundation and Goldman Sachs Foundation. *Social Impact Assessment.* 2003. http://www.riseproject.org/reports.htm.

Rockefeller, R. "Turn Public Problems to Private Account." *Harvard Business Review,* Aug. 2003, pp. 129–136.

"Runner-up, up and away." *Economist,* Dec. 14, 2005.

Sampson, R. "What 'Community' Supplies." In R. Ferguson and W. Dickens (eds.), *Urban Problems and Community Development.* Washington, D.C.: Brookings Institution Press, 1999.

Sánchez, P., and Rodríguez, M. Á. *Grupo Nueva: Proyecto 'Todos Ganamos.'* IESE case no. DG-1493. Barcelona, Spain: IESE Publishing, 2005.

Sánchez, P., Ricart, J. E., and Rodríguez, M. Á. "Social Embeddedness in Low Income Markets: Influential Factors and Positive Outcomes." Working paper, IESE Research Division, 2005.

Schmidt, R. H., and von Pischke J. D. "Networks of MSE Banks for Financial Sector Development: A Case-study in Private-Public Partnership." *Small Enterprise Development,* Mar. 2005, *16*(1), 31.

Schofield, H. W. "The Health Implications of Microcredit in Indonesia." Unpublished senior honors thesis, Harvard University, Mar. 2005.

Schumpeter, J. A. *Capitalism, Socialism, and Democracy* (2nd ed.). New York: HarperCollins, 1947a.

Schumpeter, J. A. "The Creative Response in Economic History." *Journal of Economic History,* 1947b, *7*(2), 149–159.

Schumpeter, J. A. *The Theory of Economic Development.* Cambridge, Mass.: Harvard University, 1934.

Sebstad, J., and Chen, G. "Overview of Studies on the Impact of Microenterprise Credit." Washington, D.C.: Assessing the Impact of Microenterprise Services (AIMS), USAID, 1996.

Seekings, J., and Nattrass, N. *Class, Race and Inequality in South Africa.* New Haven: Yale University Press, 2005.

Seelos, C., and Mair, J. "The Sekem Initiative." In *Improving Management: A Selection of the Best Cases from IESE Business School.* Barcelona: IESE, 2005a.

Seelos, C., and Mair, J. "Social Entrepreneurship: Creating New Business Models to Serve the Poor." *Business Horizons,* 2005b, *48,* 247–252.

Seelos, C., and Mair, J. "Sustainable Development, Sustainable Profits." *European Business Forum,* Winter 2005c, *30,* 49–53.

Sen, A. "Does Business Ethics Make Economic Sense?" *Business Ethics Quarterly,* 1993, *3,* 46–48.

Serra, J. "The Political Economy of the Brazilian Struggle Against AIDS." Lecture at the Institute for Advanced Study, Princeton, N.J., Oct. 2003.

Sharan, H. "Sustainable Energy for Rural Progress Through Employment and Power Partnership Program (EmPP)." Presentation prepared for Eradicating Poverty Through Profit: Making Business Work for the Poor Conference, World Resources Institute, San Francisco, Dec. 12–14, 2004. http://www.nextbillion.net/node/252.

Sheth, J. N., Newman, B. I., and Gross, B. L. "Why We Buy What We Buy: A Theory of Consumption Values." *Journal of Business Research,* 1991, *28,* 225–244.

ShoreBank Corporation. *Annual Report.* Various years. www.sbk.com.

Sidley, P. "South Africa Considers Supplying Antiretroviral Drugs to AIDS Patients." *British Medical Journal,* 2002, *923,* 325.

Simanis, E., and others. "Strategic Initiatives at the Base of the Pyramid: A Protocol for Mutual Value Creation." Draft dated Feb, 17, 2005. www.bus.umich.edu/BOP-Protocol/BoP_Protocol.pdf (accessed Nov. 15, 2005).

Simanowitz, A., and Walter, A. "Ensuring Impact: Researching the Poorest While Building Financially Self-Sufficient Institutions, and Showing Improvement in the Lives of the Poorest Women and Their Families." In S. Daley-Harris (ed.), *Pathways out of Poverty.* Bloomfield, Conn.: Kumarian Press, 2002.

Singh, R. "A Mirage at the Bottom of the Pyramid?" *Indian Management,* Oct. 2005, p. 46.

Slevin, P. "Mbeki Says Diplomacy Needed for Zimbabwe. S. African Urges Softer Approach Toward Mugabe." *Washington Post,* Sept. 23, 2003, p. A18.

Smith, A., and Smith, A. W. *The Theory of Moral Sentiments.* Oxford: Clarendon Press, 1976.

Snodgrass, D. R., and Sebstad, J. "Clients in Context: The Impacts of Microfinance in Three Countries: Synthesis Report." Washington, D.C.: Assessing the Impact of Microenterprise Services (AIMS), 2002.

Softec. *Mexican Housing Overview 2003.* Mexico City: Prisa, S.A. de C.V, 2003.

South African Financial Sector Charter. 2003. http://www.banking.org.za/documents/2003/OCTOBER/Charter_Final.pdf.

Stark, E., and Flitcraft, A. H. "Spouse Abuse." In M. L. Rosenberg and M. A. Fenley (eds.), *Violence in America: A Public Health Approach.* New York: Oxford University Press, 1991.

Statistics South Africa. "Earning and Spending in South Africa: Selected Findings and Comparisons from the Income and Expenditure Surveys of October 1995 and October 2000." Pretoria: Statistics South Africa, 2002.

Sustainability. "The 21st Century NGO: In the Market for Change." UNEP publication. London: Sustainability, 2003.

Swanstrom, T. *The Crisis of Growth Politics: Cleveland, Kucinich, and the Challenge of Urban Populism.* Philadelphia: Temple University Press, 1985.

Tambunting, J. P. "A Journey with the Philippino Entrepreneur." Speech to the Management Association of the Philippines (MAP), Manila, 2004.

Tichy, N., McGill, A., and St. Clair, L. (eds.). *Corporate Global Citizenship: Doing Business in the Public Eye.* San Francisco: New Lexington Press, 1997.

Triodos Bank. *Annual Report.* Various years. www.triodos.com.

Tucker, R. S. "The South African Financial Sector Charter: A Private Sector Contribution to the Reconstruction and Development of Post-Apartheid South Africa." Unpublished manuscript, 2005.

Tufano, P., and Schneider, D. "H&R Block and Everyday Financial Services." HBS case no. 9-205-013. Boston: Harvard Business School Publishing, 2005.

U.S. Agency for International Development. "Innovative Approaches to Slum Electrification." Washington, D.C.: USAID, 2004.

UN AIDS. "Progress on Global Access to HIV Antiretroviral Therapy, an Update on '3 by 5.'" 2004 Report on Global AIDS Epidemic. UN AIDS, World Health Organization, June 29, 2005.

UN-Energy. *The Energy Challenge for Achieving the Millennium Development Goals.* UN-Energy, 2005.

United Nations Development Programme (UNDP). *Energizing the Millennium Development Goals: A Guide to Energy's Role in Reducing Poverty.* New York: UNDP, 2005a.

United Nations Development Programme (UNDP). *Human Development Report 2005.* New York: UNDP, 2005b.

United Nations Development Programme (UNDP). *World Energy Assessment, Overview 2004 Update.* New York: UNDP, 2004.

United Nations. *Millennium Development Goals Report.* New York: United Nations, 2005.

Upton, D. "ITC's e-Choupal Initiative." HBS case no. 9-604-016. Boston: Harvard Business School Publishing, Oct. 2003.

Vachani, S., and Smith, N. C. "Socially Responsible Pricing: Lessons from the Pricing of AIDS Drugs in Developing Countries." *California Management Review,* 2004, *47*(1), 117–144.

Venkatesh, S. *American Project: The Rise and Fall of a Modern Ghetto.* Cambridge, Mass.: Harvard University Press, 2000.

Von Hippel, E. *The Sources of Innovation.* New York: Oxford University, 1988.

Wal-Mart. "Wal-Mart Facts Sheets." http://www.walmartfacts.com/doyouknow/ (accessed Nov. 11, 2005).

Wennekers, A., and Thurik, A. R. "Linking Entrepreneurship and Economic Growth." *Small Business Economics,* 1999, *13,* 27–55.

Willard, B. *The Sustainability Advantage: Seven Business Case Benefits of a Triple Bottom Line.* Gabriola Island, B.C., Canada: New Society Publishers, 2002.

Wilson, F., and Ramphele, M. *Uprooting Poverty: The South African Challenge.* New York: Norton, 1989.

Wilson, W. J. *The Truly Disadvantaged: The Inner City, the Underclass, and Public Policy.* Chicago: University of Chicago Press, 1987.

Wolfenson, J. *The Other Crisis.* Washington, D.C.: World Bank, Oct. 1998.

Wood, G. D., and Sharif, I. A. *Who Needs Credit? Poverty and Finance in Bangladesh.* Dhaka, Bangladesh: University Press Limited, 1997.

World Bank. "India: Policy and Finance Strategies for Strengthening Primary Health Care Services." Report no. 13042-IN. Washington, D.C.: World Bank, 1995.

World Bank. *World Development Indicators 2001.* Washington, D.C.: World Bank, 2001a.

World Bank. *World Development Indicators 2004.* Washington, D.C.: World Bank, 2004.

World Bank. *World Development Indicators 2005.* Washington, D.C.: World Bank, 2005.

World Bank. *World Development Report 2000/2001: Attacking Poverty.* New York: Oxford University Press, 2001b.

World Bank. *World Development Report 2004: Making Services Work for Poor People.* Washington, D.C.: World Bank and Oxford University Press, 2003.

Wu, C. C., and Fox, J. A. "All Drain, No Gain: Refund Anticipation Loans Continue to Sap the Hard-Earned Tax Dollars of Low-Income Americans." Washington, D.C.: Consumer Federation of America, 2004. http://www.consumerfed.org/pdfs/Refund AnticipationLoanReport.pdf (accessed Sept. 24, 2004).

Wu, C .C., and Fox, J. A. "Picking Taxpayers' Pockets, Draining Tax Relief Dollars." Boston: National Consumer Law Center and Consumer Federation of America, 2005. http://www.nclc.orginitiatives/refund_anticipation/content/2005RAL report.pdf (accessed Nov. 11, 2005).

ABOUT THE CONTRIBUTORS

Ablaza Jr., Gerardo C. . . . . Globe Telecom, Inc.

Ahmed, Fauzia Erfan . . . . Women's Studies Program, Indiana University

Ahwireng-Obeng, Frederick . . . . . . Wits Business School

Anupindi, Ravi . . . . Stephen M. Ross School of Business, University of Michigan

Aquino, Antonino T. . . . . Manila Water Company, Inc.

Arboleda, Luis Fernando . . . . management consultant

Austin, James E. . . . . Harvard Business School

de Ayala II, Jaime Augusto Zobel . . Ayala Corporation

Berger, Gabriel . . . . Universidad de San Andrés

Beshouri, Christopher. . . . . McKinsey and Company

Blas, Lisandro . . . . IAE Business School, Universidad Austral

Bloom, David E. . . . . Harvard School of Public Health

Budinich, Valeria . . . . Ashoka: Innovators for the Public

Chance, Zoë . . . . Harvard Business School

Chu, Michael . . . . Harvard Business School

Crane, Christopher A. . . . . Opportunity International

D'Andrea, Guillermo . . . . IAE, Austral University

Deshpandé, Rohit. . . . . Harvard Business School

Dikkers, Melchior . . . . IAG/PUC-Rio (Pontifical Catholic University of Rio de Janeiro)

Epstein, Marc J. . . . . Rice University

Farkas, Maria . . . . University of Michigan

Fedato, Cristina. . . . . CEATS/FIA/USP—Center of Social
Entrepreneurship and Administration
on the Third Sector

Fernández, Gerardo Lozano . . . . . EGADE—Tecnológico de Monterrey

Fischer, Rosa Maria . . . . School of Economics, Management, and
Accounting, São Paulo University

Flores, Juliano . . . . Social Enterprise Knowledge Network at INCAE

García-Cuéllar, Regina . . . . Harvard Business School

Goldberg, Ray A. . . . . Harvard Business School

Gómez-Samper, Henry. . . . . Instituto de Estudios Superiores de
Administración—IESA

Goodman, John . . . . Ogilvy & Mather

Guthrie, Doug. . . . . New York University

Herman, Kerry. . . . . Harvard Business School

Hill, Linda A. . . . . Harvard Business School

Jácome, Wilson A. . . . . IDE Business School

Jhirad, David J. . . . . World Resources Institute

Kanter, Rosabeth Moss. . . . . Harvard Business School

Khanna, Tarun. . . . . Harvard Business School

Kulkarni, Anil B. . . . . S. P. Jain Institute of Management and
Research

Leguizamón, Francisco A. . . . . INCAE Business School

Leonard, Herman B. . . . . Harvard Business School

Loría, Luis E. . . . . Economic Environment & Enterprise (e3)

Mair, Johanna . . . . IESE Business School

Manno Reott, Kimberly . . . . Ashoka: Innovators for the Public

Márquez, Patricia . . . . IESA

Marwaha, Kapil . . . . S. P. Jain Institute of Management and
Research

McQuarrie, Michael. . . . . University of California, Davis

Meghji, Nadeem . . . . Harvard Business School

Mondschean, Thomas S. . . . . DePaul University

Mookerjee, Ajay S. . . . . Harvard Business School

Motta, Paulo Cesar. . . . . IAG/PUC-Rio (Pontifical Catholic University
of Rio de Janeiro)

Mukhopadhyay, Jipan K. . . . . S. P. Jain Institute of Management and
Research

Ncube, Mthuli. . . . . Wits Business School

Paladino, Marcelo . . . . IAE Business School, Universidad Austral
Porteous, David J. . . . . Bankable Frontier Associates, LLC
Portocarrero, Luis Reyes . . . . TIA, SA—Ecuador
Prado, Andrea M. . . . . INCAE
Rajan, Rohithari . . . . Hindustan Lever Limited
Reficco, Ezequiel. . . . . Harvard Business School
Ricart, Joan E. . . . . IESE Business School
Rodríguez, Miguel A. . . . . IESE Business School
Romano, Kristine . . . . McKinsey and Company
Rose, David T. . . . . H&R Block
Rufin, Carlos. . . . . Babson College
Sánchez, Pablo . . . . IESE Business School
Schmidt, Stéphanie. . . . . Ashoka: Innovators for the Public
Schneider, Daniel . . . . Harvard Business School
Scoffier, Ann . . . . City *First* Bank of D.C., N.A.
Scott, Bruce R. . . . . Harvard Business School
Seelos, Christian . . . . IESE Business School
Segel, Arthur I. . . . . Harvard Business School
Sehgal, Dalip . . . . Hindustan Lever Limited
Sinha, Kunal. . . . . Ogilvy & Mather
Sivakumar, S. . . . . ITC Limited
Tucker, R. S. . . . . Standard Bank of South Africa
Tufano, Peter. . . . . Harvard Business School
Welch, Carolyn . . . . Board of Governors of the Federal Reserve
                                                           System
Woollam, Annie . . . . World Resources Institute

ABOUT THE EDITORS

V. Kasturi Rangan

Malcolm P. McNair Professor of Marketing and Cochair, Social Enterprise Initiative
Harvard Business School

Kash Rangan is the Malcolm P. McNair Professor of Marketing at the Harvard
Business School, and until recently the chairman of the Marketing Department
(1998–2002). He has taught in a variety of MBA courses, including the core first-year
marketing course and the second-year electives Business Marketing and Channels
to Market. He has also taught marketing in the Advanced Management Program for
senior managers. Currently, Rangan teaches the elective courses Social Marketing
and Business Approaches to Serving Bottom-of-the-Pyramid Markets. In addition, he
teaches in a number of focused executive programs: Channels to Market, Business
Marketing Strategy, Strategic Perspectives on Nonprofit Management, and Governance
for Nonprofit Excellence.

Rangan's business marketing and channels research has appeared in such management journals as *Journal of Marketing, Harvard Business Review, Sloan Management Review,
Journal of Retailing, Management Science, Marketing Science,* and *Organization Science.* He
has authored five books, which include *Transforming Your Go-to-Market Strategy: The Three
Disciplines of Channel Management* (with Marie Bell), *Going to Market* (with E. Raymond
Corey and Frank V. Cespedes), and *Business Marketing Strategy* (with Benson P. Shapiro
and Rowland T. Moriarty). In addition to his interest in business marketing, Rangan

is actively involved in studying the role of marketing in nonprofit organizations, specifically how it influences adoption of social products and ideas. He has written a number of case studies and articles on the topic. He served as one of the founding cochairs of the Social Enterprise Initiative at Harvard, whose faculty study and teach the challenges of nonprofit management. His research on this topic has appeared in *Nonprofit Management and Leadership, Harvard Business Review,* and elsewhere. His current research is aimed at developing a customer-centric approach for addressing the needs of the poor.

Rangan has a bachelor of technology degree from IIT (Madras), 1971; an MBA from IIM (Ahmedabad), 1973; and a Ph.D. in marketing from Northwestern University (Evanston, Illinois), 1983. From 1973 to 1979, he held several sales and marketing positions for a large multinational company in India.

John A. Quelch

Lincoln Filene Professor of Business Administration
Senior Associate Dean
Harvard Business School

John A. Quelch is senior associate dean and Lincoln Filene Professor of Business Administration at Harvard Business School. Between 1998 and 2001 he was dean of London Business School. Prior to 1998, he was the Sebastian S. Kresge Professor of Marketing and cochair of the marketing area at Harvard Business School. Quelch's research focus is on global marketing and branding in emerging as well as developed markets. His current research projects involve understanding the brand power of global nongovernmental organizations and formalizing appropriate marketing and customer metrics for periodic review by boards of directors. He is the author, coauthor, or editor of twenty books, among them *The New Global Brands, Global Marketing Management* (5th edition), *The Global Market, Cases in Advertising and Promotion Management* (4th edition), and *The Marketing Challenge of Europe 1992* (2nd edition). He has published articles on marketing issues in such leading management journals as *Harvard Business Review, McKinsey Quarterly,* and *Sloan Management Review.*

Quelch is a nonexecutive director of WPP Group, Pepsi Bottling Group, and Inverness Medical Innovations. He also serves pro bono as chairman of the Port Authority of Massachusetts and as a nonexecutive director of ACCION International, a leading microfinance lender. He has been a consultant, seminar leader, and speaker for firms, industry associations, and government agencies in more than fifty countries. He was born in London, was educated at Exeter College, Oxford University (B.A. and M.A.), the Wharton School of the University of Pennsylvania (MBA), the Harvard School of Public Health (M.S.), and Harvard Business School (D.B.A.). In addition to the United Kingdom and United States, he has lived in Australia and Canada.

Gustavo Herrero

Executive Director, Latin America Research Center
Harvard Business School

Gustavo Herrero obtained his undergraduate business degree from the Universidad
Argentina de la Empresa in Buenos Aires in 1972. After working for two years at Ford
Motor Company, he attended the Harvard Business School as a Fulbright Scholar,
obtaining his MBA there in 1976. After graduation, he worked in the United States
and Paraguay for two years and moved back to Argentina in 1978, where he has lived
since. Over the following twenty-one years, he held various management positions in
Argentine companies. Between 1987 and 1999, Herrero was successively the CEO of
Argentina's largest wool textile mill (IVA S.A.) and of Argentina's leading paper and
packaging manufacturer (Zucamor S.A./Papel Misionero S.A.). In 1999, he left
Zucamor and Papel Misionero (on which boards he continues to serve) to become
executive director of the Harvard Business School Latin America Research Center,
based in Buenos Aires. As head of the Center, he works closely with HBS faculty who
do research throughout Latin America, developing both intellectual and social capital for the school. He has contributed to the writing of more than twenty HBS teaching cases since 2000.

　　　Herrero belongs to the board of directors of various Argentine companies and sat
on the board of directors of the Harvard Business School Alumni Association in Boston.
He serves on the board of directors of ACCION International and on the board of
trustees of LASPAU. He also serves on the board of advisors of the University of São
Paulo's Centro de Estudos em Administração do Terceiro Setor (CEATS) in Brazil,
and of the Instituto de Estudios Superiores de Administración (IESA) in Venezuela.
He is also a member of the consultative boards of the Centro de Implementación de
Políticas Públicas para la Equidad y el Crecimiento (CIPPEC) in Argentina, and of
Harvard's David Rockefeller Center for Latin American Studies Regional Office in
Santiago, Chile.

Brooke Barton

Research Associate
Harvard Business School

A research associate for the HBS Social Enterprise Initiative, *Brooke Barton* organized
the HBS Conference on Global Poverty: Business Solutions and Approaches, held in
December 2005. She also writes case studies on questions of corporate social responsibility (CSR) in developing countries; her research interests include stakeholder engagement in extractive industries, socially responsible investment, and CSR reporting.
In addition to work at HBS, she advises companies on CSR reporting as a consultant

for Ceres, a network of investment funds, environmental organizations, and other public interest groups working to advance corporate environmental stewardship. Previously, she was a communications officer for ACCION International, a microfinance NGO. She holds a master's degree from the Fletcher School of Law and Diplomacy at Tufts University, where she studied corporate social responsibility, and a B.A. in economics from Duke University. She speaks Spanish and Portuguese.

Index

Don't talk consumption, talk investment. w/
SEED

New deliv. model → "castes" of SEED at
open air markets? put in indiv. Sacks-
amt. that consumer wants? Good bc.
we need to look at new delivery
models. Or, dispensers, such as cereal
dispensers at hotels?!

p. 48 = ∅

p. 200 — # of Cooperatives

p. 229 — Relevance to CBC

p. 185 — Milk districts → farm districts??

p. 372 — Importance of buying from, not
just selling to, poor people.

p. 281 = *

Idea? CARE $ is for ag microfinance
for ? ?

pps 293 +4 — exs. of good spinoff
businesses